THE CONSTITUTION AS JUNCT

(A Re-examination of th
Foundations for Constitut__.... Law Study in
Nigeria)

By

R.A.C.E. Achara

LL.B. (Hons.) [Nig.], B.L. [NLS], LL.M. [Nig.],
Ph.D. [Nig.]
Professor of Constitutional Law,
Enugu State University of Science
And Technology, Nigeria.

Head of Department International Law and
Jurisprudence Nnamdi Azikiwe University, Awka

Winner of the 2004 Resident Fellowship of the
Five College African Scholars Program,
University of Massachusetts, Amherst.

Based on the doctoral thesis that won the
University of Nigeria
Postgraduate Prize for Law

achrace@yahoo.com

First published by AuthorHouse 05/17/05

ISBN: 1-4208-4946-8 (sc)

Library of Congress Control Number: 2005903371

Printed in the United States of America
Bloomington, Indiana

This book is printed on acid-free paper.

Dedicated to Chima Ubani, with whom I have never met; Olisa Agbakoba, SAN, an enigmatic presence; and all others who pushed 'rationality' and 'pragmatism' aside in the battle of wills against Nigeria's military terrorists.

Acknowledgments

This is the most pleasant part of my exertions. I owe my first debt of gratitude to Professor Ofori Amanquah, then of the University of Jos: not for the content of the work, but for the psychological impetus for its embarkation. As external examiner for my LL.M. degree in April of 1993, his enthusiastic reception of the Dissertation; his award of an "A" grade for it; and, his rather flattering insistence that I should go for a doctorate and immediately take up a lectureship could not but encourage further research.

I also owe Mr. Z.C. Anyogu for his part in determining me in the field of research to undertake. In 1995, as Acting Dean of Law at the Nnamdi Azikiwe University, Awka (NAU), he invited me to join the teaching staff, and, by assigning to me the Constitutional Law class, indirectly resolved my dilemma as to choice of research topic. It is true that since, at least, the June 12 debacle of 1993, I had seriously pondered the constitutional implications of force to law. However, it was not until the stage for preparation of my lecture notes, that I starkly apprehended the enormity of the problem.

I have immensely benefitted from the prodigious output of Western researchers in this and in related fields. But for the [now removed] British Council library at Enugu, access to these materials would have been denied. Thanks must therefore go to both the authors and to the British Council for their inestimable input to this work.

This work has undergone almost countless revisions. I have severally revised the manuscripts, the typescripts, and even the computer prints. It started as the PhD Thesis, which I submitted to the University of Nigeria in September of 1999. It was rather belatedly examined and passed on 26 September 2001 due to the unbelievably incompetent, slow and insensitive administrative processes. The anguish of delay has however been ameliorated by the outcome of the exercise. At the convocation ceremony of 7 October 2002, the enthusiastic response from the examiners was made an even happier recompense when the thesis won the University's Postgraduate Prize for the Faculty of Law.

Tradition demands that I thank Prof. B. Obinna Okere as my Ph.D. supervisor. But Professor D.I.O. Ewelukwa deserves special thanks for graciously agreeing to offer, beyond the call of duty, a second supervisory guidance on this topic that mingles Constitutional Law with Jurisprudence.

Because of the interdisciplinary slant of the research, I had sought and received help from a diverse background of scholars. I thank Prof. Ilochi Okafor, S.A.N., the then Dean, faculty of law, and now Vice Chancellor, NAU; the Hon. (Dr.) Justice C.C. Nweze of the Enugu State High Court; and Dr. O.C. Okafor, Assoc. Professor at the Osgoode Hall Law School, Ontario, Canada. Each of the last-named five read the entire work and offered useful criticisms. Others read the 31-page seminar condensation of the thesis. They too, deserve the highest gratitude. In this regard, I especially thank the post-graduate law seminar held at the University of Nigeria, Enugu Campus on 15 November 2000.

Before the seminar presentation, Professor I.E. Nwana of the Yitzak Rabin Centre on Biotechnology, NAU; Professor S.N.C. Obi of the

Department of Commercial and Property Law, NAU; Professor Agu U. Ogan (rtd.), F.A.S., Drs. H.M.G. Ezenwaji and Assisi Asobie of the Biochemistry, Zoology and Political Science Departments of the University of Nigeria, respectively; all read the seminar paper and offered very useful suggestions. Mrs. Edith Nwosu and Samuel Nwatu, Esq., as well as Dr. G.O.S. Amadi, Professor E.I. Nwogugu and Mrs. M.C. Anozie had previously done so too. I thank them most sincerely.

Numerous other persons have contributed in clarifying my thoughts by incisive arguments and oral disputations: Ugochukwu Ukpabi comes immediately to mind and, in this regard, Nnamdi Otukwu too. The constant proddings and briefings by my elder brother, Wing Commander Bond Achara, have been invaluable, especially on methodology. He is currently undertaking a doctoral research in Public Administration in the Department of Political Science, University of Benin.

I seize this opportunity to also thank all others who have patiently borne my curt and near-rude unsociability for these past 11 to 12 years of research. My gratitude goes too to the owners and staff of the Zodiac Hotels, Enugu, for the inspiring ambience of their poolside at which many an idea in this work found release. My first two secretaries, Nneoma Ogbonna and Amaka Mbah [RIP] typed much of the work. The author with the assistance of Mercy Eziechi principally did the computer typesetting. My later secretary, Nneka Ogbuja, was most useful in facilitating the seminar preparations and in typing the final amendments at the thesis stage in 2001. I thank everybody for all the help.

Professor Gaius Ezejiofor, S.A.N. [RIP], has always sought to simplify my language structure and Professor C.O. Okonkwo, S.A.N., has never relented in making me believe that I may, eventually, have some prospects in the academic sphere. The speed and scrupulous attention to detail with which Professor A.O. Obilade of the University of Lagos assessed the examination draft of the thesis is truly remarkable and deserving of deep-felt gratitude. It reconfirms my unshakable belief in the stupidity of tribal prejudices in Nigeria. Wicked delays came from my tribesmen. It took the professionalism and disinterestedness of one from another tribe before a date was finally confirmed for my examination.

In the end, however, credit for facilitating the repose and resources to complete the research that has turned this into a book must go to the Five College African Scholars Program (ASP) with the financial support of the Bill and Melinda Gates Foundation. Of some 400 applications from university lecturers all over Africa, the ASP kindly chose this project to enable me stay with three other African scholars for some four and a half months at the University of Massachusetts, Amherst, USA. The kindness, unsurpassable charity, friendliness and good nature of all my hosts kindled, for me, warmth out of the winter snow.

I am especially grateful for the privilege of making the acquaintance of Profs. John Lemly and Cathy Melhorn, Linda and Prof. Ralph Faulkingham, Profs. David and Catharine Newbury, Carlene Edie, David Mednicoff, Joye Bowman and John Higginson. Profs. Rowland Abiodun, Mitzi Goheen, Elliot Fratkin, Fred Holmquist, Stephen Clingman, Nathan Therien, Holly Hanson and Liz Garland all made the trip a grand learning experience. I will also treasure the intellectual gift of meeting with Prof. John Brigham and the benefits, culinary and intellectual, this has brought me. I thank him especially for the effusively kind words by which he has encouraged my work. I will forever cherish the charming facility by which Barbara Morgan (with the cheerful assistance of Annette L. Demers of the law library at Harvard), Dr. Stern and the other research and ILLIAD librarians of W.E.B. du Bois Library at UMass, were able to bring the technology of information retrieval to my wide-eyed sensibilities. Anthony Shrock of AuthorHouse Publishing must take credit for nudging me out of my lethargy. Except for this author's representative of those publishers, I probably would have failed to return to the final editing required to put the book project back on track.

In the event, for all the errors I yet suffer to remain, there is none to be blamed but me.

Preface

It may well be appropriate to start with an apology. The work explores a fairly abstract field and, consequently, the language of discourse and methodology tilt slightly beyond the traditional forms of legal science. A conscious attempt has been made to reduce obscurity, but the philosophical content of constitutional theory has not always been a compliant collaborator.

The fear that the abstract language of the opening chapters may dissuade continued reading, has suggested the movement of Chapter 2 to the tail end of the work. But this would scuttle the order of logical presentation. As an alternative, it may be suggested that after Chapter 1, the reader could choose to proceed directly to Chapters 3, 4 and 5. Thereafter, the turgid language of Chapter 2 may, more easily, be tolerated.

The seven chapters of the book fall into three unarticulated categories. I identify the problems and suggest, in the first two chapters, methodological tools for their solution. And, having explained there, that Constitutional law is best studied in three stages - how a constitution is born, lives, and dies - I, in that sequence, critique the current orthodoxy in the three subsequent chapters. The last of the three categories of the book consists of Chapters 6 and 7. Here, I make the case for a change of paradigm. Chapter 6 expatiates my theory, principle or doctrine of preponderant force. With that doctrine, conclusions are then drawn in Chapter 7.

A particular difficulty has been the current technique of study whereby a constitution is determined by the mere self-assertions of a document of that name. Since the American example of a written constitution, this reification of text has acquired some twenty-three decades of authority. Habit is difficult to break. It will naturally take some time to persuade a change of mind-set. This book hopes to serve as a gentle prod in that direction.

To gain the reader's attention about the importance of the problem, I need only highlight a glaring but common contradiction arising from the current approach to the study of Constitutional law. In Nigeria, the document known as the 1979 Constitution has, various times, been held different from, and inferior to, military laws known as decrees. This has been so despite the continued affirmation that a constitution is the supreme law. These mutually repellent propositions cannot concurrently, stand. But, in Nigerian constitutional scholarship, no attempt has been made to clearly resolve the antinomy. Surely, therefore, the student is entitled to some scepticism about the epistemological stability of the current foundations of Constitutional law.

It is to re-evaluate the theoretical bases of Constitutional law that this research has been directed. It is hoped that the difficulties highlighted will help to bring some clarity even if the problems are yet to be fully resolved.

CONTENTS

CASES

STATUTES

1. General Introduction.

This book will argue: (a), that Constitutional Law cannot fruitfully be taught or studied except within a multidisciplinary framework; (b), that methodological form is not merely a protuberance on theoretical substance but, in Constitutional Law, part of substance itself. Further, (c), that what we may call "textual fetishism" is the single most debilitating phenomenon affecting the objective, pragmatic and rational appreciation of constitutions and, thus, the study of Constitutional Law. It will also argue: (d), that the central task of the constitutional jurist is to ascertain the meaning, source and scope of a constitution, the way it distributes and operationalizes power, and its patent and latent provisions for change.

However, a significant challenge has been how to summarize and present the vast but largely disparate pieces of relevant information as a consistent whole. Chapter 2 discusses the first three arguments referred to at the start of this work as (a), (b) and (c).[1] Chapters 3, 4, and 5 respectively address the

---

[1] "(a)" is the autonomy debate whether law can fruitfully be understood and studied without reference to the study of the larger society; "(b)" is the exploration of the tensions between form and substance as well as the influence of style to the content of the work; "(c)" is a discussion about a fundamental point relative to this book. It considers whether legal textualism, the traditional method of legal study, does not unduly overrate the written word and thus undermine research efforts based on practical observations and common-sense.

arguments referred to under (d). Argument (d) is about the proper boundaries of Constitutional Law. The claim is that a necessary and sufficient treatment considers Constitutional Law under three broad headings:

1. The theory of provenance[2] (dealing with the sources and meaning of constitutions and distinguishing these from the sources and meaning of Constitutional Law);

2. The theory of distribution and operationalization[3] (dealing with the structural and substantive allocation and activation of sovereign powers); and

3. The theory of change[4] (concerned with the expressed as well as the unarticulated provisions for altering constitutions).

In Chapter 6, the book espouses what it describes as the doctrine of preponderant force. Thereafter, it assesses the result of applying this doctrine to the existing method for studying Constitutional Law, at least, in Nigerian universities. This appraisal is in Chapter 7 and it is there that conclusions are offered.

PROBLEMATIZATION.

The book has substantially been prompted by the perplexity faced in November of 1995 when the author was called upon to teach Constitutional Law at university level. Confused, one's self, by the plausible but contradictory stand-points of different jurists

---

[2] At Chapt. 3.
[3] At Chapt. 4.
[4] At Chapt. 5.

(even on the same constitutional issues), it was difficult not to see the greater danger this would probably pose for one's students. However, even more directly, the Nigerian presidential election of 12 June 1993, and its fallout have served to introduce, perhaps a mite too roughly, the extraordinarily complex relationship between doctrinal legal knowledge, on the one hand; and the logic of force, on the other. Hopefully, however, June 12 would also have brought to the fore previously unarticulated associations of law with Political Science, Sociology, Philosophy and Ethics.

The phenomenon of at once feeling two mutually antagonistic impulses as to what is ethically right, on the one hand; and what is constitutionally or legally sound, on the other, is particularly intriguing. Like a great many Nigerians, one[5] was unconvinced by the reasons for annulment. Despite this, however, it would probably have been disingenuous not to conclude that the annulment was constitutional and legal in spite of very learned views to the contrary.[6] These problems have suggested, therefore, a deeper enquiry into the relationship between force and law.

---

[5] The hypocrisy of the royal plural or of the third-person form of reported speech is a bit tiresome and disrupts in some ways, the sincerity of certain forms of exploratory research reporting. Following the current practice in a lot of socio-legal writing, I seek the reader's leave to use the first person singular; only alternating styles when this becomes too autobiographical.

[6] For example, see Chief Gani Fawehinmi, *June 12 Crisis: The Illegality of Shonekan's Government,* (Lagos, Nigeria: Nigerian Law Publications Ltd., October, 1993) v: "...illegal annulment by Babangida of the people's verdict of June 12, 1993."

The book is not primarily directed at Constitutional Application - that very exciting and, some may say, polemical part of Constitutional Law that interprets and expounds the norms of an already identified constitution.[7a] Rather, it is devoted to Constitutional Theory: that more complex aspect of Constitutional Law whose intersections with Political Theory, Jurisprudence and Legal Theory deal mostly with fundamentals and universals (especially about the identification, meaning, nature and scope of constitutions in general).[7b] It starts out by highlighting particular constitutional antinomies and the difficulties and contradictions that attend any attempts to resolve these under the text-venerating methodologies currently used for Constitutional Law study. In trying to provide coherence, the book postulates its doctrine of preponderant force and seeks to demonstrate, when tested against the same problems, that this doctrine has theoretical and methodological superiority over the current constitutional orthodoxies.

Although Nigeria is used as the principal model for the study, the principles deduced are

---

[7a] Administrative Law is the most noticeable. It deals with that part of Constitutional Application, which concentrates on executive power.

[7b] The difference usually manifests in how the question is framed. The current, but mainly Western, controversies about the nature of marriage do provide a rough but useful analogy. 'Does the Constitution of the Commonwealth of Massachusetts authorize a same sex marriage?' - This would be a matter for Constitutional Application. 'Should it?' - This would be a matter for Jurisprudence and Legal Theory; but, 'Can any constitution do so - is this within the province of a constitution?' - This would surely be a concern for Constitutional Theory.

propounded as capable of general application. As background, the book starts with the following reconstruction of the legal and constitutional conundrum that is the holding, the nullification, and the subsequent clamour for reinstatement of the nation-wide election of June 12, 1993.

June 12[8]: The Legal Historiography.

Since 1 January, 1914, when virtually all the territory now known as the Federal Republic of Nigeria came, for the first time, to be under a constitutionally, united administration, the constitutions for the country have been imposed by the one or the few upon the many. From 1914 to the end of September of 1963, Nigerian frameworks of governance have been handed down by foreigners (sometimes, with the collaboration of a minuscule percentage of empowered indigenes). The 1963 Constitution, which lasted from 1 October 1963, until 16 January 1966,[8a] was the first autochthonous Nigerian constitution. But it was not made by the people (the many). It was imposed by the empowered few. All the subsequent written constitutions of the country, including the 1979 Constitution, have been made by military decree.[9] The latter point

---

[8] 'June 12' refers to the Nigerian presidential election of that date in 1993. It also serves as a useful shorthand for the surrounding events and pronouncements directly or indirectly related to the election and its controversial nullification by the military government then in place.

[8a] Although Decree No. 1 of 1966 post-dated its commencement to 17/1/66, this legal fiction need not detain us.

[9] E.g., Decree No. 1 of 1966; Decree No. 32 of 1975; Decree Nos. 25 and 26 of 1978 and Nos. 104 and 105 of 1979. Decree No. 1 of 1984; Decree No. 17 of 1985;

emphasizes the establishment of a nearly forty-year culture of decrees as the ultimate law of the land.[10]

On 27 August 1985, a military coup d'état effected the demise of the previous constitution.[11] Under the new one,[12] Nigeria

---

Decree No. 12 of 1989 (which was eventually never operationalized); Decree No. 61 of 1993; Decree No. 107 of 1993 and Decree No. 24 of 1999. General Gowon claimed, controversially under the same Decree No. 1 of 1966, a smooth succession to General Aguiyi Ironsi. But there could have been no doubt that Gen. Obasanjo concluded a smooth constitutional succession to Gen. Murtala Mohammed under the very same framework of governance as was provided by Decree No. 32 of 1975.

[10] It is to be noted that contrary to the implications of some texts, constitutions are not such merely because a well-printed document is so designated. A constitution is the prevailing, effective, framework of government in any polity (whether written, partly-written or even unwritten). When a government is based on supremacy of directives in decrees, the instrument or unwritten phenomenon that imposes that framework is the constitution even if it is not so named.

[11] The Constitution (Suspension and Modification) Decree No. 1, 1984. In what may be considered an undue reliance on the written word over what in fact subsists, Prof. Niki Tobi [now, JSC] in his *Legal Impact of the Constitution (Suspension and Modification) Decree 1984 on the Constitution of the Federal Republic of Nigeria 1979* (Calabar: Centaur Press Limited, 1985), 9, argues that the 1979 Constitution subsisted, subject to some tinkering, after the coup of 1984. Surely, this proposition by the learned jurist might benefit from some re-evaluation. All the Nigerian coups, by their own force, each abrogated the immediately preceding constitution. The parts "retained" are more properly speaking, parts of the new constitutional decree just as if a lifeless draft were incorporated to the principal decree by reference.

[12] The Constitution (Suspension and Modification) (Amendment) Decree No. 17 of 1985. Although No. 17 of 1985 says that No. 1 of 1984 subsisted (subject to amendments), the true legal position is that the coup of

acquired her first military president, Major
General Ibrahim Badamasi Babangida ('IBB,'
later, a self-promoted, full General). The new
constitution provided for the supremacy of
decrees. A future decree could override the
enabling constitution-decree itself. Even the
decree creating the 1979 Constitution was of
this nature.[13] Acting within the then current
1985 Constitution, the new regime promulgated
Decree No. 54 of 1992,[14] which cosmetically[15]
altered the existing framework of government.
By this decree, the apex organ of the
government, the "Armed Forces Ruling Council"
(AFRC), was replaced with the "National Defence
and Security Council" (NDSC). The "Transitional
Council," headed by, and entirely composed of,
civilians,[16] was also set up as the prime
national executive body. The main function of
the Transitional Council was to ensure "a
smooth handing over process from the Federal
Military Government to the civilian
administration ..."[17]

The civilian administration was to come
into being concurrently with the (now moribund)

27/8/1985 totally abrogated that latter constitution.
The new constitution, i.e., Decree No. 17 of 1985,
merely incorporated and thus resuscitated some parts of
the now dead Decree No. 1 of 1984.
[13] Although Decree No. 25 of 1978 enacted its schedule as
the 1979 Constitution, the constitutional amendments
effected by Nos. 26 of 1978 and 104 and 105 of 1979, all
prove the supremacy of later decrees.
[14] The Constitution (Suspension and Modification)
(Amendment) Decree, No. 54 of 1992.
[15] Power essentially remained where it was. The civilians
were mere delegates. But little was delegated.
[16] See B.O. Nwabueze, *Nigeria '93: The Political Crisis
and Solution* (Ibadan: Spectrum, 1994) at 20.
[17] *Ibid.*, s. 4(b) of Decree 54, 1992.

1989 Constitution on 27 August 1993.[18] Consequently, the life of the Transitional Council as well as the military regime, could not, under the decree, transcend that date. One of the perplexing provisions of the applicable laws is section 2, sub-section (5), paragraph (c), of the decree:

> 2 (5) The chairman and members of the Transitional Council who shall all be appointed by the National Defence and Security
> Council shall –
> (a) ...
> (b) ...
> (c) not be eligible to hold any political appointment for a period of 12 months after the end of the period of the transition to civil rule.

Chief Ernest Shonekan who was appointed chairman of the Transitional Council was controversially also appointed on 26 August 1993, the Head of State after the dissolution of the Transitional Council. Curiously, critics have not made much of this seeming breach.[18a]

---

[18] By s. 1 of the Constitution of the Federal Republic of Nigeria (Promulgation) (Amendment) (No. 2) Decree, No. 56 of 1992: "The Constitution of the Federal Republic of Nigeria (Promulgation) Act, as amended, is hereby further amended by substituting for the commencement date "2nd January, 1993," wherever it occurs in the Act a new commencement date "27th August, 1993": The Supreme Court affirmed this new commencement date in its decision in *Att.-Gen. of Anambra State and ors. v. Att.-Gen. of the Federation and ors.* (1993) 6 N.W.L.R. (part 302) 692. See also, Chief Gani Fawehinmi, *June 12 crisis...*, *supra*, 12 and 13.

[18a] A possible explanation is that the abrogation of the Transitional Council also repealed the entire provisions

The appointment to the office of Head of State was, surely, a political one. Perhaps, however, the mere expiration of life of the Transitional Council was not equivalent to "the end of the period of the transition to civil rule." The point however goes both ways. If apologists of the military contend that the "Interim National Government" instituted[19] after General Babangida "stepped aside" did not introduce a civilian government but was merely a continuation of military rule, they must also accept the view, shared by many critics of the military administration, that Chief Shonekan's interim government was a diversionary sham.[20] It must be thus seen as one only set up to reduce the unprecedented degree of political pressure the military had had to endure since the date of the annulment.[21]

---

of its enabling decree. The preclusionary provision thus got thrown out, too.

[19] Under the Interim Government (Basic Constitutional Provisions) Decree No. 61, 1993.

[20] Chief Gani Fawehinmi on Wednesday, October 27, 1993, described Shonekan's interim government as "Conceived in an unprecedented treachery, born in perfidy and illegality," *June 12 crisis...*, *op. cit.*, 2. Also, see Dare Babarinsa, "The Emperor's Script," *Tell*, No. 36, September 13, 1993: "... Shonekan's unusual regime is a government in transit ... a footnote in the story of Ibrahim Babangida ..."

[21] The nullification was communicated through an unsigned press release published on 23/6/1993 by Mr. Nduka Irabor (Press Secretary to the military Vice-President). On its face, however, the President signed the formal instrument of nullification the previous day. It was to commence on 22/6/1993 and was entitled: "Presidential Election (Basic Constitutional and Transitional Provisions) (Repeal) Decree No. 39, 1993."

The Election.

On 1 January 1993, President Babangida signed into law the Presidential Election (Basic Constitutional and Transitional Provisions) Decree[22] of 1993. Three sections of that decree appear to be the most relevant for our present purposes. These are:

I. *Section 1, sub section (1),* which provides in part that "there shall be for the federation, a president …;"
II. *Section 18,* which says that election to the office of the president shall be held throughout the Federation on a day to be appointed by the commission;[23] and,
III. *Section 19,* which emphatically states in two subsections, as follows:

(1) Notwithstanding the provisions of the Constitution of the Federal Republic of Nigeria 1979, as amended, or any other law, no interim or interlocutory order or ruling, judgment or decision made by any court or tribunal before or after the commencement of this Decree, in respect of any inter-party or intra-party dispute or any other matter before it shall affect the date or time of the holding of the election, or the performance by the commission of any of its functions under this Decree or any guidelines issued by it in pursuance of the election.

---

[22] Decree No. 13 of 1993. Signed, and stated to commence, on 1 January, 1993.
[23] The National Electoral Commission (NEC) is also referred to in the Decrees concerning elections as "the Commission."

10

(2) Subject to subsection (1) of this section, a court or tribunal, as the case may be, may continue with any proceedings before it after such election and make any decision as is reasonable in the circumstance.

The Commission confirmed the date of the presidential election as Saturday, 12 June 1993. The two (statutory) political parties had each selected their presidential candidates:[24] Chief Moshood K.O. Abiola, for the Social Democratic Party (SDP); and Alhaji Bashir O. Tofa, for the National Republican Convention Party (NRC).

Significantly, Chief Arthur Nzeribe, a candidate at the nullified presidential primaries preceding that in which Chief Abiola was selected, acting through a certain Chief Abimbola Davies, sued (under the aegis of their 'Association for Better Nigeria' (ABN)) challenging Abiola's selection. Ikpeme, J., of the Abuja High Court issued an interlocutory order of injunction[25] on 10 June 1993. The order was to restrain the commission from proceeding with the election on the date fixed. Relying on section 19, subsection (1), of Decree 13,[26] however, the National Electoral Commission

---

[24] This was done under the Presidential Primary Election (Basic Transitional Provisions) (Amendment) Decree No. 17 of 1993.

[25] See the 337-page book by the Federal Government of Nigeria: *June 12 and the Future of Nigerian Democracy* (Nigeria: Fed. Min. of Information and Culture, 1996) at 106 to 110: *Abimbola Davies (for himself and as representing the members of "The Association for Better Nigeria") v. N.E.C. and 3 ors.* (FCT/HC/M/299/93).

[26] Decree 13 of 1993, supra.

declared that the election would, nevertheless, proceed.

Humphrey Nwosu, a professor of political science and Chairman of the Commission, had earlier instituted a peculiar system for the election. This system was one of the options proffered by the Commission to the ruling military in order to avoid electoral loopholes detected in earlier elections. This system, chosen by the military, was styled "option A4."[27] One of its incidents was that results would be declared at each rung of the electoral ladder starting from the many polling stations in which votes would immediately be counted and declared, up to their collation at the national level.

The results declared after the elections at all the polling stations in the country showed that Chief M.K.O. Abiola of the SDP scored a total of eight million, three hundred and forty-one thousand, three hundred and nine (8,341, 309) votes. Alhaji B.O. Tofa of the NRC scored only five million, nine hundred and fifty-two thousand, eighty-seven votes (5,952,087). The SDP candidate had more than fifty percent of the votes in twenty of the thirty-one units of reference[28] and in terms of spread, had more than a third of the votes in twenty-nine of the thirty-one units of

---

[27] See, Prof. Charles U. Ilegbune, "The Legitimation of Government in Africa," in E.E. Uzukwu, ed., *Democratization Process in Africa (Multiethnicity and African Nation States)*, Beth 5/2: 1993 (Enugu: The Ecumenical Association of Nigerian Theologians [EANT], 1993) 46 at 51, fn. 19.

[28] The 31 units of reference were the (then) 30 states of Nigeria plus the Federal Capital Territory, Abuja. In addition to the absolute majority of the entire votes cast, only a quarter of the votes in each of at least two-thirds of the states would have been sufficient.

reference. He scored more than twenty-five percent of all the votes cast in each of the units of reference except in Sokoto State where he scored 20.79 percent.[29]

By this result, the SDP candidate ought to have been returned as duly elected. But he was not. The electoral guidelines and laws expressly provided that all the results were inchoate until collated at the national level and announced officially by the returning officer for the election, in this case, the chairman of the Commission,[30] who had publicly declared the election as "free, fair, peaceful and orderly!"[31] The foreign monitors, the local and foreign press, as well as the general populace were generally of the same sentiment. The returning officer then proceeded to announce each result as soon as the relevant state chairman of the Commission brought it to him.

On 15 June 1993, Dahiru Saleh, C.J., declared that the election was invalid having been conducted in defiance of a court order;[32] and, on 16 June 1993, the military government suspended the announcement of further results. One week later, a decree[33] annulled the

---

[29] Source: Chief Gani Fawehinmi, *June 12 crisis...*, *op. cit.*, 143 (Appendix 'c').
[30] Professor Humphrey Nwosu, Chairman of N.E.C., Returning Officer for the presidential election.
[31] Chief Gani Fawehinmi, *June 12 crisis...*, *op. cit.*, 13: citing Prof. Humphrey Nwosu's comment on Cable News Network (CNN, of 12/6/93).
[32] See, *June 12 and the Future of Nigerian Democracy*, *op. cit.*, at 111. Also see, "Hard Sell," *Tempo*, 20 June, 1996, 11 and 12, esp. at 11.
[33] The Presidential Election (Basic Constitutional and Transitional Provisions) (Repeal) Decree, No. 39 of 1993, s. 1(2): "... any ... thing done ... pursuant to the

election. This was after the announcement of the fourteenth state result (which, with the others, tallied with the "unofficial" ones earlier announced at the lower levels).

The public outrage following this nullification was unprecedented. Even the Commission, a body generally considered the stooge of the ruling military, felt so thoroughly peeved as to challenge, in court, Saleh, C.J.'s nullification order and Ikpeme, J.'s injunction in favour of ABN interests. The matter was still pending at the Kaduna Division of the Nigerian Court of Appeal when the military decreed the nullification. A string of decrees was made with the effect of nullifying all previous, pending, and future, court processes, proceedings and decisions on the said election.[34] Ostensibly, the Commission's appeal was thereby nullified but so, also, were the rulings of 10 June 1993, and of 15 June 1993, by Ikpeme, J., and Saleh, C.J., respectively.

Other interesting events have attended this epochal election. These include the declaration of 11 June 1994, by which Chief Moshood Abiola named himself the President of the Federal Republic of Nigeria; the "surrender" of the SDP victory by its leadership; the creation of an interim government; and the declaration by Dolapo Akinsanya, J.,[35] that the interim government

---

Decree repealed by subsection (1) of this section shall … be … null and void and of no effect whatsoever."

[34] Decrees 39, 40, 41, 42, 58, 59, 60, and 61 of 1993. See especially, the Presidential Election (Invalidation of Court Order, etc. [sic]) Decree No. 41 of 1993.

[35] Lagos State High Court decision of 10/11/93, unreported suit No. M/573/93: *Bashorun M.K.O. Abiola and anor. v. N.E.C. and Att. Gen. (Fedn.)*. See its C.T.C. in

along with its enabling decree[36] was invalid and void. We might note also General Sani Abacha's military coup d'état of 17 November 1993, which removed the interim government allegedly by the "resignation" of Chief Ernest Shonekan, its erstwhile head. Another important fact was the acceptance of the new regime by Chief Abiola's running mate, Alhaji Babagana Kingibe. He accepted a ministerial post in General Abacha's new government and retained that status a long time.[37]

Those are the facts. This book argues that we can, under the present approach to Constitutional Law study, make anything of them. Depending on the perspective adopted, one may argue that the nullification was both illegal and unconstitutional or, the opposite: that it was legal and constitutional. Indeed, a learned Senior Advocate of Nigeria[38] has even submitted that although unconstitutional, that the annulment was legal![39] In making this

---

June 12 and the Future of Nigerian Democracy, *op. cit.*, at 192 to 215.

[36] Interim Government (Basic Constitutional Provisions) Decree No. 61 of 1993.

[37] He remained a Minister until July 1998, when General Abdulsalami Abubakar dissolved the federal cabinet a month after the unexplained but quiet death of General Sani Abacha on 8 June, 1998.

[38] Chief Enechi Onyia, S.A.N., O.O.N., oral interview granted me on 13/6/96. The author takes this opportunity to acknowledge and thank the learned S.A.N. for granting him [from October 1987], pupillage privileges in chambers for the first five years of the author's practice as a legal practitioner.

[39] This is supported by A.W. Bradley, et al, *E.C.S. Wade and A.W. Bradley: Constitutional and Administrative Law,* 10th edition (U.S.A.: Longman Inc., 1986) 25 et seq.: "... conduct may be unconstitutional without being illegal ..." See also, John Alder, *Constitutional & Administrative*

remarkable argument he drew a distinction between *de facto* actions, which he considered legal but unconstitutional; and *de jure* ones which he viewed as both legal as well as constitutional. He stated that the people had accepted the 1989 Constitution[40] along with the promise of the military to disengage by 27 August 1993 (on which date that constitution was to take effect). In summing up, he said that as far as the "people" had accepted the election of 12 June 1993, as effected under the framework in place for actualizing the 1989 Constitution, the nullification was unconstitutional. However, as far as the nullification was by the military government, which was in actual control of the state at the time, the nullification was legal.

This argument is, with respect, difficult for some of us to appreciate or accept. The book disputes the approach, the premise and the conclusion. The approach borrows from the subjective Humpty Dumpty.[41] It assumes the flexibility of words as shaped by the unspecified and mutable feelings of the speaker (in varied and varying contexts). It is premised on a hotly disputed assumption that the same thing can at once be legal and yet unconstitutional. Also, in terms of its conclusion, it fails to explain what

---

Law (Houndsmills, Basingstoke … London: Macmillan Education Ltd., 1989) 67 (but contrast with 17).

[40] Constitution of the Federal Republic of Nigeria, 1989. See (Decree 12 of 1989) (moribund for all time).

[41] "When I use a word … it means just what I choose it to mean – neither more nor less." Re-quoted by Eric Young, "Developing a System of Administrative Law?" in Peter Robson and Paul Watchman, eds., *Justice, Lord Denning and the Constitution* (England: Gower Publishing Co. Ltd., 1984) at 157.

considerations were used in affirming either that the 1989 Constitution was accepted or made by the people; or, in fact, what he means by 'constitution' in the light of his implication that military governments were, *ipso facto,* unconstitutional.

The problem of approach is fundamental. The current fixation in Nigerian Constitutional Law study is the narrow, uni-disciplinary perspective. Most jurists and practitioners restrict enquiry to doctrinal legal knowledge. This method excludes otherwise helpful insights that could be drawn from the advances made in other disciplines.

One incidence of sole reliance on doctrinal legal knowledge is the conscious or unconscious reification, or even deification, of the written word. Instead of considering the written material as, in some cases, part of the topic to be researched, constitutional jurists most times regard legal text as not just one resource but the only source. Under the following headings: "The autonomy debate," "Methodology: form versus substance" and "Legal textualism: overrating the written word," the book, in Chapter 2, expatiates on this phenomenon.

Premises established after the sub-structural discussions in Chapter 2 will be used as bases for later arguments and conclusions. It might be noticed that the book employs some styles it disparages - for example, copious and sometimes repetitive reference to authorities.[42] This is inevitable.

---

[42] See, Robert H. Abrams, "Sing Muse: Legal Scholarship for New Law Teachers" (1987) 37 J. of Legal Educ. at 8: "a caution about the writing and research process is in order: legal scholarship and legal annotation are two different occupations. Do not burden research and

We have to be conscious that in order to push through certain proposals, we might be required to go through the structures preset by what those proposals seek to reform. We try however to be brief and to exclude as much deadwood as we can get away with under the present state of the subject.

drafting efforts with the compulsion to cite (let alone discuss) every relevant datum, be it case, statute, or law review article. If someone wants an annotation, they will seek out an annotation. The burden of legal scholarship is to shape ideas, not to catalogue their previous incarnations."

2. Foundational Structures and Processes.

In every polity, the constitution depends on the wielder(s) of preponderant force. In so far, therefore, as Constitutional Law is all about the study of constitutions: how they are created, operationalized, changed and regenerated, any comprehensive portrayal of the subject must demonstrate and highlight the centrality to it of the principle of preponderant force.

But, how are we to coherently present the principle from within the restrictive framework offered by the traditional methodology for the study of Constitutional Law? The current approach is to limit analysis to the written resources available. Usually, this would come in the form of: a written constitutional document (including materials, which sometimes are described as constitution-decrees), ordinary legislation (including non-constitution-decrees), and/or case law.[1] Were

---

[1] A fourth category is the unwritten constitutional convention. This category has not yet had any significant impact in Nigeria as a modern state with a written constitution. See, Viscount Radcliffe in *Adegbenro v. Akintola* [1963] 3 W.L.R. 63 (excerpted verbatim in D.O. Aihe and P.A.O. Oluyede, *Cases and Materials on Constitutional Law in Nigeria* (Ibadan: Oxford Univ. Press, 1979) 11, *et. seq.*). The justified inclusion of this category by Joye and Igweike would seem to apply more to a general, rather than the peculiar, Nigerian, analysis of a constitution. See, E. Michael Joye and Kingsley Igweike, *Introduction to the 1979 Constitution* (London and Basingstoke: The Macmillan Press, 1982) 6 and 7: "... all constitutions consist of a combination of written and unwritten rules. These ... are found in the following sources: (1) a written document

we to rely solely on these sources, many constitutional phenomena would be impossible to rationalize. For example, in terms only of the pre-existing written sources, it would be difficult coherently to explain the legal basis for what transpired between 17 and 18 November 1993 in Nigeria's topmost reaches of power.

The then Nigerian Secretary of Defence announced on 18 November 1993, that the (nominal) Nigerian Head of State had resigned[1b] and, consequently, that he was taking over government. Simultaneously, the said Secretary of Defence, General Sani Abacha, abolished all pre-existing democratic and governmental structures.

No matter which of the sources one may rely on, there was simply no provision, which could legally justify such a state of affairs. At that time, the 1979 Constitution had earlier

---

officially designated as the constitution; (2) statutes which have to do with the basic organisation of the government, sometimes called 'organic laws'; (3) judicial decisions; (4) conventions (customs and practices) …" In the 4th of the monthly colloquia I instituted as head of the Dept. of Intl. Law and Jurisprudence, Nnamdi Azikiwe University, Awka, the two lead speakers seemed to agree that the lawyers' dress code in Nigeria depended essentially on unwritten convention. The difference of opinion between all participants lay in determining what this convention exactly consisted in, especially since those we were copying were mostly discarding the practice and the earliest Nigerian lawyers who borrowed it had left too soon after their study in England to fully appreciate the bases of the peculiar choices of jacket, trousers, or suit colours they fleetingly saw. See, R.A.C.E. Achara, ed. *The DOILJ Discourses* (Awka: Dept. of International Law and Jurisprudence, NAU, 2004) 4th Monthly Colloquium [3 Nov. 2004].

[1b] The alleged resignation was on 17/11/93 and the Secretary of Defence made his broadcast the next day on national radio and television.

been suspended[2] and the 1989 Constitution was yet inoperational.[3] However, we must concede that by the constitution-decree creating the interim government, "the most senior minister shall hold the office of the Head of the interim government"[4] at the death or resignation of the said HIG.[5]

But even at that, any such 'most senior minister' could only validly take over as HIG within the limited framework of the then existing powers. Nothing in the pre-existing constitution and laws anticipated the sort of absolute powers, including supreme law making power, claimed that day by General Abacha.[5a] It

---

[2] By Decrees 58 and 59 of 1993.

[3] See, Decree 62 of 1993. Also, B.O. Nwabueze, *Nigeria '93: The Political Crisis and Solutions* (Ibadan: Spectrum Books Limited, 1994) at 63: " It must be emphasized that there was no other constitution in force in Nigeria during the interim period, the 1979 Constitution (as preserved and modified by Decree 1 of 1984) having been suspended or repealed by Decrees 58 and 59 of 1993, and the commencement of the 1989 Constitution having since 23rd August, 1993, been postponed to 1st April, 1994 by Decree 62 of 1993."

[4] See s. 48 of Decree No. 61 of 1993. However, there were no 'Ministers' in the Interim Government. The official designation was 'Secretary;' although this may be taken as an insubstantial, technical, objection. The major controversy has been one of motive. Prof. B.O. Nwabueze has questioned s. 48 which he calls "a somewhat curious but pregnant provision" (at 60). "General Abacha is known to be," he says (at 83), an "ambitious person (his ambition for the presidency was well-known, but knowing this, why did President Babangida retire all the Service Chiefs and leave him still in office?)." See: B.O. Nwabueze, *Nigeria '93…*, *op. cit.*, at 60 and 83 respectively.

[5] Head of the Interim Government, 'HIG.'

[5a] There was no pretence (except for Shonekan's "resignation" of 17/11/93) to suggest that General Abacha ever intended to take over as HIG. In fact, his

21

is not even clear that he was the most senior minister in so far as Secretaries of the Interim Government took office at the same time and there was no other referent provided for judging seniority.

As for case law, it is doubtful whether the doctrine of necessity could go so far as to authorize the overthrow of the interim constitution[6] when there was no military threat or civilian violence so grievous as to warrant that doctrine on the standard set in *Lakanmi*.[7] Relying on *Lakanmi*, the events of 17 and 18 November 1993, did not amount to a revolution within the meaning assigned to that term in International law.[8] The same result should

---

first act included the abolition of the Interim National Government itself.

[6] Interim Government (Basic Constitutional Provisions) Decree 1993 (otherwise called Decree No. 61 of 1993). At s. 1(7) it even purports to bind future constitutions and limit the normal powers inherent in preponderant force: "The provisions of this Decree shall not be altered, varied, modified or amended by any other decree, law or enactment." The existence of Decree 107 of 17/11/93 mocks the sheer arrogance of this futile provision.

[7] *E.O. Lakanmi and anor. v. Attorney General (West) and ors.* [1971] 1 U.I.L.R. (pt. 1) 201 to 223.

[8] Consider, Niki Tobi, *Legal Impact of The Constitution (Suspension & Modification) Decree, 1984 on the Constitution of the Federal Republic of Nigeria, 1979* (Calabar: Centaur Press Limited, 1985) at 7. Here, the learned author agrees that: "... customary international law and jurisprudence recognise successful revolutions as a proper and effective means of changing a legitimate government if certain basic requirements are fulfilled ..." Also, the Nigerian Supreme Court in *Lakanmi's case* (*supra*) held at 215 that: "... a revolution occurs when 'there is an overthrow of an established government by those who were previously subject to it' or 'where there is a forcible substitution of a new ruler or form of government'...." Since the previous HIG went through the

substantially manifest from applying various cases on the change of government by other than "constitutional" means.[8a]

A similarly unique situation arose in respect of the take-over of the Nigerian government on 16 January 1966. The Major Nzeogwu-led coup d'état happened on 15 January but the 'take-over' was by, as it were, loyal troops the next day, on the 16th, at the invitation of a rump of the government. The Supreme Court was, on these facts, unable to

---

motions of resigning and handed over to a member of the same Interim National Government under the colour of section 48 of the constitution (Decree 61 of 1993), it would seem to follow, that there has thus been no revolution. This is especially so as there was no 'overthrow' and no 'forcible substitution.' However, this sort of pedantry will impress only traditional legal analysts that insist on closing their senses to other than written legal sources. See Chapt. 5 (infra) for this book's attempt to distinguish between a revolution and what it terms a devolution.

[8a] For example, *State v. Dosso* [1958] 2 S.C.R.180; *Uganda v. Commissioner for Prisons, Ex parte Matovu* [1966] E.A.L.R. 514. Consider also the case of *Federation of Pakistan and ors. v. Moulvi Tamizuddin Khan* (Writ Petition No. 43 of 1954 delivered on 9/2/55 by the Federal Court of Pakistan (Appellate Jurisdiction) on appeal from the Chief Court of Sind per Mohammed Munir, C.J. (leading). The case is fully reported in, Sir Ivor Jennings, *Constitutional Problems in Pakistan* (London and New York: The Syndics of the Cambridge University Press, 1957) at 77 to 238; *Madzimbamuto v. Lardner-Burke* [1969] 1 A.C. 645; *Lakanmi v. Att. Gen. (West)* (1971) 1 U.I.L.R. (pt. 1) 201; *Jilani v. Government of Punjab* Pak. L.D. [1972] S.C. 139 (which apparently overruled *State v. Dosso* (supra)); *Mir Hassan v. The State* Pak. L.D. [1969] Lah. 786; *Sallah v. Attorney General (Ghana)*; etc. A very good bibliographical compilation of texts and cases on this point will be found in Prof. M.A. Owoade, "The Legality of Illegal Regimes in Nigeria" (1993) *Brainfield Law Journal*, Vol. 1 No. 1, at 84 et. seq.

hold that there was a revolution.[9] The court held that the change of government was a mere interim handover of power. It may be implied that the coup of the 15th was then still a real and violent threat, which, by the doctrine of necessity, justified the handing over of power to the loyal troops on 16 January 1966. Even then, that sort of violence was obviously absent in the "resignation" of 17 November 1993.[9a] This suggests that not even case law could coherently explain the take-over of 17 November in the guise it was presented. However, the change of government was successful and has been as effective as any other revolutionary change effected by violence or a threat of violence. If the researcher adopts only traditional methods of constitutional study, therefore, she would come up with either of two conclusions. Under the Interim constitution-decree No. 61 of 1993 (which she may continue to regard as subsisting), she could conclude that the actions of the 17th and 18th were illegal, unconstitutional and, thus, void.[10]

---

[9] See *Lakanmi's case* (*supra*) at 215: "It is no gainsay that what happened in Nigeria in January 1966 is unprecedented in history. Never before, as far as we are aware, has a civilian government invited an army take-over … We disagree with the learned Attorney-General that these events in January 1966 are tantamount to a revolution."

[9a] This is so notwithstanding the unsubstantiated excuse by General Abacha and his colleagues that a part of the armed forces had become restive. See, B.O. Nwabueze, *Nigeria '93…, op. cit.* at 80: "…They spoke about the restiveness of the rank and file in the military…" (Shonekan's resignation text to the nation).

[10] The judgment of the Hon. Mrs. Justice Dolapo Akinsanya of the Lagos High Court declaring Decree 61 of 1993 and the interim government of Chief Ernest Shonekan as null and void a week earlier on 10/11/93, adds yet another

Alternatively, the researcher may have to impose a procrustean interpretation[11] to show, in some way, that those events were conformable to the case-law authorities defining a revolutionary change of government.

A more honest appraisal would accept that the problem is meta-legal and would require

---

embarrassment to this already complex and convoluted matter. This is the case of *Bashorun M.K.O. Abiola and anor. v. N.E.C. and Att. Gen. (Fedn.)* reported by certified true copy (CTC) in *June 12 and the Future of Nigerian Democracy, op. cit.,* at 192 to 215.

[11] A similar ambiguity must attend the televised start of judicial proceedings against the deposed Iraqi president, Saddam Hussein. It was like a theatre of the absurd. The *CNN* live broadcast was on Thursday, 1 July, 2004, and the proceedings gave the tyrant every opportunity to ridicule the judiciary. A new constitution had [ostensibly] not yet been written for Iraq after the illegal invasion of that state by the USA, UK and a few other nations. These 'coalition forces' had breached Iraqi territorial sovereignty without the express mandate of the United Nations' Security Council. This invasion of 19 March 2003, had led, some 9 months later, on 13 December, to the capture of Saddam Hussein. The invaders handed sovereignty back to an executive body of unelected Iraqis on 28 June 2004, but this time, with the support of the United Nations. At all times material to these events, the Iraqi judiciary consisted of judges appointed under the old constitution under which Saddam [claimed he] was elected. He was immune from trial under that, now dead, Baathist-based, constitution. It is the continued reliance of the entire world on text-dependent constitutional orthodoxy that has led to the complications so well harnessed by President Saddam Hussein in challenging the jurisdiction of the Iraqi investigating judge. Instead of acknowledging the overthrow of Saddam's Baathist constitution immediately the invaders became successful, the world seems bent on accepting the emergence of a changed constitution only when the formalities of a new document has been concluded - complete with its appropriate constitutional nomenclature!

recourse to other departments of knowledge for answers; or, it would borrow such knowledge and transform it to a form that it could call its own. Areas of law may still exist, to which the closed, self-referential, methodologies of traditional legal science remain appropriate or, at least, sufficient, but in this book we argue that such open and philosophically dependent areas as general jurisprudence and Constitutional Law demand, for an accurate treatment, a cross-, inter-, or multi-disciplinary focus.

David Schiff has well said, that:

> The lack of an explicit theoretical perspective gives to any particular research the dubious nature of its being built on unsound hypotheses.[11a]

This chapter is therefore devoted to laying the methodological and structural foundations for the book's thesis that Constitutional Law is dependent on, and ought all through to be considered along with, preponderant force. In developing this "explicit theoretical perspective," one is determined at this early stage to dispose of the more technical, background, points. This course of action seems logical for at least two related reasons: (1) the methodological premises will be utilized in future chapters and explanation at the outset dispenses with repetition; also, (2) immediate treatment will promote the free flow of the entire argument.

[11a] David N. Schiff, "Socio-Legal Theory: Social Structure and Law" (1976) 39 Mod. L. Rev., No. 3, 287 to 310, esp. at 291.

The Autonomy Debate.[11b]

"Our perceptions are mediated by our conceptions."[11c] How we engage with legal issues will, in all probability, depend upon our preconceptions of what law is. Some consider law in isolation of all other social sub-systems, attributing to it a life, all its own: "the law is," Raymond Wacks thus observes, "law unto itself."[12] A view based on this conception would clearly require fewer resources of research, which, for Constitutional Law, have been itemized by Joye and Igweike.[13]

A broader perspective would see law as an unfailing mirror image of the organized coercive structure of its peculiar polity. It would regard law as a structure which itself is structured by the larger society. This view of law when applied to Constitutional Law will naturally find expression in the reliance upon a broader spectrum of analytical sources. The researcher following this approach would appreciate the traditional sources offered by Joye and Igweike without necessarily accepting them as exhaustive. The researcher with this

---

[11b] See, similarly, R.A.C.E. Achara, "Constitutional Law and the Autonomy Debate: Synthesis from Autopoiesis" (1998-1999) 7 Nig. J. Rev. 206.

[11c] Valerie Kerruish, *Jurisprudence As Ideology*, Maurice Cain and Carol Smart, Series eds., *Sociology of Law and Crime* (New York: Routledge, 1991) at 167. Consider also, N. Poulantzas, *Political Power and Social Classes* (London: New Left Books and Sheed & Ward, 1973). See also, A. Jaggar, *Feminist Politics and Human Nature* (Sussex: The Harvester Press, 1988).

[12] Raymond Wacks, *Swot Jurisprudence*, C.J. Carr, Series ed., 4th ed. (Great Britain: Blackstone Press Ltd., 1995) at 173.

[13] Joye and Igweike, *Introduction to the 1979 Nigerian Constitution*, *op. cit.*, at 6 and 7 (see fn. 1, supra).

frame of mind would, in the search for truth, feel no difficulty in relying upon insights offered by other branches of knowledge to test the adequacy of even the traditional materials.

Such a broad perspective would permit a conversion of the resource into, becoming itself, part of the topic for research. For example, section 1, subsection (2) of the 1979 Constitution[14] stipulates that:

> The Federal Republic of Nigeria shall not be governed, nor shall any person or group of persons take control of the Government of Nigeria or any part thereof except in accordance with the provisions of this constitution.

Under Joye and Igweike's classification, this provision is a primary resource for Constitutional Law in Nigeria. However, for the analysis of the military revolution of 31 December, 1983, where no provision of the said written constitution was relied upon to overthrow the existing government (and to promulgate the Constitution (Suspension and Modification) Decree No. 1 of 1984), it would be permissible under the broader perspective, to treat this primary resource[15] as itself, part of the topic to be investigated. To embark on this reversal of resource and topic, empirical insights already accumulated by the Symbolic Interactionists in the field of criminology,[15a]

---

[14] Constitution of the Federal Republic of Nigeria, 1979. Schedule to the Constitution of the Federal Republic of Nigeria (Enactment) Decree (No. 25) of 1978. This Decree took effect on 21/9/78. The 1999 Constitution has an identically worded subsection.
[15] That is, s. 1 (2) of the 1979 Constitution.
[15a] See, David Schiff, loc. cit., at 288.

might readily be borrowed. Under this approach, the law is not law unto itself but adopts a multi-disciplinary perspective - borrowing eclectically when appropriate.

Professor Hans Kelsen may be impugned or credited as the most comprehensive propagator of the theory that requires that legal science be studied as a distinct and independent discipline (divorced from its social science cousins such as history, ethics, political science, economics, sociology and so on). It must, at once, be pointed out that it was not part of Hans Kelsen's doctrine that law *is* independent of the society. He only proposed that it *ought to be* studied in such a way as to abstract its principles from their underlying sociological and other sub-structural bases. It is important to highlight this. Kelsen did not (and perhaps, could not) entirely divorce law from society.

The distinction is one between substance and method. Substantively, the Pure Theory of Law[16] does not claim the independent existence of law from society.[17] Methodologically however,

---

[16] Hans Kelsen, *The Pure Theory of Law*, Max Knight, transl. (Berkeley: University of California Press, 1967). (See also the second edition by the same translator. It has the same bibliographical data except for the year of publication, i.e., 1970. We shall specify "2nd edition" when referring to the 1970 edition; otherwise, all reference is to the 1967 version).

[17] After all, societal forces or an entity within society cannot but have created the grundnorm. The Pure Theory is therefore, dependent on sociological fact despite Kelsen's protestations to the contrary. See further, Richard Tur, "The Kelsenian Enterprise" in Richard Tur and William Twining, eds. *Essays on Kelsen* (Oxford: Clarendon Press, 1986) 150 at 182. In quoting Sawer, *Law in Society* (Oxford, 1965), Kelsen is described as 'engaging in sociology when writing his Pure Theory

it requires that law be abstracted from society and, its peculiar normative attributes, studied as an independent body of knowledge. It will be difficult to locate any serious legal thinker that maintains, substantively, an absolute thesis of law's independence from society.

Seen in this light, it is difficult to attribute too much importance to the pseudo-battle between the tendency of legal thought which maintains that law is an entirely normative body of knowledge existing independently from any ethical or societal structuring; and, the opposite tendency which asserts that law is created, modified, and entirely structured, by social processes. This latter view maintains the dependence of law on society and consequently maintains that no fruitful analysis of law can be made without first analyzing the peculiar society or polity which constitutes its sub-structure. This tendency of thought is what is referred to as the sociology of law; the perceived tension existing between it and the independence theorists (within the traditional schools of jurisprudence) is what is termed the autonomy debate.

Sociology of law might even be distinguished from sociological jurisprudence. The difference is a matter of perspective and emphasis. While sociological jurisprudence proceeds from the standpoint of a lawyer investigating the social relations, effects, and impacts, of the law, sociology of law or legal sociology adopts the methodology of a

---

notwithstanding his indignant denials'. I have drawn all these sources from the scholarly but humorous account of Professor Raymond Wacks in his: *Swot Jurisprudence, op. cit.,* esp. at 70.

sociologist concerned with that narrow aspect of society called law. David Schiff presents an illuminating, even if difficult-to-read, article on the subject.[18] He marshals a strong argument for what might be considered a more fundamental difference between sociological jurisprudence and the sociology of law. In one reading of his position, he seems to contend that the sociology of law involves not simply the change of emphasis pointed out above, but also the interesting postulate that while other traditions of independent law (including sociological jurisprudence) are primarily concerned with the question: "What is law?" legal sociologists, asserting as they are the entire dependence of law on society, are primarily concerned with a totally different venture: "What is society?"

Drawing, in this relatively new field,[19] from the earliest published materials including the thoughts of Weber, Durkheim, Erhlich, Bredemeier (whose theory borrowed from Parson's works on social systems), Comte and Freud from whom Jhering and Pound are thought to have borrowed their views which started sociological jurisprudence, and contrasting these with Kelsen's Pure Theory, Schiff very ably constructs a compelling textual picture of the history and growth of juristic and sociological analyses of the relations between law and society. However, the hitch is his apparent extension of the existing frontiers of the sociology of law to one solely concerned with "What is Society?" The problem adds dimension

---

[18] David Schiff, "Socio-Legal Theory: Social Structure and Law" (1976) 39 Mod. L. Rev., No. 3, 287 to 310.
[19] Just about 100 years old as a distinct legal tradition.

in the fact that following this thesis, Schiff draws the conclusion, which was logical from his quite extra-ordinary premise, that a correct definition of society inevitably leads to *the* definition of law. Law, in other words, was equivalent to society![20]

In this matter, Kelsen's critique of Eugene Erhlich becomes most apposite, for:

> ... If we define law simply as order or organization, and not as a coercive order (or organization), then we lose the possibility of differentiating law from other social phenomena; then we identify law with society, and the sociology of law with general sociology...[21]

But, is law really as broad as all society? Is not law, even intuitively speaking, understood as just one part of the larger idea of society? Is morality law? Is not morality part of the societal fabric? If morality is not, *ipso facto*, law but yet part of society, is this not one viable evidence that there is a logical disjunction between law and society? Only as metaphor can Schiff's postulate be properly appreciated. In the innocuous language of hyperbole, David Schiff, it may be argued, asserts the unity of law with society only to emphasize his point as to the centrality of the

---

[20] David Schiff, "Socio-Legal Theory...," *loc. cit.*, at 303.
[21] *Ibid.*, at 307 quoting Hans Kelsen, *General Theory of Law and State* (1945 ed.) at 26. Future reference, except otherwise stated, shall be to the 1949 edition, to wit: Hans Kelsen, *General Theory of Law and State*, transl. Anders Wedberg (Cambridge, Mass: Harvard University Press, 1949) (20th Century Legal Philosophy Series, vol. 1).

sociological focus to any meaningful analysis of law: its creation, its operation, its amendment, its nullification and its regeneration. The more restrained language of earlier paragraphs seemingly support this alternative reading of his extended thesis:

> According to a socio-legal approach, analysis of law is directly linked to the analysis of the social situation to which the law applies, and should be put into the perspective of that situation by seeing the part the law plays in the creation, maintenance and/or change of the situation.[22]

His acceptance of a logical, conceptual, and factual difference between society and law (which is only part of the larger society), is made in even more specific language:

> The methodology of a sociology of law does not start with the primacy of legal rules, nor with rules as such, or laws or a legal system. The methodology is determined by an initial understanding of society, of the social system. The aim being to analyze social structures and social institutions, *law being one such institution (there are clearly many others)*.[23]

From these quotations, Schiff could not have seriously intended to construct a theory equating law to society. Surely, society, which

---

[22] David Schiff, "Socio-Legal Theory...," *loc. cit.*, at 287.
[23] *Ibid.*, at 294 (our emphasis).

is comprised of many social institutions, cannot possibly also be at par with one of the many such "social institutions" it comprises.

Yet, another standpoint is that which contends that autonomy is distinct from the idea of independence. While the string is fully cut in a situation of independence, autonomy accepts the string's intact existence but without the puppeteer's dominant control of it.[23a] This argument is advanced for attenuating the damage, to independence theories, effected by the idea that all laws necessarily stem from society. The logic here is that while law may not be independent (in the context of existing in an entire vacuum from society), it may nevertheless be autonomous (in the sense that its operations are regulated and identified by rules peculiar to it in contradistinction to those applicable to other sociological phenomena). A fairly good representation of this view of the autonomy debate is taken from an observation, again, offered by David Schiff:

> A theory of law is independent[24] of the social order according to the methodological assumptions of that theory, i.e. that law is normative and has its own existence. Whilst a theory of law is dependent on the social order according to

---

[23a] Like the "Ajonkwu" masquerade of Ovim, in the Abia State of Nigeria, the rope attached to its waist and held by its strongest attendant helps to restrain some of its more ferocious forays but does not really control it.

[24] 'Independent', in a second reading, should be understood here as 'autonomous' to appreciate the full import of the argument.

the methodological criteria adopted, i.e. law is a phenomena [sic] within society.[25]

The latter representation of the autonomy debate is easier to defend. Law cannot entirely be divorced from its environment; its society.[26] This remains true not only in respect of its impact after creation but, additionally, even so, at the time of its creation and/or its unarranged death.[27]

Analytical positivism has traditionally been the chief claimant to the throne of independent law. At the risk of generalization, theorists that march to its drum believe that law is to be studied from within parameters set by law itself. It considers that law is normative, logical and necessary as distinct from other social sciences that are causal, factual and contingent. The dichotomy in this is regarded as so important that analytical positivists generally consider that the study of law should be by methods distinct from those of other social sciences.

The chief claimants to dependent law have generally been the various and variegated schools under the 'Sociology of Law' banner. To

---

[25] David Schiff, "Socio-Legal Theory…," *loc. cit.*, 292.

[26] Even the most extreme standpoint to the contrary: the "Pure Theory," nevertheless, exhibits some connectedness to society.

[27] Arranged 'death' of law will include 'self-referring' provisions on amendment. For the dispute as to the logicality or illogicality of self-referring laws, see the opposing arguments, respectively, by Professors H.L.A. Hart and Alf Ross in H.L.A. Hart, "Self-referring laws" *Essays in Jurisprudence and Philosophy* (New York: O.U.P., 1983 and 1988), Essay 7, 170 to 178 esp. at 175: "Professor Alf Ross… takes the view that neither a statute nor a constitution can state the conditions for its own amendment."

these, might be included (apart from general sociologists (with a bias for law) such as Durkheim, Erhlich and Duguit) theorists of the Socio-Economics School[28] such as Marx and Pashukanis, and those of the Historical School of jurisprudence such as Von Savigny.[29] In recent times, however, the independence theorists of law have received an ally from the most unlikely source: sociology of law. Niklas Luhmann, a professor of Sociology in the University of Bielefeld, in collaboration with Gunter Teubner, has put forward an addition to the rich theoretical library of legal concepts.[30] Under the neologism, "autopoiesis," it is, in a remarkable departure from the stand-point of mainstream sociologists of law, argued that law is law unto itself and any societal or environmental factors which it considers relevant, are ingested by the legal

---

[28] Their theory of law 'withering away' with the state suggests a conceptual dependence of law to the state. The legal economics school, in so far as it refers to scholars who make an analysis of law from an economic standpoint, should be wide enough to embrace both the socialist and communist jurists mentioned above as well as the capitalists such as Judge Richard Posner. Prof. John Brigham of the University of Massachusetts, Amherst, has, in January of 2004, reminded me however, of the outrage this sort of conjunction might cause to jurists from those vehemently opposed ideologies. And this has led me to distinguish the former with the title of: 'Socio-Economics School.'

[29] Savigny's Volksgeist imports, even if metaphysically, a dependence of law on the psychological factors of the people's united will.

[30] Niklas Luhmann, "The Unity of the Legal System" in Gunther Teubner, ed., *Autopoietic Law: A New Approach to Law and Society* (Berlin: de Gruyter, 1988) 12 to 35. See further, Niklas Luhmann, "Legal Argumentation: An Analysis of its Form" (1995) 58 Mod. L. Rev., No. 3, 285 esp. at 292.

system and turned up for use in a form peculiarly adapted to itself. [31]

The debate, it would seem, has come full circle. Nevertheless, from the positivist's claim for independence to the other pole of dependence arguments, and now, across to autopoietic autonomy, the points in the conceptual triangulation (forgive the mixed metaphors) seem blunted by the inevitable relativism of a debate fashioned by the imprecise instruments of non-recursive language.

The principal merit in an autopoietic view of law is that it positively conflates the best points from the different poles of the autonomy debate. There is surely some truth in the argument that law has its peculiar logic (for example, a child less than seven years old is absolutely incapable of committing a crime under the Criminal Code).[32] This logic of law

---

[31] For similar reasoning, consider J. Fitzgerald, ed., *Salmond on Jurisprudence*, 12th ed. (London: Sweet & Maxwell, 1966) 72 to 73: "Even to [purely factual] questions the law will, on occasion supply predetermined and authoritative answers. The law does not scruple, if need be, to say that the fact must be deemed to be such and such, whether it be so in truth or not ... The eye of the law does not infallibly see things as they are. Partly by deliberate design and partly by the errors and accidents of historical development, law and fact, legal theory and the truth of things may fail in complete coincidence. We have ever to distinguish that which exists in deed and in truth from that which exists in law" (square brackets and words therein, courtesy of Valerie Kerruish, *Jurisprudence as Ideology, op. cit.* at 124).

[32] See s. 30 of the Criminal Code. See further, C.O. Okonkwo, *Okonkwo and Naish on Criminal Law in Nigeria*, 2nd ed. (London: Sweet & Maxwell, 1980) at 92, 97, 119, 197, and 172. The Criminal Code is the Schedule to the

disregards actual physical possibilities (just as does the rule of evidence,[33] which stipulates that the statutory identification of a fact as conclusive proof of another remains so irrespective of what in actual fact may be the case). In the light of such examples, it seems a bit naïve to insist that law is not, in some respects, autonomous. However, to generalize this would probably reduce the pungency of the equally valid observation that in many respects, the logic of law is a reflection of the logic of its foundational society. As an example, the entire interpretive jurisdiction of judges and the whole body of reasoning authorizing customary law springs entirely from the core usages, reasoning, practices and logic of the larger society.

A more telling example of law's dependence is the rule, popularized by Kelsen, that "an extra-constitutional" change is validated by its own success. This rule of law is, in fact, a rule of common sense. Had *State v. Dosso*[34] not so decided, the successful change of the Pakistani government would, nevertheless, have resulted in practice, to a recognizably valid law-creating fact. The case merely declares this teleological truth.

To choose one view against the other unnecessarily curtails the wide vista of research resources. We may accept, as do the dependence theorists that much law is essentially fashioned by its peculiar, constituent, society. Nevertheless, we must at

---

Criminal Code Act, cap. 77, Laws of the Federation of Nigeria, Vol. V, 1990.

[33] See s. 4(c) of the Evidence Act, cap. 112, L.F.N., Vol. VIII, 1990.

[34] Per Mohammed Munir, C.J. *The State v. Dosso* [1958] 2 S.C.R. 180 or [1958] S.C. Pak. 533.

the same time, insist, as do Salmond and other independence theorists, that law generally creates its own truths.[34a] This method is more a synthesis than it is a subjective eclecticism - it takes care to avoid the undisciplined thought processes of undue relativism while at the same time avoiding attachment to the, truth-eliding, closed-systems inherent in any self-referential body of dogmatisms.

This broad view of law permits us entry into the heartlands of philosophy, political science, ethics, sociology, jurisprudence, etc. In considering questions in the field of Constitutional Law, insights from all these subjects (and more) will freely be borrowed. In borrowing them however, an attempt will be made to transform the data into a form recognizably legal. Professor Brigham, that most thoughtful of thinkers on the relationship between law and politics, has once said that "Politics imbricated with law raises issues as to what we call politics and what we call law."[35] And we are not at all certain that it is possible to conceive of Constitutional Law in a framework entirely devoid of, say, political science. Chief Obafemi Awolowo, a foremost Nigerian statesman, Constitutional Lawyer, and sage has once considered the matter in a different situation and concluded that "The making of a

---

[34a] See P.J. Fitzgerald, ed. *Salmond on Jurisprudence* (*supra*, at fn. 31 of this chapter).

[35] John Brigham, *The Constitution of Interests: Beyond the Politics of Rights* (New York and London: New York University Press, 1996) at 135. I still treasure the autographed copy, which Prof. Brigham so kindly presented to me on 28 Jan. 2004 at his Thompson Hall office, University of Massachusetts, Amherst.

country's constitution is applied political science ..."[35a]

A similar case can be made regarding the relation of philosophy to Constitutional Law. The very attempt to distinguish between the different disciplines or to define, interpret or analyze the nature of either subject is, itself, a philosophical "problematic."

The somewhat detailed rationalization of the broad-based methodology of this book is, in advance, to anticipate, the now gradually fading objection of traditionalists that any exposition of "law" must restrict itself to statutes, court decisions, and books on these written by lawyers. In so far as some sort of discipline is required to determine what actually fits the description of "law," "statutes," "courts," "decisions," "lawyers," etc., it seems that so far shall all serious researchers continue to require assistance from fields other than that one (law) which is the subject of analysis.[36] After all, "unaided, one cannot see one's own eyes."[37]

[35a] Obafemi Awolowo, *Thoughts on Nigerian Constitution* (Ibadan: Oxford University Press, 1966) 26. See also Valerie Kerruish, *Jurisprudence as Ideology*, *op. cit.*, at 90: "... the question of law's legitimacy is a question of the conformity of its institutions and practices to political principles" (Our emphasis). Further on this point, consider Mark Tushnet, *Red, White and Blue: A Critical Analysis of Constitutional Law* (Cambridge, Massachusetts and London, England: Harvard University Press, 1988) at viii: "...understanding the work of the Court therefore requires that we give it a political analysis."

[36] Richard A. Posner, "The Decline of Law as an Autonomous Discipline: 1962 - 1987" in (1987) 100 Harv. L. Rev., No. 4, 769: "...the overall progress of disciplines other than law in illuminating law has been striking and cannot but undermine the lawyer's

Methodology: Form Versus Substance.

Knowledge is related to the knowledge of knowledge roughly in the same way as the constitution is related to Constitutional Law. While the one is substantive reality, the other is the formalistic methodology adopted to fully appreciate that reality.

In ideal circumstances, objective truth or knowledge would be attainable or knowable. However, we operate, as humans, in very much less than ideal circumstances and must be content with subjective approximations of truth or knowledge.[38] This brings to the fore the vital importance to any research project of that aspect of epistemology known as methodology (or approach). There is objective truth but so long as there remains human uniqueness, limitations and distinctive perspectives, it can only subjectively be perceived or appreciated.

If objective knowledge were readily apparent, it would be used as referent to test the validity of any thesis. Since it is not, the least a researcher should do is to present, at the outset, the theoretical bases of his

---

(especially the academic lawyer's) faith in the autonomy of his discipline."

[37] Valerie Kerruish, *Jurisprudence as Ideology*, op. cit., 41: "… a view from … which all is visible - except the mechanism of its own gaze."

[38] Considering the limits of our powers of perception and observation, it becomes apparent why no one perspective seems able to transcend the target of reasonable criticism. One view taken of an elephant from its rear will reveal the "incorrectness" of another picture properly taken from its side. See also, Mark Tushnet, *Red, White and Blue* …, op. cit., at 119: "… there are transcendent truths but … the human capacity to apprehend those truths is limited …"

ideas of truth so as to provide for his audience, access to some sort of referent with which to examine the consistency and logicality of such theses and conclusions.

Knowledge is essentially subjective. No matter how clear something appears to you, it is not knowledge to the other person unless he too comprehends it. There are three principal categories or forms through which knowledge usually manifests. There is rationalism or intuitionism by which knowledge is perceived through *a priori* flashes of insight. There is empiricism or sense perception, which relies on experience or history to determine truth or knowledge. There is also pragmatism, which unlike the earlier two essentialist approaches relies on consequences to test validity of information and knowledge.

Within these broad categories, there are yet variations. For example, "classical rationalism" has been vilified for its over-blown claims[39] in contrast with views of "rational intuitionists" such as John Maynard

---

[39] Criticizing the French rationalists of the 18th Century, the tone of John Maynard Keynes in his second dissertation (1908) is especially sarcastic: "... Its formulae were deemed applicable to all questions alike, to trial by jury, the perfectibility of the human race or the existence of God – to all those questions ... which seemed to the French rationalists the most pressing of their time." See, R.M. O'Donnell, *Keynes: Philosophy, Economics & Politics: The Philosophical Foundations of Keynes's Thought and their Influence on his Economics and Politics* (Houndsmills ... and London: The Macmillan Press Ltd., 1989) at 99. Also see, *Ibid.*, at 93, the author's distinction between Keynes's "critical but constructive form of rationalism ... and classical rationalism, whose claims were sometimes exaggerated and preposterous."

Keynes (who is grouped with Moore and others as "Cambridge rationalists"[40]).

The more important point however is that, in practice, none of these broad categories can usefully stand by itself. Empirical investigations do not start-off without some sort of pre-conceived notion as to the expected result, which eventually, may or may not be borne out by the accumulated data. The preconceptions are rationalistic. The point is even more manifest in the realization that the recognition of the appropriate data to collect within the researcher's empirical enterprise is, itself, an essentially intuitive action. Valerie Kerruish has, thus, well said that "If inquiry is being made ... a researcher will have to decide what data to collect ... such decisions are theory dependent."[41]

Similarly, it is evident that Immanuel Kant's "Synthetic *a priori*"[42] or direct knowledge independent of analysis, still requires experience or empirical assistance to graduate from intuitive to confirmed or confirmable knowledge. Research work entirely

---

[40] *Ibid.*, at 81: "There are, of course, varieties of rationalism, and Keynes's own phrase 'Cambridge rationalism' might conveniently be used to distinguish his from other versions." At 97 and 98, "two of the strongest influences on Keynes ... sympathetic to rationalism ... Moore and Russell..." were, together with "Whewhell, Sidgwick, Whitehead and Boad," lumped together with him in this philosophical category. See further at 99: " ... 'Cambridge rationalism and cynicism' ... "

[41] Valerie Kerruish, *Jurisprudence as Ideology* , *op. cit.*, 92/93.

[42] Immanuel Kant, *Critique of Pure Reason*, Phillip Wheelwright and Peter Fuss, eds., *Five Philosophers* (New York: The Odyssey Press Inc., 1963) 214 to 275, esp. at 217. See also R.M. O'Donnell, *Keynes...*, *op. cit.*, at 96 and 97.

based on rationalism or the researcher's intuitions alone is a most absurd conception, especially if it is to be exposed to the rigours of academic scrutiny. In seeking the essence of something, the researcher will inevitably call in aid both his "mental muscles"[43] as well as the confirming materials of experience or empirical facts.

Pragmatism is not really concerned with ascertaining the true essence of things. It rather concentrates on results. This approach is only slightly different from empiricism. While empiricism is concerned with finding what `is' under given circumstances, pragmatism is rather engrossed with *how* what `is' becomes suitable to the goal or object in view. It is function-oriented and not therefore a traditionally preferred academic method of enquiry (geared towards knowledge of the nature of the subject matter). Even though different from empiricism and rationalism, pragmatism is nevertheless dependent in some degree to both. What is suitable in any particular case is a rationalistic stipulate of the perceiver. To confirm this judgment (of suitability), empirical considerations become indispensable.

To summarize, therefore, empiricism and rationalism are not practically divisible except on matters of emphasis. They both go to the question of essence or the "is" while pragmatism is a functional "ought" device,

---

[43] R.M. O'Donnell, *Keynes…*, *op. cit.*, 92. This memorable metaphor is attributed to Keynes's praise of one of Moore's papers: `The whole thing has simply been produced by mental muscles and by keeping his nose to the stone when anyone else would have given way … If he doesn't […] and if he lives forever I think there's no doubt the riddle of the universe will be printed' (emphasis and square brackets, ours).

which seeks to apply the results obtained by the essentialist methodologies of rationalism and empiricism. The ought of pragmatism is utilitarian [and, usually, objectionable to the deontological philosopher] - but that is a different issue.

This interconnectedness of the three approaches afore-mentioned should lead any researcher to question the wisdom in their practical (as opposed to theoretical) disjunction. As an aid to sharp, precise, analysis, the separation may be helpful; but in practice, their extreme isolation, one from the other(s), is an obstacle to the research process and, consequently, a hindrance to truth discovery (and the practical use of such truth in solving live, human problems).

To say this however, is not to excuse the indiscriminate jumbling of these three approaches. This seems to be another example of the methodological pitfalls into which the present approach to Constitutional Law study in Nigeria stumbles. There is hardly any lucid separation of the critical from the expository. Even when raw essences are being highlighted scant, if any, attention is paid to distinguishing the categories fitted for more pragmatic than empirical or rationalistic emphasis (and vice-versa). One result has been a less than coherent account of the boundaries of Constitutional Law and an even less comprehensible analysis of its core concepts.

In Constitutional Law, approach (or form) is as important as substance. Analogizing to that ancient fable of the blind men describing an elephant, it is possible for different researchers to come to different conclusions as to the nature of a constitution (the substance) depending on the different perspectives adopted in their search (within the peculiar constitutional-law framework (the form) they have each adopted).

An ideologically unstructured starting point breeds unfortunate results. Empiricism has traditionally aligned itself with textualism unlike rationalism, which is more in tune with realism.[44] A solely empirical format would, for example, lead Professor Jadesola Akande[45] to rely on the preamble in the 1979 Constitution in order to assert that "We the people ..." first proclaimed thereat automatically proves it was the first autochthonous constitution made by the Nigerian people in their mass. This conclusion seems oblivious to the reality of military puppeteering leaning to the contrary view.[46] A realistic approach by Professor Elias goes beyond the text. He is able to question Akande's conclusions by reference to reason as justified by other relevant data. In this, he is able to assert that the deliberate non-compliance with the amendment procedure specified in the 1960 Constitution resulted in the 1963 version being the first homegrown Nigerian constitution.[47]

---

[44] *Ibid.*, at 88: "Traditionally, empiricism has allied itself with nominalism, and rationalism with realism."

[45] Dr. [now Prof.] Jadesola O. Akande, *The Constitution of the Federal Republic of Nigeria 1979 with Annotations* (London: Sweet & Maxwell, 1982) unnumbered sixth page of the "General Introduction" and at 1.

[46] Consider the tinkering by the ruling military junta through Decrees 104 and 105 of 1979 on the draft constitution; the severely restricted suffrage and unbalanced composition of the Constituent Assembly; etc.

[47] Judge T.O. Elias, *Judicial Process in the Newer Commonwealth* (Lagos, Nigeria: University of Lagos Press, 1990) at 139.

In relation to autochthony and provenance (but not necessarily to chronology), these different approaches have resulted in conflicting conclusions as to the ordinal primacy of those constitutions. A teleological approach would do more. It could question, for instance, whether ontologically speaking, the 1960, 1963 and 1979 documents were, in fact, constitutions.

The teleological form of constitutional knowledge is mostly concerned with circuitous concepts and conceptions. To the extent that its causes are predetermined by its consequences, it may be vilified or applauded as a closed-system. However, this closed-system is restricted only to one of its two levels of assessment. On its second level of less abstraction, it is not a closed-system. It, for example, asserts on the first level, that *the constitution is any framework of governance produced by the person(s) at the relevant time in possession of the preponderant force within the relevant polity or legal system.* This definitional format produces a closed-system admitting no conceptual alterations. But on the second level, which is derived from the first level, itself, there is ample room to agree or disagree as to what in fact, is the particular framework of government at any particular time; who, in fact, is in possession of the preponderant force; and, what degree of force constitutes the preponderating quantity at any particular time. The possibility of error on the second plane does not necessarily falsify the premise postulated on the first. Adoption of this methodology has the advantage of streamlining basic concepts and thus disciplining research efforts to easily ascertainable standards of uniformity without necessarily imposing at the same time, the un-academic regime of unquestionable, unbending, dogma.

A researcher using the teleological format would, thus, for determining autochthony, consider the relevant documents of 1960, 1963, 1966, 1967 (Aburi), 1975, 1978, 1979, 1984, 1985, 1989, 1993, 1995 and 1999 to see: one, whether each amounts actually to a framework used in governance at anytime? (Here, the 1989 and 1995 documents would automatically disqualify themselves). Two, whether each was produced by the person or persons in possession of preponderant force in Nigeria at the relevant time? (This would seem to be so for all afore-mentioned documents including the Aburi-brokered confederal constitution, which was produced by the jointly held preponderant force of Colonels Gowon and Ojukwu. (It must be noted at the outset that preponderant force does not discriminate between actual and only apparently perceived versions.) Three, and finally, whether their maker(s) are, or were, Nigerians? (Only the document of 1960 was made by foreigners.) From the above, therefore, a teleological approach would concur with the realist methodology of Professor Elias to hold that the 1963 document was the first Nigerian, autochthonous constitution. It would however arrive at this conclusion in a clearer and more convincing way.

A review of Constitutional Law literature reveals a troubling lack of certitude as to the topics properly within its ambit. This is another area where form stunts substance. The major trend is to pattern most textbooks against the topics treated by the relevant written constitution (at the time of writing). In respect of the Constitution of the Federal Republic of Nigeria, 1979, this is the approach adopted by Professors B.O. Nwabueze[48] and Jadesola Akande.[48a] In respect of the (still-born) 1989 Constitution, the same approach has been adopted by Professor P.A.O. Oluyede,[49] but to a wider extent.

The approach presents some epistemological embarrassments. As a theory of knowledge for Constitutional Law, it is necessarily limited in focus to a particular type of constitution – the written version – with the added confusion that must arise when the Constitutional Law student attempts to apply its concepts to a different type – for example, the unwritten constitution of the United Kingdom of Great Britain and Northern Ireland.

Similarly, it suffers, as an academic contribution, a more serious setback in the speed of its obsolescence. In the space of barely three years, textbooks patterned against the 1979 Constitution became obsolete or, at best, misleading as a proper guide to the knowledge of immediately succeeding military constitutions of Nigeria. This confusion has on

---

[48] B.O. Nwabueze, *The Presidential Constitution of Nigeria* (London: C. Hurst & Co. in association with Nwamife Publishers Ltd., 1982) see, esp., p. v, *et. seq.*
[48a] Jadesola Akande, *Introduction to the Nigerian Constitution with Annotations*, (*supra*).
[49] P.A.O. Oluyede, *Peter Oluyede's Constitutional Law in Nigeria*, 1st ed. (Ibadan, Nigeria: Evans Brothers (Nigeria Publishers) Limited, 1992). At xvii, Professor Oluyede recognizes that " … time … is [of] the essence of any book on constitutional law …" (square brackets and word therein, ours).

many occasions, led even Justices of the Supreme Court to confound concepts suited for a democratically inspired 1979 Constitution to fact-situations clearly more appropriate for applying the precepts of a military constitution.

Professor Oluyede's position is even more untenable. In 1992, when his book was published, the 1989 Constitution, which was billed to come into force that year, had had its commencement date, further postponed to 1993. Even then, it was further postponed in August 1993,[49a] to 1 April 1994. Before that date, the Abacha coup d' etat of 17 November, 1993, had effectively ensured that that so-called 1989 Constitution never, for even one day, subsisted as a real, active, constitution of the Nigerian state.

Even foreign texts seem to suffer this remarkable lack of certitude as to the appropriate subject boundaries for Constitutional Law study. The topics and chapter divisions vary according to the country of the author.[50] Even where two authors come from the same sovereign state, there is no assurance that there will be congruence in

---

[49a] Decree 62 of 1993 (made to commence on 23/8/93) postponed the commencement of the 1989 Constitution to 1/4/94 but before that time, on 17/11/93, a new legal order was emplaced by Decree 107 of 1993 which entirely put into irrelevance the still-born 1989 Constitution. See further, B.O. Nwabueze, *Nigeria '93: The Political Crisis and Solutions* (Ibadan: Spectrum, 1994) 71.

[50] See for example, Mark Tushnet, *Red, White and Blue…* , *op. cit.*, (fn. 35, supra) and compare its contents with those of A.W. Bradley's, *E.C.S. Wade and A.W. Bradley: Constitutional and Administrative Law* tenth edition (New York: Longman Inc., 1985 and 1986).

their choice of topics. *O. Hood Phillips' Constitutional and Administrative Law*[50a] has admitted the difficulty. In a somewhat despairing tone, the learned editors of this long-lasting textbook have admitted that caprice plays a major part in the selection of topics for Constitutional Law.

A different approach is to pattern the text against abstract ideas and concepts of Constitutional Law and, only then, using particular constitutions as examples, to elucidate the ideas discussed. Except for higher degree treatises devoted to specialized scrutiny of any particular constitution, this approach is surely more appropriate than the former for textbooks of Constitutional Law. Professor B.O. Nwabueze adopts this pattern in his *Ideas and Facts In Constitution Making;*[51] *Military Rule and Constitutionalism;*[52] *A Constitutional History of Nigeria;*[53] etc.[54]

[50a] O. Hood Phillips and Paul Jackson, *O. Hood Phillips' Constitutional and Administrative Law*, Sixth Edition (London: Sweet & Maxwell, 1978) 10: '… it is largely a matter of convenience what topics one includes in Constitutional Law …'
[51] B.O. Nwabueze, S.A.N., *Ideas and Facts in Constitution Making, The Morohundiya Lectures*, First series (Ibadan: Spectrum Books Limited, 1993).
[52] B.O. Nwabueze, *Military Rule and Constitutionalism in Nigeria* (Ibadan: Spectrum Books Limited, 1992).
[53] B.O. Nwabueze, *A Constitutional History of Nigeria* (London: C. Hurst & Company, 1982).
[54] To be included in this important genre of constitutional texts may be such works as: Okay Achike, *Groundwork of Military Law and Military Rule in Nigeria* (Enugu, Nigeria: Fourth Dimension Publishers, 1978 and 1980); Abiola Ojo, *Constitutional Law and Military Rule in Nigeria* (Ibadan: Evans Brothers (Nigeria Publishers) Ltd., 1987); D.I.O. Ewelukwa, *Historical Introduction to*

But an even better approach would try to supply a nexus between the topics so as to evince a consistent and coherent whole. Instead of the disparate concepts one is disjointedly fed by even the very erudite and analytically sharp texts of Professor Nwabueze, one would be given a textbook of general constitutional concepts and ideas which starts off from a logical beginning that smoothly dove-tails into the subsequent chapter, and the next - consistently maintaining a unifying theme, up to the concluding sentence.

There are advantages to this approach. Apart from its self-evident facilitation of understanding, it, more importantly, reins in the wild horse of erratic, topic-inclusions to the equestrian corral of core areas properly fitted for Constitutional Law study. It may well be of some use that the mutable membership of some Nigerian executive bodies be cursorily treated to buttress a point or be analyzed under a course in Public Administration (or such like). But a full treatment of same as a distinct topic in the short time allocated to Constitutional Law study would not only be diversionary, it would clearly be wasteful. The treatment of the nature, definition and scope of constitutions and of Constitutional Law should be sufficient to show that, in fact, such a topic as executive bodies is, properly speaking, only a secondary part of Constitutional Law.

The book proceeds on the hypothesis that a teleological approach should permit the

---

Nigerian Constitution (Awka: Mekslink Publishers Ltd., 1993); etc.

adoption of a single concept to unify the whole course. This unifying theme is our doctrine of preponderant force, which shall be explained in some detail at Chapter 6. It will attempt to show that Constitutional Law can and should be treated in an essay-like treatise of consistent and coherent argument rather than in the disjointed snippets we are presently accustomed with. It will also seek to demonstrate that topics appropriate for inclusion in Constitutional Law study are to be determined by preponderant force rather than the present haywire, capricious, and somewhat irrational, inclusion of every topic under the sky of public law and administration. In this enterprise, the book will show, or seek to show, that the most emphasis in Constitutional Law should be placed on the fundamentals from which all else depend, to wit; meaning and source of constitutions. The current attitude of many Constitutional Law publicists in Nigeria is to vaguely dismiss these fundamental introductory topics in a few, unfocused paragraphs of scant or no philosophical content.

The lackadaisical treatment is painful. In his 670-page book,[55] for instance, Professor P.A.O. Oluyede cites at Page 1, definitions of "constitution" offered by two English constitutional jurists (Professors Wade and Hood Phillips). Relying only on these clearly different definitions, the learned Professor, without any attempt whatsoever at analysis, declines to offer his own; resting content with

---

[55] P.A.O. Oluyede, *Peter Oluyede's Constitutional Law in Nigeria*, 1st ed. (Ibadan: Evans Brothers (Nigeria Publishers) Limited, 1992).

only a perfunctory description of barely five lines. In this attitude of mind, there appears to be an unspoken assumption that the written word is sacred and inviolable whenever it proceeds from authority (formal or informal). This veneration of text has led to the uncritical acceptance of two divergent (although, not altogether antagonistic) definitions of the same concept. This undiscriminating attitude or approach is a form, which will inevitably structure the eventual substance of the conclusions. In Constitutional Law, the undue reverencing of the written word manifests in so many ways and presents so many research problems, that we have extracted it for discussion in a separate sub-chapter to which we shall now proceed.

Legal Textualism: Overrating the Written Word.

No doubt, in this age of documents, the importance of writing can hardly be overstated. Law, like other institutions of this modern age, has come to depend largely on writing for preparation, storage and communication of its content and norms. There is a danger however that this important creation of the human intellect may be reified to the extent that analysts may well forget that its value is not ontological but merely instrumental. In extracting the written word from its underlying conceptual base and creating for it, a life all its own, a huge disservice is, by many researchers, done to the academic quest for truth. This reification is what we may call: "textual fetishism"[56] or "legal textualism."

This sub-chapter suggests that legal textualism is probably the single most debilitating phenomenon in any quest for a truly realistic theory-construction in the field of Constitutional Law. To this end, it demonstrates, or attempts to demonstrate, that writing is not even an essential ingredient of law. It calls attention to the fact that even for written legislation, so long as there remains the hermeneutic or interpretive function of the judge and the final executor, so long shall it remain true that what is written is not necessarily what in actuality is the case. It then attempts to show glaring examples of a clear lack of fit between what is written from what actually exists and point to the blissful disregard of this disjunction by many Constitutional Law theorists in their stubborn insistence on "constructing sameness from difference."[57]

Text is no essential part of the law or of the constitution.

The preliterate political community is the easiest proof that writing is not an essential ingredient of law. Surely, they had laws. In

---

[56] We have had occasion to consider this phenomenon in a slightly different context. See, R.A.C.E. Achara, "Textual Fetishism and the Ambiguities of Constitutional Definition," in I.A. Umezulike and C.C. Nweze, eds., *Perspectives in Law and Justice* (Enugu: F.D.P., 1996), Chapt. 12, 274 to 295.

[57] Apologies to Valerie Kerruish, *Jurisprudence as Ideology*, *op. cit.* at 110.

addition, if they could neither read nor write, their laws were, surely, not made or communicated by the medium of text. If this is true, if laws existed before writing was invented,[58] then, surely, writing is no essential part of the law.

A more involved, yet intriguing, proof depends for its validity on an attitudinal and mental pedestal. Just as the abstract, psychological, phenomenon of a constitution is distinct from the more concrete manifestations of Constitutional Law, so also is it possible to see the law as separate from its manifestation in writing.

In a sense, all 'written law' is merely the evidence of actual, inherently unwritten, law. When they are presented as decrees, acts, subsidiary legislation, rulings [as recorded in the proceedings], enrolled judgments, law reports and even legal textbooks, these forms by which law usually manifests, can merely be seen as the primary and secondary resources for discovering the actual or metaphysical will of the wielder(s) of a country's constituent power. The abstract will may be expressed directly, where the constituent power is in the same hands as exercise day-to-day administration; or, it could be indicated indirectly, as where constituent power, i.e., the power to make a country's constitution, acts through delegates (in the legislature, in

---

[58] Derek Roebuck, *The Background of the Common Law* (Hong Kong: Oxford University Press, 1983 and 1988) at 14: "The rules are unwritten … The greatest technological advance, so far as the law is concerned, is the use of writing … "

the executive and in the judiciary) to whom only limited power is conferred.[58a]

This idea has an interesting intellectual history.[59] In his *General Theory of Law and State*,[59a] Kelsen has drawn a distinction between the norms of a legal system and things he describes as rules of law in a descriptive sense:

> It is the task of the science of law to represent the law of a community, i.e., the material produced by the legal authority in the law making procedure, in the form of statements to the effect that 'if such and such conditions are fulfilled, then such and such a sanction shall follow.' These statements by which the science of law represents law, must not be confused with the norms created by the law making authorities. It is preferable not to call these statements norm, but legal rules. The legal norms enacted by the law creating authorities are prescriptive; the rules of law formulated by the science of law are

---

[58a] See, for instance, A.V. Dicey, *Introduction to the Study cf the Law of the Constitution*, 10th ed., E.C.S. Wade, ed. (London: Macmillan & Co. Ltd., 1965) at 155.

[59] As poignantly outlined by Professor Hart. See, H.L.A. Hart, "Kelsen Visited" in his *Essays in Jurisprudence and Philosophy* (New York: Oxford University Press, 1983 and 1988) at 286 esp. at 287 to 295.

[59a] See, Hans Kelsen, *General Theory of Law and State*, Anders Wedberg, transl. (Cambridge, Mass: Harvard University Press, 1949) (20th Century Legal Philosophy Series, vol. 1) 45.

descriptive. It is … 'legal rule' or 'rule of law' … in a descriptive sense.[60]

Professor Alf Ross of the *law as fact* school has not always been tolerant of meta-physical and hair-splitting legal ideologies and, in this particular case, reviles Kelsen's "talk of rules in a descriptive sense as both confused and confusing."[61]

Rising to Kelsen's support, however, Professor Martin Golding asserts that although the use of the term has been unfortunate, confusion is, yet, easily dissipated by calling in aid the distinction, known to modern logicians, between the 'use' and the 'mention' of words. Without yet reading Golding's view, Hart describes how, in an oral debate with Kelsen in November of 1961, he had urged the same argument as the proper clarification for the rather confusing proposition.

When you 'use' a word, modern logicians take you as assuming that your audience also understands that word. When a teacher of law tells her students that: "if X, then Y," she implies that they already know what 'X' means. A mere 'mention' of a word is different. The teacher assumes that the students want to learn the meaning of 'X' and, in her lecture, talks about, rather than deploys, the word. Instead of: "If X, then Y," she would rather explain, for example, that: "the letter 'X' is a prohibited activity [under such and such a law] and if it happens, the sanction, 'Y',' follows."

---

[60] *Ibid.* See, similarly, although less clearly translated, Hans Kelsen, *Pure Theory of Law*, Max Knight, transl. (Berkeley and Los Angeles: Univ. of California Press, 1967) para. 16 in Chapt. III: "Legal Norm and Rule of Law," 71 to 75.

[61] See, H.L.A. Hart, "Kelsen Visited", *loc. cit.*, 291.

To make sense of Kelsen's rather cryptic construction, therefore, Golding and Hart suggest, here, that the reference was to the nature of the job of law teachers. Unlike the real legislators, teachers have to describe, i.e., 'mention,' rather than take the words for granted and thus directly 'use' legal norms. Hart reports his surprise that Kelsen rejected even this explanation, and, after many years of reconsideration, he now sees, that Kelsen was right and, that the use and mention distinction was probably, too crude as an explanation of this recondite formulation.[62]

The phrase, in Hart's opinion, is better explained by the substantially more nuanced interpreter-analogy. The lawmaker says "Burn this tyre, this stove and this tent on the pathway," and the interpreter tells those whom he believes do not understand either the language or what was said that, they should, "Clear out all things cluttering the road." In this format and tone of voice, the interpreter seems to be prescribing his own norms of behaviour. But Kelsen's phrase shows he is merely describing (perhaps, even more clearly) what the real lawmaker has commanded.

In spite of this brilliant review by Hart, we may yet see that more remains to clarify the "rule of law in a descriptive sense." In our reading, Kelsen has touched on a deeper and more fundamental insight than Golding and Hart have recognized. In his usually abstruse language,[63] he seems to have struck upon an

---

[62] *Ibid.* 292 and 293.

[63] This complaint against Kelsen's style is common. See for example, Raymond Wacks, *Swot Jurisprudence*, C.J. Carr, series ed. 4th ed. (Great Britain: Blackstone Press Ltd., 1995) at 69: " ... Hans Kelsen (1881-1973) is probably the least understood [legal theorist]... Much of

important piece of epistemological evidence without clearly grasping the sheer magnitude of its logical import.

While Golding, Hart and, perhaps, even Kelsen himself, fixed their attention only on the limited scenario of outsider-experts objectively assessing in their own language, things which are unquestionably recognized as "laws" (legal norms), we submit that the focus should have been enlarged to accommodate both that scenario as well as one in which the official (insider) representation (in writing or otherwise) of the legislator's normative stipulates is also seen as not the legal norm itself but also part of the rules of law in a descriptive sense.

Seen from this perspective, the Government Printer's publication, for instance, of Decree No. 107 of 1993 might be seen only as a persuasive representation of the stated will of General Sani Abacha's ruling coalition. It is primary evidence, but by no means, conclusive proof, of what in November 1993, was laid down as the new constitution of the Nigerian legal system. The legal norm of Decree 107 may possibly have been misrepresented in the written form by which that unwritten phenomenon was presented by the Government Printer. Writing is, thus, not an essential part of law.

Again, quite apart from the above postulation of a divide between law and (its written representation) written law, even where writing has had an impact on the legal plane,

---

this is due to his use of fairly difficult and abstract conceptual language ... " (square brackets and words therein, ours).

it has historically and logically had very little influence on 'laws' at the constitutional level and, even less or none, at the political plane (in which constituent power resides). A fuller explanation seems, at this stage, necessary.

Laws do not exist outside a politico-legal system. A close study of any such system will show three planes: the political, the constitutional and the legal (in the descending order of their manifestation).

The political plane is the arena in which constituent power is the battle-prize. Constituent power is the authority to make the constitution and is thus, effectively, the legitimizing authority for all laws and exercise of all sovereign or governmental powers. Whenever (and this is usually the case) there is no unanimity of opinion upon whom the status rests, the issue is resolved by force[64] or the threat, or perceived threat, of force. The person or group of persons (whether the one, the few or the many) whose force or assumed force preponderates over those of other contender(s) become(s) the validating source of the constitution and all laws emanating therefrom.

By the very features of this plane, as outlined above, it is evident that its determinations of constituent status are not to be logically sought in any normative stipulates of whatever authoritative provenance: each determination is a phenomenological existence

---

[64] This could be mental, psychological, physical, economical, spiritual or any other type of force standing alone or in any combination.

that simply happens and lends itself only to observation. Any theories (including this one) about it are only attempts at explanation not prescriptive constructs of any legislative character.

The constitutional plane is second in the hierarchy. This plane consists of a core-area as well as an upper and a lower level of fringe materials, which respectively mix with the political and the legal planes. If Constitutional Law is not to run amok with an indefinite number of topics,[65] it is only material within this plane that ought to constitute its object of focus. Any materials from the other planes should only serve to illustrate some point at issue and not constitute an elaborate topic for Constitutional Law treatment.

This second or middle plane is, itself, vertically divided at the core area into the fields of legislative legitimation, executive legitimation, and judicial legitimation. Especially in its core area, the constitutional plane does not normally impose sanctions. It essentially sets forth boundaries for the exercise of sovereign powers. By stipulating which body, for example, is entitled to exercise legislative power, it impliedly asserts that others will not be acting legitimately if they legislate. This plane

---

[65] Because all valid laws inevitably proceed from the constitution, every legal topic or problem can quite logically be subsumed under Constitutional Law lectures. If literally construed, therefore, the subject would perniciously be inundated with topics more properly treated in specialized courses of law such as Criminal Law, Property Law, Administrative Law, etc.

suggests a series of promises not backed by legal sanctions issued by the constituent power against itself (when governing directly) or against its direct or principal delegates (when governmental powers have been delegated to specified person(s) or bodies). It must be recognized that the nature of sovereign power is not to be confused or equated with its (variable) location at any given time, place or context. There is nothing to conceptually prevent the allocation of, say, the legislative and judicial aspects of sovereign power to one person while assigning executive powers to a body of a few or many. The determination of location is usually a question of practical convenience not one of ideological certainty. Any or all or a combination of some of these powers are distributed at the constitutional plane by whomsoever the uncertainties of the political plane throws up as the wielder of constituent power. This plane legitimizes the exercise of legislative, executive and judicial powers within the framework it sets.

It is important to remember that on this plane it is constituent power that, so to say, directs itself.[66] The regulations here, unlike those at the legal plane are usually not in the nature of sanction-backed prescriptions from a lawgiver to his obedient subjects. The "promises" of restraint or "boundary-marks" to limit the areas of power evinced on this plane are, in the Kelsenian sense, not commonly

---

[66] Indeed, the *Chambers 20th Century Dictionary* of 1983 defines "constitution" as "a system of laws and customs established by the sovereign power of a state for its own guidance."

"legal" norms.[66a] These mostly sanctionless norms are, therefore, to be sharply distinguished from the legal norms found at the lowest plane.

The legal plane is the one in which we have prescriptions for shaping desired patterns of behaviour as well as sanctions thereon, to encourage compliance. This is possible essentially because it is on this plane that rules are predominantly directed at those John Austin's theory would consider as "political inferiors."[67] The expressions of sovereign-will at this level, not being exclusively self-directed, give the requisite latitude for inclusion of sanctions. The rules found in this plane reflect the quintessential attributes of the Kelsenian legal norm.

Table 1, below, attempts a graphical illustration of this theoretical construct. At this stage, it serves merely as background to the observation that while, historically and logically, the three planes manifest in a

---

[66a] Hans Kelsen, *The Pure Theory of Law*, J. Warrington, transl. (Berkeley: University of California, 1970) 2nd ed., 4: " 'Norm' is the meaning of an act by which certain behaviour is commanded, permitted or authorized." But elsewhere Kelsen distinguishes the ordinary norm from the legal norm. Professor Wacks puts it quite concisely in his *Swot Jurisprudence*, *op. cit.* at 72: "… legal norms differ from other norms in that they prescribe a sanction."

[67] John Austin, *The Province of Jurisprudence Determined and the Uses of the Study of Jurisprudence* with an Introduction by H.L.A. Hart (1832 and 1863; London: Weidenfeld and Nicolson, 1954) 9: "The matter of jurisprudence is positive law: law, simply and strictly so called: or law set by political superiors to political inferiors." See, also, Raymond Wacks, *Swot Jurisprudence*, *op. cit.*, at 49.

descending order, writing has had its impact on the politico-legal system in an ascending order of progression. Nevertheless, writing has had less impact at the constitutional level than it has had at the legal plane and almost no impact at all at the political plane.

Why, one may ask, is this so? Of the various possible explanations for this, the most credible may be outlined as follows:

(a) Writing is an instrumental invention of relatively young age – some 8,000 years old[67a] in a world some biologists and physicists claim to have existed for over 3,000 million years. (b) This instrument is primarily for use in communicating and recording information. The older devices of the spoken word and sign language are similarly effective, or even more effective, tools of communication.[68]

[67a] "… the first known writing dates from 6,000 B.C.": *The Concise Columbia Encyclopaedia* (Columbia: C.U.P., 1991) in *Microsoft Office Professional & Bookshelf* (1987-1994) computer diskette. The author is thankful to his former colleague, Dr. Yvonne King of Philadelphia, USA, who supplied him with this valued reference at the Faculty of Law, Nnamdi Azikiwe University, Awka, on 13/5/97 and 15/5/97.

[68] In this respect, consider the rather poetic presentation of the same point by Walton, J., in *Grant v. Southwestern and County Properties Ltd.* [1974] 3 W.L.R. at 231. His tone is musical: "… It appears to me that written or printed words are, after all, only encapsulated sound." In a sense, he however notes, "badly encapsulated sound, in that they often do not, when they purport to be a record of direct speech, embody the tone of voice, the inflexions, the subtleties of phrasing and pauses, which form the warp and woof of real life conversation."

Table 1: *THE COMPLETE POLITICO-LEGAL SYSTEM.*

A	POLITICAL PLANE	B
	[CONSTITUENT POWER]	
	[SOURCE OF CONSTITUTION]	
	[AREA OF PREPONDERANT FORCE]	

L		C
	CONSTITUTIONAL PLANE UPPER LEVEL	

K	M	N	D
	CONSTITUTIONAL PLANE		
	[THE CORE-AREA OF SOVEREIGN POWER DISTRIBUTION]		
J	P	O	E

	CONSTITUTIONAL PLANE	
	LOWER LEVEL	
I		F

H	LEGAL PLANE	G

KEY:

1. ABGH: The politico-legal system.

2. ABCL: The political plane.

3. LCFI: The expanded constitutional plane.

4. KDEJ: The core constitutional plane.

5. IFGH: The legal plane.

6. KMPJ: Area of legislative legitimation.

7. MNOP: Area of judicial legitimation.

8. NDEO: Area of executive legitimation

9. LCDK: Twilight zone between the political and constitutional planes.

10. JEFI: Twilight zone between the legal and constitutional planes.

11. ABDK: Expanded political plane.

12. JEGH: Expanded legal plane.

The uniqueness of writing therefore consists only in its permanent or semi-permanent capacity for storage and retrieval of information (i.e., its capacity to record); (c) writing is most desired by the law-maker at the plane in which recording is, from his own perspective, of most value, to wit, the legal plane. The reason seems self-evident: the legal plane is primarily or even entirely the area at which the lawgiver fashions standards of behaviour he wants the relevant populace to follow. It is for him, as well as for them, of utmost importance that there is uniformity in what is communicated to the general populace. This is more so because sanctions usually attend breaches of the rules made in this plane; (d) the constitutional plane, on the other hand, is one mostly concerned with non-sanctioned statements of intent as to how the source of power wishes the populace to be governed. Until very recently, the common practice was direct exercise of sovereign powers by the wielder of constituent power himself and this practice still exists today in almost all military dictatorships.

By its nature, any writing is a limitation, however slight, on the otherwise arbitrary power left mutable by vague and undocumented promises. It is quite understandable, therefore, that the constituent power would ordinarily avoid putting into writing, matters in this limiting (constitutional) plane. Writing has come to the constitutional plane only after a sustained challenge to one-man constituent power as mounted by other effective locations of power in the polity. The Athenian constitution offered by Solon in 594 BC[68a] was only because of the successful clamour by the lower classes. The clamour was against perceived impositions by the erstwhile rulers. The Magna Carta was not documented until the rich nobles forced the issue (in 1215) from John, the new Norman King

---

[68a] Aristotle, *The Athenian Constitution*, John Warrington transl. (London: Dent Everyman, 1959) 247 to 249. Quoted in Anthony Arblaster, *Democracy* (England: Open University Press, 1987) 15.

of England. The pressures of the War of Independence led to the creation of the Articles of Confederation[69] as the first constitution of the United States of America. This was effected by the few empowered men that held sway in her Continental Congress. In 1787, for the first time in human history, not only was an independent state's constitution preserved for posterity in writing, also, that charter of power was created by the many as their act and deed not only in theory but in reality. James Madison described it brilliantly in 1792:

> In Europe, charters of liberty have been granted by power. America has set the example and France has followed it of charters of power granted by liberty. This revolution in the practice of the world may with an honest praise, be pronounced the most triumphant epoch of its history and the most consoling presage of its happiness.[70]

---

[69] In 1776 John Dickinson's draft of the plan for confederation on behalf of the relevant sub-committee of the Continental Congress came to nought as disagreements by the delegates led in August of that year to deferment of further deliberations. See, A.J. Langguth, *Patriots: The Men Who Started the American Revolution* (New York: Simon and Schuster, 1988) 370-371. It took five whole years after Independence before agreement was finally reached. After Maryland's acceptance, the Articles of Confederation became, in 1781, the first written constitution of the United States of America (see, *Ibid.*, 518).

[70] Quoted by Bernard Bailyn, *The Ideological Origins of the American Revolution* (Cambridge, Mass: The Belknap Press of Harvard University Press, 1967) at 55.

(e) The political plane is in an even more markedly different category as regards the impact, or lack of impact, of writing on the politico-legal system of rules. The rules in this plane are, in a manner of speaking, not even normative. Unlike the legal plane, which hands out legal norms, or the constitutional plane, which issues ordinary, sanctionless norms, the political plane prescribes nothing. If it does anything, it is merely to observe.

There is no rule specifying who is entitled to make constitutions or be the source of power in any polity. This book suggests that entitlement to this status just happens - it is not pre-stipulated by any norm.[70a] This phenomenon is what the doctrine of preponderant force seeks to elucidate. Writing at this plane serves no practical purpose but this has not prevented some rather sanguine attempts to document the impossible.

In section 1, subsection (2), of the 1979 Constitution, it is provided as follows:

> The Federal Republic of Nigeria shall not be governed, nor shall any person or group of persons take control of the Government of Nigeria or any part thereof, except in accordance with the provisions of this constitution.

[70a] There is a sense here in which the declaration in Daniel 4, verse 17, of the *Holy Bible* attains some sort of ominous significance: "… the Most High ruleth in the kingdom of men, and giveth it to whomsoever he will, and setteth up over it the basest of men."

Professor Niki Tobi has criticized this provision[71] and one has to agree with the learned professor that the provision is quite useless. It is not only impractical, it is simply vacuous. If the "person or groups of persons" actually "take control," that provision of the "constitution" as well as other laws of the preceding politico-legal system will automatically lapse.[72] If the overthrow bid is unsuccessful, the above provision will not apply, as it does not deal with attempts. Section 1, sub-section (2), is thus a clear demonstration of the futility of writing for matters properly within the province of the political plane.

The impact of writing on laws is, from the foregoing, relative to the particular plane of analysis. No matter how important written

---

[71] Professor Niki Tobi, *Legal Impact of the Constitution (Suspension and Modification) Decree, 1984 On the Constitution of the Federal Republic of Nigeria, 1979* (Calabar: Centaur Press Limited, 1985) at 4, 5 and 6: "…it is useless … In any case, the so-called section 1(2) is dead and probably dead forever" (p. 6). See also, Justice Niki Tobi, "Keynote Address" delivered on 24/8/92 at the Annual General Conference of the Nigeria Bar Association held in Port-Harcourt, at 13, 14 and 15: "… section 1 (2) provision was … pretence … " (p.14). Niki Tobi, JCA (now, JSC), was the chief draftsperson for the 1999 Constitution and it is not a little peculiar that s. 1(2) has re-emerged thereat - some 7 years after his accusation that it was an insincere "pretence" by those who drafted the 1979 Constitution; and 14 years after his prophecy that it is "probably dead forever."

[72] See, Professor Tobi, *Ibid.*, 7: " … customary international law and jurisprudence recognise successful revolutions as a proper and effective means of changing a legitimate government …." "It is by now," Justice Tobi concluded (*ibid.* at 13), "a well established principle of both customary international law and municipal law of most jurisdictions … "

legislations at the third plane may be, it is dangerous to assume that the same importance should be attached to writing in the constitutional plane. Strict enforcement of laws evidenced in writing at the third plane, does not necessarily mean that the same assiduous implementation would follow constitutional rules when they are based only on some piece of official document that is called a constitution. Then, again, the impact of writing, to press upon constituent power compliance with its constitutional promises, should also not be under-rated. We only argue that a proper balance should be struck in order to repress the tendency of some analysts to regard the written word as the sole determinant of what actually is the case.

INFLUENCE OF THE HERMENEUTIC JURISDICTION.[72a]

Perhaps the most potent argument against an undue veneration of written law is the existence of the interpretive jurisdiction in the courts and, in a subsidiary sense, in the executive. Separation between the lawgiver and the agency for law execution automatically creates room for law interpretation. By the very nature of things, including problems of polysemy, limited ability of conveying thought in written or oral language, possibility of improper motives, and such-like, interpretation cannot but sometimes lead to intentional or unintentional misinterpretations.

[72a] An earlier draft of this sub-chapter formed the basis for my article published as: R.A.C.E. Achara, "The Jurisprudence of Hermeneutics (Judicial and Executive Functions of Interpretation as a Limit on the Legislative Powers for Ousting Jurisdiction)" (2001) *UNIZIK Law Journal*, vol. 1, no. 3, 79.

The making and the enforcement of laws are the cardinal attributes of sovereign power. The normal case has been that the same lawgiver also enforces. From the Jewish and Christian perspective, the earliest legal norm was made and enforced by the very same authority.[73] Due, *inter alia*, to increase in the subjects of laws, it became necessary to divide the functions. The sovereign lawgiver makes laws and appoints agents (mainly soldiers and palace servants) to enforce them. It is these agents in their various degrees of dignity and rank that are collectively called the executive.

As laws grew more complex, it became increasingly apparent that the quality of knowledge required to appropriately decipher them was one higher than could reasonably be expected from every foot soldier or barely literate courtier or servant. The executive was distinguished such that its cream of the highest rank, devoted to the discipline of legal interpretation,[74] was separated from the

---

[73] See, Genesis 3, verses 1 to 6; as well as, Genesis 3, verse 17.

[74] See Prof. Thayer, *A Preliminary Treatise on Evidence at the Common Law* (1898) 207, cited in Sir Patrick Devlin, *Trial By Jury*, The Hamlyn Lectures, 8th Series, 1956 (London: Stephens & Sons Ltd., 1966 and 1978) 121 and 207. At 121, Devlin, L.J., states in a non-judicial capacity that: "… in England the judges have always, in theory, been great ministers of the crown … ." This puts the judiciary in the class of executives as has been done for pre-1979 Nigeria by Dr. F. Olisa Awogu. See, Olisa Awogu, *The Judiciary in the Second Republic of Nigeria 1979-1983* (Onitsha: Pacific College Press Ltd., 1984) viii: '… before the 1979 Constitution … the court functioned as a Department of the Executive, popularly known as the "Judicial Department" … even after the Supreme Court of Nigeria had become a final court of appeal …'

others charged with the day-to-day administration of mostly uncontroversial laws. Alexander Hamilton has made the point in a different context. Writing under the pseudonym "Publius" (which he shared with James Madison and John Jay), he comments, that:

> It has been frequently remarked with great propriety that a voluminous code of laws is one of the inconveniences necessarily connected with the advantages of a free government ... there can be but few men in the society who will have sufficient skill in the laws to qualify them to the station of judges.[75]

This cream of the executive gradually became more specialized and has since been known as the judiciary.

It is important to remember that laws directly interpreted by the judiciary before enforcement in particular cases, constitute a minuscule percentage. The lower level interpreters, i.e., the (non-judiciary) executives administer the vast majority of cases calling for interpretation of the laws. The major distinction is in the claim by the judiciary to the ultimate competence in matters of legal interpretation. The executive may, thus, interpret laws if the affected citizen or other authority accepts the outcome. Where there is disagreement, the executive's interpretive power is subordinated to those of the courts.

---

[75] "Federalist No. 78" in James Madison, *et al*, *The Federalist Papers*, Isaac Kramnick, ed. (1788; England: Penguin Books, 1987) 85 to 487 esp. at 441/442.

The brief theoretical construct above invites the conclusion that in all practical terms, insofar as the judiciary enjoys the exclusive power to make definite pronouncements on what amounts to the will of the sovereign power within the relevant polity, it, the judiciary, is in effect, the ultimate power or at least, the agency closest to the polity's sovereign powers. Given the importance of this power, one may legitimately inquire: what is this authority to interpret laws, this hermeneutic jurisdiction?

The nature and historical origins of the field of hermeneutics, exegesis or interpretation is a very wide one but has been well documented.[76] A detailed study of this vast body of knowledge is presently uncalled for and need not detain us. Attention may however be

---

[76] See for example, D. Rasmussen, *Symbol and Interpretation* (The Hague: Martinus Nijhoff, 1974); K. Mueller-Volmer, *The Hermeneutic Reader* (Oxford: Continuum, 1985); R.E. Palmer, *Hermeneutics* (Evanston: North-Western University Press, 1969); Ricoeur, *Hermeneutics and the Human Sciences: Essays on Language, Action and Interpretation*, J.B. Thompson, transl. (Cambridge: Cambridge University Press, 1981); E.D. Hirsch, *The Aims of Interpretation* (Chicago: University of Chicago Press, 1978); J.L. Austin, *How to Do Things with Words* (Oxford: Oxford University Press, 1962); L.F. Hartman, "Exegesis" in *New Catholic Encyclopaedia*, vol. 5 (Jack Heraty & Associates, 1967); R.O. Madu, *African Symbols, Proverbs and Myths: The Hermeneutics of Destiny* (New York, 1992); Ricoeur, *Conflict of Interpretation: Essay in Hermeneutics*, Don Hide, ed. (Evanston: Northwestern University Press, 1974); and, Ricoeur, *Interpretation Theory: Discourse and the Surplus of Meaning* (Fortworth: Christian University Press, 1925). All cited by R.O. Madu, *Problem of Meaning in Philosophy and Theology: The Hermeneutic Solution*, (Enugu: Anic Printing Press, 1995) 48, 50 and 51.

called on this subject to a remarkably lucid booklet by Reverend Father (Dr.) Raphael Okechukwu Madu.[77] It is not only a concise guide, but much more, it provides a useful and scholarly bibliography of other sources of information about this arcane subject.

At pages 11 and 12 of the booklet, the author traces the etymological origins of hermeneutics to Hermes (the Greek god whose major role was that of messenger of the gods to mortals). Madu most efficiently demonstrates the link between hermeneutics, exegesis and interpretation[78] and the importance this has (for his seminarian audience) to philosophy and theology. The booklet demonstrates deep scholarship but sometimes the marked enthusiasm for his project leads the author to some quite avoidable inanities. For example, the erudite Reverend asserts with astonishing certitude that one

> … may not hesitate to propound that hermeneutics is not only a search for proper and deep meaning but is itself the meaning that is sought.[79]

If it is really the medium of search, can it, logically speaking, also be the object sought? Should it not be either the one or the other? We need not join Dr. Madu into the extremities he attempts, by this summation, to lead us. Hermeneutics is the means not the end. It is the search-instrument for meaning not the truth-value sought.

---

[77] R.O. Madu, *Problem of Meaning …, Ibid.*
[78] *Ibid.*, 13.
[79] *Ibid.*, 17/18.

Having said that, having touched on the substance of the law-interpreting power which may be attributed to judges, one comes to the realization that even if a lawmaker himself writes the law, even if his meaning were conveyed in precise language and his audience, highly educated; it remains the case, nevertheless, that his stated desire can be subverted (intentionally or ignorantly) so long as there remains any other person or body invested with interpretive jurisdiction over that law.

This can happen various ways. Just as written and unwritten legislation can be subverted, so can the interpretation by judges be undermined (by future judges or by administrators enjoined to execute such judgments).

In very picturesque language, James Madison has in the Federalist papers,[80] described the inherent imperfections that must attend communication of meaning from source to audience when done with the medium of imprecise text or language:

> All new laws, though penned with the greatest technical skill and passed on the fullest and most mature deliberation, are considered as more or less obscure and equivocal, until their meaning be liquidated and ascertained by a series of particular discussions and adjudications ... But no language is so copious as to supply words or phrases for every complex idea, or so correct as not to include many

---

[80] "Federalist No. 37," *op. cit.* 245.

> equivocally denoting different ideas …
> When the Almighty himself condescends to
> address mankind in their own language, his
> meaning, luminous as it must be, is
> rendered dim and doubtful by the cloudy
> medium through which it is communicated.

In respect of hermeneutics in case law, none
can state the point any much better than has
Paul Watchman.[81] Again, we borrow large chunks:

> The process may appear to be one of
> procrustean conceptualism but, as the
> judgment of Lord Reid in *Conway v.
> Rimmer*[82] illustrates, seemingly
> authoritative precedents can be
> distinguished … other methods … are to
> argue that the rule laid down was wider
> than necessary for the decision, that the
> decision is obscure, that the decision is
> in conflict with other authorities or
> legal principles, that the reasoning of
> the judge was deficient in some respect,
> or that the judge primarily had one fact
> situation in mind when he made his
> judgment and his reasoning therefore
> cannot by analogy be applied to the fact
> situation in the present case. The list is
> not exhaustive.

Indeed, it is not:

> … The open textured nature of the rules
> which the judiciary work with, whether in

---

[81] Paul Watchman, "Palm Tree Justice and the Lord
Chancellor's Foot" in Peter Robson and Paul Watchman,
eds., *Justice, Lord Denning and the Constitution*
(England: Gower Publication Co. Ltd., 1981) at 27.
[82] [1968] A.C. 910 at 950.

statutory or common law form, mean that their support cannot be certain.[83]

These rules permit appeals to natural law, fundamental human rights and such other concepts that imply, in the words of Lord Devlin of Westwick, the idea of "The law above the law."[84]

An intriguing reaction to the hermeneutic jurisdiction has been an irritated backlash by the lawmaker. He simply legislates away the court's power to manipulate what he perceives to be his clear, unambiguous directives. This can take the shape of a positive conferment of exclusive jurisdiction to another court, tribunal or other authority, or it could be by the more offensive method of negatively precluding the courts from looking into a specified area of adjudicatory subject.[84a] The

---

[83] Peter Robson, "Problems of Judicial Proof" in Peter Robson and Paul Watchman, *loc. cit.* at 45.

[84] Lord Devlin "Foreword" in J.L. Jowell and J.P.W.B. McAuslan, eds., *Lord Denning: The Judge and the Law* (London: Sweet & Maxwell, 1984) vii.

[84a] See for e.g., *Att. Gen. of Bendel State v. Agbofodoh and ors.* [1999] 2 S.C.N.J. 111 esp. at 144. In *Abaribe v. Speaker Abia State H.A.* [2001] CHR 225, esp. at 254 and 255, Pats- Acholonu, J.C.A., denies that s. 188 (10) of the 1999 Constitution amounts to an ouster of jurisdiction. Impeachment is, he says, the normal province of the legislature; and the preclusion of the court's interference in that section is merely a re-statement of facts. The 2nd limb of the statement seems especially doubtful. The constitution gives and takes. It gave adjudicatory functions to the courts in s. 6 and in chapt. VII. The same constitution can, and has taken that function from the courts in relation to impeachments, simple! It is an ouster without the normally negative connotations that attach to that term.

instrument for this is what is known as the ouster clause.

This has however, not entirely put the courts to vanquished flight. In a remarkable show of intellectual resourcefulness, the judiciary, "the least dangerous branch," has maintained that so long as any court remains so, it has an inherent power to consider the validity of even these ouster clauses. The principle is ingenious. The courts have simply asserted the logical point that to be able to find that their jurisdiction has been ousted, it must be admitted that they have jurisdiction to make that declaration. Moreover, if there is power to say there is no power, this necessarily implies the power to hold that there is power. Thus, as was stated by the Supreme Court in the celebrated case of *Barclays Bank of Nigeria Ltd. v. Central Bank of Nigeria,*[85] "a court may, by statute, lack jurisdiction to deal with a particular matter, but it has jurisdiction to decide whether or not it has jurisdiction." The jurisdiction to determine its own jurisdiction is the most effective power held by the judiciary over the legislature.

Between a clear, unambiguous, legislative pronouncement and a determined insistence by the judges to interpret such proclamation into something different, what is valid law is rather a political than a legal question. One

---

[85] [1976] All N.L.R. 326 at 335, per Fatayi-Williams, J.S.C. (as he then was). See also, *ARCON v. Fassassi (No. 4)* (1987) 3 N.W.L.R. (pt. 59) 42 at 45/46 (per Kayode Eso, J.S.C.); *Aladegbemi v. Fasanmade* (1988) 3 N.W.L.R. (pt. 81) 129 at 155. Also, consider *Wilkinson v. Barking Corp.* [1948] 1 K.B. 721 esp. at 725.

approach, in jurisdictions with an omnicompetent legislature, is to make a law retrospectively nullifying the offending court judgment. This was done in Nigeria by the promulgation of the Federal Military Government (Supremacy and Enforcement of Powers) Decree No. 28 of 1970. This legislation was specifically to nullify the Supreme Court decision that invalidated some decrees (legislative judgments) when purportedly the jurisdiction of the court had earlier been ousted.[86] Following the reasoning in *Lakanmi* against *ad hominem* laws targeted at particular individuals rather than general subjects, it may be wondered whether the retrospective annulment of that particular Supreme Court decision in *Lakanmi* would not itself, be *ad hominem* and void? If so declared by the courts what would have been the reaction of the military government in the face of such an open challenge to its acquired right to constituent power at the time? Fortunately or not, this judgment-annulling decree[87] was never tested in the courts[87a] and we may never know the answer to the above questions except by analogy to any similar future legislation.[87b]

---

[86] The Supreme Court decision referred to is *Lakanmi v. Att. Gen. (West), supra.*

[87] The Federal Military Government (Supremacy and Enforcement of Powers) Decree No. 28 of 1970.

[87a] But see the *obiter dictum* of Karibi-Whyte, J.S.C., in *Military Governor of Ondo State v. Adewunmi* (1988) 3 N.W.L.R. (pt. 82), 280 at 305: "... the contrary view of this court in ... Lakanmi ... which was promptly and unequivocally rejected by the Federal Military Government ... Decree No. 28 of 1970 ..."

[87b] The Interim Government (Validation, etc.) Decree No. 23 of 1994 is one such decree. This decree of 17/11/94 expressly nullifies the judgment in suit no: M/573/93 (i.e., Akinsanya, J.'s, decision in *Bashorun Abiola and*

A similar situation has arisen in England. The omni-competent Parliament had made it clear that it would not brook any adverse decisions in a case then pending at the judicial division of the House of Lords concerning a claim against the government for compensation by a foreign company. Characteristically, the judges refused to be intimidated and gave judgment to the plaintiff in that case of *Burmah Oil v. Lord Advocate.*[88] In no distant period, Parliament asserted its sovereignty by promulgating the War Damage Act[89], which, in clear words, nullified retrospectively the House of Lord's decision in *Burmah Oil*. Like the Federal Military Government (Supremacy and Enforcement of Powers) Decree, the War Damage Act has, not been challenged in court. If we agree with Madison[90] that "all new laws ... are considered as ... obscure and equivocal, until their meaning be ascertained by ... adjudications," we must conclude too that the judgments purportedly avoided by those legislations have, at worst, only been rendered questionable[91] as extant, binding, legal authorities.

---

anor. v. N.E.C. and anor. (supra) avoiding the Interim Government (Basic Constitutional Provisions) Decree No. 61 of 1993). But it too has not yet been tested for validity in court. The possibility that the courts will declare Decree No. 23 of 1994 as null and void, being *ad hominem*, cannot yet be ignored.

[88] [1965] A.C. 75.

[89] The War Damage Act, 1965.

[90] Federalist No. 37, supra (see fn. 80).

[91] The fact that 25 years later (on 13/6/95) the Nigerian Court of Appeal relied on reasoning in *Lakanmi* to strike down another *ad hominem* military decree is particularly significant: *Guardian Newspapers and ors. v. Attorney General of the Federation and anor.* (1995) 5 NWLR (pt.

However, this is not an end to the matter. One has to consider the executive branch as a preponderating factor in this politico-legal power equation. It is the peculiar province of the executive to directly enforce or administer laws (a large majority of which are directly implemented without the mediating process of judicial interpretation). Indeed, even when controversial laws are sent up for authoritative judicial interpretation, it still falls on the executive to implement them after the said clarification. The application or administration of judgments and other laws involve interpretation and although the judiciary has nominal finality in this field, the executive can use its own hermeneutic powers to subvert (legislative and) judicial pronouncements almost in the same way as the judiciary may, if it desires, undermine laws made by the legislature.

To undermine a judgment, the executive can simply disobey it, refuse to enforce it, delay its implementation or subvert its meaning by a contrary interpretation. The first two broad methods of challenge are relatively crude and appear to be found more readily in societies where the one or the few who fuse legislative and executive aspects of sovereign power in the same location hold constituent power. The latter methods of challenge are subtler and more likely to be found in democratic societies where the executive is separated from the legislature and more inclined to respect the

---

398) 703. The powerful but sometimes contradictory leading judgment was by Pats-Acholonu, J.C.A. (now, JSC), and the fact that he admits that Decree 28 of 1970 "overturned" *Lakanmi* accentuates, rather than diminishes the point. See esp. 739 (paras. C and D).

sensibilities of the general populace against open disobedience of court orders. Examples here are hazy but still helpful. In Nigeria, under a military imposed civilian dictatorship, the judgment of Dolapo Akinsanya, J., in *Bashorun M.K.O. Abiola and anor. v. N.E.C. and anor.*,[91a] was ignominiously disobeyed to the extent that it invalidated the appointment of Chief Ernest Shonekan as Head of State and required the immediate operationalization of the 1989 Constitution. In spite of the many questionable pronouncements in this very bold judgment, one would have expected an appeal or a more subtle challenge to it if Nigeria had been a more developed polity. Rather, the Chief Justice of Nigeria himself, in contempt of the very judiciary he was supposed to lead, invited Chief Ernest Shonekan to attend and speak (as Head of State) at a conference organized for judges and which Justice Dolapo Akinsanya was expected to attend!

Justice Pats-Acholonu and his brave colleagues at the Lagos Division of the Court of Appeal ordered the government, in *Guardian*,[91b] to open the premises of the Guardian Newspapers, which it had sealed; but this was ignominiously ignored. It took another couple of months before the legislative branch of the military government, promulgated, on its own terms, a de-proscription legislation, which it, wearing its executive hat, then enforced to reopen the sealed newspaper house. The examples are legion and include the brazen display of one Major-General Musa Bamaiyi, who in defiance of the orders of Belgore, C.J., of the Federal

---

[91a] *Supra.*
[91b] (1995) 5 NWLR (pt. 798) 703, *supra.*

High Court, found it in himself as a major functionary of the executive to write the learned trial Chief Judge emphatically stating that he would not obey the court's order. He did not stop there but proceeded to request the Chief Judge to keep off cases involving the government agency in which Bamaiyi was Chief executive as well as to advise other judges under the learned Chief Judge to keep off as well (purportedly for their lack of jurisdiction over his agency).[92]

In the United States of America, although many states' executives were opposed to *Abington School District v. Schempp*[93] (which held that "school-initiated prayer in public schools was unconstitutional"[94]), they usually criticized, but did not openly disobey it. However, by deliberate misinterpretation and delays, the practice continued in some schools 20 years later into "the 1980s."

It would incredibly be jejune to seek an explanation of these matters in simple legal norms. It is an area, which the Americans imaginatively describe as the "political question." We shall try, later in this work, to develop the analysis. The book deploys it here simply to emphasize the immense influence of the hermeneutic jurisdiction of judges and of administrators on writing. We conclude this chapter by describing legal textualism in some

---

[92] The committal proceedings for contempt of court was appealed against by the government agency (NDLEA) rather than the alleged contemnor, Major-General Musa Bamaiyi (the Chief Executive of NDLEA). See the *Guardian* Newspapers of 20/2/97.
[93] 374 U.S. 203 (1962).
[94] Mark Tushnet, *Red, White and Blue…, op. cit.* at 150.

detail through examples and end with the call for a balanced view.

TEXTUAL FETISHISM, A JAUNDICED VIEW, AND THE NEED FOR BALANCE.[94a]

To keep focused within our 'June 12' model, we shall give examples of 'legal textualism' or 'textual fetishism' from within that framework. We shall especially rely on two text writers: Chief Gani Fawehinmi and Professor B.O. Nwabueze. They have each written respectively for and against the notion that the June 12 election-nullification was unconstitutional and we shall draw from arguments (mostly peripheral to that substantive issue) with which each has advanced or sought to advance his viewpoint. For case law, the book will call attention to some parts of Mrs. Justice Dolapo Akinsanya's rather remarkable judgment in the earth-shaking case of *Bashorun M.K.O. Abiola and anor. v. National Electoral Commission and anor.*[94b]

The goal is to demonstrate the untidy nature of thought that comes from sole reliance on methods of legal textualism to solve constitutional problems. In this enterprise however, it may also be seen that some error must result from assuming that writing serves no useful function at all in constitutional analysis. This would be a jaundiced view. Psychologically, it is not evidently controversial to remark that, many people

---

[94a] See, similarly, R.A.C.E. Achara, "Bare Text and the Constitutional Case for Abiola" (2003) vol. 1, no. 1, *Nigerian Bar Journal*, 71.
[94b] *Supra.*

regard obligations or norms encapsulated in writing as more hallowed than when evidenced in merely ephemeral vocalizations.

In his *June 12 crisis…* (supra), Chief Gani Fawehinmi advances three principal arguments for his view that the civilian government of Chief Ernest Shonekan, emplaced by the military in order to legitimize the earlier nullification of the June 12 election, was invalid. These arguments constitute the three chapters of his book and are as follows: (a), that the then military president signed the enabling constitution for that government when he had legally ceased to have such legislative competence. Also, (b), that the appointment of the head of the new government (and consequently his entire executive), was illegal in so far as the appointment was not made under the (impugned) interim constitution. Finally, (c), that the implications of fraud surrounding the time of publication of the constitution[95] vitiated it and, consequently, nullified any thing done thereunder.

Argument (a) seems to be an elaboration of (c), which contends that from all the questionable circumstances including: the publication of the (26 August, 1993) Interim Constitution in the gazette of 23 August, 1993 (i.e., 3 days before it was signed); the statement by the Federal Attorney General on 27 August, 1993, that the said constitution was still in draft; the evidence of differences between that draft and the actual constitution:

---

[95] Decree No. 61 of 1993 (supra).

> The irresistible conclusion is that Decree No. 61 of 1993 was CERTAINLY not signed on the 26th of August, 1993. It was signed into law after the 28th August, 1993.[96]

These two arguments seemed to have impressed the learned trial judge in *Bashorun M.K.O. Abiola's case* (supra) and she consequently held the Interim Constitution and government, invalid. In an acerbic criticism of both the motive and substance of this judgment, Professor B.O. Nwabueze, a principal draftsman of that constitution, lampoons the two arguments as entirely lacking in merit. He contends that only the unused argument '(b)' is sustainable. But, even here, he argues, the defective appointments cannot justify the calamitous outcome inherent in the judgment.

To avoid undue repetition, the book will briefly outline the arguments as made by Chief Gani Fawehinmi. Thereafter, it will highlight relevant comments by Akinsanya, J., and/or Prof. Nwabueze on the point. It will try after this to evaluate the weight of the argument and make any necessary criticisms. The aim, throughout, will be to emphasize the nature and dangers of textual fetishism or legal textualism to constitutional law study. The rather boisterous tone of criticism only reflects the extreme distaste the author has for that illogical method of enquiry and is meant to accentuate the urgency for radical change.

ARGUMENT (a).

---

[96] Chief Gani Fawehinmi, *June 12 crisis...*, at 117.

By Decree No. 59 of 1993, President Babangida suspended and/or repealed Decree No. 1 of 1984 (as variously amended). Decree No. 1 of 1984 was the military constitution of the previous regime of Major-General Buhari. With a few amendments under Decree No. 17 of 1985, the new regime "retained" Decree 1 as its own constitution. By this Decree, the legislative authority of the Federal Military Government was to be exercised by decrees signed by the President (Head of the Federal Military Government). Decree 59 was, on its face, to commence on 26 August 1993. The Interim Government (Basic Constitutional Provisions) Decree No. 61 of 1993 was also billed to commence the same day.

Chief Fawehinmi's argument is that the law does not take account of fractions of days in construing the effective commencement time of a statute.[96a] By indicating 26 August 1993, as the commencement date, Decree 59 effectively took effect from midnight of the 25th and, thus, deprived President Babangida of his erstwhile competence to sign any subsequent decrees. By this reasoning, President Babangida was incompetent, on 26 August, to sign Decree 61 of 1993.[96b]

[96a] S. 2(3) of the Interpretation Act, 1964 (now in L.F.N., 1990). *Tomlinson v. Bullock* [1879] 4 Q.B.D. 230 at 232 (per Lush, J.): "… the law takes no notice of the fractions of a day … an Act which comes into operation on a given day becomes law as soon as the day commences."

[96b] See Gani's, *June 12 crisis …*, *op. cit.* at 21: "After signing Decree 59 of 1993 into law, President Ibrahim Babangida no longer had legislative competence to sign any other Decree into law and by Decree 59 of 1993, the military regime ended. Any other Decree signed into law after … was thereby void. The void Decrees are … No. 60

In a 24-page judgment displaying arguments and supporting authorities strikingly similar to those advanced by Chief Fawehinmi, Justice Dolapo Akinsanya of the Lagos High Court came to the same conclusion (ostensibly relying on the submissions of plaintiffs' counsel) in the case of *Bashorun M.K.O. Abiola and anor. v. N.E.C. and anor.*[97] Professor B.O. Nwabueze has torpedoed this argument, judicially endorsed by Akinsanya, J., as "completely erroneous."[98]

Professor Nwabueze's trenchant criticisms do not clearly discriminate arguments (a) and (c). However, in a staccato-torrent of fiery disapprobation, the learned professor considers most of the points raised in all the arguments. Broadly speaking, those directed against argument (a) are three in number (when a related argument which seems more appropriate to (c) is excluded).

First, he argues, the learned judge failed to appreciate the difference in status between Decree 61 of 1993 and ordinary statutes, which, ostensibly, she thought she was dealing with. Secondly, thought Professor Nwabueze, Justice Akinsanya failed to see that the validity of Decree 61 was not justiciable. This is because of real-politics and because of that decree's specific and unambiguous ouster clause. Thirdly, and finally on argument (a), Professor Benjamin Nwabueze faults the reasoning of Mrs.

---

of 1993 … and Decree No. 61 of 1993 …." Also, see 33 (Ibid.).

[97] See, *June 12 and the Future of Nigerian Democracy, op. cit.*, 192 to 215 (inclusive). Fawehinmi was nowhere acknowledged as the source of the learned judge's information.

[98] See, *Nigeria '93 …, op. cit.*, at 67.

Justice Dolapo Akinsanya (and consequently, the reasoning of Chief Gani Fawehinmi) by emphasizing the difference between, on the one hand, President Babangida's power to sign decrees (which he admitted was at an end on the repeal or suspension of Decree 1 of 1984) and, on the other hand, the power of the Federal Military Government to have its decrees authenticated by its head (Babangida) irrespective of the existence of any written law in that behalf.

The third criticism is founded upon the first limb of the second criticism and both may conveniently be treated together. Although argument (a) seems quite untenable, yet, substantial criticisms of it by Professor Nwabueze are no less immune from censure.

It is difficult to justify the first criticism on its own terms. The substratum upon which it is based[99] is not even remotely borne out by the evidence. In the entire 24-page judgment, Mrs. Justice Dolapo F. Akinsanya took care to analyze the issues and never suggested that her conclusions was hinged on any misapprehension of the constitutional status Decree 61 claimed for itself. The misconception seems to have come from the learned professor himself. He went into a lot of trouble to assert uncontested points in proof of this criticism. The basis of the judgment was not that Decree 61 did not contain organic provisions creating the relevant governmental

---

[99] *Ibid.*, 62: "The initial error was the failure on the part of the court to appreciate the status of Decree 61 of 1993 and treating it like an ordinary statute … it had all the attributes requisite in the definition of a modern written constitution."

offices highlighted. Rather, it was concerned, as was the originating summons upon which the suit was brought, on whether at all, that piece of printed words, was authorized by the appropriate person required to elevate it to the status it claimed. The learned professor could surely not be suggesting here that courts would be precluded from investigating the validity and status of Decree 61 if, for example, the Chief of Air Staff had purported to have written and signed it? It is rather unhelpful to claim, as does Professor Nwabueze:

> That since at the time the learned trial judge heard and determined the present suit, authority to do so must have derived from some constitution, it could not have derived from any other constitution than the basic law embodied in Decree 61 of 1993.[100]

Why not? Are all constitutions necessarily written? If it were proved that Decree 61 was made days after General Babangida left office and was, for example, signed not by him but by the Federal Attorney-General, would we, following Professor Nwabueze's argument, be constrained nevertheless to hold that the judge's authority derived from such an impugned document? Could we properly say we had no constitution only because all the written ones had been vitiated? What, after all is the whole basis of the interpretive jurisdiction of courts?

Undoubtedly, if the learned trial judge found, as she could have, that Decree 61 of

---

[100] *Ibid.*, 63.

1993 was a validly subsisting representation of the will of the holders of preponderant force in the Nigerian polity of that period, it would have been her duty to strike out the suit and affirm her inability to question its validity. It would however be stretching the point too far to say that she was precluded from carrying out the investigation and finding out whether this state of affairs, indeed, existed.

It is for the same reason that the second limb of the second criticism by Professor Nwabueze seems questionable. He argues that Justice Akinsanya erred in proceeding to judgment despite the ouster of her jurisdiction:

> By a provision in the decree which is couched in language so unequivocal and umabiguous [sic] as to leave no loophole at all for judicial activism.[101]

The learned trial judge did, in fact, consider this ouster clause and, consistent with the view she took of the entire decree, held it "ineffective."[102] This position hardly deserves the learned professor's rebuke, that the judgment "amounts simply to a palpable refusal to respect and apply the law."[103] In the circumstances of this case, where Professor Nwabueze has earlier admitted that the

---

[101] *Ibid.*, 66. See also, s. 1(2) of Decree 61 of 1993: "No question as to the validity of this Decree shall be entertained in any court of law in Nigeria."

[102] See 21 of Certified True Copy (CTC) of the judgment in M/573/93: *Bashorun M.K.O. Abiola and Ambassador Kingibe v. National Electoral Commission and Attorney General of the Federation* (see fn. 97 *supra*, esp. at 212).

[103] *Nigeria '93 …, op. cit.*, 66.

nullification of the June 12 election was *unjust*, it appears unduly harsh that the judge should be accused of being "subversive of the rule of law"[104] when, in fact, the decree was an instrument to perpetuate injustice and the judge's accuser was its principal draftsman.[105]

The most supportable point is contained in the first limb of the second criticism. As the foundation for this also energizes the third criticism, we may discuss them together, while, only tangentially, pointing to the unnecessary baggage with which textual fetishism has almost bogged down the force of the criticisms. The first limb of the second criticism simply asserts that:

> The legality or validity of the Interim Constitution of 1993 (i.e., Decree 61) is not justifiable [sic, "justiciable"] for another reason. It was enacted by the FMG by virtue of the constituent power seized from the Nigerian people in a military coup. It established a new legal order ... The military legal order ... rested on force, and its termination cannot be governed by law.[106]

If we remove some of the minor and totally unnecessary irritants in this otherwise, excellent statement of the true position, we shall arrive at the single point, which

---

[104] *Ibid.* Rule of Law is now a perverted concept embraced alike by democrats and dictators. The use of that term in Prof. Nwabueze's circumstances would seem more fitted to its modification for use by dictators, i.e., "Rule by Law."

[105] See, *Nigeria '93..., op. cit.* at 59.

[106] *Ibid.* at 65 and 74.

destroys the entire basis of not just argument (a) by Chief Fawehinmi but also, his arguments (b) and (c). Much confusion of thought in constitutional analysis stems, as we shall attempt to demonstrate in subsequent chapters, from a failure to appreciate the true relationship of force with law. If Justice Akinsanya and Chief Fawehinmi had understood what Professor Nwabueze here expounds, they would have seen the futility of their arguments. With or without any written authority in that behalf, at that time, Decree 61 was the will of those wielding constituent power and, thus, the constitution of Nigeria. The reasoning is quite uncomplicated if a proper historiography of Nigerian constitutional development is taken from the 17th day of January, 1966.

On that date, General Aguiyi-Ironsi's Decree 1 of 1966[107] retrospectively commenced. That decree expressed the will of the wielder of preponderant force at the time. It created the offices of the new Federal Military Government and distributed powers. In short, "it had all the attributes ... of a modern, written constitution"[108]. However, the question to Chief Fawehinmi and Akinsanya, J., would be this: "who authorized Ironsi to sign that constitution into law? By what legal authority did he act? If there were no prior decree enabling him in that behalf, could it still be argued that without Decree 1 of 1984 (or more accurately, Decree 17 of 1985), that President Babangida became thereby entirely powerless?

---

[107] Constitution (Suspension and Modification) Decree No. 1 of 1966.
[108] Apology to Prof. Nwabueze, *Nigeria '93 ...,* 62.

Was his power to sign decrees brought about by a lifeless document or was that document merely in affirmation of his power, which derived from preponderant force? What of Gowon's Decree 8 of 1967 after the Aburi accord with Ojukwu? In unilaterally repealing that decree, which required the consent of all the regional governors, what was Gowon's warrant? Decree No. 32 of 1975 was the constitution for General Mohammed's regime but by what authority was it made? The same may be asked of Buhari's Decree 1 of 1984. If there was no previous law enabling the making of that admittedly legal decree, what is the sense in arguing that in its absence, no future decrees can legally be made? This is textual fetishism at its worst. A piece of paper denuded of all but its historical significance is held on to, despite clear evidence to the contrary, as the extant, binding, supreme regulator of conduct within the relevant polity. Such unmaintenable misjoinder of a fictional, theoretical, premise with a factual, practical, existence will never fail to present legal science in the most ludicrous light.

Professor Nwabueze is therefore essentially correct in this instance although some of the frills he adds to spruce up the point are misleading. For instance: (i), the FMG[109] that enacted Decree 61 of 1993 did not seize constituent power from "the Nigerian people," it seized it from another cabal of the military establishment. (ii), the "termination" of the "military legal order" can, indeed, depending on the peculiar circumstances at any particular time, "be governed by law" as was

---

[109] "Federal Military Government."

demonstrated by the constitutional handover effected by General Obasanjo's government to the President Shagari regime as well as the transition on 29 May, 1999, from General Abdulsalami Abubakar to President Olusegun Obasanjo.

A more irritating embellishment to the, otherwise, sound basis of Limb One of the second criticism is its unhappy extension into Criticism Three. In Professor Nwabueze's rather unconvincing words:

> Whilst the FMG's power to make Decree 61 of 1993 did not derive from Decree 1 of 1984 and could not be affected by its repeal or suspension, President Babangida's power to sign Decree 61 of 1993 admittedly derived from it.[110]

This concession is an odd one. If at this stage, Professor Nwabueze is still prepared to deny President Babangida's power to sign decrees just because of the repeal of Decree No. 1 of 1984 (which, in any case, he is by Decree 17 of 1985, deemed himself to have made), one wonders whether the learned professor has properly understood his own correct argument in (limb one) of Criticism Two above?[111] It is the same logic of force that authorized Babangida to make the repealing decree that also authorizes him, even one year later, if still in possession of preponderant force, to sign yet another decree (even when contrary to the previous one). The insidious

---

[110] *Nigeria '93 ...*, *op. cit.*, 66/67.
[111] *Ibid.* 66/67 and 74. But contrast with 75: " ... his power to sign decrees had not been lost ... any more than the power of the FMG to make laws ... "

distinction between the FMG's power to make, and Babangida's power to sign, Decree 61 is, in the circumstance, utterly misleading and unmaintenable.

ARGUMENT (b).

Here, Chief Fawehinmi's argument is that, even assuming the legality of its enabling constitution (that is Decree 61 of 1993), the interim government of Chief Shonekan was, nevertheless, unconstitutional and ought to be so declared. The reasoning seems clear enough. Decree 61 provided for a Head of Interim Government and a cabinet of Ministers to be appointed by the HIG. But there was no provision as to how (whether by election or by appointment) the all-important office of HIG was to be filled. Chief Gani Fawehinmi makes very much of this omission. In very firm words, he feels able to claim that:

> The constitutional foundation on which the appointment of the nation's Head of Government and Commander-in-Chief is rooted is that the *appointing authority* and the *manner* of the *appointment* must be expressly legislated.[112]

He embarks on a constitutional history of previous heads of government and commanders-in-chief of Nigeria since 1914 and concludes that:

> The appointment of Chief Ernest Shonekan as Head of Interim Government, Head of State, Chief Executive and Commander-in-

---

[112] See, *June 12 crisis ...*, *op. cit.* at 43.

Chief of the Armed Forces is void and therefore illegal because there is no *appointing authority* provided for in Decree No. 61 of 1993.[113]

Professor A.B. Kasunmu, S.A.N., was the leading counsel for the plaintiff in the *Bashorun Abiola case*. He offered substantially the same argument in that case except for a cosmetic difference in terminology. While Gani's term was "appointing authority," Professor Kasunmu's was "appointing officer."[114] In fact, it may be pointed out that both also castigated Shonekan's appointment on the alternative argument that Decree 61 was invalid. This latter point falls under argument (a). But we shall be more concerned here with the argument, which assumes the validity of Decree 61 but yet questions the said appointment as not having been anchored on any of its provisions.

Akinsanya, J., in her judgment, considered,[115] but failed to make a finding on, argument (b) as (alternatively) framed by Professor Kasunmu. She only dealt with the defective "appointing authority" for the "Secretaries" (or Ministers) and considered the defective appointment of the HIG only within the framework of argument (a). In her own words:

Having resolved that Decree No. 61 of 1993 is void, the said decree is not capable of creating an office held by Chief Ernest

---

[113] *Ibid.*, at 90/91 (emphasis is his).
[114] At 8 of the C.T.C. of judgment. Excerpted in *June 12 and the Future of Nigerian Democracy, op. cit.* at 199.
[115] *Ibid.* at 212 (21 of C.T.C.).

> Shonekan or the offices of the secretaries
> 115

Professor Nwabueze criticizes this approach of the learned judge. While he concedes the validity of argument (b),[116] he denigrates the vitiation of Shonekan's appointment on the invalidity of Decree No. 61 of 1993.[117] Argument (b) seems to have been better articulated by Professor Nwabueze than by Chief Fawehinmi:

> ... The drafting group had accepted my suggestion that the only effectual method of appointing the Head of the ING is to designate him by name in the Decree...so the provision was printed with a blank space left for the name, but the entire provision completely disappeared from the Decree as finally enacted ... All it says is that "there shall be for the Federation a Head of the Interim Government ..." The Decree says nothing about his appointment.

> By what authority, then, was Chief Ernest Shonekan appointed as Head of the ING? No appointment to an office created by the Decree could validly be made before the Decree took effect ... Chief Shonekan could not have been appointed by or under the Decree, since it does not designate him by name as the Head, and no provision is contained therein for the appointment of the Head. It follows that his appointment as Head of the ING in [sic, "is"] invalid ... The appointment to the offices of minister, which under the Decree could

---

[116] See, *Nigeria '93 ..., op. cit.* at 61.
[117] *Ibid.*, 62. See also, 70 (on the invalidity of the appointment of Secretaries as per Akinsanya, J.).

only be made by the Head, are also automatically invalidated ...[118]

This argument by Chief Fawehinmi and Professor Kasunmu, coupled with Professor Nwabueze's acceptance thereof, seem, amazingly, to elide the answers provided by our own constitutional history. It is true that neither Kasunmu nor Nwabueze attempted to supply any historical authority for this ponderous proposition but Chief Fawehinmi did. It is however quite regrettable that despite finding glaring instances in which there was a recognized Head of State and yet no statutory, "appointing authority," he yet felt committed to his inflexible thesis that under Public Law: "For every appointment there must be an appointing authority."[119]

It is irksome to be forced through 54 pages of print only to find that the only relevant authority cited in favour of this proposition (*Thornton on Legislative Drafting* at pages 215-216), is merely a textbook which itself is phrased in an unmistakably directory tone. Thornton's book merely recommends to legal draftsmen that "care should be taken with respect to: - (a) the identification of the appointing authority..."[120] "Waste work! Waste work! [all this is] abominable waste-work!"[121]

---

[118] *Ibid.*, 61.

[119] See, *June 12 crisis ...*, *op. cit.*, 92. Also, see: 43 and 73.

[120] Quoted (*Ibid.*) at 95.

[121] Apology to Chinweizu, et al, *Toward the Decolonization of African Literature* (Enugu: Fourth Dimension, 1980) vol. 1, 182.

Assuming, without conceding, the existence of a statute which demands that all such appointments should expressly provide for an appointing authority, what would be its constitutional worth in the face of this contrary framework set by the recognized, effective, wielder of preponderant force? Again, it all boils down to the previous answer given in respect of argument (a). The constitution is the supreme "law" in any polity. The wielder of constituent power makes it. Constituent power resides in the person or persons in control or apparent control of the preponderant force in the relevant polity. At the time Decree 61 was made General Babangida and his junta wielded preponderant force and, thus, held constituent power in the Nigerian polity. The constitution we had could be formulated thus: "whatever is expressed by the junta through Babangida should be regarded as the ultimate law and this has competence to vary earlier laws." The expressions of this will are, for convenience, sometimes, to be made in writing by an instrument called a decree. However, this does not derogate from unwritten expressions of the junta's will since decrees can legally be published by means other than writing. In fact, their validity and procedure for creation could not legally be questioned in Nigeria.[122]

In repealing or suspending Decree 1 of 1984, the worst that can be said was that General Babangida reverted to his unwritten, unregulated, position of absolute ruler. In

---

[122] See, *Guardian Newspapers case* (*supra* at fn. 91) esp. at 750 to 751 (per Ayoola, J.C.A. [now, JSC], concurring with Pats-Acholonu, J.C.A. [now, JSC]).

appointing Chief Shonekan as HIG and in making Decree 61 of 1993 to create a new framework of government to be headed for a certain period by this HIG, he was clearly expressing the constituent power resident in his person by virtue of his preponderant force. The "absoluteness" of power in a military constitution leads to much difficulty for the analyst. However, this is no reason to distort the true position. Sometimes, the written decrees reflect the true intendment of the makers; but sometimes, they do not. In that situation, it is futile to insist on the empty document in the face of a more solid and yet contrary unwritten practice. This unwritten practice must be deemed, within the context of arbitrary power, to constitute yet another amendment to the military constitution in terms consistent with the original understanding that all future decrees can amend the previous ones. Another way of saying this is that the new desire is in effect, analogical to a new coup d' etat each time it is effected.

It is within this context, that one can appreciate why there was no appointing authority for the Head of the Federal Military Government in January, 1966, yet, Aguiyi-Ironsi's self-appointment to that office was, nevertheless, considered lawful. Similarly, Gowon's appointment on 1 August 1966, to the same office, after the death of Ironsi on 29 July 1966, did not have any written authority yet, it was considered legal for the nine years he ruled. The same point must be made as respects General Murtala Mohammed who became the Nigerian Head of State after the military coup d' etat of 29 July 1975. We say this because Decree No. 32 of 1975, which was the military constitution for Murtala Mohammed's regime, has been put in such a light, by Chief Fawehinmi, as might suggest to the unwary that its provision in section 8(d) thereof, for an "appointing authority," means that Murtala's appointment was made by a statutorily designated authority.[123] This is obviously not so when it is remembered that Decree 32 of 1975 was signed into law by Murtala Mohammed two and half months (15 October, 1975) after he had already become Head of State without any prior legislative warrant.

General Olusegun Obasanjo was the first military Head of State appointed under a statutorily prescribed authority: Decree 32 of 1975. Generals Buhari and Babangida had both become Heads of State before, themselves, signing into law, the military constitutions that provided for appointing authorities for their respective offices. Decree 107 of 1993 makes no pretence as to any appointing authority for General Sani Abacha and yet Chief Fawehinmi recognizes that that tyrant has been, for some five years, the constitutional, Nigerian, Head of State since 17 November 1993. In a suit he filed in 1996, Chief Gani Fawehinmi described the 1st respondent, General Sani Abacha, as "(The Head of State and Commander-in-Chief of Nigeria)."[124] Argument (b) is, therefore, constitutionally unsound.

---

[123] See, *June 12 crisis …, op. cit.,* at 72 and 73.

[124] See, *Chief Gani Fawehinmi v. General Sani Abacha and 3 ors.* (1996) 9 N.W.L.R. (pt. 475) 710. But consider especially, 754G (per Pats-Acholonu, J.C.A., concurring, obiter): "… I observe that one of the respondents is the Head of State … section 267 of the constitution … provides immunity against … the President or the Head of

In the peculiar circumstances, a better argument would challenge the constitutionality of Shonekan's appointment (as well as those of his secretaries or ministers) on the ground that President Babangida had, in fact, lost constituent power before the appointment. Additionally or alternatively, that Shonekan's government had failed to become, *grosso modo*, effective due to the flurry of challenges to its legitimacy right from its inception on 26 August 1993.[125] By the foregoing, we aim to show that any meaningful challenge to the very essence of constituent power must necessarily be determined on a plane outside the established legal sphere. It is a matter that is more properly fitted for the political plane where the sole referent for objective validity is, in our submission, effectiveness.

ARGUMENT (c).

The final argument by Chief Gani Fawehinmi is another example of applying logic designed for the settled, legal plane to problems arising from the hotly contested and undefined, political plane. Like some portions of the earlier arguments, the reasoning would be brilliant if the problems were merely interpretive of settled, defined,

---

State. It is wrong in law to have joined him as a party."
[125] Viewed in this light, argument "(b)" could be considered one of the legitimate challenges against the regime from the perspective of the political plane. Its relevance is the faculty to sensitize the masses into rendering ineffective the impugned government's actions (not by any existing legal framework, but by the unregulated force of public opinion at the supra-legal plane).

constitutional or legislative issues. But they are not. The very power of interpretation is also at stake when the point is validity of the constitution itself. Chief Fawehinmi's argument here is mostly a matter of evidence rather than one of substance. The substantive portion is covered by his argument (a) to the effect that if Decree 61 was signed on a date after Babangida had left office, it was made without any legal or constitutional authority and consequently, was invalid and void. Before this legal outcome becomes relevant, it would be incumbent on the learned Chief to first establish the factual bases for it. In argument (c), he tries to do this under two heads, to wit:

(I) "the national events that took place at Abuja on the 26th and 27th of August, 1993"[126] (which must include):

    (1) the ceremonial pulling-out of the former president from the military and the swearing-in ceremony of Chief Shonekan as the new Head of State on 26 August, 1993, by the Chief Justice of Nigeria,

    (2) the Federal Attorney-General's statement to reporters on 27 August, 1993 (the date the interim ministers was sworn-in by Chief Shonekan), that the Interim Constitution was still in draft and his hedgy statements suggesting that the contents thereof were still subject to confirmation;

---

[126] Chief Gani Fawehinmi, *June 12 crisis …*, op. cit. at 97.

and,

(II) "the [discrepant] facts disclosed on the face of Gazette No. 23, vol. 80 of the Federal Republic of Nigeria"[127] (which must include):

(1) the fact that the gazette containing the Decree was, on its face, published on 23 August, 1993 (i.e., three days before it was purportedly signed on 26 August, 1993),

(2) the fact that contrary to the assertion of the Federal Attorney-General on 27 August, 1993 (that the draft gives full and unrestricted legislative powers to the National Assembly), the published Decree No. 61 had in it, section 4, subsection (8), which gave the Federal Executive Council a reserved power to assume legislative powers whenever it is "impracticable or impossible … for the National Assembly to legislate on any matter."

These points are no doubt, very weighty. It is possible to explain the inconsistencies away on other grounds. For example, one could say that the draft referred to by the Federal Attorney-General was, in the context, used to differentiate the official manuscript of Decree 61 signed on 26th from the printed copy, which would thereafter be mass-produced for public consumption after his speech of the 27th. In addition, that the gazette containing Decree 61 was mistakenly dated the 23rd instead of 26

---

[127] *Ibid.*

August 1993 (or a later date). Alternatively, that the validity of Decree 61 signed on the 26th is not affected by the fact that only its draft was published on the 23rd. This may especially be so in view of the fact that the published draft reflected an intention that it should take effect on 26 August 1993 (on which date it is expected that the President would sign it). Further, it could simply be said, as has Professor Nwabueze, that the numbering of gazettes is a merely clerical function with no legislative impact on the temporal priority of laws contained therein. As for the changed text, it is possible to argue that section 4(8) does not contradict the Federal Attorney General's statement.

On the evidence, depending on his assessment of the opposing cases, a judge should be quite competent to lean one way or the other. We would, on these facts, have found against the respondents who were the makers of the gazette and decree but we should not be very hasty in castigating a judge who would take a different view of the evidence. Justice Akinsanya dealt with the matter on a slightly different pedestal. She did not consider whether Decree 61 was made *after 26 August 1993*. Rather, she considered whether it was made *on the 26th* but after Decree 59 of the same date. From all the conflicting evidence, she resolved her doubt on the side of the applicants: "the presumption is that they were signed in the sequence of their numbering..."[128]

---

[128] See, *June 12 and the Future of Nigerian Democracy*, *op. cit.* at 211 (20 of the C.T.C.).

Professor Nwabueze shows that the numbering sequence is irrelevant and powerfully buttresses this by reference to Decree 62 of 1993, which was signed on 23 August 1993, and had the effect of postponing the commencement of the 1989 Constitution to the end of the interim period on 1 April 1994.[129] All these make for an interesting legal chess-game but become entirely useless when the substantive question about the consequence of these evidential facts is considered. The answer, when it comes to this, is the same as for the earlier arguments. Fraud or no fraud, evidence of mistakes or not; the only relevant consideration is the locus of preponderant force on 26 August 1993. This force constitutionalizes any prior errors.

In some polities, especially, those with a substantial ceremonial or ritual history, writing is sometimes venerated to a pedestal normally higher than pragmatism warrants. In some instances, this is recognized and downplayed by the courts as undue technicality, which should not be allowed to subvert the needs of substantial justice.

In England, the Queen (or King) in Parliament is the law-making authority. There is a formula in writing by which it is expressed that the three parties have contributed:

---

[129] Decree 62 of 1993 in point of fact was not made available to the public until after the Federal gazette containing Decree 61 of 1993 was published. Prof. Nwabueze's argument is not so potent on this score if the sequence of numbering is considered and if Decree 59, indeed, determined IBB's powers to sign/make subsequent decrees (after No. 59).

> Be it enacted by the Queen's Most
> Excellent Majesty, by and with the advice
> and consent of the Lords Spiritual and
> Temporal, and Commons, in this present
> Parliament assembled, and by the authority
> of same, as follows.[130]

This formula need not be used so long as all three parties to the statute are recorded as having participated. Omission of any party on the record[131] (such as the Queen) as was done in the *Prince's Case*[132] has led the courts to hold that the purported Act of Parliament was invalid.

The United Kingdom has many constitutional rules that seem to justify such textual fetishism. One is the "Enrolled Act Rule." By this rule, the courts cannot question the validity of an Act of Parliament, which on its face satisfies the conditions. In other words, even if the formula were false in fact, once they see endorsed on the face of the document that all necessary assents have been obtained, the courts would enforce it.[133] However, this

---

[130] Sir Ivor Jennings, *The Law and the Constitution*, 5th ed. (England: The English Language Book Society [ELBS] and Hodder and Stoughton, 1933 and 1979) 138.

[131] But since the Parliament Acts of 1911 and 1949, there are circumstances in which the assent of the Lords may be dispensed with, for example, as respects Money Bills (so certified by the Speaker of the Commons).

[132] [1606] 8 Co. Rep., 14.

[133] See for example, *Hall v. Hall* (1944) 88 Sol. J. 383; *Edinburgh and Dalkeith Railway v. Wauchope* (1842) 8 Ch. & F. 710; *Manuel v. Att. Gen.* [1983] Ch. 77. See generally for all the cases cited above: John Alder, *Constitutional & Administrative Law* (Houndsmills, Basingstoke … London: Macmillan Education Ltd., 1989) 67.

point should not be stretched further than it will go. It does not derogate from the principle of preponderant force. In fact, it demonstrates that principle. It only shows that those with preponderant force in the United Kingdom prefer to live under this mystifying bondage of fictional rules. It does not mean a new regime cannot change the whole set-up and insist on a congruence between the rules that govern the government and the actual practice of those rules.

We say this to warn the researcher against plunging into the other extreme to textual fetishism. It would be a jaundiced view to deny that instances exist where writing is actually and operatively venerated beyond the pedestal reality reserves for it. Appreciation of the limitations in hanging on to either of these two extremes brings in a balanced perspective. The constitutional jurist who strives for accuracy must adopt this latter perspective because of the need for balance in this course of study. If I look at my watch and answer your enquiry as to time: "It is 10pm," textual fetishism would consider it an end of the matter. A better research method would require more. It would consider other evidence; especially when there are circumstances pointing to a contrary conclusion. For example, you look out the window and see the blazing sun, you notice the hands of my analogue watch are not moving, you look at the digital wall clock and it says 2pm, etc. The point is not that my 10pm claim may not be correct. It is just that academic rigour requires some sort of corroboration since we cannot sensibly rule out honest mistake or mischievous falsehood. Despite their time-constraining deadlines, even journalists would require confirmation from

other sources before going on air or to press
with any second-hand stories.

3.   The Theory of Provenance.

We shall attempt by this chapter, a critical examination of the meaning and source of "constitution" and of "Constitutional Law." If Edward Corwin is right that:

> Constitutional Theory ... may be defined as the sum total of ideas of some historical standing as to what the constitution is or ought to be ... [1]

then, the reader may well consider this chapter as devoted in essence, to core concepts of Constitutional Theory. However, we shall not feel bound by any limitations of history or "historical standing." The novelty of the idea will be considered if not an extra merit, then at least, as deserving equal consideration in this bid to clarify concepts.

CONCEIVING CONSTITUTIONS.

There is usually a conflation of the constitution with Constitutional Law. This, to us, is a big mistake. The lack of discrimination seems to consist in a carefree preconception that they are synonymous notions. Anozie[2] writes, for example, that

---

[1] Edward S. Corwin, *American Constitutional History* (1964) quoted in Geoffrey Marshall, *Constitutional Theory*, H.L.A. Hart, ed., *Clarendon Law Series* (New York: Oxford University Press, 1971 and 1980) beside the "Contents" page.

[2] M.C. Anozie, *Notes on Constitutional Law*, vol. 1 (Enugu: Professional Business Services, 1998) at 3.

> Constitutional Law ... is that branch of jurisprudence dealing with formation, construction, and interpretation of constitutions.

But not stopping there, she seems to assume its identity with the constitution and continues that: "It is a body of rules that govern or regulate the government of a country." Surely, this cannot be free from difficulty. The law concerning the constitution suggests it is different from what it is the law of. The subject-matter of the investigation cannot be the same thing investigating it.

The indiscrimination has a long ancestry spanning many decades and is given grand and magisterial cover by the eminence of some of its perpetrators.[3] Nevertheless, the approach is still wrong. Constitutional Law is not the constitution. Rather, like Yardley,[4] one would more readily agree that Constitutional Law is "...that law which is concerned with the constitution of the country." With this sort of circular definition, the importance of the term "constitution" becomes even more pronounced. Without an understanding of that term, one cannot fully understand what Constitutional Law means, either. So, one may reasonably proceed

---

[3] For e.g., John Austin, *The Province of Jurisprudence Defined*, H.L.A. Hart, ed. (1954) 258-259. Cited in Geoffrey Marshall, *Constitutional Theory, op. cit.*, 3 and 4. See also J. Fitzgerald, *Salmond on Jurisprudence, 12th ed.* (London: Sweet & Maxwell, 1966) esp. at 83.

[4] D.C.M. Yardley, *Introduction to British Constitutional Law 6th ed.* (London: Butterworths, 1984) 3. Because of Yardley's understanding of the term "law" (as stated in his footnote thereat), I shall have to disagree with this definition of Constitutional Law even though it seems methodologically clearer than Anozie's.

by asking the deceptively simple question: "What is the Constitution?"[5]

THE AMBIGUITIES OF CONSTITUTIONAL DEFINITION.

In any organization of human beings there is, descriptively speaking, some sort of understanding as to the normative rules to guide the conduct of the governors and their relationship with the governed as well as with outsiders.[6] Essentially, this understanding defines the mode of government of the group. It could be written or unwritten. It may impose limits to the power of the governing group or permit "absolute" power. It could expressly provide the method for its own amendment or keep silent on change. When it provides change procedures, it may make the steps to entail deliberate rigour or allow for very easy alteration. Perhaps, the most important observation is that this understanding forms the basis for the legal system of such a polity. It is the referent for legality and, in that objective sense, legal validity. In other words, it is the foundational rule from which other rules (validly) proceed. It may be seen as prescriptive in its requirements and

---

[5] Charles Inglis, in Bailyn, *op. cit.* at 175. See further, R.A.C.E. Achara, "Textual Fetishism and the Ambiguities of Constitutional Definition" in Justices I.A. Umezulike and C.C. Nweze, eds. *Perspectives in Law and Justice* (Enugu: Fourth Dimension Publishers, 1996) 275 and 288, n. 2a.

[6] Compare with Thomas Paine, *Rights of Man* (1791-1792) Henry Collins, ed. (England: Penguin Books Ltd. (Pelican Classics), 1969 and 1976) at 213: "Every society and association that is established, first agreed upon a number of original articles, digested into form which are its constitution … and the government of that society then commenced."

normative specifications but, as to its essential nature or existence, it would seem to be peculiarly descriptive.

NOMENCLATURE.

The English name for what we have just described is "constitution."[6a] But there is no sacrosanctity to this name. If in Nigeria we choose to call it by another name such as "Omenala," this would be just as good.[7] The important thing to appreciate is the concept behind the name. So, what is this concept behind the name, "constitution"? To properly appreciate the concept, we propose now to investigate its definitional ramifications in more detail.

THE FOUR DEFINITIONAL APPROACHES.

Paine's (truncated) stricture "that men mean distinct and separate things when they speak of constitutions..."[8] is almost as easy to justify as his complete sentence. This is more

---

[6a] Solomon O. Ukhuegbe partially traces its etymological origins to Roman Jurisprudence. See his: "The Word "Constitution": From Antiquity to our Time," Chapt. 2 in Epiphany Azinge, ed., *New Frontiers in Law* (Benin City: Oliz Publishers, 1993) at 22.

[7] It could be called "charter," "instrument of government," "basic law," etc. See, for e.g., Solomon Ukhuegbe, *loc. cit.*, at 23 and 25. The Constitution of the Republic of Ireland is called 'Bunreacht na hEireann'. To reflect the Good Friday Agreement of 1998, on 2 Dec., 1999, its Arts. 2, 3, and 29 were amended, inter alia, to accept reunification with Northern Ireland only by peaceful means.

[8] He adds: "...and of governments." See, Thomas Paine, *Rights of Man*, Henry Collins, ed. *Pelican Classics* (1791-2; England: Penguin Books Ltd., 1969 and 1976) at 207.

so as "constitution" has been defined in countless ways by numerous writers and speakers – sometimes, in more than one way by a single person. These numerous definitions may usefully be organized into four principal categories.[9]

THE FIRST DEFINITIONAL APPROACH.

In the first place, some definitions would have us believe that a constitution is any norm or will (individual or institutional) which is identifiable as the locus and foundation for legislative and, generally, governmental authority in any given political society or polity. This implies that a constitution cannot be a written instrument: that which is written is not the essence of the term; merely the evidence. This category of definitions looks more at the source of sovereign power than its product. It argues that the name "constitution" is not ontologically referable to a piece of paper just because it is so named. It becomes a constitution only when it satisfies the requirements, that is to say, by reflecting accurately the will of the person or group actually in control of the relevant polity.

It is rare to find in the books postulations fully expository of this genre of definitions. However, there are snippets, some second-hand insinuations, and widespread oral indications leading to this conclusion. Richard Bland provides a good enough model: "a legal

---

[9.] See, R.A.C.E. Achara, "Textual Fetishism and the Ambiguities of Constitutional Definition," *loc. cit.*, esp. at 275 – 279.

constitution, that is, a legislature."[10] The view equates the constitution with the institutional will of the human members of the ultimate source of laws and is duplicated by Bernard Bailyn. In an unclear attribution to Andrew Eliot,[10a] Bailyn distinguishes the thoughts of some American patriots[11] from the confused ones of James Otis but observes that "others were referring to constitutions ... as parliament ... "[12]

In heated political discourse, one may likely hear the piece of cynicism that a dictatorial head of government actually constitutes the constitution regardless of any existing piece of paper, which, to the contrary, bears that title.[13] The argument is quite compelling when a constitution is seen as, or understood to be, the supreme, overriding *source* of laws in any polity. Where a written "constitution" exists but is routinely ignored and circumvented by an identifiable, alternative source of power, it is difficult to convince any intelligent

---

[10]. "The Colonel Dismounted or the Rector Vindicated" (Williamsburg, 1764) quoted in Bailyn, *op. cit.*, 176, fn. 17.

[10a] "A sermon preached to his Excellency Francis Bernard ..." (Boston, 1765) cited in Bailyn, *Ibid.* at 180 and 181, fn. 22.

[11] See for e.g., A.J. Langguth, *Patriots: The Men who started the American Revolution* (New York: Simon and Schuster, 1988) 1 to 637.

[12] Bailyn, *op. cit.*, 180. See similarly, Thomas Paine, *Rights of Man*, *op. cit.*, at 94 (critically quoting Edmund Burke).

[13]. "The British constitution can be defined in eight words: 'What the Queen in Parliament enacts is law' ": Vernon Bogdanor, *Power and the People: A Guide to Constitutional Reform* (London: Victor Gollancz, 1997) at 11.

observer that it deserves to continue bearing that name. If it does, then the claim that a constitution is the supreme basis of law must be reconsidered. Both conceptions cannot, without contradiction, co-exist. The major problem with this category however, is its fluidity. It is easy to criticize. Where constitution is mutable will; actually, in effect, there is none.

THE SECOND DEFINITIONAL APPROACH.

The second category of definitions identifies a constitution by reference to the product conferred by the sovereign source of power. This approach considers as "constitution" all those written charters and/or all those unwritten practices, which together identify the reality of the working of the government in relation to its various powers and in relation to those governed.

The second definitional approach is an improved version of the first category. The ever-changing will of the constituent power is divorced here from his more stable stipulate, which is referred to as the constitution. The constitution is thus concretized and becomes easier to locate and identify. Unlike the previous where even declaration does not guarantee continuance, identifying a constitution with the declaration or practice of the constituent power, introduces some sort of solidity to the concept and facilitates analysis and referential use of the material. It is true that even under this category a constitution can still be amended. Nevertheless, there is a fundamental change of its nature vis-à-vis the first definitional approach. For example, if the constitution is deemed the will of, say, General Sani Abacha, nobody can convincingly claim knowledge of what it is at any particular point in time (including, sometimes, General Abacha himself). If he declares his will this minute, the possibility that on declaring it, it has changed in his mind, renders immediately doubtful the present accuracy of the earlier declaration. But even though he can change his declarations or it may be stated who or what can amend them, if it is agreed that it is his declaration of what is in his mind that constitutes the constitution (rather than the undeclared desires of his will), then there is a radical change in the nature of the concept. The declaration (oral, practical, or written) is identifiable, concrete and capable of analysis. Its most felicitous attribute is a palpable referent (until amended) by which even the conduct of the source of that constitution may be tested.

This second category of definitions is wide enough to accommodate written, partly written and unwritten conceptualizations of "constitution." It had been the traditional and time-honoured definition of a constitution until the narrow, naturalist-inspired,[13a] assaults on its fortifications by the American revolutionaries of the 18th Century. Professor Bernard Bailyn, that outstanding Harvard political historian, offers this explanation:

[13a] See Bailyn, *op. cit.*, 188: "ultimately," he rationalized, from the writings of the colonists, "the entire legitimacy ... must rest on ... the abstract universals of natural rights."

The word "constitution" and the concept behind it was of central importance to the colonists' political thought ... and so great was the pressure placed upon it in the course of a decade of pounding debate that in the end it was forced apart, along the seam of a basic ambiguity ...[14]

However, before assessing the other side of this ambiguity, it is well to highlight some of the examples of the traditional view; that is to say, the second definitional approach to the definition of constitutions.

One example is the definition offered by Henry St. John (Viscount Bolingbroke)[14a] who in his "Dissertation on Parties" identifies the constitution as:

That assemblage of laws, institutions, and customs, derived from certain fixed principles of reason, directed to certain fixed objects of public good, that compose the general system according to which the community hath agreed to be governed.[15]

For his own part, John Adams considers a political constitution to be in the nature of:

---

[14] Bernard Bailyn, *op. cit.* at 67. See further R.A.C.E. Achara, "Textual Fetishism and the Ambiguities of Constitutional Definition," *loc. cit..*, *passim.*
[14a] I am grateful to Solomon O. Ukhuegbe for the full name and title of Bolingbroke. See, *loc. cit.*, at 22.
[15] Quoted by Prof. Bernard Bailyn, *op. cit.* at 68, fn. 12. Also quoted by Kachikwu and Ozekhome in [1978-1988] 3 Nig. J.R. at 78

> A frame, a scheme, a system, a combination
> of powers for a certain end, namely, - the
> good of the whole community.[16]

Bolingbroke's reference to "reason" and communal agreement is, with Adams's incorporation of the requirement of purpose, an acceptable but not a necessary ingredient for admittance to this class of definitions. They each demonstrate the vastness and multitudinous ramifications of the members of this definitional category rather than state the qualifying ingredients for admittance. By not specifying writing, both definitions imply that a constitution can be written, partly written or entirely unwritten.

For an ontological model of this class, we may have to return to the 20th Century and approach Nigeria from whence Professor Benjamin Nwabueze quite simply asserts a constitution to be "the frame or composition of a government..."[17] In elucidation, he observes that: "in origin, therefore, government and a constitution are two inseparable notions."[17]

There are various such definitions of this class; and Hatchard, Ndulo and Slinn may be placed in this category:

---

[16] Bailyn, *Ibid.*

[17] B.O. Nwabueze, *Ideas and Facts in Constitution Making* (Ibadan: Spectrum Books Ltd., 1993) 1. This is directly opposite to Thomas Paine's disjunction of those two concepts in his: *Common Sense* (ostensibly, first published anonymously as "Letters on Four Important Subjects") and also in his more popular: *Rights of Man, op. cit.*, vol. II, Chapt. 4.

A constitution ... is the supreme and fundamental law that sets out the state's basic structure including the exercise of political power and the relationship between political entities and between the state and the people.[17a]

These all seem unified by the realization that a constitution is the prevailing, effective framework of government in any polity – whether a good framework or a bad one. Those definitions which talk of ideals such as Bolingbroke's source of "reason" and communal consent as well as Adams's "good of the whole community" must be taken as specific types of constitution within the wide vista offered by the second definitional category. The less narrow the definition the better. The *Chambers English Dictionary* provides a good example: "*Constitution* ... a system of laws and customs established by the sovereign power of a state for its own guidance ..."[18]

The editors of Professor Stanley de Smith's *Constitutional and Administrative Law* descriptively present an even clearer model:

[17a] John Hatchard, et al, *Comparative Constitutionalism and Good Governance in the Commonwealth: An Eastern and Southern African Perspective* (Cambridge: The Press Syndicate of the University of Cambridge, 2004) 12. Unfortunately, it is not apparent from the widely diffused equation of a constitution to its written matrix [all over Chapt. 2], that the authors have remained faithful to the correct definition they have offered here at p. 12.
[18] Sidney I. Landau, et al, eds., *Chambers English Dictionary* (Edinburgh: W. & R. Chambers Ltd., 1990 and 1992) 305.

> Since Britain has a regular system of government, with a complex of rules defining the composition, functions and interrelationship of the institutions of government, and delineating the rights and duties of the governed, Britain does have a constitution ...[19]

The constitution is in this way, identified with the existence of "a regular system of government."[19a] De Smith's editors recognize here that a constitution remains so even if it permits unlimited, dictatorial, government - provided there is a government.

Some such definitions, although tied to the idea of government, place their emphases on the medium of communication. Some time is taken to explain that this governmental device is not only to be found in written codes but in fact, to be found coupled with unwritten practices. E.A. Freeman writes, for example, that:

> We now have a whole code of precepts for the guidance of public men which will not be found in any page of either the statute or the common law but which are in practice hardly less sacred ... In short, by the side of our written law, there has

---

[19] Harry Street and Rodney Brazier eds., *Constitutional and Administrative Law de Smith* 5th (new) ed. (London: Penguin Books Ltd., 1985 and 1987) at 18.

[19a] O. Hood Phillips defines a constitution as: "the system of laws, customs and conventions which define the composition and powers of organs of the state, and regulate the relations of the various state organs to one another and to the private citizen." Quoted by D.C.M. Yardley, *Introduction to British Constitutional Law*, Sixth Edition (London: ButterWorths, 1984) 4, fn. 2.

grown up an unwritten or conventional constitution.[20]

Professor Wheare is of a similar sentiment. Kachikwu and Ozekhome[21] report him as acknowledging that:

> To confine a constitution to the bare statement of the rules which establish the principal political institutions of the state may seem unduly austere.

In the context, the real austerity would consist in the exclusion of non-written "rules." These, in the nature of things, find no space in the formal written constitutions but constitute the less glamorous, essential, facilitators of the 'austere' written ones.

Professor Bailyn provides very detailed and exciting documentation of the historical standing of the views of "constitution" encapsulated within what we have classed as the second definitional approach. It however seems anti-climactic that his textual peroration upon its age-ordained claim to superior standing is unwittingly consigned to a mere footnote:

> The conception of "constitution" as the arrangement of existing laws and practices of government may be traced back through the literature of the early eighteenth and seventeenth centuries.[22]

---

[20] *The Growth of the English Constitution* 1st ed. (1872) 110. Quoted by Kachikwu and Ozekhome in (1978-1988) 3 Nig J. R. at 86.

[21] *Ibid.* at 100.

[22] Bailyn, *op. cit.*, 68, fn. 12. Notice, however, that Prof. Jan-Erik Lane in his *Constitutions and Political*

This seeming disrespect for age as a validator of argument may well be a throwback to Paine. In his staccato-style of stinging strictures, Paine has rubbished the idea of age as an enhancement of argument. In one instance, he vilifies such an approach as "a superstitious reverence for ancient things"[23] where man is deceptively led to "the sepulchre of precedents, to deaden his faculties ..."[23] He considers this sort of argument as opposed to reason and as an instrument of institutions of very weak intellectual base such as monarchy and the organized church. Paine speaks thus his terrible curse: "The ragged relic and the antiquated precedent, the monk and the monarch, will moulder together."[23]

Perhaps, it is Paine who has launched the most severe attack on the view that a constitution need not be in writing: "Wherever," he writes, "it cannot be produced in a visible form, there is none."[24] Moreover, it is perhaps, most fitting that in an apology for the second definitional approach, its superior validity claims should be hinged, not on antiquity of those definitions but on grounds more conformable to the intellect. Footnote or not therefore, Bailyn's summarization of the second category can positively still be tested against the other

---

Theory (Manchester and New York: Manchester University Press, 1996) at 40, traces a somewhat different definition one- to two hundred years earlier than this. "During the sixteenth century" he writes, "the term 'constitution' received the conceptual content it still has today meaning a set of institutions that limit the exercise of state power."

[23] Paine, *op. cit.*, at 218.
[24] Paine, *op. cit.*, at 93.

definitional approaches by criteria of reason and pragmatism. However, this conclusion we must postpone until after the examination of the remaining two categories.

THE THIRD DEFINITIONAL APPROACH.

The third definitional approach, which we have identified for the categorization, regards a constitution as a written charter of non-justiciable aspirations of government having political, rather than legal, consequences.

We are not sure that this category can be divorced, in its ancestry, from the views of the principal British constitutional theorists ranging from Austin, Dicey, and Wade, through to Jolowicz, Jennings, and Yardley. In so far as their ideas of the constitutional convention commits them to an argument of its political, but not legal, enforceability, it is possible to claim that the extension of this very same idea to a "written" constitution is dependent on, or at least traceable to, their own version.

In referring to this sort of constitution, Harry Street and Rodney Brazier refer to J.F. Triska[25] to explain that: "Much of [such a] constitution is 'programmatic', an affirmation of dogma or of objectives to be realized one fine day"[26]. To elaborate, they assert that

---

[25] J.F. Triska, ed., *Constitutions of the Communist Party States* (1968) quoted by Harry Street and Rodney Brazier, eds., *Constitutional and Administrative Law de Smith* 5th ed. (London: Penguin Books, 1971 and 1987) at 16, fn. 3.
[26] Harry street and Rodney Brazier, *Ibid*. See also, Jan-Erik Lane, *Constitutions and Political Theory, op. cit.*, esp. at 118/119.

"Quite often the text, or much of the text, of a constitution is not intended to be taken literally …"[26] Given these limitations, one is slightly taken aback by reading not quite three sentences beneath, the apparently discrepant claim that:

> Although written constitutions differ widely in their purposes, form and content, they will normally … have two characteristics in common … fundamental law of the land; and … higher law … in that the law … will be hierarchically superior to other laws and will not be alterable except by a specially prescribed procedure for amendment.[27]

If constitutions of the third class were written (as they are) it follows that they are fundamental laws, higher than and superior to other laws and even unalterable except by some peculiarly rigid mechanism different from the more flexible mode for amending "lesser" laws. This is obviously incorrect. Although there are some written constitutions with this character, those classified under the third definitional approach of our present theoretical construct do not possess this feature.

The classic example of the third category is the constitution of the (now moribund) communist haven of U.S.S.R. Two learned commentators have observed that even though "one can point to the constitution of the U.S.S.R. which guarantees individual rights and the procedures for the exercise of governmental functions …," nevertheless,

---

[27.] *Ibid.* at 16 and 17.

> This 146-article constitution … by its language and tone … make it abundantly clear that no legally enforceable code of fundamental rights is thereby established …[28]

Similarly, Professor Nwabueze's assertion that a constitution may largely consist only of "lofty declarations of objectives and a description of the organs of government in terms that import no enforceable legal restraint"[29] may be based on the peculiar nature of the "constitution" of the former Soviet Union as well as those of its East European Satellites.

Some states provide a variant of this type of constitution. Instead of an outright and total toothlessness, one or two chapters of the otherwise court-enforceable, written, constitution are specifically made non-justiciable. An instance is Chapter II of the Constitution of the Federal Republic of Nigeria, 1979. Consisting of ten sections numbered 13, 14, 15, 16, 17, 18, 19, 20, 21, and 22, this chapter is titled: "Fundamental Objectives and Directive Principles of State Policy." Strangely, it peremptorily enjoins, in its very first lines[30], that:

---

[28] E.I. Kachikwu and M.A.A. Ozekhome, "Extending the Frontiers of Constitutionalism: Should Constitutions Contain only Legal Rules Stricto Sensu?" (1978-1988) 3 Nig. J.R., 86 to 105, esp. at 89.

[29] B.O. Nwabueze, *Constitutionalism in the Emergent States* (1973) quoted *Ibid.* at 87.

[30] I.e., s. 13. See similarly, Chapt. II (ss. 13 to 24) of the 1999 Constitution.

> ... All organs of government, and ... all authorities and persons, exercising legislative, executive or judicial powers ...

should "Conform to, observe and apply the provisions of this chapter of this constitution." While in section 6, subsection (6)(c), of the very same constitution, the judicial powers of the Nigerian Courts are ousted over the consideration of any matters contained in chapter II (including section 13). Although the peculiar wording of section 6(6)(c) gives space for creative interpretation and, thus, judicial enforcement of section 13,[30a] our present task is quite different. Chapter II is employed here only as analogy in the explication of the third definitional category for the definition of constitutions.

India is one other jurisdiction, which has devoted a portion of its written constitution to the communication of expressly posited, non-justiciable, fundamental objectives and directive principles of state policy. Unlike Nigeria, however, India has by the hermeneutic genius of its Supreme Court, found a way of "indirectly" enforcing those allegedly non-justiciable (mostly, second- and third-generation) rights in court. Professor B.

[30a] However, the Lagos Division of the Nigerian Court of Appeal in *Archbishop A.O. Okogie v. Att. Gen. (Lagos)* [1981] 2 N.C.L.R. 337 held (as reported by Kachikwu & Ozekhome (1978-1988) 3 Nig. J.R. at 103) that: "section 13 has not in any way made chapter II of the constitution justiceable because of the express (p)rovisions of s.6(6)(c) ...."

Obinna Okere has fully examined this remarkable trend and we need not be detained by its further discussion here.[31]

Constitutions, which fall under this category, are, by no means, commonplace. It is rare to discover any non-dictatorial polity, which undertakes the exertions, and expense usually associated with formulation of a written constitution only to expressly declare that what it has laboured to procure should yet be unenforceable in its own courts. The more usual thing is to find states whose constituent power has been usurped by one man or a junta; and these, feeling too embarrassed to put to international glare the robbery they have committed against their nation, pretend to leave intact (or slightly amended) the empty-shell of a previously extant written constitution. They do this while, in fact, ruling by an unwritten or partially written constitution antagonistic to the supremacy claims of the visible, pre-existent one. It is in such circumstance that a written constitution would, in these modern times, fall under the class of the third definitional approach. Since the fall of the bastion of

---

[31] See, B. Obinna Okere, "Fundamental Objectives and Directive Principles of State Policy under the Nigerian Constitution" (1978-1988) 3 Nig J.R. 74 to 85 esp. at 82, 83 and 84. He discussed the *Dorairajin rule* A.I.R. [1951] S.C. 226; *Golak Nath's case* [1967] SCR. 762; etc., to show that the courts have only after continuous constitutional amendments, backed down from their insistence that fundamental rights supersede the directive principles. But that is not my point. I seek only to emphasize here the fact that despite the implication of non-justiceability, they have yet been enforced in practice and have risen to even challenge fundamental rights provisions.

communism in the late 1980s, the age of the self-declared, non-justiciable constitution would seem to have passed.

THE FOURTH DEFINITIONAL APPROACH.

The fourth and final definitional category is probably the most widespread in modern times. To be one, three necessary and sufficient conditions are required. In form, it must be visibly permanent or semi-permanent; in content, it must be superior and a veritable limit to ordinary governmental power; and in its provenance, it must be fundamentally a delegation of people-power; not a usurpation of the one or few.

We spoke of a historically evolved ambiguity in the conceptualization of constitutions. This we did at the tail end of the discussion about the second definitional approach, quoting Bernard Bailyn in support[32]. The second part of this ambiguity is the notion of constitution we now class as the fourth definitional approach. It is restrictive in scope, belligerent in stance, revolutionary in conception and rather intolerant in methodology. This view of what a constitution is has gained ascendancy in the intellectual history of thought for a little over two centuries now; and this, relatively speaking, is quite recent. We have had occasion elsewhere,[33] and for a substantially different

---

[32] See, fn. 14 of this chapter (*supra*).

[33] R.A.C.E. Achara "Textual Fetishism and the Ambiguities of Constitutional Definition" in I.A. Umezulike and C.C. Nweze, eds., *Perspectives in Law and Justice* (Enugu: Fourth Dimension Publishers, 1996) 274 to 295 esp. at 278, 290 and 291.

purpose, to explore the birth, infancy and maturity of this novel notion. To reduce the trouble of too many cross-references however, we shall endeavour here a summary reconstruction.[34]

There was not, it is true, a pre-existent model for the sort of constitution developed by the American colonists after their revolution of the mid- to late- 18th Century. But it is equally true that to formulate the constitution, the ideological leaders of this revolution did not proceed from a total, intellectual, *tabula rasa*. They had the privilege of at least 150 years of Coke, Hobart and the like: fiercely jealous guardians of judicial independence (some would say, judicial arrogance, meddlesomeness and impertinence).

The origins of this definitional approach can be traced to the, then, prevalent doctrines of natural rights, which are said to have descended from the deity and are inherent in man (and woman). The claim is that it is law higher than positive, secular, law; and thus, overriding it. Rodee, Anderson, Christol and Greene[35] have traced this idea to the Stoics and attributed its assimilation into western philosophy, to the erudite contributions of the great Roman statesman, Cicero. However, this archival reconstruction is not of immediate interest in this exposition. We must come closer to present times, and focus, in the 17th

---

[34] On this subject, I owe a big debt to Prof. Bernard Bailyn. See his, *Ideological Origins of the American Revolution, supra.*

[35] C.C. Rodee, T.J. Anderson, C.Q. Christol, and T.H. Greene, *Introduction to Political Science* 3rd ed. (Tokyo: McGraw-Hill Kogakusha Ltd., 1976) 4.

Century, on some of the more important judge-made doctrines of the English common law upon which much of Nigerian constitutional jurisprudence depends.

In *Dr. Bonham's case,*[36] Coke, C.J., stated (albeit *obiter*) that:

> When an Act of Parliament is against common right and reason, or repugnant, or impossible to be performed, the common law will controul [sic] it, and adjudge such act to be void.

Similarly, in *Day v. Savadge,*[37] Hobart, C.J., in the Court of Common Pleas, reaffirmed the "supreme" limiting power of the British constitution (or common law) over the "sovereign" power of parliament (but also *obiter*). He is quoted as saying[38] that: "Even an act of parliament made against natural equity, as to make a man judge in his own cause, is void in itself," because, *"jura naturae sunt immutabilia"* and, they are, *"leges legum."*

All these laid the foundation for the idea of rules superior to the unjust or 'anti-natural' dictates of a reigning sovereign (whether a monarch or a legislative assembly). In context, however, the judges did not intend the full radical import of their pronouncements above. No direct annulment was claimed. This infant idea took its first hesitant steps towards maturity with theorists who, at once,

---

[36] [1610] 8 Co. Rep. 114 at 118.
[37] [1615] Hobart 85 at 87.
[38] O. Hood Phillips and Paul Jackson, *O. Hood Phillips' Constitutional and Administrative Law,* 6th ed. (London: Sweet & Maxwell, 1978) 49 and 50.

confusedly admitted and denied direct constitutional limitation of the governing authorities. In the *Writs of Assistance Case* of 1761, for example, James Otis had in his character of legal advocate as well as political gadfly, "struck a bold and confident note"[39] when he declared that an Act of parliament "against the constitution is void." Otis even went so far as to assert that it was the duty of the courts to "pass such acts into disuse" for the "reason of the common law [could] control an act of parliament."

With these, Otis intended to badger Thomas Hutchinson, the inexperienced new Chief Justice of the Massachusetts Bay Colony[40], against the grain of lay thought. But (mixing metaphors), he did not go the whole hog. The exercise in logic could hardly avoid the implication that there was, thus, a fixed, superior, constitution over and above the reigning, sovereign, legislative institution; and, the courts was duty-bound to apply this as a limit to any contrary parliamentary provisions. Otis only accepted the contention of Emmerich de Vattel that:

> The constitution of the state ought to be fixed; and since that was first established by the nation which afterwards

---

[39] See Bailyn, *op. cit.* at 176.

[40] See., A.J. Langguth, *Patriots…*, *op. cit.*, 13, 14 and esp. 15: "Despite his lack of training as a lawyer, Hutchinson had been appointed by Governor Bernard three months earlier to replace the Chief Justice who had died … For thirty years, Massachusetts lawyers had been struggling to win respectability for their calling, and many were disgusted that their profession's highest honour had gone to a man who was reading elementary law texts at night to prepare for court …"

trusted certain persons with the legislative power, the fundamental laws are excepted from their commission.[41]

However, he failed to draw the full implications we have earlier outlined. Chained mentally by the constitutional rhetoric of the 17th Century, which glibly maintained supremacy of the parliament, Otis would find himself solely accepting that these corrections or nullifications were capable of performance only by the very same "sovereign" parliament (but in its judicial character). "If the supreme legislative errs, it is informed by the supreme executive in the King's Court of Law." Parliament was thus part of the constitution and not its creature. Its power was "uncontrollable but by themselves and we must obey." This ideological jumbling of 17th century conservatism with 18th century radicalism has been poetically captured by Professor Bailyn's portraiture of Otis as: "Quoting Coke together with Vattel without grasping the implications of their conjunction ..."[42]

Intellectual maturity of this novel notion of a superior, antecedent, government limiting, constitution gradually developed in fits and starts. But it is to the sheer heat generated by the American revolution that credit must go for the additional requirement that such a constitution must be an "act of all" (based on people-power). It was no longer sufficient that the limitation be left to the interpretive genius of the judicial branch of the governing body; nor yet left for charitable bestowal by

---

[41] See, Bailyn *op. cit.* 175 to 180.
[42] *Ibid.* esp. at 180.

individual Kings[43]. Writers like Thomas Paine had already started to insist that any "constitution" made by the government was a contradiction in terms and illegitimate. *Ex definitione*, Paine contends, a constitution must be an act of the people and not of the government for the government it will create is yet non-existent.

> A constitution is a thing *antecedent* to a government, and a government is only the creature of a constitution. The constitution of a country is not the act of its government, but of the people constituting a government.[44]

Even more explicit is the "second Pennsylvania pamphlet" of 1776[45], wherein Obadiah Hulme's book; *An Historical Essay on the English Constitution*[46] is liberally used. This pamphlet declares how constitutions are to be formed "By a convention of the delegates of the people appointed for that express purpose" and they are, Bailyn narrates, never to be "added to, diminished from, nor altered in any respect..." Except by "the power which first framed" them.

---

[43] See, James Madison (1792) in Bailyn, *op. cit.* 55: "In Europe, charters of liberty have been granted by Power. America has set the example and France has followed it of charters of power granted by liberty ..." See also, John Dickinson, *An Address to the Committee of Correspondence in Barbados ...* (Philadelphia, 1766) quoted in Bailyn, *op. cit.* At 187: "... even the great declarations like magna carta - do not create liberties; ... only declaratory ... and in affirmance of them."

[44] Thomas Paine, *op. cit.* at 93 (emphasis, his).

[45] "The Genuine Principles of the Ancient Saxon or English Constitution" cited in Bailyn, *op. cit.* at 183.

[46] *Ibid.* at 183 and 184. Published in 1771.

One thing may be said here before we continue. Sheer common sense requires a discrimination between analysis and recommendation. But these theorists, Paine especially, ignore this distinction. Thomas Paine writes with the compelling magic of heart-stirring language. He appeals to the heart but is, on more sober reflection, stumped by a restrained assessment of the mind. A careful survey of his full text will reveal the contradictory conclusions of his meretricious sophistry.

It is significant, for example, that while Paine argues that a government cannot exist until there is a constitution,[47] the examples he proffers of the model approach by the Americans between 1776 and 1781 prove the contrary. The Continental Congress (formed in "September 1774"[48]) governed for seven years until 1781 when the Act of Confederation, which it framed was adopted. The adoption was not by the people in convention or referendum but by, the several governments of the then thirteen constituent states! In the light of this, Paine's lambasting ridicule of the constituent pretensions of the Bill of Rights as rather "a bill of wrong, and of insult,"[49] appears to be confused if not patently hypocritical. There is no clear warrant for his discriminatory denunciation of its provenance through the then existing "convention parliament" by: "A bargain, which the parts of the government made

---

[47] Paine, *op. cit.*, 210: "To suppose that any government can be a party in a compact with the whole people, is to suppose it to have existence before it can have a right to exist."

[48] *Ibid.*, 209.

[49] *Ibid.*, 215.

with each other to divide powers, profits and privileges."[49a] To make that criticism stick, there would be need for similar censure against the Act of Confederation, which was surely, also, a bargain, which the parts of the government (the Continental Congress and the various states' governments) "made with each other to divide powers, profits and privileges."

We should not be misunderstood as not sharing with Paine his clearly progressive sentiments regarding America's gift to the world of an improved system of creating people-sensitive governments (and thus good constitutions). Rather, we question the analytical propriety of conflating what is properly a recommendation with what clearly is an observable phenomenon. It is an advocacy where it should be an analysis. It proffers a prejudice when it should communicate a conclusion.

Having said this, we may continue the analysis of the fourth definitional category by observing that in its zenith of development, there was a requirement that its contents be recorded in permanent or semi-permanent form.[50] Before this age of audio-visual technology, the most advanced instrument for keeping records was writing and this was insisted upon. But we cannot now say that in this day and age, an "unwritten" magnetic cassette tape-recording of

---

[49a] *Ibid.*, 209.

[50] See Arthur Lee, "Monitor III" *Virgina Gazette* (r), March 10, 1768, cited by Bailyn, *op. cit.* 189. See further, Paine, *op. cit.*, 93: "A constitution … has not an ideal but a real existence … wherever it cannot be produced in a visible form, there is none."

a constitution would, for lack of writtenness, fail to qualify for admittance into the fourth definitional category. It may however be observed that with the long use of writing, the document, rather than the unwritten rights and rules guaranteed thereby, had now casually come to be solely regarded as the constitution[51]. In our "Textual Fetishism and the Ambiguities of Constitutional Definition," we have attempted to call the attention of the unwary analyst to the possible dangers; because,

> Without sufficient grasp of the underlying history of this idea, there is great danger of its misapprehension and, consequently its misapplication.[52]

The main model of the fourth definitional approach is that provided by Professor K.C.

---

[51] Many consitutional scholars of American extraction now write as if the document not the unwritten rules constitutes the constitution. See for e.g., Mark Tushnet, *Red, White and Blue: A Critical Analysis of Constitutional Law* (Cambridge, Massachusetts: Harvard University Press, 1988); Ronald Dworkin, *Taking Rights Seriously* (London: Duckworth, 1977 and 1987) esp. at chapt. 5. But see to the contrary, the more subtle distinctions by earlier American writers like John Dickinson, "Address to the Committee of Correspondence in Barbados" (1766) in Paul L. Ford, ed., *Writings of John Dickinson* (1895) 261 and 262. Quoted in Bailyn, *op. cit.*, at 187. He wrote that charters, like most aspects of the law are "declarations but not gifts of liberties." Kings and Parliaments cannot give "the rights essential to happiness." We claim them, he said, from a higher source. They are not annexed to us by parchments and seals … even the great declarations like Magna Carta do not create liberties: they must be considered as "only declaratory of our rights, and in affirmance of them."

[52] R.A.C.E. Achara, "*Textual Fetishism...*" *loc. cit.*, at 278.

Wheare in the first edition of his book entitled: *Modern Constitutions.* We emphasize the edition because in the second edition as quoted by Bradley, a subtle modification has been made, which substantially transforms the definition away from the fourth definitional category.

Kachikwu and Ozekhome quote K.C. Wheare [first edition of 1960] to the effect that a constitution is: "A selection of the legal rules which govern the government ... and which have been embodied in a document."[53]

The first thing to note is the identification of constitution with supreme, written law. However, another thing to note is the absence of any requirement as to source. It does not say that the supreme, written, law not made by people-power is thereby not the constitution. Nevertheless, this may plausibly be inferred. The one or few necessarily carry on government. For any rules to be set out in writing and for these to actually (and not just in claim) "govern the government" They would necessarily have to be predicated on an authority superior to the one or few; that is, the many (or people-power). The above argument is admittedly a bit of a stretch. Wheare's definition could have covered better all the requirements for the fourth approach if it had expressly specified people-power as its required source of authority. It did not. Nevertheless, as model, it is still a very

---

[53].K.C. Wheare, *Modern Constitutions* 1st ed. (with revisions) at 2 in E.I. Kachikwu and M.A.A. Ozekhome, "Extending the Frontiers of Constitutionalism: Should Constitutions Contain Only Legal Rules Stricto Sensu?" (1978-1988) Nig. J.R. at 87, fn. 4.

useful tool for explaining definitions of this class.

Interestingly, as the years went by, it would appear that Professor Wheare realized the sheer empirical dysfunction of his definition vis-à-vis the real world. He could not but recognize that a definition of constitution, which totally excludes unwritten ones, is a definition bound, itself, to be ridiculed for unseriousness. In his second edition of the book therefore, he seems to have made amends: "Constitution" says Bradley, quoting Wheare[54]:

> Refers to 'the whole system of government of a country, the collection of rules which establish and regulate or govern the government'. In this sense, the United Kingdom has a constitution since it has a complex and comprehensive system of government.[55]

This time he provides a definition, which incorporates polities under written, partly written and even wholly unwritten, rules. This implicit self-censure anticipates our own evaluation of the relative worth of the four definitions. By moving from the fourth approach to the second, Professor Wheare seems, as we do ourselves, to agree that the second definitional approach is the most plausible, pragmatic and empirically sustainable choice.

[54.] K.C. Wheare, *Modern Constitutions*, 2nd ed. (1966) at 2; cited in A.W. Bradley's 10th ed. of E.C.S. Wade and A.W. Bradley, *infra*, fn. 55 (See also its Bibliography at 747 for date and edition of Wheare's said book).

[55.] E.C.S. Wade and A.W. Bradley, *Constitutional and Administrative Law Tenth edition by A.W. Bradley* (New York: Longman Inc., 1985 and 1986) 4 and 5.

There are quite a few reasons for the conclusion that the second approach seems best to reflect the idea of what amounts to a constitution. These can be summarized as follows:

1. Unlike the first approach, which is flawed by inability to foretell its ever-manipulable scope, the second is wide enough to allow for express rules divorced from the source. These can, thus, objectively be used to test for validity even where the contraventions emanate from the source.

2. Also, unlike the third and fourth which seem to restrict a constitution to only written charters (thus excluding constitutions such as those of pre-literate societies and even those of the modern polities of United Kingdom, Saudi Arabia and Israel), the second category of definitions includes writing but goes further to provide room for unwritten or partly-written frameworks of government.

3. Undoubtedly, confusion is enhanced by mixing what is properly a recommendation with what is the essence of a constitution. The third and fourth approaches should merely be seen as instances of specialized types of constitution, which it may be possible (and for the fourth, even prudent) to recommend for use. Nevertheless, it would be very limiting to suggest that either of them qualifies, in model, to the essential characteristics and appropriate attributes of a constitution. It is to the advantage of the second approach that it is not as restrictive as the third or the fourth. In fact, any written constitution which is merely declarative of legally unenforceable

principles of government (as was the constitution of the former U.S.S.R.); or any written constitution which, by its entrenched rights and strict divisions of power, is a limit on absolute governmental power (as is the case with the current United States' constitution); can, quite easily, fit in and be absorbed by the wide scope provided by the second definitional approach.

SUMMATIVE ANALYSIS.

The term "constitution" may be understood by perspective. It is constitution in name only when a perspective of the third approach is adopted. It is ontologically so when the first or second is used. It is defined by function and effect when the fourth approach is relied upon. We are intrigued by the similarity of the theoretical construct produced by Professor Hans Kelsen on this same matter of constitutions. There are "slight" variations between our different schemes of thought. However, we have found the similarities more exciting than the differences.

In a somewhat defensive tone, Kelsen offers a spirited reply to some critical commentary by Professor Stone.[56] A few portions of this reply[57] are relevant and quite

---

[56]See, Julius Stone, *Legal System and Lawyers' Reasonings* (1964) and, esp., Julius Stone, "Mystery and Mystique in the Basic Norm" in 26 M.L.R. 34 excerpted and cited by Lord Lloyd of Hampstead, *Introduction to Jurisprudence*, M.D.A. Freeman, co-ed., 4th ed. (London: Stevens & Sons, 1979) 69-73 and 326.
[57] Hans Kelsen, "Professor Stone and the Pure Theory of Law" (1965) 17 Stan. L.R. 1,130. Excerpted in Lord Lloyd of Hampstead, *Ibid.* at 325 to 328.

illuminating for the present topic. "I have always," Professor Kelsen complains,

> and not only in the second edition of my *Reine Rechtslehre* clearly distinguished between the basic norm presupposed in juristic thinking as the constitution in a legal-logical sense and the constitution in a positive legal sense …[58]

By this, it may be said that Kelsen has produced a scheme of thought, which divides into two broad categories the perspectives by which the meaning of a constitution can be viewed. The first, the "*legal-logical sense,*" by which Kelsen meant the un-posited basic- or grund- norm, grants objective legitimacy to otherwise undifferentiated coercive commands or norms that bear the same "subjective" meaning (no matter from whose authority they emanate). He explains and gives an example:

> The problem that leads to the theory of the basic norm … is how to distinguish a legal command which is considered to be objectively valid, such as the command of a revenue officer to pay a certain sum of money, from a command which has the same subjective meaning but is not considered to be objectively valid, such as the command of a gangster. The difference consists in that we do not consider the subjective meaning of the command of a gangster as we consider the subjective meaning of the legal command of a revenue officer - as its objective meaning because we do not presuppose in the former case -

---

[58] *Ibid.*, 326.

as we presuppose in the latter case - a basic norm.[59]

We have before now commented upon Kelsen's (or his translator's) obscurantist and peculiarly painful language-structure. We shall however do our best to act the Sydney Smith "middle-man"[60] and attempt to step-down his involved message in more commonplace language.

In the above passage, Kelsen is only trying to offer a solution to the old jurisprudential, political and philosophical, perplexity arising from the question: "What is the basis for attributing legal validity to one manifestation of force rather than another in any given polity?" If I pay my tax only because I fear prosecution and imprisonment, why should my submission to the bandit arising similarly from fear of punishment, not have the same legal connotation? Why should the bandit's sanction-backed demand be regarded as illegal when the tax-official's own sanction-backed demand is termed lawful?

Kelsen's solution is the concept of the basic norm - what he calls the constitution in the legal-logical sense. Contrary to his espousal of pure legal methodology, Kelsen reaches into the realms of meta-physical and indeed, mystical contemplation for what he calls "objective" meanings and "subjective"

[59.] *Ibid.*, 327.
[60.] Original refers to Bentham. See, Sydney Smith, "Bentham's Book of Fallacies" in (1825) 84 *Edinburgh Review*, xlii, 367. Quoted by H.L.A. Hart, *Essays on Bentham: Studies in Jurisprudence and Political Theory* (Oxford: Clarendon Press, 1982) 1.

meanings of acts[61a]. He claims, first, that an act or conduct means different things in law as distinguished from fact. One woman, for example, utters a sombre speech from an elevated courtroom bench and it means that the man standing in the dock beneath is liable to die by firing squad. Another powerful woman (politician) utters the same sentence in her private residence directed at one of her thugs and it means that the man should be shot to death by the chief thug. Kelsen explains that the utterances of the women mean, consequentially, the same thing in fact (the subjective meaning) but only those of the first woman has any legal validity (the objective meaning). The legal consequence arises, and is based on various conditions. For example, that the first woman has previously been appointed a judge under the existing laws of that polity; that there is a law forbidding a certain conduct which the docked man has breached; that there is yet another law which enjoins judges in that polity to sentence to death any persons who contravene such laws. All these constitute the "conditioning circumstance"[61] upon which the legal validity of the judge's death sentence is the "conditioned consequence"[62]. Even if the man in the dock is not killed after the first

---

[61a] Personally, I consider Kelsen's usage particularly unhappy. Even in his context, "objective" should have done better service for "subjective" and vice-versa. See my own usage of objective legitimacy and of subjective legitimacy in R.A.C.E. Achara, *Meta-Constitutional Conceptions: Subjective Legitimacy in the Jurisprudence of June 12* (Enugu: Mike Lawrence Publishers, 1998) esp. at Chapts. 3 and 4.

[61] Hans Kelsen, "The Pure Theory of Law" (1934-35) vols. 50 and 51 L.Q.R. Excerpted in Lord LLoyd of Hampstead, *op. cit.*, esp. at 308.

[62] *Ibid.*

woman's utterance, Kelsen argues that, the lack of enforcement does not alter the peculiarly legal validity of that utterance or sentence. This assumption, by the legal system, that the sentence remains valid regardless of any contrary factual situation is what Kelsen means by the "objective" meaning of phenomena in the legal sphere. It is a differentiating feature between the coercive norms of the law and those of ordinary citizens and sub-institutions within a given polity. Identifying from where this feature descends is therefore, of central importance to any legal system judged by Kelsen's thesis.

Kelsen's argument is that the basic norm is the un-posited presupposition in any legal system that so and so lineage of norms is validly made. The validity is judged by form not by content. Each norm is traced up to its ultimate justifier in form. This ultimate justifier is the grundnorm, the basic norm, and it is based simply on actual effectiveness of the system set up.

Critics of this thesis point to the amorality of its reasoning. If the person who made the laws under which the first woman (judge) was appointed and acted is, by and large, ineffective in coercing the enforcement of the system he set up, the death sentence is legally invalid and retains only its ("subjective") factual import. If the second woman (politician) has successfully executed a coup d' etat and her unwritten, arbitrary, decrees now constitute the means of effecting the legislative, executive and judicial stipulates of the relevant polity, then the death-sentence to be executed by the chief thug is based on the effective basic norm.

148

Consequently, it is not just factually effective (subjective meaning) but also, no matter how distasteful, legally and normatively valid (objective meaning). Kelsen continues and says that the basic norm:

> Is not a norm of positive law … it is not a norm "posited," i.e., created by a real act of will of a legal organ, but a norm *presupposed in juristic thinking.*[63]

He rightly joins Hughes[64] in deducing that the basic norm is, thus, not a content of the legal system or constitution but rather, an observation *about* the legal system or constitution. In our own summation, we see the basic norm as *descriptive* of the "posited" constitution whereas the "posited" constitution itself contains also *prescriptive* norms for regulation of actual conduct.

Kelsen's scheme is divided into two. First, the constitution in the *"legal logical sense"* which we have described above; and second, its *"positive legal sense."* By this term, he means the man-made, supreme, organic, rules within a given polity (whether by legislation or by custom).

Although not contradictory, Kelsen is not quite consistent. He leaves his two-tier categorization and, in (Max Knight's translation of the second edition of) his *Reine Rechtslehre*[65], moves into a scheme of three

---

[63.] "Professor Stone and the Pure Theory of Law," *ibid.* 326. Emphases are supplied by Kelsen, himself.

[64.] G. Hughes, 59 Calif. L.R. 695 at 704. Cited *Ibid.*

[65.] Hans Kelsen, *The Pure Theory of Law*, Max Knight transl., *op. cit.* (1967). Excerpted in Lord Lloyd of

tiers. Under "The Hierarchical Structure of the Legal Order," the sub-head entitled "The Constitution" is discussed, such that:

> Considering only a national legal order, the constitution represents *the highest level of positive law*[66]. "Constitution" is understood here in its *material sense*, that is we *understand by constitution the positive norm or norms, which regulate the creation of general legal norms.* The constitution may be created by custom or by … a legislative act.[66a]

For the "material" constitution, Kelsen recognizes that it may consist of both written and unwritten precepts, which, when codified by the appropriate authority, result in what is known as "a written constitution." Kelsen does not stop there. A further distinction is made between the "material" constitution and what he calls the "formal" constitution.

> The constitution in the *material sense* must be distinguished from the constitution in the *formal sense*, namely a document called "constitution," which, as written constitution, may contain not only [organic law] … but also norms concerning other politically important subjects …[67]

Hampstead, *ibid.* It is not clear whether this criticism should not be reversed in terms of chronology. Kelsen's 2nd edition of *Reine Rechtslehre* was published in 1960 - five years before his two-tier categorization in "Professor Stone and The Pure Theory of Law" was.

[66] This is to retain the classification of legal-logical (transcendental or unposited) constitutions.

[66a] *Ibid.*, 335 (my emphases).

[67] *Ibid.* I have supplied the emphases, square brackets and words therein.

Having regard to what Kelsen says a few lines beneath; it is difficult to distinguish between a written constitution, in the "material sense" and a document called "constitution" in the "formal sense." The written constitution of this formal sense is said to "include any desired content" and also:

> Regulations according to which the norms contained in this document may be abolished or amended – not like ordinary statutes, but by a special procedure and under more rigorous conditions ... primarily to stabilize the norms designated here as "material constitution" and which are the positive-legal basis of the entire national legal order.[68]

With such requirements for a merely "formal sense" of constitution, one wonders what remains to distinguish it from the substantive version called constitution in the "material sense"?

Kelsen's final category is identical to what in his earlier two-tier classification, he has termed: constitution in the "legal-logical" sense. Here, however, he gives it a new name, to wit: "[C]onstitution in the *transcendental-logical sense.*"[69] Our point is that no matter the Kelsenian scheme, the two-tier or three-tier classification can, with slight modifications, be reconciled with our four-tier approach. Considering his two-tier schema of thought, one can approximate his constitution in a legal-logical sense (the basic norm) to

---

[68.] *Ibid.*

[69.] See, *Ibid.* at 336. Square brackets, letter therein and the emphasis are mine.

our first definitional approach, and his constitution in a positive legal sense, to our second, third and fourth approaches (in combination).

His three-tier approach is more academically rigorous. It is clearer and methodologically more enlightening than the other which fails to discriminate the different shades of meaning within conceptualizations of constitution in the positive legal sense. We have earlier pointed out the ostensible confusion of thought between his classification of written constitutions under the *"material"* sense as against an almost identical classification of rigid, written, constitutions within the *"formal"* sense of the word. Nevertheless, the 3-tier classification is epistemologically more helpful than the other is. Under this classification, however, the approximations are not quite as sharp when compared with our four-tier approach. In broad terms, Kelsen's constitution in a "material" sense approximates our second definitional approach. In addition, his constitution in the "formal" sense may be identified roughly with our third and, especially, fourth definitional approaches. It is constitution in a "transcendental-logical" sense that bears the closest affinity with the schematic rendition of our own construction for it is, in all-important respects, identical with our first definitional approach to the definition of a constitution.

Graphically, therefore, Kelsen's two-tier and three-tier schematic constructions can be approximated to our four-tier approach as demonstrated in Tables 2 and 3 below:

Table 2:

(Under Kelsen's "Professor Stone and the Pure Theory of Law" of 1965):

Kelsen's 2-tier approach:

Constitution in the Legal-logical Sense	Our 1st Definitional Approach.
Constitution in the Positive Legal Sense.	Our 2nd, 3rd and 4th Definitional Approaches.

Table 3:

(Under Kelsen's: *The Pure Theory of Law* of 1967):

Kelsen's 3-tier approach:

Constitution in the Material Sense	Our 2nd Definitional Approach.
Constitution in the Formal Sense	Our 3rd and 4th Definitional Approaches.
Constitution in the Transcendental-Logical Sense	Our 1st Definitional Approach.

One of the biggest defects in Kelsen's definitional schemes is his failure to express a preference. To avoid the same pitfall, we should say that a constitution is best illustrated by the 2nd definitional approach and may be defined as the prevailing, effective, framework of government within any polity or association of persons. This conclusion opens up exciting new ways for considering and elucidating another major piece of this work, to wit, "Constitutional Law." We may now investigate that notion.

WHAT IS CONSTITUTIONAL LAW?[69a]

"The world is a noisy place."[70] It becomes even noisier when enmeshed in philosophical debates as to what is what in abstract subjects. This is the attitude of mind to adopt when considering the meaning of Constitutional Law. There is no one interpretation decreed by divine providence. Various definitions can plausibly pass the "giggle-test" even if many others cannot. It is in the course of this ideological shouting-match that it is possible to fashion out one, which best signifies the general, common sense, agreement of persons that have bothered to seriously contemplate the subject. This will not, of course, abolish the odd definition or the other whose author resists the force of more persuasive, opinion.

There are three plausible perspectives by which one can view "Constitutional Law." The

---

[69a] Earlier drafts of this sub-chapter constituted the basis for my similarly titled article published as R.A.C.E. Achara, "What is Constitutional Law" (2004) vol. 4, no. 1, *UNIZIK Law Journal* 38-51.
[70] John Morison and Leith Philip, *The Barrister's World and the Nature of Law* (Buckingham: Open University Press, 1992) at 102.

most common is that it is the body of rules, customs, and practices which fix, determine, and identify the boundaries and locations of the several powers of government in any given polity. The second is that it is the academic or juristic study concerned with the analysis or explication of the nature of constitutions generally as well as particular examples of such constitutions. The third viewpoint is that "Constitutional Law" is equal parts, both. It is the systematic study of the observable situation of the sovereign structure and its processes; yet, it is made up of actual law that regulates and serves as a structuring structure of current governmental institutions and sovereign practices.

This area is by no means easy to understand. It is important to make this admission at the very start. A failure, at the outset, to appreciate the demarcation between what the "constitution" *is* from what "Constitutional Law" is *about* has led the worthiest constitutional theorists into the most appalling confusions of thought. It is easy to be misled even while appearing sensible. If Maitland, Holland, Dicey, Jennings and Marshall (amongst others) have, however, it will be no big disgrace to fall into the same error. Nevertheless, we need not.

Constitutional Law is, in nature, an academic and juristic enterprise. From this perspective, we can then expound upon its scope. We can clearly identify at this stage that its proper object is the constitution. And, we can explain that in this enterprise, it is appropriate to consider not just the observable, extant, framework of government which just happens currently to exist; but, additionally, the instruments of logic and reason (natural and artificial) which operators of the system have applied in trying to identify, shape, and systematize the rules of that observable constitution.

This is all very confusing so we should like to highlight the pitfall of previous writers to help concentrate the mind upon the appropriate detour for correct solution. Geoffrey Marshall starts with an interesting categorization, for example, but veers off to an unfortunate elaboration informed by his confounding of Constitutional Law with the constitution. He explains that the question "what is Constitutional Law ...?"[71] is motivated by various purposes:

> One motive for seeking a definition of Constitutional Law had been simply to settle conventional questions of usage within the legal system for purpose of exposition - to mark, for example, the boundaries of constitutional and administrative ... law.[72]

This motive is attributed to Maitland and classified as the "internal compartmental convenience of the working and teaching lawyer."[73] We call it the "academic motive" for short.

> Another point to the question 'What is Constitutional Law?' has been to establish or refute the existence of a clear distinction [in this field] between rules of strict law on the one hand and rules

---

[71] Geoffrey Marshall, *Constitutional Theory*, H.L.A., Hart, ed., *Clarendon Law Series* (New York: O.U. P., 1971 and 1980) 3.

[72] *Ibid.*

[73] *Ibid.*, 7.

established by political practice or constitutional convention on the other.[74] Dicey is accused of exemplifying this motive, which Marshall describes as the 'professional motive.'[75] This category is considered to be another "form of demarcation dispute" which in effect, is concerned "not so much [with] the internal business of the law as its frontier with political science, political sociology, and political theory"[76].

In the final category, Marshall contends that

> The dispute has merged at times into a more general question about the eligibility of Constitutional Law to count as positive law...[77]

at all. Austin's jurisprudence is taken as model for this category. Marshall dubs it the "philosophical or jurisprudential motive."[78] We call it the 'jurisprudential motive' for short.

The interesting thing about this schematic construction is its subtle re-direction of the debate away from what is important, that is, the meaning and essential nature of the term "Constitutional Law," to, what is substantially irrelevant to the present enquiry, that is, the speculated motives of earlier jurists who have attempted enquiries into this difficult terrain of analytical jurisprudence. Therefore, while we may see no substantial reason to accept or challenge Marshall's particular attributions of motives to particular writers, we may yet remain unsatisfied with the result of the exercise. We may still justifiably express

---

[74] *Ibid.*, 3 (square brackets and words therein are mine).
[75] *Ibid.*, 7.
[76] *Ibid.* (square brackets and word therein, mine).
[77] *Ibid.* at 3.
[78] *Ibid.*, 7.

doubt whether the question he started out to answer ("what is Constitutional Law...?") has not been drowned-out in the ten-page-sea of unrequired motivational enquiries. In fact, all the motives (not just one) must be operative for a proper and true analysis.

The editor of the 12th edition of that ever-green master-piece of clear-thought, *Salmond on Jurisprudence*, sensibly starts off by first identifying the core-concept, that is, the constitution, before attempting a description of the secondary subject, that is, Constitutional Law. To him,

> The organization of a modern state is of extraordinary complexity, and it is usual to regard it as divisible into two distinct parts. The first, essential, and basal portion is known as the *constitution* of the state. The second has no generic title.[79]

Having said this, he then proceeds to assert that: "Constitutional Law is, as its name implies, the body of those legal rules which *determine* the constitution of the state."[80]

If we adopt Marshall's scheme of thought (although we see no vital reason why), we could classify the Salmond/Fitzgerald definition under the "academic" as well as the "professional" motives. There is, indeed, no good reason why we should not conjoin the "professional motive" with and under the "academic" one. Having thus satisfied Marshall's concerns about *animus* we may then

---

[79]J. Fitzgerald, *Salmond on Jurisprudence*, 12th ed. (London: Sweet & Maxwell, 1966) at 83. (Emphasis, supplied in the original.)
[80] *Ibid.* (Emphasis, mine.)

revert to our original worry as to *nature and ontology*. Here, the classification we set out at the start of this part of the enquiry may usefully be called into play. Of the three plausible perspectives we identified, the present definition apparently falls most nearly within the first.

Salmond had "spoken" of "...those legal rules, which *determine* the constitution..."[81]. This, by itself, suggests that it is Constitutional Law itself, which, so to say, "fashions," "makes," "creates" or "fixes" what then becomes the constitution. We cannot more vehemently disagree. From what we have said from the very beginning, it must have become apparent that as the "prevailing, effective, framework of government in any given polity," the constitution cannot be based on any rules fixed beforehand: it just happens as a phenomenological fact, not a prescriptive norm. In that case, as far as the word "determine" is used in the sense suggested above, Salmond's definition of Constitutional Law must be rejected.

The logical sequence adopted by Salmond's definition would have effected an irreproachable definition if by "determine" he had meant: "describe and identify" rather than his denotation, which is "prescribe and decide the contents of." The ambiguity has therefore been particularly unfortunate.

Salmond had attempted to rationalize his ambiguous definition: intelligently, but, nevertheless, unconvincingly. First, he concedes:

We have here to face an apparent difficulty and a possible objection. How,

---

[81] *Ibid.* (Our own emphasis.)

it may be asked, can the constitution of the state be determined by law at all?[82] The answer should have been a rhetorical: "It cannot." Instead, Salmond proceeds to offer exceptions (constitutions granted on independence to former colonies and constitutions made upon the "self-referring"[83] authority of a previous one).

"Apart from such cases," Salmond (or his editor) concludes:

> Every constitution has an extra-legal origin and *the resulting Constitutional Law* depends on the pre-establishment *de facto* of actual usage and operation.[84]

But this conclusion is not quite logical. Until there is a disjunction between the constitution of the newly independent colony and the laws of its previous sovereign, the so-called "constitution" is not ontologically so. If, however, nationalist pressure has, as it were, compelled the previous sovereign to enact an independence constitution for the ex-colony, it is this extra-legal political fact that creates the new constitution and not necessarily, the empty textual signification of authoritative grant. We have explained this more extensively in our "Textual Fetishism and the Ambiguities of Constitutional Definition."[85]

---

[82] *Ibid.*, 84.

[83] See H.L.A. Hart, "Self-referring Laws," in his *Essays on Jurisprudence and Philosophy* (New York: O.U.P , 1983 and 1988) Chapter 7, 170 ff.

[84] J. Fitzgerald, *Salmond on Jurisprudence op. cit.* at 84. (The first emphasis is mine; the second is supplied in the original.) Use of "resulting" shows that Salmond (wrongly) conflates "the laws of the constitution" with "Constitutional Law."

[85] See Chapt. 12 in I.A. Umezulike and C.C. Nweze, eds., *Perspectives in Law and Justice,* (Enugu: Fourth Dimension Publishers, 1996) esp. at 281.

As to the second exception offered by Salmond, it is not necessarily true to say that a "constitution" based on the amendment section of a previous one, has dependent legal existence. No. Professor Alf Ross[86] of the Vienna Law School has creatively condemned any such belief as superstitious and "magical"[87]. The point is, he says, citing logicians, that "no proposition can refer to itself"[88] and therefore, "no statute or constitution can provide for its own amendment"[88]. In other words, if the Independence constitution is made upon the procedure set forth by the colonial one, "it is not possible to regard the new ... as derived from it"[89]. "Any such derivation," Professor Ross argues:

> Presupposes the validity of the superior norm and thereby the continued existence of the same, and by derivation cannot be established a new norm which conflicts with the source of the derivation.[90]

The argument is thus, this: if the new constitution claims its authority from the old one, it means that the old one is still in existence and that the new one is just an actualized manifestation of what has all the time been in place. If it is asserted that the new one actually has independent force, it means the old one has been killed by what Ross calls an "alegal act"[91]. Professor Hart disputes the foundations of Ross's reasoning. The debate merely re-echoes the meta-physical question of

---

[86] Alf Ross, *On Law and Justice* (London: 1958) 80 to 84. Quoted in H.L.A. Hart, "Self-referring Laws", loc. cit.
[87] *Ibid.* at 175.
[88] *Ibid.*, 176.
[89] *Ibid.*
[90] *Ibid.*
[91] *Ibid.*, 175.

God's omnipotence. If God is omnipotent, does this not mean that he has the power to make himself no longer so? If he can make himself so, can he really be said to be omnipotent? Any answer can be correct depending on the temporal frame adopted. Yes, God's omnipotence implies power to diminish his own power. This is logically correct at the time before exercise of his omnipotence in that way. He is only not omnipotent when judged after the exercise. Therefore, while still in contemplation, he retains full omnipotence even to diminish his own power. However, this does not mean lack of omnipotence until it is actually done. So too, Hart may argue, with old and new constitutions. Ross may yet remain unimpressed. He may still point in agreement and say "that's exactly our point: the transformation is an 'alegal' and 'magical' phenomenon quite different from natural experience!"

Coming back to earth, Constitutional Law is better expounded when it is conceptually separated from the constitution itself: i.e., its object of knowledge. The extent of enquiry to be carried out by Constitutional Law should be distinguished from what Constitutional Law is, in nature. It is this failure that has led to Marshall's misdirected investigation of the motives of earlier writers.

John Austin has pursued the right methodology but, like Salmond, has been stumped by a similarly ambiguous verb. Professor John Austin, that most misunderstood and mistreated of the legal sages, had defined "Constitutional Law" as:

> The positive morality or the compound of positive morality and positive law which *fixes* the constitution or structure of the supreme government – which *determines* the

162

character of the person or the respective characters of the persons in whom for the time being the sovereignty shall reside.[92]

Salmond's verb is "determine." Austin has used both "fixes" and "determines." The resultant ambiguity in one as in the other is regrettable. But, then, it may be said that Austin's usage is less ambiguous. In his context, there is something to be urged for seeing "fixes" as more descriptive than prescriptive. Overall, however, his analysis must suffer the same fate as Salmond's. We must have to reject his definition of Constitutional Law for not clearly separating the object of study from the instrument used for that study.

In placing Maitland in the class of the "academic motive," Marshall relies on his criticisms of others rather than positive contributions by Maitland to the debate. This is yet another reason why we should be suspicious of Marshall's motive-based methodology. What is material is the nature of Constitutional Law. Maitland's criticism of other writers such as Austin and, inferentially, Holland[93] concentrates on subsidiary issues. It assumes knowledge of what Constitutional Law is and, leaving that ontological enquiry, engages in territorial disputes with other subjects within and without the academic province of law. So, instead of searching for any foundational definition of Constitutional Law by Maitland, much time is

---

[92] John Austin, *The Province of Jurisprudence Determined*, H.L.A. Hart, ed. (1954) 258 to 259. Quoted by Geoffrey Marshall, *op. cit.* at 3 and 4. (Both emphases are mine.)
[93] T.E. Holland, *Jurisprudence* (Oxford: Clarendon Press, 1916). See, H.F. Jolowicz, *Lectures On Jurisprudence*, J.A. Jolowicz, ed. (London: The Athlone Press, University of London, 1963) esp. at 329.

spent quarrelling over whether or not the boundary line of Administrative law and Constitutional Law is not merely a matter of "degree"[94].

We must not be misunderstood as rejecting the use of these "boundary" arguments. We only say that their epistemological positioning is not quite right in terms of priority. Attention first should be to the nature of the definition before these extras are relied upon to elaborate. We do not say, for example, that Maitland should not be classed under the "academic/professional" genre. All we say is that he has earned this classification not because his criticism of other writers emphasizes "the preferences of the Cambridge law examiners"[95] but because he, in fact, describes "Constitutional Law" with the implication that it is, basically, a sort of study – a systematic body of knowledge about the constitution. It is within this framework that he then quarrels about the limitedness in the scope of study Austin's definition imposes:

> Most certainly any student set to study Constitutional Law would be ill-advised if he was to trust that his examiners would not go beyond Austin's definition. To take one instance, the question whether the King has power to tax without the consent of Parliament would be very generally treated as a grave and typical question of Constitutional Law, but it does not fall within Austin's definition.[96]

---

[94] *Ibid.* at 330.

[95] See, Geoffrey Marshall, *op. cit.* at 6.

[96] F.W. Maitland, *Constitutional History of England*, 531 to 532. Quoted in Geoffrey Marshall, *op. cit.*, at 6.

A model of the academic/professional category could be the definition offered by Simpson. In his witty but, yet, intellectually profound book (written under the 'Invitation Series'), Professor Simpson[97] explains that

Constitutional Law is primarily concerned *to investigate and expound* the degree to which the ideal of the rule of law, that is the ideal of government through law, is reflected in the existing legal arrangements through which government is carried on. Hence it is concerned first of all with power, *in particular with the legal rules* according to which governmental powers are distributed between the legislature, the executive and the judiciary. *Its subject matter here is the legal structures and institutions through which government operates.*[98]

The scope of Simpson's Constitutional Law is, of course, too narrowly stated. Nevertheless, his slant is clearly accurate. He seems to understand what the others misapprehend, that the true nature of Constitutional Law is instrumental rather than normative. It assesses the constitution by means of organizing-concepts, which it systematically fashions for the purpose of elucidation. The first step is to understand this disjunction. It is only thereafter that any meaningful debates can be carried on as to whether a particular jurist's instruments of analysis are too wide or yet too narrow.

We personally see Simpson's definition as too narrow. Not because it does not set a

---

[97] A.W.B. Simspson, *Invitation to Law* (Oxford: Basil Blackwell Ltd., 1988) esp. at 83 to 110.
[98] *Ibid.* at 101. (All emphases, mine.)

proper goal for Constitutional Law-study; but, rather, because it seems to exclude other possible goals. We, for our part, would advocate the use of the ideals of the rule of law to study the constitution; and this type of study should certainly qualify to the term: "Constitutional Law." But a different jurist, perhaps the special legal adviser to the leader of a dictatorial military regime, may set as his goal for the study of constitutions, the possibilities and precedents for justifying arbitrary power. His study would still qualify as "Constitutional Law" even if, as Pollock would say, it were so much "The worse for the definition."[99]

We should be willing to classify Sir Ivor Jennings within the academic/professional approach to the definition of "Constitutional Law." This is based upon the view he expressed in the first edition of his *Principles of Local Government*. In Sir Ivor Jennings's view:

> ...Constitutional Law *contains* the rules *relating* to the organization and function of the legislative and administrative organs of the state ...[100]

This passage is omitted in later editions and casts doubt whether Sir Ivor retains this view. In any case, we have emphasized his use of the word "relating," in the context, to show that Constitutional Law is essentially "about" the constitution. Despite the use of the term "rules," one will, from the whole

---

[99] Quoted by Pats-Acholonu, J.C.A., in *Guardian Newspapers Ltd. and 5 ors. v. The Attorney-General of the Federation and Inspector General of Police* (1995) N.W.L.R. (pt. 398) 703 at 735.

[100] Sir Ivor Jennings, *Principles of Local Government*, 1st ed. (1931) 41 et. seq. Quoted in Jolowicz, *op. cit.*, at 330, fn 3. (Emphases are mine.)

circumstances, realize that Jennings only meant by that, instrumental devices for systematic organization of the norms of the constitution not that the study itself imposes "rules" properly so-called.

The discussion so far demonstrates the tenuous lines separating the various approaches. Some authors may convincingly be placed within any of the categories. We see the difficulty and hope that by continued discrimination, the major point will be emphasized even if the actual differences remain blurred.

Deep thought upon the subject cannot but agitate the mind as to the propriety of excluding legal rules of the constitution from the essential nature of Constitutional Law. Surely, a constitution, by whatever conceptualization, consists of normative prescriptions apart from its descriptively observable qualities. What shall we call these but Constitutional Laws? Quite apart from this, what shall we make of the simple (some may say simplistic) view by Yardley and many others that, by its very nomenclature, "Constitutional Law" means "that law which is concerned with the constitution"?

This concern is probably the major rationale for Albert Venn Dicey's own formulation. Marshall gives a good account of Dicey's theory[101] even if much of his criticisms thereof are based on a misplaced concretion. "Dicey's thesis" Marshall elucidates with admirable brevity, is that "Constitutional Law

---

[101] Professor A. V. Dicey, *Introduction to the Study of the Law of the Constitution*, 10th ed. by E.C.S. Wade (1959) cited by Geoffrey Marshall, *op. cit.* at 9. And also cited by Harry Street and Rodney Brazier, *op. cit.*, 30, fn. 4.

consists only in those rules affecting the structure and powers of government which are enforceable in courts of law."[102]

This would retain the methodological qualities of the academic/professional genre for which we entertain an obvious bias. It does this by the first limb of the definition, which adopts an analytical posture as far as it, in the context, uses the word "affecting" to demonstrate that Constitutional Law is more *"about"* than it *"is"* the constitution. The scope (only those enforceable in courts of law) is of merely secondary importance. The really important thing is that Constitutional Law "consists" of one of the various rules "affecting," that is, "about" the prevailing, effective, framework of government (or the constitution). It implies that the constitution consists of both legally enforceable and non-legally enforceable rules. Its selection of the legally enforceable aspects as the only concern of the epistemological "rules" of Constitutional Law will not upset anything fundamental in our own schematic constructions. The approach is thus still predicated on the academic/professional category even if its scope is open to criticism for undue narrowness.

Dicey seems here to understand that political conventions and political morality are not posited. They exist by their own force: the result of the inevitable grappling of political forces in any agglomeration of human society. He may recognize that it is these un-posited norms, which principally constitute the constitution. Being so, it is useless to talk of rules to regulate them. Since there are, in

---

[102] Geoffrey Marshall, *Ibid.*

fact, some rules effectively implemented by courts of law concerning the actual working of government, he considers that these should properly come under Constitutional Law study, not those implemented by the unsystematic pressures of legislative or executive power. The judiciary is, in its official pronouncements, thus seen as manifesting the constitution itself. These pronouncements are, Dicey suggests, the proper object of Constitutional Law study. Other parts of the constitution: those the courts do not enforce; even if they may be deemed to be a part of the constitution, are not in the range of Constitutional Law and thus, he says: "Need trouble no lawyer nor the class of any professor of law."[103]

Upon criticisms of the unduly narrow scope of his definition, Dicey has clarified that it is to "the law of the constitution" rather than to "Constitutional Law" that his strict definition refers. Marshall remarks that this was done "confusingly."[104] This criticism is rather uncharitable and, perhaps, based upon a misapprehension. There is less confusion in the clarification than Marshall seems, here, to realize. Dicey was on firmer grounds by this distinction than even attained in his main thesis. It is true that an obstinate commentator may, without fear of grammatical censure, insist on referring to legally enforceable directives of the constitution as "Constitutional Law." But from the foregoing discussion, a more accommodating researcher would probably accept the clarificatory

---

[103] A. V. Dicey, *op. cit.*, 31. Quoted in Geoffrey Marshall, *op. cit.*, at 9, fn. 1.
[104] Marshall, *Ibid.*

relevance of regarding these directives such as to separate them from the different notion of "Constitutional Law" (which is not "law" but only studies these "legally enforceable rules" as well as political conventions).

It is mainly because of Dicey's distinction that the third perspective seems so plausible. Constitutional Law is here, considered equal parts, a systematic study of constitutions as well as actual "laws" made by or concerning the constitution. In this respect, Hood Phillips and Paul Jackson have, like Yardley, taken first of all the simplistic approach of asserting that "The Constitutional Law of a state is *the law relating to* the constitution of that state …"[105] But not long thereafter, they have added that:

> Although constitutional conventions are not laws as here defined, a *study of them is essential* to the understanding of a constitution … and a description of the more important conventions is always included in *books on British Constitutional Law.*[106]

This perspective suggests an inter-relationship between the *law* and *the study* of constitutions. Gerraint Parry and Michael Moran, quoting Sheldon Wolin, have put this most elegantly (although in a political context). As for political science, the message has implications for Constitutional Theory:

> … 'the designation of certain activities and arrangements as political, the characteristic way we think about them,

---

[105] O. Hood Phillips and Paul Jackson, *O. Hood Phillips' Constitutional and Administrative Law* sixth edition (London: Sweet & Maxwell, 1978) 3 (opening sentence of the book).My emphasis.
[106] *Ibid.*, 4. My emphases.

and the concepts we employ to communicate our observations … none of these are written into the nature of things but are the legacy accruing from the historical activity of political philosophers'. But … political philosophers do not simply make things up as they go along. Before we have political thought there are arrangements and practices to think about. In this way the realm of politics is created by both practitioners and thinkers.[107]

Although we agree that the third perspective is plausible and empirically justifiable, we still submit that it leads to unnecessary confusion, as does the first perspective of the foregoing discussion. The second perspective appears most acceptable in terms of methodology and we would urge its adoption in preference to the other two. We believe that under the third, Dicey's distinction between "law of the constitution" and "Constitutional Law" should, for clarity, be maintained.

In addition, to show that Constitutional Law is the academic study concerned with constitutions, it is plausible to rely on other legal subjects. It is analogous, for example, to Evidence law, Contracts law and Torts law. These are academic disciplines devoted respectively to the study of the laws of evidence, contracts and civil wrongs. Constitutional Law suffers the same sort of terminological confusion as afflicts these other subjects, to wit, a failure to distinguish the subject from the object of

---

[107] See, Gerraint Parry and Michael Moran, "Introduction" in Parry and Moran, eds., *Democracy and Democratization* (New York: Routledge, 1994) 1 and 2.

study. But in Constitutional Law, the conflation has even deeper dimensions due to the peculiarity of the thing studied.

Evidence, and contracts are phenomena regulated by norms of law that may, respectively, be described as the laws of evidence and the laws of contracts. These normative laws are what Evidence law and Contracts law as academic disciplines would then consider and study. But the constitution is not exactly of this class. The constitution is not just the phenomenon but is also the self-regulatory law, which Constitutional Law is then called upon to study. Let us try to explain.

Evidence, for example, is different from the law made to regulate it. And, although both the phenomenon known as evidence and the norms enacted or pronounced to regulate it may be considered in an academic subject, such a study is distinguishable from either. *Evidence* is any proposition, condition, statement or thing, which induces belief. *Laws of evidence* are legislation and judgments enacted or pronounced to determine the nature, extent or status of evidence acceptable to the state. *Evidence law* is the academic or professional examination or study of these regulatory laws of evidence. This may apply too to the field of contracts. A *contract* is any agreement or exchange of promises between two or more persons. The court decisions or legislative enactments that determine those cognisable for judicial enforcement are *laws of contract*. But *Contract law* is the academic discipline that studies laws of contract. Analogically, *Constitutional Law* could be viewed in the same light. It could be considered the academic discipline concerned with understanding normative, regulatory, *laws of the constitution*, that is, laws made by the legislature or judiciary to regulate the phenomenon called *constitution*.

But it is not as simple as that. There seems a slight variation in the field of Constitutional Law or, at least, in the object of its study. While for lower-level legal studies there appears to be a three-tier category, for Constitutional Law, there are usually only two. Because no superior governmental authority regulates the constitution, its self-regulatory, normative, aspect should be copulated in one category with the ordinary phenomenal part. Constitutional Law then studies this singular object. As is the modern trend, governmental power is sometimes, however, delegated by the wielders of constituent authority to persons other than they. In this circumstance, the laws of the constitution would amount to enforceable, normative, stipulates of that distinct and distinctive kind. As for the ordinary class of laws, there would thus be three rather than just two tiers.

This conceptual framework is not to suggest that anything is syntactically wrong in calling Evidence law study, by the name, Evidence. Nor, for that matter, is there anything ungrammatical in describing the legislator's law of evidence by the title, evidence law. We would make ourselves clear. Our purpose is to attain more clarity than has hitherto been achieved in this subject. It is for this, that these conceptual and nominal distinctions are proposed.

Two remarkable conclusions can be made from this three-tier classification. First, it has implications for the scope of the relevant subject depending on whether the researcher deals only with the middle tier of state imposed norms of law or goes deeper to the factual phenomenon of the social citizen. Secondly, because the constitution normally has no middle tier of state imposed norms outside of it, Constitutional Law, unlike most other legal subjects, is constrained to by-pass norms of law to study the actual, factual, phenomena. In the result, different analytic devices would be called for. Here, the uni-disciplinary, text-reverencing, methodologies of lower-order legal subjects would require re-evaluation. We must permit our minds the enormous resources and insights gained by other disciplines whose subject matter is similarly not constricted by legal norms. Since a constitution is not made by the legislator's law but by the politician's constituent power, its study cannot properly be restricted to resources of law. After all, "unaided, one cannot see one's own eyes."[107a]

The traditional legal sciences all have a normative starting point although they may have different slants or emphases. Sociological jurisprudence may, for example, glean insights from the fact of evidence but only in aid of an elucidation of norms at the sphere of the laws of evidence. The crude positivist would insist only on the legal norms, i.e., the laws of evidence, as the sole object of study. For him, the questions should be: "What does the Evidence Code say? Have the courts had anything to say about the matter? How have professors of Evidence law assembled and explained the relevant statutes and case-law?" Any reference

---

[107a] Valerie Kerruish, *Jurisprudence as Ideology*, Maureen Cain and Carol Smart, eds. *Sociology of Law and Crime* (New York: Routledge, 1991) at 41.

to the phenomenal sphere of evidence would be considered an impure extravagation.

The Naturalist still depends on norms of law but sees these norms with the tinted glasses of his own construction. It will only be a norm of law when it satisfies the natural lawyer's subjective tests of reason and democracy. The Naturalist would study the laws of evidence but insist that these norms are not laws unless they satisfy conditions he has pre-set. It is the Legal Sociologist who looks with equal respect at both the norms of law and the facts on ground. Evidence would be married to the laws of evidence. The norms are not treated as disembodied spirits. The approach of the Sociology of Law (an approach forming the crux of Realism, Critical Legal Studies, Critical Race Theory, Feminist Rights theories, Post-Modernism, Post-Structuralism, and other such mental indulgences with which many Western scholars would now occupy an idle hour) tries to effect a rapprochement between norms in books and facts on ground.

Current constitutional scholarship fails to discriminate the three tiers. Progress in the field is stumped by the consequent mix-up. The methodologies barely suitable for three-tier areas are unreflectively imposed for service in the two-tier constitutional field. The resultant muddle is predictable. Constitutional Law studies all of the constitution. It is not like the positivist's Evidence law that may quite successfully restrict itself only to the analysis of state-imposed norms regulating things that may induce belief. The constitution is, itself, both the norm imposed as well as the phenomenon that imposition shapes. Constitutional Law must study both or what is studied would remain incomprehensible and incomplete. In Evidence law, it may be enough to pick the Evidence Act and analyse the import of its normative provisions. It would not similarly be sufficient in Constitutional Law to pick up the '1999 Constitution' and immediately proceed with an analysis of its normative prescriptions. First things first. First of all, we ought to establish what makes the 1999 document the current constitution.[107b] The norms are useless unless they actually are the norms of *the* constitution. To find the true situation, we must look beyond the document of 1999.

In conclusion, we might observe that our theory of the three planes[107c] leads logically to the inference that law is only a specialized offshoot of politics; legal science and legal theory, merely part of political science and political theory. The enceinte zone between the parent (political science) and the offspring (legal science) is embodied in the specialized field of study known as Constitutional Law. From this, we retain the conclusion derived from an epiphany at the early stages of this research[108] that, "Constitutional Law is both political, as well as legal science. The constitution is an aspect both of politics as of law. Constituent power and preponderant

---

[107b] Schiff, *supra*, explains how the Symbolic Interactionists in the field of Criminology have mastered this reversal of roles between topic and resource.

[107c] See, Chapt. 2 (*supra*), esp. Table 1. See also, R.A.C.E. Achara, *Meta-Constitutional Conceptions: Subjective Legitimacy in the Jurisprudence of June 12* (Enugu, Nigeria: Mike-Lawrence Publishers, 1998) esp. Fig. 1 at 38.

[108] At 9.13am of 14 November 1994. Private research notes of that date, 3.

force are concepts both susceptible to epistemological methodologies of political theory as well as of jurisprudence and legal theory."

Constitutional Law is concerned with the analysis and study of constitutions of sovereign states or semi-sovereign societies (such as Palestine).[109] It may be defined as the system of rules and concepts formulated by academics and lawyers for the more effective identification, understanding and appreciation of the relevant constitution under investigation as well as the nature and attributes of constitutions generally. The study may or may not set goals for which it is expected that particular constitutions should strive; it may or may not mark out boundaries outside which it will not enquire; but it will demonstrate and reflect its heuristic and epistemological nature. Its peremptorily prescriptive pronouncements ought not be thought the constitution but merely descriptive of it.

An understanding of what is meant by constitution helps explain to the perplexed student the, sometimes, disparate results which usually arise from the application of identical rules of Constitutional Law to different localities. Because the prevailing, effective framework of government is fundamentally different, say in Iraq from what it is, say in Israel, the application of, for instance, the Constitutional Law principle of freedom of religion will most probably yield amazingly

---

[109] This is simply common-sense. There are various types of constitution. The "law" attached to "constitutional" is there to show that it is not the constitution of, say, "the palm-wine drinker's association of Adelabu Street" that is the object of its study.

discrepant results. We aim to discuss this in the next chapter but first we should like to conclude the present investigation under the theory of provenance with a brief commentary about the sources of Constitutional Law and of constitutions.

SOURCES.

When Dias says `the word "source" has more than one meaning',[110] he may be taken in the context to mean that it has "more than one use." He outlines three uses of the word. First, as reference material; second, as origin; and finally, as stamp of formal authority. He points to the third use as most relevant for identification of legal material. He explains that the first class (which will give information about a rule) refers to things such as textbooks. The second class, on the other hand, would refer to provenance of that rule's content. He did not offer an example of the second class (which may well be such things as custom, a dictator and such like). Anyway, the judiciary is central to Dias's thesis.

Dias regards conflation of the second and third uses as particularly problematic and seeks to distinguish them. Unlike the second, he explains, the third is predicated on "criterion [sic] of validity"[111] accepted by the courts of the relevant polity as imparting the quality of "lawness" to otherwise, ordinary propositions. These law constitutive media may well be the courts themselves (through judicial decisions), the legislature (through statutes)

---

[110] R.W.M. Dias, *Jurisprudence* 4th ed. (London: Butterworths, 1976 and 1983) 15.
[111] *Ibid.*

and Dias adds, "immemorial custom."[112] There is a glaring contradiction in the inclusion by Dias of the last item and the error is by no means lessened by the example for it. Under that item, Dias asserts that:

> By convention the writings of certain ancient jurists, the latest of whom is probably Foster, 1762, can also be quoted as "English law," but only as "law" at their respective periods ...[113]

It is difficult to reconcile this example with the earlier differentiation of the first class from the third. The first incorporates textbooks, which this last item of the third class seems also to include. Quite apart from this, unlike the filtering media of courts and parliaments, immemorial custom seems to depend for its status, on the very same law-constitutive authority of the former two institutions mentioned. It does not give its stamp of authority of lawness to any proposition unless the courts so recognize or the legislatures so enact. It is therefore a specie not easily attributable to the third class. The major weakness of Dias's classification is its assumption of unproved premises.

The word "source," he writes, `may refer to the source of information of a rule ...'[114]. This circularity assumes, without explaining, what `source' actually means. With this woolly foundation, the theory is constructed and predictably, confusion ensues. No convincing argument is offered, for example, for Dias's preference for the third class. Why, it may be

---

[112.] *Ibid.*, 16.
[113.] *Ibid.* fn. 3.
[114] *Ibid.*, 15.

asked is it the third or "last sense which is relevant in identifying legal material"[115] rather than the other two? Textbooks (in the first class) are surely as relevant as court judgments (if not more so) in "identifying" (if not in "making") law[116]. In any case, what is the criterion for determining the "criteria of validity"? Who or what should tell us that it is through the medium of the court or the medium of parliament that propositions must pass to gain the stamp of lawness? What validates that proposition? Are these foundational enquiries (based on the second class) not more relevant than those of the third class in "identifying legal material"?

Various jurists have investigated the topic of source of law with various degrees of illuminating thoroughness but almost all the modern writers would seem to fall back on Salmond. Dias's account is only a truncated version. With reference to the fuller classification, Dias apologizes for the later editors, who had, themselves, first abridged Salmond's original.[117] Various writers have given different representations of Salmond's thesis - sometimes lucidly and accurately and other times opaquely and disjointedly. Professor Ogwurike's exposition of source[118] for

---

[115] *Ibid.*

[116] See for e.g. Harry Street and Rodney Brazier, *op. cit.* at 39: "It is fair to say that in the diffuse field of Constitutional Law the opinions of authorities are resorted to more often than in other branches of English law."

[117] *Ibid.*, 16 esp. at fn. 5 referring to the 10th, 11th and 12th editions of Salmond's *Jurisprudence* whose 7th edition was the last by the author himself.

[118] C. Ogwurike, *Concept of Law in English-Speaking Africa* (New York: NOK Publishers International Ltd., 1979) Part II, Chapts. 1 and 2, esp. at 23.

instance, appears to be a botched mimesis of Salmond borrowed from the clearer representation of that author by Jolowicz.[119] The account by E.C.S. Wade and A.W. Bradley[120] is doubly censurable. It ostensibly borrows, without attribution, Salmond's distinction between legal and historical sources of law[121] and it does this rather unclearly.

From the foregoing, it seems reasonable to start the enquiry by at least a summary account of Salmond's classification of the subject. It may seem strange to say that on this matter, *Salmond on Jurisprudence* is not the best material for fully expatiating the view of Sir John Salmond[122]. Only a truncated version remains since the editorship of that magisterial treatise by Professor Glanville Williams in the tenth and eleventh editions and by P.J. Fitzgerald in the twelfth.[123] We shall rely on Jolowicz for the omitted portion of Sir John's thesis and return to Fitzgerald's twelfth edition of *Salmond on Jurisprudence* for the rest.

Jolowicz's account reveals that the major classification of "source" by Salmond is between "formal" and "material" sources and not as his later editors would suggest, between "legal" and "historical" sources. "A formal

---

[119] See, H.F. Jolowicz, *op. cit.*, Part Two, esp. the "Introductory" at 191 to 194.
[120] *Op. cit.*, Chapt. 2 esp. at 12.
[121] J. Fitzgerald, *Salmond On Jurisprudence* 12th ed., *op. cit.* at 109: "sources of law can be classified as either legal or historical."
[122] *Ibid.*
[123] Sir John's last personal contribution was for the 7th edition.

source," he quotes directly[124] from Sir John Salmond himself:

> Is that from which a rule of law derives its force and validity. It is that from which the authority of the law proceeds. The material sources, on the other hand, are those from which is derived the matter, not the validity of the law. The material source supplies the substance of the rule to which the formal source gives the force and nature of law.[125]

The distinction between legal and historical sources is only a sub-classification under material sources of law. Salmond's claim is that the only formal source of law is: "The will and power of the state as manifested in courts of justice."[126] However, he divides material sources of law into two: the legal and the historical. The legal: "Are those sources which are recognized as such by the law itself,"[127] while the historical "Are those sources lacking formal recognition by the law."[128]

In fact, Fitzgerald suggests a third genre. He terms it the "literary source." He seems as unconvinced by this classification as his reader must be and this may well explain his consigning its explication to a mere footnote[129]. In one breath, he says that "literary sources" are "the sources of our knowledge of law ... the original and

---

[124] H.F. Jolowicz, *op. cit.*, 191, fn. 2.
[125] See, Sir J.W. Salmond, Jurisprudence 7th ed. (London: Sweet & Maxwell Ltd., 1924) 164.
[126] *Ibid.* Quoted by Jolowicz, *op. cit.*, at 191 and 192.
[127] Fitzgerald, *Salmond On Jurisprudence* 12th ed., *op. cit.*, 109.
[128] *Ibid.*
[129] *Ibid.* 112, fn. (c).

authoritative sources of such knowledge, as opposed to later commentary or literature." However, not two sentences later, he gives an example that is quite the opposite:

> The sources of English law are the statute book, the reports and the older and authoritative text-books, such as Littleton. The literature … comprises all modern text-books and commentaries[130]

It is possible that Fitzgerald intends neither confusion nor contradiction. By including textbooks in both, he might have intended the distinction to lie with the terminology. For literary sources, he intended only the old textbooks such as Blackstone's Commentaries, etc. While for the modern textbooks such as Dicey's, Wade's, Salmond's, Jennings's, de Smith's, etc., he uses the term "literature" as opposed to "literary sources." If this is so, one may still wonder why there is no attempt to distinguish the "literary sources" (old text-books) from the historical sources. After all, he had stated at the outset that the "literary sources" was offered "in addition to the historical and legal sources of the law …"[131]

We shall have no choice than to ignore this attempt at supplying a third sub-division. It fails either internally (for self-contradiction) or externally (for offering no useful improvement on what have earlier been proffered).

Salmond's classification almost falls into the same extent of profligacy Street and

---

[130.] *Ibid.*
[131] *Ibid.*

Brazier have allowed themselves.[132] He makes further divisions even within the "legal" sub-division. But prudently, as preamble, he first explains that such sub-, sub-divisions are factually dependent on particular legal systems and, consequently, variable. "We cannot" he asserts, "deduce from the nature of law, the nature of its *legal* sources, for these are merely contingent and not necessary"[133]. They differ, he argues, "In different systems of law and even in the same system in different periods of its growth.[134] Having set this preambulatory caveat, he then suggests that "In general" the legal sources of law may consist of the following:

(a) A written constitution;

(b) Legislation;

(c) Judicial precedent;

(d) Custom; and,

(e) Writings of experts.

Joye and Igweike, writing from the particular Nigerian legal system of 1979 to 1983, seem substantially to agree with this enumeration. In their book on the 1979 Constitution, they have included as sources of the written and unwritten rules of the constitution, all but the last item, above.[135] *Salmond On Jurisprudence* demonstrates the complexity of this topic by further explaining that for the peculiar, unwritten, constitutional system of England, there are two chief sources: legislation and precedent; and, two subsidiary sources (if special laws such as

---

[132] Harry Street and Rodney Brazier, *op. cit.*, 34 to 49.

[133] Fitzgerald, *op. cit.*, at 112 (the emphasis is mine).

[134] *Ibid.*

[135] E. Michael Joye and Kingsley Igweike, *Introduction to the 1979 Nigerian Constitution* (London and Basingstoke: The MacMillan Press, 1982) 6 and 7.

local, conventional and autonomic laws are considered separately from the general law). He terms these subsidiary sources "custom" (for customary law) and "agreement" (for conventional law). In all therefore, Salmond's expostulations of the legal sources of English law are:

(i) Legislation;
(ii) Precedent;
(iii) Custom; and,
(iv) Agreement.

All these are indicative of great learning and impressive erudition. Unfortunately, however, the discussion is flawed by a misapprehension of what the basic object of the enquiry is. The first thing should be to find out what is meant by the word "source" rather than to assume its meaning and upon that shaky pedestal, engage in a wasteful wrestling match upon the relative eminence of each "source" identified. The first thing has not yet been done. It is only after it is that the status and priority of each becomes of any relevance. It is only in the middle of his discussion that Fitzgerald even attempts a definition of "a source of law" and having regard to how he had since used that term, one would quite agree that there is no little confusion on the matter. As premise, he says that:

> Every legal system contains certain rules of recognition determining the establishment of new law and the disappearance of old.[136]

Then, he proffers the opinion that:

---

[136] Fitzgerald, *op. cit.*, 110. Compare this with Dias's third category of a source as the stamp of formal authority: *supra*, fns. 110 and 111.

> A source of law … is any fact which in accordance with such basic legal rules determines the recognition and acceptance of any new rule as having the force of law.[137]

This is circular and logically confusing. It does not tell us what is meant by "source" but, rather, assumes the term as uncontroversial. If we were told what was meant by "source," we should have been able, for example, to more directly question why those "basic legal rules" themselves should not be seen as the real "source of the laws" rather than the "fact which in accordance with such basic rules determines" the new rules now stamped as law.

If "source" means "origin," we shall see immediately, the magnitude of error the later editors of Salmond have committed by deleting the "formal/material" distinction in which the formal source considers the ultimate origin of laws as their source. If it means reference-material normally consulted for the identification of law, it would be futile and a barren exercise to persist in the debate whether or not historical sources are as authoritative as legal sources. The matter will simply not arise. The question will just be this: "Is it referred to by courts and jurists when seeking to identify law?" If it is, it is a "source" of law whether or not the court, the academic writer, or even Professor Hart's "bad man," considers that there are other sources which, when available and opposed to it, are more compelling. It will therefore seem that Fitzgerald's definition regards 'source' as "stamp of authority" of lawness. If so, it is

---

[137] Fitzgerald, *Ibid.*

unacceptably narrow and, besides, the restrictive definition is not borne out by his own discussion.

We propose that a more logical methodology be adopted for this topic. The steps must be sequential. We should first stipulate what we mean by source and following from that, we can then indulge ourselves in consequential luxuries of classificatory prioritizations (if necessary and if thereafter it is still possible).

Our research reveals that the word "source" has, relevantly, two principal connotations. First, it can be viewed as: "That from which any thing rises or originates."[138] Secondly, it can be considered as: "Any person, publication, etc. providing information."[138] Depending on which perspective is adopted, the sources of a constitution and of Constitutional Law may be differently appreciated. The first perspective seems better suited for a discussion of the sources of a constitution while the second perspective makes better sense for the topic "sources of Constitutional Law."

An examination of the views of many constitutional writers as well as other jurists who have pondered the subject will reveal that the meaning popularly fixed for "source" is the second perspective. This explains the rather peremptory dismissal of Salmond's attempts (under his "formal sources") to bring in the perspective of ultimate origins. However, we shall adopt the two perspectives and offer the use of the first and second for discussing the constitution and Constitutional Law

---

[138] Sidney I. Landau, et al, eds., *Chambers English Dictionary* (Edinburgh and New York: W. & R. Chambers Ltd., 1990 and 1992) 1,405.

respectively. The reason for this use will be best appreciated by a reference to the definition of a constitution as the prevailing, effective framework of government. In addition, the point is emphasized by referring to our definition of Constitutional Law as the academic and juristic study of the constitutions of sovereign or semi-sovereign polities.

As a reference to the written material and person(s) for which it is conceived that reliable information can be obtained, the source of Constitutional Law is quite wide. Of course, the principal source would be, where there is a written constitution, that constitution. But the most interesting proposition that results from our enquiry is that unlike other areas of law such as Criminal law and Property law where the state-ordained institutions such as the legislature and the courts rank highest in practical importance, in Constitutional Law, the most important source appears to be the writings of jurists. A cursory glance at law books will somewhat buttress this admittedly unorthodox assertion. Like books on Jurisprudence and Legal theory which deal with ultimate foundations of knowledge, textbooks on Constitutional Law will be seen to make more reference to works of other constitutional writers than they do to case law or statute. This is hardly accidental. For while a Professor C.O. Okonkwo, S.A.N., may feel justified to cite section 24 of the Criminal Code in proof of a proposition of Criminal law, he would probably concede the insufficiency of that legislation if the question becomes: "What law authorized the makers of the written constitution, which constitution then enabled the making of the

Criminal Code"? In this, he would seek solution, not in the self-declared legal sources themselves but in the welter of professional opinion as to what constitutes the constitution that then authorizes legislation and adjudication. Thus, any relevant material can be a source of Constitutional Law. The most important are the textbooks and these identify others.

This is probably why Fitzgerald concedes that:

> The line between legal and historical sources is not crystal clear … the distinction between legal and historical sources, while useful as a starting-point, must not be pressed with too procrustean zeal.[139]

SOURCE AS LOCATION FOR INFORMATION.

It is not the source of Constitutional Law that presents the bigger problem. Rather, it is how to identify the source of the constitution. Under the second perspective of viewing "source" (which seems the more popular), there appears, amongst Nigerian constitutional jurists, a tendency to approach the subject of identification of the source of the constitution in either of two principal ways. For want of better terminology, we shall discuss these under the neologisms of "nominalism" and "formalism."

NOMINALISM.

By nominalism, we refer to the textual analysis of a self-declared constitution for its self-declared source. In the Nigerian context, the chief exponent (some may say chief

---

[139] Fitzgerald, *op. cit.*, at 110 and 111.

culprit) for this tendency of thought may well be Dr. (now Professor) Jadesola Akande. We pick on her not so much for being the first to declare this stand nor, indeed, for being the most voluble on the matter, but rather, for presenting the best target by the wide-spread availability of her medium and, more, for the unguardedness of its presentation. At the un-numbered sixth page of the "General Introduction" of her otherwise very informative work, the very learned professor insists that:

> It may, therefore, be justified to accept that only with the 1979 charter have Nigerians produced the first autochthonous constitution ... thus the preamble "We the people of Nigeria, having firmly resolved ... [sic] do hereby make, enact and give to ourselves the following constitution.[140]

Surely, this very wide statement must open the learned professor up for attack both as to the extent of her material as well as the quality of its analysis. If the word "autochthonous" still means "home-grown;" and, if a constitution means "the effective framework of government, can it not be argued that the Ironsi Decree No. 1 of 1966 constituted an earlier autochthonous Nigerian constitution? In fact, by section 57, subsection (1) of the 1960 Constitution (Order-in-Council), amendments could only validly be effected with, amongst others, the signature of the Governor-General (as representative of Her majesty, the Queen). This provision was deliberately ignored when the 1963 Constitution

---

[140] Dr. Jadesola O. Akande, *The Constitution of the Federal Republic of Nigeria (with annotations)* (London: Sweet & Maxwell, 1982).

amended the 1960 version[141]. By virtue of this breach, should Professor Akande not have realized that the 1963 Constitution was the very first homegrown Nigeria constitution? Is it not even possible to argue that in so far as the Nigerian nationalists "forced" the British government to concede full self-government through the 1960 Constitution, that, the British was merely the ministerial agency for the Nigerian constitution of that year?

The above falsifies Akande's assertion that the 1979 Constitution was the first homegrown Nigerian constitution. From the surrounding circumstances in which the 1979 Constitution emerged, the Constitution Drafting Committee as well as the Constituent Assembly served merely as the ministerial agency employed by the ruling military junta to bring about what was clearly their own charter[142]. It is important to realize that the plenitude of rights and amplitude of mature provisions contained in that 1979 Constitution do in no wise derogate from the essential nature of its cabal-based provenance.

This is not to say that the preamble in a written constitution cannot correctly convey the true source of the constitution's authority. No. The preamble to the second written constitution of the United States of America is a substantially accurate description of its provenance. There was no Constituent Assembly Decree that offered a partial representation to a limited class of citizens to deliberate on the draft constitution made by

[141] See, T.O. Elias, *Judicial Process in the Newer Commonwealth* (Nigeria: University of Lagos Press, 1990) at 139.
[142] Constitution of the Federal Republic of Nigeria, 1979.

forty-nine appointed persons. Rather, the Americans selected delegates from their already representative legislature to fashion a draft, which remained just that, a draft constitution. There were no decretals of self-imposed military rulers that the draft would be debated by only those they, themselves, appointed and directed their appointed local government councils to (s)elect. No. The Americans did not even permit their existing, elected legislatures to make such assumptions. They went through the trouble of specially electing representatives in the various states for the singular purpose of considering the draft constitution, debating every provision (without any "no-go areas") and if found necessary, ratifying the result of that exercise. It was agreed that at the ratification of nine of the extant thirteen states, the draft constitution should then take effect. It was not, as in Nigeria, an arrogant ratification after substantial doctoring by the very few and unelected members of the Supreme Military Council. Professor B.O. Nwabueze[143] played a leading role in the Nigerian exercise and to that extent, his observations are doubly authoritative. As does this book, he appears to refute the claim that the Nigerian people were the source of the 1979 written constitution.[144] We need only re-emphasize that the said 1979 Constitution was merely a schedule to a

---

[143] LL.D., N.N.M.A., S.A.N., LL.D. (Honoris causa).
[144] See, esp., B.O. Nwabueze, *The Presidential Constitution of Nigeria* (London and Enugu: C. Hurst and Coy. With Nwamife Publishers, 1982) 1, 2, 3, and 4: B.O. Nwabueze, *A Constitutional History of Nigeria* (U.S.A.: Longman, 1982) at 256 (sub-titled: "Source of the constitution's authority as law").

military decree.[145] As demonstrated by the decision of the Court of Appeal in the celebrated case of *Guardian Newspapers v. Attorney General of the Federation and Inspector General of Police*,[146] it requires only (the signature of) one person, the Head of the Federal Military Government, to make a valid decree. This is not to say that the preamble or, indeed, any other part of a written constitution can never correctly state the source of that constitution. All we say is that this auto-declaration alone should not be treated as an end to the enquiry. Further practical investigation should be undertaken to justify or refute the veracity of any such textual proclamation. If a dictator (military or civilian) gathers a bunch of his yes- men and women under the aegis of an illegitimate, pseudo-election for the purpose of manufacturing a written constitution, no amount of ink or other means of proclaiming the product of that exercise as the work of the "people" is likely to confuse and thus convince any meticulous observer.

The other approach popular with Nigerian constitutional Lawyers for identification of the source of a constitution (within this same perspective) is, as we have earlier mentioned, what we call "formalism." Formalism would make better sense if it were used for the identification of the sources of Constitutional Law rather than for the constitution itself. This will be better appreciated in the course of the following discussion.

---

[145] Constitution of the Federal Republic of Nigeria (Enactment) Decree No. 25 of 1978 as variously amended by Decrees 26, 104 and 105 of 1979.
[146] (1995) 5 NWLR (pt. 398) 703 esp. at 727B and 750B.

FORMALISM.

By formalism, we refer to that approach, which, as it were, adopts the position of a courtroom lawyer, and regards as the sources of a constitution those materials habitually adopted by the courts in coming to decisions as to what the constitutional position is at any given time.

The chief exponents of this approach may well be Messrs Joye and Igweike. In their illuminating book based upon the (then new) 1979 Nigerian Constitution, they argue quite emphatically that:

> ... All constitutions consist of a combination of written and unwritten rules. These written and unwritten rules are found in the following sources:
> (1) a written document officially designated as the constitution ...[147]

Further:

> (2) statutes which have to do with the basic organization of the government, sometimes called `organic laws';
> (3) judicial decisions;
> (4) conventions (customs and practices) [148]
> ...

This analysis, while it may sit comfortably with the average court advocate, will suffer at least two conceptual encumbrances when exposed to the analytical gaze of a legal academic. First of all, it seems to equate the constitution with what it describes as its source. This is surely

---

[147] E. Michael Joye and Kingsley Igweike, *Introduction to the 1979 Nigerian Constitution* (London and Basingstoke: The Macmillan Press, 1982) at 6.
[148.] *Ibid.*, 7.

circuitous. It does not explain what it is that entitles these four to the status of sources. It is, for example, obviously weak to say that a written document called a "constitution" is the source of the constitution without going further to explain why that particular document is entitled to so declare whereas other, perhaps better printed, documents in the country are not.

Secondly, it may be convenient to classify the sources in this formal way but the approach still leaves open to the more detailed enquirer the rationale for restricting the sources of the constitution to the above four items alone. What makes the court or court-lawyer to accept organic laws or judicial precedents or a written document (calling itself "constitution") or certain political practices that have gained the status of traditions as exclusive areas wherein the constitution is to be sourced? One may wonder why Joye and Igweike omitted the written and unwritten opinions of professional and academic experts. Even the omission of the peculiar idiosyncrasies of politicians, judges, media pundits, etc., may yet give room for plausible wonder. In summary, the two concerns we have raised against formalism can simply be put thus: "Why these four: what is so special? Why only these four: aren't there others?"

Our view is that use of the second perspective whether by way of nominalism or of formalism is, either way, deficient in pragmatic results. Formalism is helpful, but actually only when used for locating the source of Constitutional Law - not the constitution. For the source of the constitution, we suggest that the first perspective based on "origin" is more appropriate.

SOURCE AS ORIGIN.

The first perspective for assessment of the source of a constitution has many possible approaches within its broad compass. Here, we shall examine four. For convenience, we shall refer to these four approaches as the: (a), logical (b), deductive (c), inductive and (d), teleological approaches.

THE LOGICAL APPROACH.

In this approach, the source of a constitution is logically arrived at by first determining what is meant by the term "constitution." Different conceptualizations of the term quite naturally lead to different conclusions as to who or what is the source. The 1st and 3rd definitional approaches of our earlier discussion (supra) would seem to produce what we may call constitutions in the descriptive sense in that the framework of government is not rigidly or immutably effective outside the will of constituent power. Here, one cannot show that the framework of government is prescribed beforehand. Breach by the constitution-maker is not therefore, easily nullified or avoided. The framework lies in the will of the constituent power and even when it is written down, it is nevertheless subject to uncontrolled and even retroactive change. In effect, the current constitution becomes merely any accurate description of the present will of the constituent power.

In conclusion, therefore, the source of such constitution is easily ascribed to the person or group of persons presently and actually in control of the relevant polity under consideration. An example is the (military) constitution of an absolute tyrant

196

such as Shaka, the Zulu (or his murderer and immediate successor, King Dingane (the Needy One) of the Zulus)[149]. Another example is the (military) constitution of Nigeria which, from 17 November 1993, to 8 June 1998, was ostensibly located in the capricious will of General Sani Abacha, the tyrannical Head of the Federal Military Government (HFMG). An attempt has been made by Abacha to reflect in writing the provisions of this highly flexible constitution through the "Constitution (Suspension and Modification) Decree (No. 107) of 1993."[150]

On the other hand, using the second and fourth definitional approaches (earlier discussed, at chapter 3.1), we can plausibly submit that the constitutions made within those frameworks of government were prescriptive and, conceptually therefore, separable from the person or group of persons currently then in control of the state. In this way, to identify the source of such constitution, one need not start or end one's enquiry by locating the person presently heading the government. A good example is the Nigeria of late 1998. Although General Abdulsalami Abubakar took control of

---

[149] See, Dr. Peter Becker, *Rule of Fear: The Life and Times of Dingane King of the Zulu* (England: Penguin Books Ltd., (1964) 1979) esp. at 26 to 32.

[150] See, ss. 1 to 8 of this decree which leave absolutely no room for doubt about the primacy of FMG decrees and the unquestionability of the status of anything signed or purported (even orally alone) to be signed by the HFMG. See, similarly, the Bahrain Constitution of 1973 which in section 32(b) confers Legislative, Executive and even Judicial power on the Emir despite claiming in section 1 that "The system of government in Bahrain is democratic under which sovereignty lies with the people, the source of all powers": cited in Jan-Erik lane, *op. cit.* at 120.

the Nigerian State on 9 June 1998 (under the very same Decree 107 of 1993), he is clearly not the source of the said 1993 military constitution of Nigeria upon which he ascended power. The logical approach depends for its conclusions on what perspective is adopted for the definition of constitution.

THE DEDUCTIVE APPROACH.

Under this approach, the source of a constitution is by an *a priori* postulation, first asserted and only thereafter, proved by reference to observable reality. Many jurists, political scientists and historians have made postulates about the source of a constitution within the purview of this methodological approach. Even then, the examples can yet be multiplied.

It is possible, for example, to postulate a distinction based on the physical and the meta-physical categorization of constituent power. While the meta-physical sources of the constitution can thus be enumerated as including ideas such as divinity and custom, physical sources can be broken down into further broad categories such as the individual, a minority or the majority (people power).

There is a very illuminating statement made some 200 years ago by James Madison:

In Europe, charters of liberty have been granted by power. America has set the example and France has followed it, of charters of power granted by liberty ...[150a]

[150a] In peroration, he continues: "This revolution in the practice of the world may, with an honest praise, be pronounced the most triumphant epoch of its history and the most consoling presage of its happiness." Quoted in Bailyn, *op. cit.*, at 55.

Bailyn[151] explains, as have Rodee, Anderson, Christol and Greene,[152] that traditionally, power has inhered in the few while its weaker counterpart, Liberty has naturally resided with the Many. Bailyn has put it very poignantly:

> ... Power in its legitimate form inhered naturally in government and was the possession and interest of those who controlled government just as liberty, always weak, always defensive ... inhered naturally in the people and was their peculiar possession and interest.[153]

From Bailyn, above, the sense in Madison's quote becomes even clearer. Traditionally (as evidenced by the practice in Europe), the source of the constitution is (the few in) government. It is only recently (as shown first by the American and, then the, French revolutions) that the mass of people outside government have activated their, latent, dormant, preponderant-force to create constitutions. No longer would we wait for government to grant them some few constitutional advantages and devices for protection of their liberty. Instead, the governed have reclaimed all their liberty and have now, on their own, chosen to give out to government only a few powers to derogate from their plenitude of liberty.

From this combination of James Madison (1792) and Professor Bernard Bailyn (1967), the point is made that the source of the constitution is either (a) the government (i.e. power); or, (b) the people (i.e. liberty).

---

[151] *Ibid.* at 59.
[152] *Introduction to Political Science*, *op. cit.* (see fn. 35 of this chapter 3) esp. at 32 and 35.
[153] Bailyn, *Ibid.*, 59.

However, this is only one way of looking at the problem of sources within this deductive approach. Quite apart from the conceptual problem of distinguishing between the government and the people (as if those in government was not people also), this characterization of sources suffers the difficulty of insufficient categories and a lack of analytic precision.

Experience shows that it is almost entirely impossible to acquire unanimity in any large body of persons (such as is conveyed by the idea of a sovereign state or semi-sovereign polity). Who then constitutes "the people" when opinion is divided? Should it be the majority? But who constitutes the majority? In determining "the majority," should we count everybody including those less than 18 years? What of those totally incapacitated in the five senses?[154] Or, those that are mentally ill? If not, why not? Who is to decide those to be excluded from the reckoning? On what authority should this exclusion be accepted? Even when the majority is indisputably identified as such, what is the basis for applying the will of the majority in disregard of the, perhaps, more enlightened or stronger minority?

Even less perceptually clear is the distinction between "minority" and "majority" vis-à-vis the differentiation between "the few" and "the many." Both are admittedly vague. However, the latter eliminates the requirement of both a census and a referent group in the census to justify the usage. One would not need to state, for example, the number of people in a given polity before concluding that those

---

[154] Assuming that the lack of a sense of smell will not prevent breath.

identified as the source of its constitution are numerically few. But before one can justifiably group the same number as a minority, academic rigour would require the exact number from which the conclusion was arrived as well as the particular part of the total populace considered in the calculation (e.g., persons of 18 years and above under "universal adult suffrage").

Apart from the Madison/Bailyn conjunction, there are yet other propositions, which may quite easily fit into the deductive approach. Professor John Austin, for instance, argues that the ultimate source of laws is to be found in the will of a political sovereign. The difficulty in this proposition is essentially in his use of the idea of "command" and the consequent individualization and personification of his sovereign. If only an individual can claim to be the sovereign and thus, wielder of constituent power within a state, how can Austin sufficiently explain the source of broad-based, limiting, constitutions of the fourth definitional genre (such as is that of the United States of America)?

Professor Okere[155] has suggested a three-class categorization of sources of the constitution and, in this, he enjoys the support of Professor Nwabueze.[156] Quite obviously speaking from the peculiar tragedy of Nigerian experience, Okere suggests that the source of a constitution can be either of the following three institutions:

(a) The military;

---

[155] B.O. Okere, "The Constitutionality of Incorporating Certain Decrees into the 1979 Nigerian Constitution" (1980) xvi Nig. B.J. 44 at 45.
[156] Nwabueze, *supra*, fn. 144 of this chapter.

(b) The constituent Assembly; and,

(c) The people (by referendum).

Analytically, this classification is an improvement upon the "people" problematic. This is successfully carried through by qualifying the term to a reasonably identifiable group (of people), that is, those marked out by the majority rules of a referendum (probably by universal adult suffrage as is the current, dominant, practice in the world). However, the proposition is open to criticism for its limited purview. There is no reason why other sources, apart from those three, cannot also be identified.

We have earlier spoken about a physical/meta-physical disjunction of constitutional sources. The writers we have mentioned above, all seem to emphasize physical sources but Professor Hans Kelsen can be presented as proposing a principle predicated upon the meta-physical sourcing of constitutions. We have dealt too extensively on his theory of the grundnorm to permit a rehearsal here. However, it is sufficient to say, that in so far as he asserts that a positive-legal constitution is based upon a basic (or grund) norm but concedes that this grundnorm is a mental construct rather than a tangible physical entity, it follows that for him the source of a positive-legal constitution is meta-physical.

One thing will be noted about the deductive approach. It comprises under its broad compass wide and varied theoretical constructs. This diversity is its principal peculiarity. Diverse jurists and other publicists fall under this class because it permits the communication of thoughts unhindered by pre-set paradigms. The jurist proposes, and only thereafter is the reader permitted to test the resultant theoretical construct against the limits of reality.

THE INDUCTIVE APPROACH.

By this approach, the source of a constitution is, by observable facts, arrived at empirically. We are called upon to use history to elucidate the timeless present.

This approach anticipates an important topic, "constitutional history," to be briefly mentioned in the concluding chapters. It makes no pre-judgment but, rather, takes the historical situation as it finds it. For this approach, the source of the constitution is the person or institution seen to have brought it about.

The problem with this approach is however concerned with its indeterminacy and lack of a pre-set guiding test. What or who is the source of the 1914 Nigerian Constitution? Lord Lugard? The Secretary of State for Foreign and Commonwealth Affairs?[157] The local colonial administration (with Lugard at its head)? Powerful commercial concerns such as the Royal

---

[157] See the official book on British Government Departments written by Reference Services, Central Office of Information (R.S., C.O. I.) History and Functions of Government Departments (London: Her Majesty's Stationery Office (HMSO), 1993) Aspects of Britain Series, at 5, 77 and esp. 98 to 101. There is confusion whether the Ministry of War in 1801 (p. 77) which took the Home Office's responsibilities for colonies retained same under the Foreign secretary during the early and mid-20th Century or whether it was handed over to the Commonwealth office as a Department under the headship of the Secretary of State for Foreign and Commonwealth Affairs? (Or "Secretary of State for the Colonies?" See Prof. C.O. Olusanya, "Still in Search of Nationhood," The Guardian, November 11, 1998 at 15).

Niger Company? Religious powerhouses such as the Church Missionary Society[158]? What of the 1922 Constitution? Was it Clifford? Who? Was Governor Richards the source of the 1946 Constitution? Was Macpherson responsible for that of 1951? Did Lyttleton create the version of 1954? What of the Independence constitution? Should its provenance be attributed to the Queen (by her Order-in-Council) or to the Parliament (by the foundational legislative Act for a sovereign Nigeria)? Could it, in fact, be said that the source of the 1960 Independence constitution, although ostensibly attributable to the British Imperial Government, was, in actual fact, a result of nationalist pressures and thus, autochthonous?

What of the 1963 Republican Constitution? Who or what was its source (judging from the materials presented to us by empiricism and history)? Could its source be differentiated in fact from those of the 1960 version? Considering the laborious attempt to achieve the amendment under the regimen set by the 1960 version, can it usefully be claimed that the source is not consequently imperial? On the other hand, was the ratificatory signature of President Azikiwe rather than by Governor-General Azikiwe sufficient to prove its local source? Even if autochthonous, which of the locals can plausibly claim its creation? Shall we accept Nwabueze's cynical observation attributing its provenance "entirely" to:

> The prime minister and the regional premiers who, meeting for just one day,

---

[158] See, Lord Lugard's, "Declaration of the constitution of the colony and protectorate of Nigeria" on 1 January, 1914, as excerpted in Prof. D.I.O. Ewelukwa, *Historical Introduction to Nigerian Constitution* (Awka: Mekslink, 1993) Appdx. I.

agreed among themselves that a republican constitution should reproduce the 1960 imperial constitution with such amendments as would conform it to a republican status[159]?

Or, shall we adopt the more charitable analysis by Elias that apart from the "All Nigerian Constitutional Conference" (alluded to by Nwabueze), the actual source of the 1963 Nigerian Constitution was, in fact the people's elected representatives (a few months later) in Parliament, assembled[160]?

In 1966 Major-General Aguiyi-Ironsi suspended both the federal as well as the various regional constitutions. This he did by way of a Proclamation broadcast by him to the nation on 16 January 1966 (a day after the unsuccessful coup d' etat led by Major Nzeogwu)[161]. He set up a new framework of government, which he styled "The Federal Military Government." The next day, 17 January 1966, he is stated to have signed the written instrument codifying this new framework. This written constitution entitled "Constitution (Suspension and Modification) Decree No. 1 of 1966 was only fully published one and half months later[162]. Was Decree 1 of 1966 the constitution at that time, and if so, who was its source? Ironsi? The Federal Military

---

[159] B.O. Nwabueze, *The Presidential Constitution of Nigeria, op. cit.*, at 6.
[160] See, Elias, *op. cit.*, 139.
[161] See, Government Notice No. 147 of 1966. The major text of the proclamation is quoted verbatim in Okay Achike, *Groundwork of Military Law and Military Rule in Nigeria, op. cit.* at 98.
[162] On 4 March, 1966. See Achike, *Ibid.*, 123.

Government[163]? The surviving rump of the civilian cabinet of ministers and the acting President, Nwafor Orizu, who "voluntarily" handed over government to Ironsi (and the military high command)? By the Supreme Court decision in the *Lakanmi case*[164], there is an implicit (if not expressed) view that the remote source of the 1966 military constitution is the 1963 version[165] operating under the Constitutional Law and political-science doctrine of necessity (allegedly) implied in every political constitution.

Interestingly, at the time when the *Lakanmi* case was being used to debate the true source of the 1966 military constitution of General Ironsi, there had, in fact, been a further political upheaval. This, on 29 July 1966, culminated both in Ironsi's assassination and in the accession by Lieutenant-Colonel Yakubu Gowon to headship of the FMG (through his nationwide broadcast of 1 August the same year).[166] The proclamation, later challenged by Lieutenant-Colonel Odumegwu Ojukwu, dubitably claimed this headship "with the consent of the majority of the armed forces..."[167] Some commentators have suggested that the military putsch that emplaced Gowon as head of the National Military Government was actually spear-headed by Murtala Mohammed. Gowon's

---

[163] See, the preamble to the Federal Military Government (Supremacy and Enforcement of Powers) Decree No. 28 of 1970. This decree purported, *ad hominem* to nullify the Supreme Court decision in *Lakanmi's case*.
[164] [1971] U.I.L.R. 201.
[165] As operated by the surviving, elected government.
[166] Achike, *op. cit.* at 132 and 133.
[167] *Ibid.* There were at least two Generals in the heirarchically structured Nigeria Armed Forces at that time (senior to Gowon).

administration continued to operate under Ironsi's Decree No. 1 of 1966. Who or what was the source of this revalidated military constitution? Gowon? Mohammed? A junta of these two and a few other Northern-Nigerian military officers that led the coup d' etat of 29 July 1966?

Similar questions can be asked about the military constitutions used during the unelected usurpations of the Nigerian government by Brigadier Ramat Murtala Mohammed[168] (as continued by his deputy, Lieutenant-General Olusegun Obasanjo, after Mohammed's assassination); by Major-General Mohammadu Buhari;[169] by Major-General Ibrahim Badamasi Babangida (IBB);[170] and by General Abdulsalami Abubakar.[171]

The last three were predicated on the civilian constitution of the Federal Republic of Nigeria, 1979. But although the 1979 Constitution set up a framework for an elective civilian government, it was, as we have argued earlier in this work, made by the unelected military government of General Obasanjo and promulgated as a mere schedule to a decree[172].

Two (so-called) civilian constitutions made under military governments, those of

---

[168] Constitution (Basic Provisions) Decree No. 32 of 1975.
[169] Constitution (Suspension and Modification) Decree No. 1 of 1984.
[170] Constitution (Suspension and Modification) (Amendment) Decree No. 17 of 1985. Brigadier Dogonyaro's coup-day speech suggests the source was a junta. Consider, Abiola Ojo, *op. cit.*, 288.
[171] Constitution (Suspension and Modification) Decree No. 107 of 1993.
[172.] Constitution of the Federal Republic of Nigeria (Enactment) Decree No. 25 of 1978.

1989[173] and 1995 (yet a draft), went through the
motions of popular debate and, thus,
ostensible, legitimation by the many. Does this
pretence mean that the sources of those
constitutions were not Generals Babangida and
Abacha respectively? What of the pseudo-
civilian framework provided for Chief Ernest
Shonekan's interim government (after
Babangida's nullification of the epochal
election of Chief M.K.O. Abiola on 12 June,
1993)? There was very little doubt that IBB
signed that constitutional document[174]. The
doubt raised by Chief Gani Fawehinmi and by the
decision of Akinsanya, J.,[175] was mainly as to
the time when he signed it. But considering all
the evidence of a secret power-pact between IBB
and Abacha as corroborated by the suspicious
inclusion of section 48 into Decree No. 61
(that the most senior minister would take-over
from Shonekan), and the non-retirement of
Abacha when IBB left with his High Command, can
it not properly be argued that the source was
the junta of IBB and Abacha and not IBB alone?

Different conclusions can result from the
same indisputable facts depending on the person
making the observation. This is the major
limitation of the empirical approach and the
reason why the fourth approach seems the most
appealing.

---

[173] The Moribund, Constitution of the Federal Republic of
Nigeria (Promulgation) Decree No. 12 of 1989 now
reflected as C.F.R.N. (Promulgation) Act, cap. 63, Laws
of the Federation of Nigeria, 1990.
[174] Interim Government (Basic Constitutional Provisions)
Decree No. 61 of 1993.
[175] *Abiola and anor. v. NEC and anor.* (Suit No.
M/573/93). Lagos High Court Judgement of 10 November
1993.

THE TELEOLOGICAL APPROACH.

By this approach, we refer to that process of identifying the source of a constitution, which eclectically adopts the least objectionable parts of the preceding approaches. It logically, deductively, and inductively, constructs a theory whose result is unfailingly pre-determined by the concept itself.

It seeks a theoretical thread that runs through the previous approaches and discovers that it is *preponderant force.* The teleological approach claims that the source of a constitution is the current wielder of preponderant force within the relevant polity under consideration. What this means is that the theory cannot fail although the factual basis of its assessment may be defective. Once we identify the location of preponderant force, we automatically have the answer to the source of the constitution. If our assessment is wrong as to the true source of the constitution, it can only be because we have factually erred in identifying where the highest ostensible force or power in the land is situated. If we have properly identified it, we could not possible have gone wrong because, the relationship of the preponderant force to the source of a constitution is definitional.

In concluding this chapter, we would say that in these modern times where writing is rife, sources of Constitutional Law are best seen as referential in nature. The principal source is quite obviously the relevant written constitution (where there is one). Nevertheless, how does one isolate and thus identify the constitution? Again, this is easily assisted by reference-materials consisting, most times, of a written constitution law reports, legislation (on fundamental governmental structures and processes); and most importantly, the oral and written opinions of experts especially as contained in books on political science, law and philosophy.

The pre-eminence of recorded expert opinion in our scheme of thought is given some support by the interview granted to C.N.N. by U.S. Senator (then Senator-elect) Charles Schumer[176]. On the constitutional question whether President Clinton's sexual trysts with Monica Lewinsky and the lies he told a United States' Grand Jury (in order to cover it up) attained the standard for impeachment set by the constitution, the Harvard-trained lawyer relied on the authors of the "Federalist Papers" and on "Professor Black." Describing these as "the experts," Schumer concluded that the United States' constitutional impeachment standard of "high crimes and misdemeanors" had not been reached by the (admittedly reprehensible) conduct of President Clinton.

The reference materials for a constitution while helpful for discovering the sources of Constitutional Law are not as relevant when the issue is the identification of the source of the constitution itself. As we have argued, the methodology here should lean to origin rather

---

[176.]On a Cable News Network (CNN) political talk-show; "Evans & Novak, Hunt & Shields" at 5.33am (Nigerian time) of Sunday, 8 November 1998. The actual interviewers were Messrs Novak and Hunt and it was principally based on Schumer's remarkable defeat of the then incumbent Republican senator for New York State on 3 November, 1998 (after a negative and bitter campaign of calumny on both sides).

than to mere reference-materials as used for sources of Constitutional Law.

4. The Theory of Distribution and Operationalization.

Within the rubric of knowledge offered by the definition that Constitutional Law is primarily concerned with the study of constitutions, two distinct and distinctive questions immediately present themselves. The first is: "*What* is the nature of constitutions?" The second is: "*Which* type of constitution operates in the particular polity under investigation?" The first is a question of general jurisprudence and seeks an ontological response as to the very minimum ingredients that would qualify a thing to the name: "Constitution." The second is a question within particular jurisprudence. Having satisfied itself that the object considered is actually a constitution, it goes further to seek answers to the distinctive features, which would separate one constitution from another.

In the previous chapter, we have suggested an answer to the first question. In this one, we propose to offer solution to the second. The first step would be an assessment of the prevalent categorizations of different constitutions. Thereafter, we shall enquire into the possibilities and specific devices for recommending improved types based on progressive contents. This is because we divide content into form and substance. Formal content deals with classification of constitutions into various dualisms such as the written/unwritten, federal/unitary, rigid/flexible, presidential/parliamentary, etc. constitutions.

Substantive content demarcates between *liberty-sensitive* and *power-oriented* types of constitutions. The devices with which this ethical input is made to the analysis will be discussed under the title: "liberty-sensitive constitutional concepts."

CLASSIFICATION OF CONSTITUTIONS.

The different contents of constitutions as found in different polities has led many a Constitutional Lawyer as well as many a political scientist to attempt a classification. Several classifications have been suggested and these have usually been represented by way of dualisms. Some of the most commonly used dualisms have been the:

(a) Written/unwritten;
(b) Rigid/flexible;
(c) Federal/unitary; and the,
(d) Presidential/parliamentary

constitutional categories.

It is important to point out immediately that classification of constitutions does not have any inherently discoverable legal basis. Classification, in our submission, is merely a tool for easier analysis. The particular classification used is dependent on the individual preference of the particular researcher. Classifications are merely conceptual hangers for peculiar modes of appreciating and understanding the particular constitution under assessment. Although several classifications have been offered including those outlined above, the examples can be multiplied. To the list above, we can add the dualism into military and civilian constitutions. Alternatively, we can, for example, dispense with dualisms and classify into three the federal/unitary constitution into a federal/confederal/unitary classification. Even while retaining the common classification of the written/unwritten dualism, we may yet have differences of opinion as to what constitutes an "unwritten" constitution. Should it, for example, be totally devoid of writing? Or, shall we use its current term of art and accept multiple documents and unwritten conventions as together amounting to the "unwritten" category?

From the following discussion, we may come to see that much of the conclusions are merely based on prevailing professional opinion: terms of art having no necessarily distinct semantic or logical foundations.

WRITTEN AND UNWRITTEN CONSTITUTIONS.

The written/unwritten dualism presents a singularly peculiar distinction. When the principal rules of the constitution are contained in a single document, it is considered a written constitution.[1] However, this does not mean that an unwritten constitution is one entirely lacking any writing. In a remarkable disregard for semantic exactitude, professional opinion has transformed the word "unwritten" to include certain categories of writtenness. In this sense, an unwritten constitution may consist of one not embodied in any writing at all, as well as one whose rules may be found embodied both in written as well as in non-written media. Thus, the constitutions of Israel, New Zealand

---

[1] See Joye and Igweike, *op. cit.* at 6. There is a slight shift of emphasis by some publicists: `a constitution is said to be "written" when the most important constitutional Laws are specifically enacted': O. Hood Phillips and Paul Jackson, *O. Hood Phillips' Constitutional and Administrative Law* (London: English Language Book Society (ELBS)/Sweet & Maxwell, 1987) 7th ed. at 5. (Emphasis in original). See also the 6th ed., *op. cit.* 6.

and of the United Kingdom of Great Britain and Northern Ireland have been identified by Hood Phillips and Jackson[2] as the only unwritten constitutions yet remaining in what they questionably refer to as "all civilized states."[2] Professors Phillips and Jackson seem, however, a bit confused in their terminology. We argue that the written constitution is not restricted only to those enacted in "one formal document"[3] but will include the most important "Laws constituting the basis of the state ... *specified in one ... or a series of formal documents ...*"[4]. Notwithstanding this, they, somewhat inconsistently, admit that Israel has a written series of "basic laws"[5] yet, they fail to classify that state as having a written constitution.

Quite apart from the above, *O. Hood Phillips' Constitutional and Administrative Law* may be questioned on the accuracy of its enumeration of countries still retaining an unwritten constitution. In 1978 when the sixth edition was written, it may have been possible to sustain the argument that New Zealand's constitution was "unwritten." However, it was not similarly convincing when the seventh

---

[2] *Ibid.*

[3] *Ibid.*, 6 (7th ed.) and 6 (6th ed.) See especially Harry Street and Rodney Brazier, *op. cit.* at 24: `... an authoritative and reasonably comprehensive document called the "constitution" ... '

[4] *Ibid.* (my emphasis). B.O. Nwabueze, *A Constitutional History of Nigeria, op. cit.* at 89, refers to the federal and regional "Constitutions" of pre-military, independent, Nigeria to exemplify this point. But this is a misconception. In the context, there was only one constitution, i.e. the federal one. See also, Oluyede, *op. cit.* at 5 .

[5] O. Hood Phillips and Paul Jackson, *Ibid.* at fn. 10 (7th ed.) and at fn. 8 (6th ed.)

edition was published in 1987 to maintain that argument.[6] The (New Zealand) Constitution Act of 1986[7] has too convincingly incorporated the principal constitutional rules of that country in one document. Besides, Saudi Arabia ought to have been included with the United Kingdom and Israel as the three most easily recognizable countries operating "unwritten" constitutions. Professor Jan-Erik Lane boldly so asserts[8] and he buttresses the claim by reference to the fact that "In Saudi Arabia for example the constitution is derived from Shariah law legitimating monarchical autocracy."[9]

Even if a written constitution is where the principal rules of government are embodied in one document; and even if an unwritten one consists of all other types, the distinction itself is open to a very serious and practical criticism. Very little of practical value turns on whether a constitution is "written" or "unwritten" for the simple reason implicit in

---

[6] Their obsolete position is retained in the 7th ed., probably because Hood Phillips and Paul Jackson still rely on books on N.Z. written as far back as 1962 and 1967 (see, respectively, K.J. Scott, *The New Zealand Constitution* (1962) esp. Chapt. 1; and J.L. Robson, *New Zealand: The Development of its Laws and Constitution* 2nd ed. (1967) also in Chapt. 1 (cited at fn. 7 (6th ed.) and fn. 9 (7th ed.)).

[7] See, Jan-Erik Lane, *Constitutions and Political Theory* (Manchester and New York: Manchester University Press, 1996) at 6. Harry Street and R. Brazier *op. cit.* at 23 cautiously specify 1985 as when New Zealand, Israel and U.K. could accurately be classed under unwritten constitutions of the modern world.

[8] *Ibid.*

[9] *Ibid.* at 121. Shariah Law is not confined to one document or even a related series of documents as would justify the description of its derived constitution as written. It is based on four sources of which only the Koran is entirely written.

the observation by Joye and Professor Igweike that: "... All constitutions consist of a combination of written and unwritten rules."[10]

If Joye and Igweike are correct (and they seem substantially so), it follows that every modern constitution can, in practical terms, be classified (illogically) both as "written" and as "unwritten"[11] with no fundamental disequilibrium to the general body of constitutional knowledge. It is however important to qualify the general postulate by Joye and Igweike. Not all constitutions consist of written and unwritten rules. Constitutions of pre-literate societies necessarily and logically comprise of no other rules but those of the unwritten genre.

RIGID AND FLEXIBLE CONSTITUTIONS.

A constitution is sometimes also distinguished into the rigid and the flexible – the distinctive feature being the difficulty or facility of the amendment procedures provided for by the constitution itself. Change that is brought about outside the contemplation of the relevant constitution is not to be taken into

---

[10] E. Michael Joye and Kingsley Igweike, *Introduction to the 1979 Nigerian Constitution* (London and Basingstoke: The Macmillan Press, 1982) at 6.

[11] If we consider the misconception prevailing in professional opinion about the very nature of constitutions (see Chapt. 3, supra) it will be seen that many formally enacted documents bearing the name of "constitution" are, ontologically, not properly so-called. Jan-Erik Lane, *op. cit.* esp. at 119, uses the term: "camouflage constitution." From this can be derived the conclusion that despite the existence of an enacted written "constitution" the real "constitution" may remain unwritten but effective. The quintessential example of a written constitution would then be one in the fourth definitional category.

consideration when distinguishing between flexible and rigid constitutions (such change is revolutionary and will be treated later).

As the name suggests, a rigid constitution is one that is difficult to change just as a flexible constitution is one easy to alter. This again is based merely on approximation and subjective relativism. As Sir Ivor Jennings explains in exasperation:

> a classification based on a purely subjective notion like "importance" is no classification[12]

at all. The same criticism can be leveled against a classification based on the relative facility or otherwise of change.

There is very little of practical value to be said for the division of constitutions into the rigid and flexible categories. That a constitution is difficult or easy to amend is entirely a matter determined by the subjective assessment of the individual commentator. An honest appraisal by one observer may justifiably shock an equally reasonable co-commentator. Indeed, any mutable constitution, no matter how strenuous, may be justifiably classed as flexible compared with one that is immutable.

While considering the 1979 Nigerian constitution, for example, Dr. Moses Akpan[13] has boldly described it as flexible. This ought to surprise any person who has read the principal amendment sections of that written constitution[14]. Section 8 deals with amendments

---

[12] Sir Ivor Jennings, *The Law and the Constitution* 5th ed. (Great Britain: ELBS and Hodder and Stoughton, 1959 and 1979) 76.
[13] Dr. Moses E. Akpan, *Constitution and Constitutionalism, op. cit.* at 3.
[14] C.F.R.N. 1979, ss. 9 and 8.

for states creation and for boundary adjustments to existing states. It, like section 9, which deals generally with amendments of the constitution, had been suspended by the military since the last day of 1983[14a]. While still in force, section 8 required that for a new state to be created[15]

(a) Two-thirds of all the local council, state, and federal, legislators representing the territory sought to be made a state shall first forward a request in that behalf to the National Assembly;

(b) At a referendum upon the said proposal for state creation, two-thirds of the people[16] of that proposed state-territory shall approve;

(c) The approved referendum shall, then, be approved by a simple majority of state legislators at each of the Houses of Assembly in at least ten of the nineteen existing states (i.e., a simple majority of existing states);

(d) Finally, the proposal shall be approved by two-thirds of all the members of the House of Representatives and by two-thirds of all the senators (sitting separately in each of those two houses of the Nigerian National Assembly) at which stage it becomes a validly passed Act of the National Assembly creating that state.

[14a.] In the 1999 Constitution, ss. 8 and 9 have been substantially reinstated.

[15] S. 3 names 19 states and thus, any variation would amount to a constitutional amendment of that section as well as its corresponding stipulates at parts I and II of the first schedule to the said 1979 Constitution.

[16] Ostensibly, only those registered as eligible to vote (being 18 years of age or over).

Ostensibly, even though not specified,
this Act would still need to reach
The President and possibly be vetoed subject to
a reversal, under the usual rule[17] by a two-
thirds majority of votes at the National
Assembly[17].

Now, that is how the 1979 Constitution
provided for the amendment of its section 3
and, thus, the creation of a new state. Despite
this obvious rigour, Dr. Moses Akpan felt no
hesitation in, yet, declaring it flexible. Dr.
Akpan supports his rather strange conclusion
with the outcome of the presidential election
appeal decision of the Supreme Court in the
case of *Chief Obafemi Awolowo v. Alhaji Shehu
Shagari and ors*[18]. In that first and only test
of the 1979 Constitution's provisions for
election of a president, Chief Awolowo had
argued that the return of Alhaji Shagari as
duly elected President was wrong. This was, in
his view, because Shagari had not satisfied the
constitutional requirement specified in section
126, sub-section (2), paragraph (b) of the said
constitution. That paragraph specified that
despite scoring the highest number of votes,
where there are more than two candidates (as
was the case here), a candidate will be duly
elected President only if, in addition: "He has
not less than one-quarter of the votes cast at
the election in each of at least two-thirds of
all the states in the Federation."[19]

Alhaji Shehu Shagari had the highest
number of votes cast for the five presidential
candidates at that election while Chief Awolowo

[17] Consider the President's power to assent to or veto a
passed bill under ss. 54 and 55 of the 1979 Const. [same
as ss. 58 and 59, 1999 Const.]

[18] [1979] 6-7 S.C. 51 (Suit No: SET/1/79).

[19] S. 126 (2) (b) of the 1979 Constitution.

had the next highest number. The second requirement concerning geographical spread was the problem. Of the, then, nineteen states of the federation, he had at least one-quarter of the votes cast in each of only twelve states. In what may be called his thirteenth state, he scored just over 20 percent of the votes but was nevertheless returned by the Federal Electoral Commission (FEDECO) as duly elected. The basis for this return was that if only two-thirds of the total votes cast in this thirteenth state was reckoned, the 20 percent scored would constitute more than a quarter of the votes cast. In other words, two-thirds of the nineteen states amounted to twelve states and two-thirds of any other state. Chief Awolowo's argument that there could be no fractionalization of a state and that the mathematical result of twelve and two-thirds should be rounded up to the next whole number, thirteen, was accepted only by Kayode Eso, J.S.C. The other (six) Justices of Nigeria's highest appeal court agreed with FEDECO and thus, in Dr. Akpan's view, amended the clear intention, even if ambiguous text, of the framers. By this easy mode of effectively changing the constitution through the views of the majority of the Supreme Court panel (three of five or for a full court, four of seven justices), the conclusion is then reached that despite the rigidity of sections 8 and 9 of the afore-said constitution, in practice, it is yet flexible. For at least two reasons, we cannot more vigorously disagree with Dr. Akpan on this point. First of all, used as a term of art, rigidity is tested upon the formal (not substantive or real-life) provisions for change. Otherwise, the already fluid test would be rendered even more un-palpable. Secondly, the example offered is particularly unfortunate for the view sought to be advanced. If anything, *Awolowo v. Shagari* is a decision exemplifying a literal interpretation of the constitution. It is Eso, JSC's, minority judgment that would have marginally corresponded to an interpretive amendment to the clear text of the constitution.

The more definitive test for flexibility depends on form. If a body different from the normal legislator or legislature (whether by way of a special majority of the normal legislative body; or, by way of an entirely separate special legislator/legislature) is entitled to amend or veto the amendment of the constitution, then, it is said that the relevant polity has a rigid constitution. It is said to have a flexible constitution only when by means of its ordinary law-making procedure (simple majority), the normal legislative authority is also authorized to effect constitutional amendments.

Professor Jan-Erik Lane has made a comparative study of various written constitutions and come to some useful, even if debatable, conclusions.[20] He proceeds with the highly questionable, premise that for "each and every written constitution" in the world there are four immutable elements/objectives; to wit, rules for:

> (a) the nature of the state; (b) the rights of individuals; (c) the powers of the state; and (d) the process of changing the constitution.[21]

[20.] Jan-Erik Lane, *op. cit.* Chapt. 6: "Mini or Maxi Constitutions in the World," esp. 110 and 111.
[21] *Ibid.*, 110.

Relying on the (d) element, he observes that some written constitutions are made sometimes rigid in order to protect "the constitution against sudden change." His own terminology for rigidity is interesting even if only by diverting one's mind from the turgid, old, nomenclature. He describes the process as the introduction of a `degree of constitutional inertia.'[22] He outlines six institutions of such "degree" of intertia[23] but, yet, he includes total immutability in the classification. This is difficult to reconcile. If something is totally unchangeable, it cannot properly be included in the category of things which, with various degrees of flexibility, can.

Despite this indiscrimination, Professor Jan-Erik Lane's comparative analysis is a definite contribution to this body of knowledge. It clearly adds significantly to the seminal compilation (upon which he relies) offered by Blaustein and Flanz some three decades ago.[24] Just for the rigidity/flexibility exposition, he relies on not less than seventeen written constitutions picked from diverse corners of the globe. It is true that some references had become dated even as he wrote in October, 1995, but this short-coming is of very little moment viewed against the overall historical and epistemological object of this brilliant treatise (especially Chapter 6 thereof). The 1949 German Constitution and

---

[22] *Ibid.*

[23] *Ibid.* at 114, Prof. Lane specifies these types: "(a) no change; (b) referendum; (c) delay; (d) confirmation by a second decision; (e) qualified majorities; and (f) confirmation by sub-national government."

[24] A.P. Blaustein and G.H. Flanz, *Constitutions of the Countries of the World: A Series of Updated Texts* (New York: Dobbs Ferry, 1972).

the Portuguese Constitution are mentioned to demonstrate provisions on immutability. He could well have added the Ceylonese constitution as well as the particularly stupid immutability of "the law of the Medes and Persians which altereth not."[25] The former Cypriot provision for immutability[26] has proved the lack of wisdom inherent in such rigidity but it has not been relied upon in Lane's historical and comparative analysis. He has however, rested on the conclusion that:

> Such no-change rules are not frequent, because it is not considered advantageous to bind the state too closely to already existing constitutional rules. *There must be constitutional flexibility.*[27]

We propose to postpone further discussion of the rigidity/flexibility distinction of constitutions to the next chapter of this work dealing with the "theory of change." We only

---

[25] Consider the answer by King Darius the Median in Daniel, Chapt. 6, v. 12. See: *The Holy Bible* (Nashville, Camden New York: Thomas Nelson Inc: 1972) at 967.

[26] See The Cyprus Const. of 1960. See also, *Att. Gen. for the Republic v. Mustafa Ibrahim and ors.* [1964] Cyprus L.R. 195 and 227. See also, French Const. of the 5th Republic at s. 89 and see, generally, B.O. Nwabueze, *Ideas and Facts…, op. cit.* at 25.

[27] Jan-Erik, Lane, *op. cit.* at 114. I have emphasized the last sentence to signify the point I made earlier that Lane and most other jurists fall into a significant confusion in joining immutability with provisions for rigorous but, nevertheless, mutable change. See also, Justice Clark's opinion quoting President Lincoln in *Youngstown Sheet and Tube Coy. v. Sawyer* 343 U.S. 579 at 661 (1952). [The leading judgment was delivered for the US S.C. by Black, J.] Quoted [sans the date of the law report] by B.O. Nwabueze, *A Constitutional History of Nigeria, op. cit.* at 168 and 177, n. 21: "Is it possible to lose the nation and yet preserve the constitution?"

add here a few of the other written constitutions mentioned or relied upon for the discussion by Professor Lane. He mentions the Italian, Swedish, Norwegian, Finnish, Dutch and Belgian constitutions. To emphasize the breath and vision of his exertions, Professor Lane includes too, the American, Swiss, Austrian, Irish and Danish constitutions. Not stopping there, he examines those of the Czech Republic, the Slovak Republic, as well as the Romanian, Bulgarian and even, to add a contrast, the unwritten United Kingdom constitution. The amendment procedures for all the written examples are particularly rigorous but this would yet not convince a Dr. Akpan of their inflexibility.

Let us take two more examples of commonly used constitutional dualisms before drawing our own conclusions.

FEDERAL AND UNITARY CONSTITUTIONS.

Almost similarly dubious is the constitutional dualism, which seeks to distinguish constitutions into the federal and the unitary. This classification is directed at the *locus* of power in the polity under consideration. If power is located at the centre, it is called a unitary constitution and, in such cases, any powers left to the fringes are merely delegated by the centre and not from any independent source. This is different in the case of a federal constitution for, there, power is not concentrated in the centre but constitutionally *shared* between the central government and the fringe governments (which may be provinces, regions, states or even local councils) by whatever names, called.

One implication we can draw here is that a federal government cannot exist except under a constitutional framework institutionalizing limited governmental sovereignty. A federal constitution will arrange the areas of jurisdiction between the central and fringe governments as well as between the federating units amongst themselves into specified demarcational compartments. Dicey's definitions in this regard have been somewhat quaint, particularly incisive, but hermeneutically apt:

> Federalism means the distribution of the force of the state among a number of *co-ordinate* bodies each originating in and controlled by the constitution ...
>
> Unitarianism, in short, means the concentration of the strength of the state in the hands of one visible sovereign power be that Parliament or Czar' (A.V. Dicey, *Law of the Constitution*).[28]

As horizontal separation of powers refers to the division of powers between the three arms of government (the legislature, the executive and the judiciary), so does the vertical separation of powers demarcate between the central governmental apparatus (legislative, executive and judicial) at the federal level from the same apparati left with regional or federating units of the polity under consideration. But too strict an

---

[28] Rehearsed in C.F. Padfield and A. Byrne, *British Constitution*, Revised Ed. by Tony Byrne (Oxford: Made Simple Books - Imprint of Heinemann Professional Publishing Ltd., 1987 and 1989) at 3. The first emphasis is mine and underlines my submission that the relevant bodies are not co-ordinate. In a federal constitution, the central government is superior to the others and, apparently, it is vice-versa in a confederal set-up. There is vertical division between unequal governments rather than a horizontal separation between co-ordinate departments.

adherence to the federal/unitary distinction may lead to incongruous conclusions from the facts of particular experience. It becomes something of a fuss to disentangle the Diceyian elements of federalism from what many would ordinarily call a unitary state and vice-versa.

In Nigeria, for example, the colonial constitutions up to 1951 could clearly be identified as unitary. No autonomous power was, by the constitutions of 1914 (Lugard's),[29] 1922 (Clifford's), and, 1946 (Richard's), specifically assigned to the talk-shops or "debating societies" set up as regional legislatures in 1946. The difficulty arises however from the Macpherson Constitution of 1951 onwards. Did this constitution set up a federal or unitary state? Could regional legislative power properly be said in that case to have an autonomous, rather than a merely "cosmetic" (and thus delegated), basis? The regional legislatures were, it is quite true, constitutionally assigned a limited number of legislative competences[30] in addition to those the federal legislature may delegate to them[30]. However, despite those enumerated powers in schedule III, the federal legislative

---

[29] With the greatest respect to this brilliant scholar, Nwabueze was surely in some error to say that in 1914, because "the diversity of the country made it necessary to decentralise administration" of the Northern and Southern provinces "under the charge of a lieutenant-governor in Kano and Lagos" respectively, therefore, "the origin of federal government in Nigeria may be traced as far back as 1914": B.O. Nwabueze, *A Constitutional History of Nigeria*, *op. cit.* 127. Federalism does not arise merely because central government at its own pleasure, delegates some of its power to the fringe governments.

[30] Schd. III of the 1951 Constitution. See also, B.O. Nwabueze, *Ibid.*, 144, n. 8.

competence was such that it could legislate "generally on all matters within regional competence[31].

And, despite the provision of section 91 that a regional law could not be questioned in court for extravagating from matters assigned to it by the constitution or the federal legislature, the fact nevertheless remained that even within its constitutional sphere, laws passed by regional legislatures could be vetoed by the (central) Governor on the advice of the central council of Ministers[32].

With this sort of overbearing influence in favour of the centre, is it accurate to describe the 1951 Constitution as federal? It is true that section 89 required central government enactments to be laid upon the table of any regional legislature upon whose territory, that enactment would apply. Yet, this requirement was not absolute. The Governor could, by certification, circumvent this requirement in respect of bills deemed too urgent for regional consideration or those of a merely formal nature.[33]

But to describe the 1951 Constitution as unitary would also invite incredulity. Despite the seemingly disproportionate distribution of powers, it remains a fact that specific power was assigned directly from the constitution to the regions. In spite of Dicey's use of "co-ordinate bodies," it is not the extent but the provenance of legislative power, which distinguishes the federal from the unitary. In fact, the constitution of 1951 went so far as to customize for its purposes, the normally

---

[31] Nwabueze, *Ibid.*, 128.
[32] *Ibid.*
[33] *Ibid.*, 129 esp. at n. 14 and at 144/45.

implicit interpretational device known as *the doctrine of implied repeal.*[33a] Under this doctrine, a law passed by a co-ordinate legislature is deemed by implication to revoke a contrary, earlier, one.[33b] The doctrine normally has no application as between inconsistent laws made by an inferior legislature, on one hand; and a superior one, on the other hand. The law of the superior (usually, the central) legislature would normally prevail whether or not it is the earlier in point of time.

However, in 1951, the doctrine of implied repeal was no longer left to implication. And not just that, it was, by section 107,

---

[33a] See, for e.g. the English Court of Appeal decision in *Ellen Street Estates Ltd. v. Minister of Health* [1934] 1 K.B. 590. Commenting on this case, Sir Ivor Jennings, *The Law and the Constitution op. cit.* at 162 observes that "the implication that the Act of 1919 was pro tanto to be repealed was so evident that it was almost … explicit …." The maxim must remain: "*quod leges posteriores priores contrarias abrogant*" (Coke, 4 Institutes 43). See similarly, Publius (Alexander Hamilton), "Federalist Papers No. 78" in James Madison, Alexander Hamilton and John Jay; Isaac Kramnick, ed., *The Federalist Papers*, Penguin Classics (1788; England: Penguin Books, 1987) at 439: "between the interfering acts of an equal authority that which was the last indication of its will should have the preference."

[33b] By analogy, the doctrine of implied repeal has, apparently, been extended, not just to time but, to content. In *Shroder v. Major* [1989] All NLR 201, the Supreme Court *held* that in relation to specific matters specific provisions would override general provisions of a legislation. At p. 215, in the flowery concurrence of Oputa, JSC, therefore: "*generale tantum valet in generalibus, quantum singulare in singulis.*" This has most recently been reaffirmed by Niki Tobi, JSC, in *Kraus Thompson Organisation v. National Institute for Policy and Strategic Studies (NIPSS)* (2004) 121 LRCN 5011 esp. at 5020F-P.

constitutionally specified that even laws of the ostensibly inferior regional legislatures would supersede any, earlier enacted, by the (superior) federal law-makers[34]. On this view, therefore, the 1951 Constitution was federal. However, the foregoing discussion demonstrates the conceptual difficulties of classification.

Professor Nwabueze describes the 1954 (Lyttleton) Constitution as having introduced "a full-fledged" or "a thorough-going federal system."[35] The same can be said for the 1960 and 1963 Constitutions where, in fact, not only did the regions benefit from the concurrent and residual powers but, additionally, each had its own dedicated "constitution" although these was subject to contrary provisions of the central or federal constitution[36].

The 1979 Constitution seems, without much doubt, truly federal in every sense of the word, even as defined by Dicey. Non-central powers are not just those enumerated for the states in the Concurrent Legislative List[37] but they also include all residual matters not specifically mentioned in any of the lists (exclusive or concurrent) or not allotted to the centre in any other part of the constitution. This conclusion derives from the provision of section 4, sub-section (7) to the effect that:

> The House of Assembly of a state shall have power to make laws for the peace, order and good government of the state or

---

[34] *Ibid.*, 128 esp. n. 13 at 144.
[35] *Ibid.*, 130.
[36] See s. 1 *Ibid.* at 134, esp. n. 36 at 145.
[37] At the 2nd Schedule, Part II, 1st column of the Constitution, to the extent specified in the 2nd column thereof.

any part thereof with respect to the following matters, that is to say –

(a) any matter not included in the Exclusive legislative list set out in part 1 of the second schedule to this constitution ;

(b) any matter included in the concurrent legislative list .... to the extent prescribed ... ; and

(c) any other matter with respect to which it is empowered to make laws in accordance with the provisions of this constitution.

The stillborn 1989 Constitution[38] would have similarly been a "full-fledged" federal constitution. It even went so far as to create, for the first time, an autonomous, separate, (three-tier) legislative authority down to the local government level.[39] However, the military constitutions have been problematic in interpretation. The true form has evidently been unitary because of the hierarchical command structure so normal in the military establishment. Yet, the written "camouflage" constitutions used in Nigeria by the various military regimes of 1966, 1975, 1984, 1985, 1993 and 1998(?), have been quite ambivalent in the matter except for General Aguiyi-Ironsi's unification Decree[40]. This decree enacted on 24 May, 1966, lasted 3 months before it was abrogated by General Gowon on 1 September,

---

[38] Decree No. 12 of 1989, Cap. 63, L.F.N., 1990.

[39] The local government council was set up as the legislative counterpart to the local government headed by a chairman assisted by supervisory councillors (with porfolios under an amendment Decree No. 23 of 1991).

[40] Constitution (Suspension and Modification) (No. 5) Decree No. 34 of 1966.

1966,[41] after the assassination of its author in a Northern-led counter coup at Ibadan.

The Unification Decree was very explicit about its intention to institute a barefaced unitary government. In fact, the government was from the "Federal Military Government," renamed the "National Military Government" in order to clearly do away with the "federal" tag in the former appellation. Others have been ambivalent and sometimes, ambiguous. The military constitution of 1993 created by Abacha and continued in force on his death since 8 June, 1998, by General Abdulsalami Alhaji Abubakar, although it enacts in section 2, sub-section (2), paragraphs (a) and (b), that a state shall lack competence in the federal list and, except with prior consent of the federal military government, also lack competence upon concurrent matters, it is instructive that state legislative power is nevertheless, constitutionally reserved by section 2, sub-section (3) for what may be called the residual legislative powers of the federation. What is troubling to this analysis however, is the all-embracing provision of section 2, sub-section (1) which asserts without equivocation, that:

> The Federal Military Government shall have the power to make laws for the peace, order and good government of Nigeria *or*

---

[41] Constitution (Suspension and Modification) (No. 9) Decree No. 59 of 1966. This decree revived Aguiyi-Ironsi's initial constitution (Decree No. 1 of 1966) and restored what B.O. Nwabueze, *Military Rule and Constitutionalism in Nigeria, op. cit.* 114, describes as "the quasi-federal system of the constitution Decree No. 1." There was really nothing "quasi-federal' about Decree No. 1 of 1966 or any of the other military constitution-decrees (except No. 8 of 1967 [Aburi-based] between Ojukwu and Gowon) which, in practice, only delegate but do not share powers with the fringes.

> *any part thereof* with respect *to any matter whatsoever.*[42]

With this sort of vastness coupled with the interpretational device known in Constitutional Law as *the doctrine of covering the field,*[43] it would seem quite untenable to maintain residual power claims under sub-section (3) in favour of the state legislatures. In consequence, all that is left to the Military Administrator of each state is *delegated* legislative power under sub-section (2) (a) (within the constricting framework of

---

[42] Both emphases are mine.

[43] Normally, an inconsistency between federal and state laws (depending on which sphere is superior under a confederal or federal system) results in the nullification of the subordinate legislation to the extent of its inconsistency with the superior one. The Australian Courts have, however, extended this inconsistency rule to apply even where there is no substantive inconsistency. Here, having regard to the implied intention to be gleaned from the extent and detail of the superior legislation (that no other law on the matter would be entertained), the rule is derived that subordinate laws (even if consistent) should by nullified: See *Clyde v. Cowburn* (1926) 37 C.L.R. 466. See also *Lakanmi's Case* (1974) 4 E.C.S.L.R. 713 at 721/22 or [1971] 1 U.I.L.R. 201 at 208/209 and Uwais, J.S.C.'s, concurrence in *Salati v. Shehu* [1986] All N.L.R. 53 at 67. But see (*per incuriam*) per Wali, J.S.C., in *Sadikwu v. Dalori* [1996] 4 S.C.N.J. 209 at 220 where the learned Justice assumes that "inconsistency" is literally used under this doctrine. Since, at least, *Att. Gen. (Abia State) & 35 ors. v. Att. Gen. (Fedn.)* (2002) 95 LRCN 407 [the LG tenure case of March 2002], the Supreme Court has extended the doctrine of constitutional supremacy to embrace the occupied field theory. See, also, *Att. Gen. (Fedn.) v. Att. Gen. (Abia State) and 35 ors.* (2002) 96 LRCN 559-882 [The resource control case]. Even more radically, consider: *INEC & AG (Fedn.) v. Musa & 4 ors.* [2003] 1 S.C. (Part I) 106 [Ayoola, JSC, leading].

the concurrent legislative list). The 1993 military constitution (just as its ancestors of 1966, 1975, 1984 and 1985) is therefore, a unitary one despite its (and their) ambiguity and ambivalence. The *"Federal* Military Government" has been a barefaced lie. Except for the 70-day period that the "confederal constitution"[44] lasted (brokered at Aburi between Ojukwu and Gowon just before the Nigerian Civil War); as well as the brief civilian interventions[45] between 1 October 1963 to 16 January 1966; and, 1 October 1979 to 31 December 1983; the so-called *"Federal* Republic of Nigeria" has (before 29 May, 1999) been a blatant misnomer. Nigeria, in those periods, has neither been federal nor, in any coherent sense of the word, a republic.

It must be admitted that the federal/unitary dualism presents a more articulate analytical device than those previously discussed. Nevertheless, it remains bogged by imprecision caused, not least, by the problem of defining co-ordinate power as between the federal and regional legislatures. Another problem is how to determine the distinction between federal and confederal polities.

PRESIDENTIAL AND PARLIAMENTARY CONSTITUTIONS.

The last of the four dualisms we have chosen to consider here primarily distinguishes

---

[44] Constitution (Suspension and Modification) Decree No. 8 of 1967 made on 10 March, 1967, with effect from 17 March, 1967, but unilaterally revoked on 27 May, 1967, by Gowon.
[45] For just six and a half years since Republicanism in October, 1963, as compared to about 28 years, 9 months, up to the time of my first draft for this chapt. in Dec., 1998.

between an executive directly responsible to the people; and, one indirectly responsible to the people through a representative legislature. The first is presidential; the second, parliamentary. As the following discussion will demonstrate, this is another one of the dubious classifications flawed by imprecision and woolly conceptualizations.

It is possible, relying on the observation of polities which claim to be parliamentary, to distinguish this class not only through the method by which the chief executive is hired and fired, but also, by considering whether there is a conjunction or separation of the office of head of state from that of the head of government. When there is separation, it is indicative of a parliamentary constitution while a conjunction of both offices in one functionary signifies a presidential constitution.[45a] It is added that strict separation of powers arises only in a presidential system but the executive functionaries are all legislators under parliamentarianism.

The editors of Stanley de Smith's classic[45b] both agree that: "This kind of classification is not very illuminating because of the wide variation within each type of system."[45b]

Under the "parliamentary" constitution of 1995 by which Prime Minister Benjamin Netanyahu was elected, for the very first time in modern Israeli history, the head of government could not be removed merely by loss of a simple

---

[45a] E. Michael Joye and Kingsley Igweike, *Introduction to the 1979 Nigerian Constitution, op. cit.,* esp. at 121.
[45b] Harry Street and Rodney Brazier, eds., *Constitutional and Administrative Law de Smith op. cit.,* at 25.

majority support in the Knesset (the legislature). This was largely because, for the first time, the office of Prime Minister was filled through direct election by the entire electorate and not simply because a candidate was the leader of the majority party in the legislature[46].

The constitution of the post-communist Russian Republic presents another contrast to the object of smooth analysis sought by this classification. While President Boris Yeltsin's mandate derived from direct countrywide elections, day-to-day rule was, at least notionally, left to his Prime Minister. The Prime Minister in Russia is now selected and dismissible by the President but his appointment presents a feature nowhere duplicated in the rest of the world. Before the Prime Minister-designate becomes substantive head of government, the Duma, the more powerful lower house of the Russian parliament, must approve. The president is allowed to re-nominate the same person and seek approval at the Duma a second time; and if still rejected, a third time. The unique thing is that if the nominee is rejected a third time, the Duma will stand dissolved and new parliamentary elections will be held. This feature enabled an overbearing Yeltsin to force, at the third vote, the acceptance of the youngest Prime Minister by the Communist-party-dominate-Duma of 1997/98. Unlike most places elsewhere, the

---

[46] It is true that a special (60%) majority could by vote of censure, cause him, at his option, to dissolve the Knesset for fresh elections, or by an even wider (80%) vote, impeach him without dissolution of the Knesset. But this is similar to impeachment-control held over the executive president under most presidential constitutions.

Russian Prime Minister then appoints his (assisting) Ministers and not necessarily from the legislature. In other words, the Prime Minister and his Cabinet are not responsible to the Duma but to the president quite unlike the model represented by the Westminster Parliament.

Professor Lane classes "France, Finland and Portugal" as "semi-presidential systems"[47]. He relies on the fact that it is the president who appoints and dismisses the premier (who, nevertheless, still needs to retain the confidence of the legislature). "Presidential government in [much of] Europe" he concludes,[48] citing Shugart and Carey,[49] "is of the semi-presidential type, adding to presidentialism a strong dose of parliamentarism." It is possible that Lane would have added Yeltsin's Russia to this list if he had but considered that country as North-East-European.

Another aberrant example, giving doubt to the presidential/parliamentary dualism is the Kenyan constitution (a new one is proposed for ratification in 1999 and later, in 2004). In the 1988 version, President Daniel Arap Moi, an executive head of state as well as head of government, nevertheless retained a seat in the legislature. Street and Brazier[50] also show that in Tanzania the presidential system is more orthodox. However, although the president in

---

[47] Jan-Erik Lane, *Constitutions and Political Theory, op. cit.*, at 134.

[48] *Ibid.* Square brackets and words in square brackets are mine.

[49] M.S. Shugart and J.M. Carey, *Presidents and Assemblies* (New York: Cambridge University Press, 1992). See also cited, H. Doring ed., *Parliaments and Majority Rule in Western Europe* (Frankfurt: Campus, 1995).

[50] Harry Street and Rodney Brazier, *op. cit.*, at 25.

that country is not a Member of Parliament, his ministers are.

PRELIMINARY CONCLUSIONS ON CONSTITUTIONAL DUALISMS.

There are other dualisms including that between a monarchy and a republic. The distinction is the hereditary element in the accession of the head of state. The succession in a monarchical constitution is said to be dependent on consanguinity and heredity while a republican constitution, based on the *Res Publica* (public thing), allows for participation of the general electorate in determining who becomes the new head of state. Thus it is, that the United Kingdom of Great Britain and Northern Ireland has a monarchical constitution while the United States of America has a republican one.

But even here, the controversy is not rested. Thomas Paine kicks it from the very base. He offers a definition of "republic" which shatters the above character as the distinguishing feature because, if: "Republican government is no other than government established and conducted for the interest of the public ..."[51] and even if it is also added that: "... it is not necessarily connected with any particular form, but it most naturally associates with the representative form ...,"[51] then, we would be unable to deny republican status, for example, to the Kingdom of Jordan where, in spite of section 1 of its constitution to the effect that the: "Form of government shall be parliamentary with

---

[51] Thomas Paine, *Rights of Man*, Henry Collins, ed., *op. cit.* at 200.

hereditary monarchy,"[52] the benign 50-year rule of the recently deceased King Hussein has undoubtedly been "for the interest of the public." In fact, there is a "representative form" of some sort wherein:

> The king shall exercise the powers vested in him by Royal Decrees ... signed by the Prime Minister or the Minister concerned[53]

and these elected Ministers and Prime Minister:

> Shall be collectively responsible before the House of Deputies ..."[54]

If Paine's definition is adopted (which diminishes the criterion of heredity) it would result in the conclusion that a hereditary monarchy can be, at the same time, a republic. Were that to be so, the classification would entirely be meaningless; the notion of republicanism, clearly absurd.

Quite apart from the criticisms above, a more debilitating critique of these dualistic classifications is that none of the four or five types discussed truly admits of the dualistic compartmentalization adopted. The problem seems to have stemmed from Dicey's seminal classification of constitutions under those headings. However, reality suggests that instead of dividing, for example:

(a) Between written and unwritten constitutions, one would probably be more coherent to include the partly-written constitution;

---

[52] Constitution of the Hashemite Kingdom of Jordan, 1984 (Our emphasis). See also, Jan-Erik Lane, *op. cit.*, at 120. At King Hussein's sad demise in 1999, his eldest son, Abdullah, took over the crown by constitutionally recognized inheritance (or succession).

[53] See, s. 40, *Ibid.*

[54] See, s. 51, *Ibid.*

(b)   Between rigid and flexible constitutions, one should become more precise by adding the entirely immutable constitution;

(c)   Between unitary and federal constitutions, one should rather substitute the federal/confederal/unitary categories; and

(d)   Between presidential and parliamentary constitutions, one should realize and acknowledge the existence of constitutions where there is neither a direct nor an indirect responsibility of the chief executive to the electorate. Here, it is right to add the constitutions of forceful usurpation.

Similarly, even though there is the dualism based on hereditary succession, we must yet realize that military constitutions exist (like Nigeria's before 29 May, 1999),[55] which neither enthrone hereditary succession nor can, without pure absurdity, be classed among the republican genre. In this respect, we may more properly consider a tripartite typology into presidential/parliamentary/military   (or unrepresentative) constitutions.

We should not be understood as totally dismissing these analytic devices of dualistic classification as inherently useless. No, what we disparage is the attempt by many commentators to elevate them into sacred or mystical constitutional concepts (as if having a life and logic independent of the subjective requirements of the individual researcher whose tools they are). Just as there is the "sliding scale of softness"[56] (for laws), there may well

---

[55] Decree 107 of 1993 (supra).

[56] See, W.M. Reisman, "A Hard Look at Soft Law," (1988) 82 Amer. Soc. of Intl. Law Procds., 371, 374 to 377; and

be a frangible frame of flexibility for the classification of constitutions.

And just as for Kelsen, "any content may be law," for us, any content may constitute a constitution. A "sultanistic" constitution such as that of Saudi Arabia may, for instance, deny its citizens the right to a representative government; and a "religious" one such as the constitution of the Islamic Republic of Iran, 1979, may impose a state religion and subject dissenting citizens to the idiosyncratic preferences of the Ayatollah (or supreme religious leader)[57]. Yet, they remain constitutions nevertheless. A constitution may be good or bad, authoritarian or liberal. The thesis we try to defend here is that contrary to the unbending dogma in the premises to the foregoing dualisms, a constitution is neither created nor dictated by law teachers or armchair political philosophers. It is dependent on what we call preponderant force and only when this notion is fully appreciated can meaningful lessons be learnt on how to truly fashion long-lasting, liberty-sensitive, constitutions. There should be a more focused beeline for military and political control rather than the pathetic process of seeking change through the nebulous deification of concepts.

---

his, "The Concept and Functions of Soft Law in International Politics" in E. G. Bello and B.A. Ajibola, eds., *Essays in Honour of Judge Taslim Olawale Elias* (Dordrecht: Martinus Nijhoff, 1992) at 135. Cited by Obiora C. Okafor, "The Status and Effect of the Right to Development in Contemporary International Law: Towards A South-North `Entente' " (1995) vol. 7 RADIC, pt. 4, 865 at 874.

[57] Consider for eg., s. 110 of the Iran Const., 1979, which permits the Ayattolah to confirm (or reject) the President even after popular election.

The whole object of Constitutional Law study should be how to create and maintain better governments[57a]. The process is a continuing one but the experience of ages and ages of good and bad governments of the world have supplied informed observers with elements which it is thought should be adopted (from beneficial governments) or avoided (from oppressive ones). To fulfill the object of Constitutional Law, it has usually been proposed that the framework of beneficial government should preponderate a liberty-sensitive content as opposed to a power-oriented one. It is realized however, that power is required to give energy to even good governments and protect them from subversion. The problem of fashioning the best constitution has therefore been how to strike the appropriate balance.

Constitutional Law seeks to provide the solution. And, for the liberty-sensitive constitution (with just the right jots of power to effectively prop it), various constitutional concepts have been proposed by various commentators and publicists. The second part of our theory of distribution and operationalization (i.e., the theory of contents) of constitutions, shall, in the following paragraphs, examine some of these.

LIBERTY-SENSITIVE CONSTITUTIONAL CONCEPTS.

Taslim Elias, General Rapporteur for the "Law of
Lagos," repeats Pope's couplet:

[57a] "In the constitutionalist tradition," Jan-Erik Lane writes (*op. cit.* at 40), "the key question has always been whether it was possible to frame institutions that are conducive to good government."

> For forms of government let fools conte*nd*,
> what'*er* is best administered is best.[58]

However, he adds, as we must too, that:

> All will agree that forms of government
> are often as important as the art and
> practice of government[59]

It is all too easy for despotic regimes, especially in Africa of recent history, to rely, as it were, on Pope and justify their departure from tested forms of democratic, limited, government.

Raymond Wacks speaks of "The *Rechtsstaat*"[59a] and, in parenthesis, explains it as "(the state whose legitimacy is based on the `rule of law')."[60] This conception of a "right state" as attributable to congruence with the rule of law has a long history. Professor Ewelukwa has even gone so far as to assert that:

> It is difficult and, perhaps, impossible
> to say exactly when the idea of the rule
> of law was first conceived or entertained
> by man.[61]

---

[58] See, Dr. T.O. Elias, "General Report" in *African Conference on the Rule of Law, Lagos, Nigeria, January 3-7, 1961: A report on the proceedings of the conference* (Geneva: International Commission of Jurists, 1961) at 55 quoting "the poet" (i.e. Alexander Pope) with a little reservation. The quotation of course is a bit off: "… let fools contest, /What e'er …" (I have emphasized the letters, which highlight the differences).

[59] *Ibid.*

[59a] A simple translation would be "right state."

[60] Raymond Wacks, *Swot Jurisprudence* 4th ed. (Great Britain: Blackstone Press Ltd., 1995) at 172.

[61] Prof. D.I.O. Ewelukwa, "The Rule of Law" (1994-1997) 6 Nig. J.R. 1 at 10.

However, he somewhat contradicts this assertion by the further observation that:

> What is clear is that it is one of the most enduring and adorable bequests of the Greeks to the world.[61]

Surely, if we cannot say exactly when the idea "was first conceived or entertained by man," we cannot possibly be so "clear" in our minds that it was a bequest of the "Greeks to the world." This is doubly so when four pages later, the transmission to the world is attributed to the Romans.[61a] Most relevant to the present argument is the crucial point made here by Professor Ewelukwa[62] as to the distance of time covered by the concept. It is possible to generalize that the consistent idea that runs through disparate definitions of the "rule of law" is that of good government and, thus, a good constitution.

This has always seemed to be the ultimate object. There are certain sub-concepts, which are thought to be intimately related to the identification of constitutions that are dependent on the rule of law. Amongst these is the doctrine of separation of powers as well as its sub-conception, the notion of checks and

---

[61a] *Ibid.* at 14. The inexactitude inherent in such generalized attributions reinforce my sceptical view about the wisdom of isolating the study into epochs (traditional/ancient and modern/current, eras); or, into geographical divisions (African, European, Oriental, American, practices; etc.). The concept is a universal mental construct, which cuts through time and space. My project is to determine what it is; not, principally, how approximations of the term have been used. The premise is that one time or the other, it has existed in every human society. So, it is superfluous to discuss, for example, an "African rule of law." Rule of law is ontologically the same: anytime, everywhere.

[62] In relation to whom the author sat *in statu pupillari* at the University of Nigeria.

balances. Under separation of powers, certain theories also present themselves. There is federalism, for example, and theories that arise thereunder including those we have discussed earlier in this chapter. We include the doctrine of covering the field; of the pith and substance of legislation; of inconsistent legislation; of enumerated and residual powers; of vertical division as distinct from horizontal separation of powers; etc. The concept of the (substantive and formal) independence of the judiciary is also relevant and may introduce here the sub-theories of limited and full powers of judicial review. The hermeneutic or interpretive jurisdiction of the courts and the various presumptions of interpretation employed thereunder may, conveniently, also be discussed.

A controlling belief in this area is that the "absolute" powers of government should, in some way, be restricted or limited. This belief, while tied to the idea of the rule of law, finds more concrete instantiation in such principles as fundamental human rights, constitutionalism, and, strange as it may at first sound, the so-called doctrine of parliamentary sovereignty (when it is recalled, as has Sir Ivor,[63] that this doctrine was originally developed from the desire to stem the excesses of the executive, exemplified by the Crown).

We shall discuss some of these constitutional concepts with the background argument that they all have a family resemblance of sorts, which may be summarized

---

[63] See, Sir Ivor Jennings, "Was Lord Coke a Heretic?," Appdx. III in *The Law and the Constitution, op. cit.* at 318 to 329 esp. at 321.

in the notion of limited government. They all seem to adopt the attitude that for good government, the relevant polity must strive for a constitution whose content should preponderate towards the liberty-sensitive model.

THE RULE OF LAW.

"Be you never so high," Thomas Fuller proclaims, "the law is above you."[64] Here, more than 300 years ago, Fuller tries to represent the idea, which in popular circles, has come to be known as the "rule of law." However, this hydra-headed concept has been made to mean whatever, "... like Humpty-Dumpty,[65] the particular user ..." of the term chooses it to mean. It has equally been adopted by liberal, progressive, governments as it has been unfurled as the banner of even the most repressive regimes. However, the lack of clear meaning has not been restricted to the realms of political ideology. Even within a liberal democracy, for example, opinion as to its scope has by no means been homogenous. Judge Wiley Y. Daniel of the United States' District Court, District of Colorado, has, in a lecture at the Nigerian Law School,[66] expressed his insights upon this subject. And, perhaps, much to the surprise of those who would distinguish between

---

[64] Quoted with approval by Lord Denning, M.R., in *Gouriet v. Union of Post Office Workers* [1977] 2 W.L.R. 310 at 331.

[65] "When I use a word ... it means exactly what I choose it to mean - neither more nor less." See fn. 35 of Chapt. 1 (*supra*).

[66] Now published (since March, 1997). See, Judge Wiley Y. Daniel "The Rule of Law" in *Nigerian Law and Practice Journal* (Lagos: Council of Legal Education - Nigerian Law School, March 1997) 114 to 122.

a merely characteristic, even if highly publicized, contravention of the criminal law; from more systematic, policy-entrenched, breaches of the rule of law, the learned federal judge has gone so far as to characterize the Rodney King, police beating of 1991 as: " A dramatic and painful reminder of this principle."[67]

For the about 24 centuries of recorded contemplation of this concept, there is a remarkable disinclination to offer a definition of what the term is as opposed to what it does or is used for. In fact, much use of the term proceeds as if the meaning were generally known and substantially free of controversy. However, it is not as simple as that.

The principle behind the term, "rule of law," is simple enough. It is when rigorous scrutiny concentrates upon its constituent words that opinions diverge into controversy. The simple idea for the term as a whole emphasizes the need for restriction of the, otherwise, dangerously wide powers of the executive (the administration). The formulation has semantic and syntactic support; for historically, the verb form of the word "rule" is taken to refer to the executive, "the ruler."[68] The executive is, inverting Madison's and Bickel's description of the judiciary,[68a] "the *most* dangerous branch." For protection of the citizen therefore, this power of the administration ought to be limited to pre-formulated rules. The pre-formulated rule (in the political signification of its noun form)

---

[67] *Ibid.* at 114.
[68] Quoting Dicey, see Sir Ivor Jennings, *op. cit.* at 59: "… a ruler, that is, head of the executive government …"
[68a] As "the least dangerous branch" of government.

designed to promote governmental policy, while limiting capricious implementation, is what is referred to as law. The rule of law is thus, administration or execution based, in the relevant polity, upon pre-formulated rules known to both the rulers and the ruled.

In spite of this, the major problem remains the constituent term, "law." If law is merely the pre-formulated rule of action restricting executive discretion, it is, for the citizen, a yet hollow protection. This surely is so where the extent of its content is not predetermined; or, where its formulator is not institutionally controllable or separable from the implementer. But ontologically, this is a quite different question. The basic idea of the rule of law is administration controlled by the legislator's "law" or reshaped by the adjudicator's interpretational "law." In this conceptualization of the term, it is not an essential defect that the same functionary bears the three responsibilities. The requirement for separation of functionaries is merely a useful suggestion for the fuller and more effective actualization of the guiding principle behind this otherwise simple formulation.

Bracton, in his "Book of Authority,"[69] generally seems to think so too. He accepts that the king has no mortal equal in the realm but, nevertheless, that the king should be both under God and under the law. The king is thus:

> Ipse autem rex non debet esse sub homine sed sub Deo et sub lege, quia lex regem. Attribuat igitur rex legi, quod lex

---

[69] Henry Bracton, *De Legibus et Consuetidinibus Angliae*, fol. 5b, Woodbine (ed.), vol. 2, 33. Cited in Jolowicz, *op. cit.* at 382 and 57.

attribuit ei, videlicet dominationem et potestatem, non est enim rex ubi dominatur voluntas et non lex.[70]

As Bracton, so Jolowicz. Writing in the early and middling years of the 20th Century, Jolowicz observes that: "Magna Carta itself is a clear embodiment of the principle that the king is subject to law ..."[71]

Professor Ewelukwa has in his article on this subject, supplied a wider and more intellectually stimulating interpretation. In his evolutionary historicism of a somewhat imaginary reconstruction, the learned professor of law suggests a tripartite division along the epochs of time. There is thus the rule of law as understood in ancient times, which he dubs the "classical" era; as understood in mediaeval times; and also the rule of law: as conceived in the present time, which he refers to as the "modern" era.

For the ancient perception of the rule of law, which Ewelukwa attributes to the Greeks and thereafter to the Romans, he makes two very remarkable claims. In the first, he suggests that the rule of law refers to subjection of the polity only to common law, which alone, he contends, satisfies the test of "reason freed of all passion." Secondly, he asserts, the conception of law in Greek and Roman thought, had no real place for legislation. If at all there was to be legislation, it could come about only through the extremely wise law-

---

[70] See Jolowicz, *Ibid.* at 57: The king is "Under God and the Law, because the Law makes the king. Therefore the king should give to the law what the law gives to him, namely lordship and power, for there is no king where caprice rules and not the law."
[71] Jolowicz, *Ibid.* at 57.

guardians or philosopher-kings. And this, only under extreme necessity for such change. For the first claim, Ewelukwa relies on Plato and Aristotle. And for the second, reliance is placed on the textual evidence of Sir Ernest Barker.[72]

Neither logic nor the literature would seem to bear out these claims. The Greeks and no less the ancient Romans viewed law much as we now do: drawing the appropriate distinctions between customary and statutory law. They, as now, had admirers of long established customs and practices. But this has in no way made any of those societies to lose sight of the possibilities and concrete examples of bad customs, same as bad legislation; good enactments, same as worthy customs.

In a very careful reading of all the forty-four "Dialogues of Plato": from "Charmides" down to all ten volumes of "The Republic" as well as the later "Timaeus," "Critias," "Sophist," "Statesman," up to the twelve volumes of "Laws," it will be evident that Plato was engaged primarily in the object of formulating, especially in "The Republic," a model state which by novel and "better" legislation, would sweep away the then extant "bad" laws (*both* customary and statutory).[73] An

---

[72] Sir E. Barker, ed. and transl., *The Politics of Aristotle* (New York: Oxford University Press/Galaxy Books, 1962) at 128. Citing Barker with approval, Prof. Ewelukwa says that "Athenian law was an ancient body of standing rules which seldom changed, there being little or no legislation and no separate and specific legislature": Prof. D.I.O. Ewelukwa, *loc. cit.* at 12 (fn. 36).

[73] Robert Maynard Hutchins, ed.-in-chief, *Great Books of the Western World,* vol. 7: Plato, Benjamin Jowett, transl., *The Dialogues of Plato* (Chicago, London,

illuminating pointer to this comes from the dialogue conducted in the presence of Socrates between the "Eleatic Stranger" and "The Younger Socrates":

> ... The next best thing in legislating is not to allow either the individual or the multitude to break the law in any respect whatsoever.
>
> Y. Soc. True.
>
> ... A true statesman will do many things within his own sphere of action by his art without regard to the laws, when he is of opinion that something other than *that which he has written down and enjoined to be observed* during his absence would be better.[74]

Splattered all over these dialogues are clear references to legislation as the then dominant method of making laws. They are not essentially considered inferior to "national customs"[75] but are, in fact, spoken of as instruments for correcting an already deficient body of customary (and earlier statutory) law. If that be the case, the most important premise for many of Ewelukwa's major conclusions[76] has

---

Toronto: William Benton of Encyclopaedia Britannica, Inc., 1952) 1 to 799.

[74] "The Statesman." *Ibid.*, 580 to 608 esp. at 602. The emphasis is mine to show that even the philosopher king rules by legislation and not necessarily by customary law. The difference is that because of his wisdom and selflessness, he is granted what the English denied the Stuart kings: suspending and dispensing powers over existing laws.

[75] *Ibid.*, 603.

[76] See, Prof. D.I.O. Ewelukwa, *loc. cit.* at 18: "With the above assumption in the background, the rule of law in its pure and original version seems to mean or demand (a)... (b)... (c)... (d) that law in force in a state should

become, somewhat, untenable. Major reconstruction is required. If, for the classical era, Ewelukwa, had limited his claims to Aristotle and clearly emphasized that this, at any rate, was Aristotle's novel recommendation rather than a restatement of predominant Greek thought, less criticism would have resulted.

Although placed under the heading "medieval contribution,"[77] Roman thought is ostensibly regarded by Ewelukwa as more properly placed under the classical epoch "after the Greeks"[78] and as a transitional phase before the actual medieval times. Ewelukwa classes John of Salisbury (1115-1180), Henry Bracton (who died in 1268) and Thomas Aquinas (1225-1274) as together constituting the principal exponents of the rule of law in that epoch. He suggests, quite plausibly, that after the fall of the Roman Empire and the resurgent influence of Greek philosophical ideas, these writers refurbished and passed on, in the middle ages, Greek rule of law principles and Roman constitutionalism (which had similar ingredients as the Greek conceptions of the rule of law).

---

be free of human elements so as to qualify as reason free from passion or as the pure voice of God."

[77] *Ibid.*, 13.

[78] *Ibid.* This phrase must be given an interpretation different from the expectations of common language. Unless the Greeks became extinct after this time, the historical generality of the words should be understood and tolerated even if not justified.

Interestingly, the three quotations[79] selected by Professor Ewelukwa in illustrating the writings of this epoch all demonstrate the semantic claim we have made earlier: that the rule of law is, in origin, directed against the prerogative and other arbitrary powers of the executive branch.

In assessing the modern epoch, however, Ewelukwa has, apart from the semantic tendency identified above, brilliantly located two extra schools of thought. He has examined the modern epoch and has found that the rule of law is seen as an instrument formulated for the control of: (1) the executive; (2) the executive, the legislature and the judiciary; and also, that there is a tendency of thought (3) which views the rule of law as a synonym for democratic government: where the origin and actions of governmental agencies must be predicated upon the people's mandate.

It is the conclusion derived from these premises that reveals the incongruities inherent in these additional interpretations. From schools (2) and (3), Professor Ewelukwa is able to conclude that the rule of law means:

(a) That all and sundry … should be subject to the law of the land …

(In other words, the "rule of law" means "the rule of the law." This adds nothing but platitudinous circularity);

(b) That the state and its government … must have legitimate foundation and be amenable to legal control …

---

[79] *Ibid.*, 14 and 15. Referring to John of Salisbury and Bracton in G.H. Sabine, 3rd ed., *A History of Political Theory* (London: George G. Harrap & Co. Ltd., 1956) at 217; and referring to St. Thomas Aquinas in A.P. D'entreves, ed., *Aquinas: Selected Political Writings*, J.G. Dawson, transl. (New York: MacMillan, 1959) at 161.

(In other words, the people must create the state and its government and these must be subject to control of the very same government as expressed by laws);

> (c) That every act or decision of the state … must have legal foundation and submit to the direction, regulation and control of the law …

(Thus, government must be subjected to the control of government); and,

> (d) That law in force in a state should be free of human elements so as to qualify as reason free from passion or as the pure voice of God.[80]

The last conclusion entirely fails to specify any referent for isolating its active element. Who determines what laws are "free of human elements" and thus, "reason free from passion"? Unless the government is excluded from this function, the definition would be quite meaningless. Although the second and third conclusions have ignited an illuminating torch of knowledge in their people-oriented first limbs, they seem nevertheless to obfuscate matters by the indistinct "legal control" of their second limbs.

If rule of law were made to mean the legal control of "government" by the same government, it would, in analytical terms, mean very little or even amount to an inanity. If, however, it is interpreted to mean the control of the executive by the populace through institutions (governmental or not) such as the courts, the legislature, the press, the trade unions, the legal profession, etc., this would amount to very much (especially for the analyst who

---

[80] *Ibid.* at 18.

prefers clarity to vagueness). It would mean even more to the liberty-conscious citizen if it were added that the rule of law finds better expression in the control, direct and indirect, held by the people over their (s)elected representatives (appointed or elected) in all of the arms of government. However, to come to this determination, rather more in foundation would be required and called for. In this, we offer our *theory of subjective legitimacy* (to be found in any politico-legal system). We have extensively discussed this theory in our first published book[81] and can afford, therefore, to provide only a brief reconstruction here. Before this, however, we should like to first wind up the foregoing literature review.

Professor Ewelukwa's essay, to our mind, presents one of the most intellectually rewarding contributions on this subject. Not least because of its recency[82] and thus the advantage of reliance on the rich materials of preceding years. The academic value is enhanced mostly because of the logical construction of ideas into a smooth and, thus, easier to comprehend, evolutionary progression. This second merit is however, its most vulnerable spot.

---

[81] R.A.C.E. Achara, *Meta-Constitutional Conceptions: Subjective Legitimacy in the Jurisprudence of June 12* (Enugu, Nigeria: Mike Lawrence Publishers, 1998) esp. at Chapt. 3 and generally, 31 to 75. See (*infra*) text to fn. 105, etc.
[82] Published by the Faculty of Law, University of Nigeria, Enugu Campus in September of 1998.

Historical pyrrhonism,[83] the tendency to doubt any statement of fact made when neither the narrator nor his audience was alive or able by any of the senses to perceive that fact, is always a problem for the historian. But the problem becomes more acute when common sense and logic join forces with pyrrhonism to render doubtful, the reconstructed facts of a previous era. The beauty in Ewelukwa's imaginary history is the somewhat facile disregard of some possibly troubling instantiations and specificity. He, as many historians, magisterially makes very sweeping generalizations. In few sentences, he attempts to capture the disparate and divergent views of a generation (which commonsense would suggest) into a uniform and unified idea of an individual or few individuals (for which all our senses of logic must rebel). There is nothing in our experience, which would suggest validity of his neat epochal compartments. If Aristotle proclaimed in the classical era that:

> He who commands that law should rule may thus be regarded as commanding that God and reason alone should rule: [and] he who commands that a man should rule adds the character of the beast,[84]

---

[83] See. J.W. Burrow, *Gibbon*, in Keith Thomas, Gen. ed., *Past Masters* (Oxford: Oxford University Press, 1985) at 20 to 22 esp. at 20 and 21… "This could lead to suspicion not merely of the value of knowing about the past but of the possibility of knowing anything with any reasonable certainty about the past at all … mutual critical scrutiny and the desire for unimpeachable proofs was an inducement to more disciplined scholarly methods."

[84] Aristotle, *Politics*, 1287, a 18-22 (III. 16, s.5). As quoted and cited by Prof. D.I.O. Ewelukwa, *loc. cit.* at 12, fns. 34 (and 30). Square brackets and word therein, mine.

this does not prove that many others in that age held preponderantly the same view. In fact, it is quite likely that many of the ideas forced by Ewelukwa's version of history into the medieval and modern times, were widely held as well, in the classical era and vice-versa. Professor Ewelukwa's history is thus more an aid to research methodology than a factual contribution to insights of any epistemological verity.

The temporal distinctions do not really hold. Alternatively, they do not matter. Whether viewed in ancient times, the Middle Ages, or now, the important question remains: "What is meant by 'the Rule of Law'?" The preceding views have been predicated on an assumption that the rule of law is a good thing. That it is an instrument of control to limit otherwise arbitrary power - whether of the administration or some or all of the entire branches of government. But there are other views. Much of them are based on biting cynicism and a skeptical disinclination to be moved by all this enthusiasm for what is considered a deliberately contrived catch-phrase, which diverts attention from the reality of glaringly unfair social and power relations. The evolutionary history of this version of the rule of law is slightly different.

Sir Ivor Jennings[85] constructs the facts to imply that "the rule of law" originally meant no more than the establishment of law and order in any given polity. He traces the tradition from the period of the Roman Empire and suggests, with Thomas Hobbes, that in a state

---

[85] *The Law and the Constitution*, *op. cit.*, Chapt. II, s. 1, esp. at 34.

of nature, "every man is enemy to every man" and there is:

> No place for Industry ... and consequently no culture of the Earth; no Navigation ... no Commodious Building ... no knowledge of the face of the Earth; no account of Time; no Arts; no Letters; no Society; *and which is worst of all, continuall fear, and danger of violent death;* And the life of man, solitary, poore, nasty, brutish and short.[86]

Jennings's story is that under this state of security, even the law-abiding pillars of the community would resort to an arms build-up for their safety and the protection of those under them. Lesser mortals was defeated and enslaved while others voluntarily surrendered their property and persons to the protection of stronger neighbours. There was continual war and commotion and not even the strong felt secure. So,

> Kingdoms and principalities were established in which order was maintained by the king or prince[87]

and although "kings often fought with kings," at least, however,

> The people became law abiding; *the rule of law* was established.[87]

This is the version of the concept much loved by dictators and would-be dictators. It is fair, however, to absolve Jennings from inculpation in its dour ramifications. Despite

---

[86] Thomas Hobbes, *Leviathan,* Chapt. XIII. Cited and quoted by Jennings, *Ibid.* at 44 (emphasis, mine).
[87] Sir Ivor Jennings, *Ibid.* at 43. (Our emphasis.)

the tone of the narrative, it must be admitted that elsewhere in his unorthodox[88] treatise Jennings has non-heretically, adopted the form of words appropriate to the more popular acceptation. Even though he questions the imprecision inherent in the term, he leans to the view that it cannot merely mean law and order, for:

> If it is only a synonym for law and order, it is a characteristic of all civilized states ...[89]

He suggests that the rule of law should be used as:

> A phrase for distinguishing democratic or constitutional government from dictatorship ...[90]

but cautions that if so understood, it is wise at the outset to say so.[90]

Others are not prepared to so easily surrender their skepticism. This is especially so with Marxist oriented theorists. The cynical implication is that Jennings's historicism is substantially accurate. But in order to paint a more acceptable façade for the decrepit structure of unfair domination (by powerful ruling groups) and to justify continuance of this domination, it became necessary to invent the "rule of law" as a legitimating, emotive, catch phrase.

Judge Wiley Y. Daniel admits that "The underlying purpose of the rule of law has remained constant: namely, to justify the legal

---

[88] H.W.R. Wade may prefer "heretic." See his article in (1955) Cambridge Law Journal which Jennings refers to with veiled angst in the first line of his "Was Lord Coke a Heretic?" in *The Law and the Constitution, op. cit.* Appdx. III at 318.

[89] *Ibid.* at 60.

[90] *Ibid.*

system of a given society."[91] However, he makes this assertion not in a confessional, but laudatory, tone. This is not the tone of voice, which Valerie Kerruish endorses. Hers, dripping with acidic cynicism, victimized sentiments, and rebellious combativeness, instructs us that the rule of law is a now unveiled instrument used for hiding the naked truth of unjustified rule by men (and women?):

> The difficulty we confront is voicing concern at human laws ruling our lives when this is just what laws are meant to do, and when alternatives seem either reactionary or impossible. This difficulty is met, however, by making the concern more precise. It is focused on a disjunction that goes to the very heart of legitimating strategies in jurisprudence – the disjunction of the rule of law from the rule of men. The claim here is that this metaphorical expression of the impartiality of law is a metaphor whose value is spent. *The rule of law is the rule of men* and it is high time that was recognized.[92]

It is difficult to change the views of people like Valerie. Like most Marxist theorists, they would probably be more knowledgeable and informed of all the arguments one could possibly offer for the purpose of redirecting them to what one would have thought a more sensible line of thought. One could, for instance, explain that their skepticism is even

---

[91] Judge Wiley Y. Daniel, "The Rule of Law," *loc. cit.*, 114.

[92] Valerie Kerruish, Jurisprudence as Ideology, Maureen Cain and Carol Smart, series eds., Sociology of Law and Crime (New York: Routledge, 1991) at 176.

more destructive of the interests their ideology is formulated to protect. Without law, the rule of law, those on the down-side of society's power-relations would be worse off than they presently are under admittedly imperfect laws. Rather than achieve a change of heart, they would probably put the point better, and contend that:

> In a society structured by materially unequal social relations, people on the down-side of these relations would be worse off without law than they are with law ...[93]

Having made that little concession, however, they would then go ahead to destroy or do serious damage to the foundation of one's objections by answering that the:

> ... Generalization of the political value of law to an assertion that law is a necessary if not sufficient means of protecting individuals or subordinated groups from those with more power, rests on the assumption that unequal social relations are an inevitable feature of the human condition ...[93]

Further, to clinch the argument, they could argue that:

> There is no doubt that recorded history is overwhelmingly a history of societies with such structures. But first, that is no ground for saying that it always will be. Slavery remained an institutional feature of American ... society, well into the nineteenth century. An argument that slavery always has been and always will be part of the human condition could have

---

[93] *Ibid.*, 145.

been made then and it would have been the same argument. It is obviously false.[94]

Luckily, our present project does not depend for its success on unifying the hostile ideologies of the Babel-like world. We are not even sure that such an enterprise would be useful or beneficial to anyone. We are more concerned with the analytical function of isolating the essential meaning of the term "rule of law" as understood and used in Constitutional Law. We cannot, therefore, enjoy with Kerruish and other Marxists, their futuristic game of "close your eyes till dreams become real." In rejecting their total rejection of the concept, it is yet possible to retain a point raised, which is relevant to the present analysis.

It is difficult to deny that the rule of law is, in the end, rule of the law made by men and women. However, this is no disclaimer. In the use of state power, provided the men and women who actually administer the state are constrained by the law (whether made by the legislator or conclusively interpreted by the judge), the rule of law is achieved and its

---

[94] *Ibid.* The reasoning is so powerful as to invite an inclination to ignore its obviously fallacious foundations. We should not now regard law as necessary because, in future, we may find it no longer necessary. To magnify the fallacy, we may take another example and rely on its ridiculous syllogism. Because slavery once was thought a necessary part of the human condition, but now no more so; therefore, although the mouth is now thought a necessary part of the human condition, we should not so regard it because of the future possibility that eating, speaking, drinking and spitting will no longer be necessary.

disjunction from rule of men, obtained.[94a] Even Aristotle recognizes this. He does not imagine that some meta-physical beings would be brought in before a realization of the rule of law. Contrary to Ewelukwa's somewhat idealized interpretation, Aristotle's "reason unaffected by desire," meant no more than this, that because: "... the law can do no more than generalise"[95] and although: "There are cases which cannot be settled by a general statement..."[95], law, in Aristotle's conception, avoids, because of its inherent futurity, the later desires of the executor even if that executor is also the lawmaker. Because he cannot foresee whether future circumstances would not equally affect him negatively, the lawmaker is constrained to make reasonable laws. In this sort of polity, the law is deemed to be based upon "reason unaffected by desire."[96] The exclusion of the human element of

---

[94a] Compare this with the definitions offered by Obaseki, J.S.C., in *Gov. of Lagos State v. Ojukwu* [1986] 17 N.S.C.C. (pt. 1) 304 at 313 and 314 (quoted with apparent approval by Uwaifo, J.S.C., in *A.G. (Fedn.) v. Guardian Newspaper* [1999] 5 S.C.N.J. 324 at 341: "... the rule of law ... is that every thing must be done according to law. It means also that government should be conducted within the frame-work of recognized rules and principles which restrict discretionary power ... Coke(s) ... `golden and straight metwand of law as opposed to the uncertain and crooked cord of discretion' (... 4 inst. 41) ... the rule of law means that disputes as to the legality of acts of government are to be decided by judges who are wholly independent of the executive ...."

[95] See, Aristotle, *The Ethics of Aristotle: Nichomachean Ethics*, J.A.K. Thompson, transl. (Harmondsworth, Middlesex: Penguin, 1995) at 167. See also, Kerruish, *op. cit.* at 109.

[96] See, Aristotle, Politica in the Works of Aristotle, vol. 10, W.D. Ross, ed. (Oxford: Clarendon Press, 1938) III, 16 at 1,287a. Cited in Kerruish, *Ibid.*

passion and other desires in the above passage is emphasized by Aristotle's recognition that the generalized, futuristic, statements of the law, may in their rigidity, cause some injustice in exceptional instances. However, this only proves our point. In any case, Aristotle's solution is the provision of rules of "Equity as a higher form of justice … In general though, Aristotle has no doubt that the law should rule …"[97]

Even if we have found from the foregoing, what the rule of law means, and although our analytical task is thus concluded, there is yet room for censorial jurisprudence. This is where the claims of some other jurists should effectively come in. Even if the rule of law means no more than that the executive administration is subordinated to the legislature (those who make the controlling *law*) and the judiciary (those who ultimately determine what this controlling *law* requires in particular cases), it is yet open to us to criticize this etymologically based conception as rather too restrictive and inadequate for the purposes of modern government.

We may not entertain the same optimism implicit in Aristotle that the mere existence of pre-formulated law would be sufficient check upon executive arbitrariness. We may not even be too sure that despite futurity, the legislator cannot find words sufficient to exclude herself from pernicious statutes aimed at particular segments of society to which she may never belong. Moreover, there is nothing to guard against "judicial terrorism" even if the rule of law were to be an effective control of the executive. These and other problems have

---

[97] *Ibid.*

led to serious thought about how to improve the protection offered by the notion.

At a conference organized at New Delhi by the International Commission of Jurists (ICJ) (almost exactly 46 years ago as we now write),[97a] "185 judges, practicing lawyers and teachers of law from 53 countries"[98] "(including Lord Denning and Mr. Justice Devlin)"[99] came to the conclusion, in what is now known as the "Declaration of Delhi,"[100] that the rule of law should apply not just to the legal control of the executive, but also in relation to legislative and judicial powers (as well as the legal profession and the criminal process in a special way):

(i) The legislature: there is a right to representative and responsible government; and there are certain minimum standards or principles for the law, including those contained in the Universal Declaration and the European Convention, in particular, freedom of religious belief, assembly and association, and the absence of retroactive penal laws;

(ii) The executive: especially that delegated legislation should be subject to independent judicial control, and that a citizen who is wronged should have a remedy against the state or government;

[97a] "Done at Delhi" on the "10th day of January 1959." See, the "Declaration of Delhi" *infra.*, fn. 98.
[98] See, "Declaration of Delhi" in *African Conference* … (fn. 50) *op. cit.* at 12.
[99] See, O. Hood Phillips, 6th ed., *op. cit.* at 18.
[100] "Declaration of Delhi" (1959) 2 Jo. Int. Com. of Jurists, 7 to 43. Done at Delhi the 10th day of January, 1959. See, O. Hood Phillips, 6th ed., *op. cit.*, esp. at 17 and 18. See further, *African Conference on the Rule of Law*, Lagos, Nigeria, January 3-7, 1961…, *op. cit.*, at 13.

(iii) The criminal process: a "fair trial" involves such elements as certainty of the criminal law, the presumption of innocence, reasonable rules relating to arrest, accusation and detention pending trial, the giving of notice and provision for legal advice, public trial, right of appeal, and absence of cruel and unusual punishment;

(iv) The judiciary and the legal profession: this requires the independence of the judiciary and proper grounds and procedure for removal of judges; and [to] impose a responsibility on an organized and autonomous legal profession.[101]

Earlier than the Declaration of Delhi, the ICJ had held a similar conference in June of 1955 from which they came out with resolutions designated as the "Act of Athens."[102] The first one in the African Continent was held at Lagos and on 7 January, 1961, the conference came out with the "Law of Lagos" to the effect, amongst other declarations, that:

1. ... The Rule of Law cannot be *fully realized* unless legislative bodies have been established in accordance with the will of the people who have adopted their constitution freely;

2. ...

3. That fundamental human rights, especially the right to personal liberty, should be written and entrenched in the

---

[101] See, quoted verbatim from O. Hood Phillips, *Ibid.* at 18.

[102] See, *African Conference on the Rule of Law... op. cit.,* at 13.

constitutions of all countries and that
such personal liberty should not in
peacetime be restricted without trial in a
court of law...[103]

While it is true that before the British
Human Rights Act of 1998, both Nigeria and the
United Kingdom were in breach, it is
interesting to observe that judged by clause 3
of the Law of Lagos, the Nigerian Military
regime had been in closer compliance. The
military regime incorporated written,
fundamental, human rights into Decree 107 of
1993 (although these were not entrenched)[104]
while, the U.K. had neither a written charter
of such rights nor, therefore, any provision
for their entrenchment. This would probably
amuse General Sani Abacha's apologists although
we are not sure it would raise any equivalent
mirth among the British lobby for a written
constitution.

A more important observation is that the
various resolutions of the ICJ conferences seem
to have expanded the requirements for the rule
of law. The authority gained by the numerical
size and professional status of the
participants give to the expansion of this
concept more force than have individual
authors. It is upon these therefore that the
extended conclusion by Ewelukwa may find
anchorage that is more convincing. In the
context of the modern age, therefore, the rule
of law may be seen as no longer based on legal
control of executive power alone. Perhaps, the
most potent requirement is that in clause 1 of

---

[103] *Ibid.* at 11. The emphasis is mine to show that the
Law of Lagos in clause 1, admits that realization of the
ideal can be attained in progressive stages.
[104] Constitution (Suspension and Modification) Decree No.
107 of 1993, s. 1(3).

the Law of Lagos: that law-making power should depend on popular consent. This has so much bearing upon our theory of subjective legitimacy as to encourage us now, to briefly discuss it.

At the start of this work, we endeavoured to introduce to the reader, the problem of "June 12." When only the legal control of executive power is considered a sufficient definition of the "rule of law," June 12 demonstrates that for the citizen, this is inadequate protection. To briefly rehearse the problem, we recall that after the popular election of Chief M.K.O. Abiola on 12 June 1993, the all-powerful legislator whose law enabled and structured that poll repealed the enabling-law on 22 June 1993. This had the effect of canceling everything Chief Abiola's victory was legally predicated upon.

Although the annulment-implementing executive actions were effected within the framework of a "pre-formulated rule" (at that time made by the legislative authority of the Nigerian state), this could only be cold comfort to Abiola and the electors. This is especially so when it is recalled that the very same person, General I.B. Babangida, represented both the executive implementer of the rule as well as its legislative formulator. It is possible from the foregoing, to argue that the annulment did not contravene the rule of law. Such claim should shock right thinking citizens and amaze even persons within the brutal circles that carried off this insensitive nullification.

As an expansion of the original conception of the *rule of law*, our argument is that the *"rule of men"* involves administration tempered in no way by legislative or judicial restraints (as could be said of the government of Dingane, "The Needy One," King of the Zulus). However, better described as *"rule by law"*[104a] is the sort made by the same functionary as executes the country's laws (where there is formal but not substantive subordination of the executive to pre-formulated rules of whatever content). Both of these should be distinguished from rule where the executive is controlled, both formally as well as substantively, by the laws of a popularly selected legislature and of a judiciary whose tenure is dependent on the direct or indirect desires of the people. In this context, laws are such and become legitimate only when there is popular approval[104b] both as to who makes them and as to how they are made. In this sense, the direct election of the executive is desirable, but, as in the Westminster model of parliamentarism, not necessary.

Subjective legitimacy provides a philosophical and jurisprudential justification of this model of the rule of law. It recognizes a distinction between (a) constituent power; (b) the constitution; and, (c) legislative and other governmental powers derived from the

---

[104a] For use of the phrase to signify rule through dictatorial laws, see, the very telling commentary by Prof. C.U. Ilegbune, "The Legitimation of Government in Africa" (Beth 5/2: 1993) 46 to 63.

[104b] Consider Rainsborough's assertion in the *Putney Debates* of October, 1647 (between the radicals and conservatives of General Cromwell's) army that: "Every man that is to live under a government ought first by his own consent to put himself under that government ... the poorest man in England is not at all bound in a strict sense to that government that he hath not had a voice to put himself under." Quoted by Bernard Manin, *The Principles of Representative Government* (Cambridge: C.U.P., 1997) at 84.

effective constitution currently in force. It recognizes that at (a), there are no rules to regulate how power to ultimately determine the content of a constitution can be acquired. The docile majority may, in their apathy, let it slip into the hands of the one or the few. In that case, there is likelihood, but not certitude, that constitutional provisions would be skewed in favour of arbitrary authority to the executive. Conversely, in its constitutional allocation of legislative, executive and judicial power, a free, informed, and alert citizenry could not possibly fail to secure and allot such as would conduce to the curtailment of administrative caprice.

Subjective legitimacy admits, for analytical consistency and methodological clarity, that a law made even under the machinery of one-man constituent-power remains just that, a law. It reviles natural law attempts, which obfuscate enquiry by claiming that such laws, when they fall short of certain tests of approval, become therefore, no longer laws.[104c] When the laws are made consistently with the provisions of the extant, effective, constitution, they are constitutional. When, at the time of enquiry, the constitution is that of the actual holder of preponderant force, it is objectively legitimate. However, this is no end to the matter. An objectively legitimate and constitutionally valid law may yet be

---

[104c] Consider, e.g., Okere's summarization of Thomas Aquinas's thesis that "an unjust and unreasonable law, and one which is repugnant to the law of nature, is not law but a perversion of law": B. Obinna Okere, "The Relationship of the Church and the State and Dichotomy Between Law and Morality" in C.C. Nweze and C.O. Ugwu, eds., *The Catholic Clergy Under Nigerian Law* (Enugu: Hamson Publishers, 1998) 16-39, esp. at (30 and) 31.

subjectively illegitimate. In this, popular approval again rears its persistently stubborn head. The theory considers, *ex definitione*, that nothing is subjectively legitimate unless it has the approval (express or implied) of the general populace. Therefore, even when constituent power is wrested from the citizenry by a rambunctious rebel or a mutinous military, the new constitution (e.g., Decree 17 of 1985) may, objectively speaking, legitimate a June 12 annulment-decree and validate its executive implementation. But in so far as the election-annulling decree has been made and sustained in direct and strident opposition of the generality of the populace, subjectively speaking, it is illegitimate and no person needs feel obliged to abide by its stipulates.[105a]

When rule *of* law is distinguished from its factually similar counterpart, "rule *by* law," the theory of subjective legitimacy has illustrative parallels with it. As an instrument for supplying the defect in the original conceptualization of the rule of law, subjective legitimacy has, in our submission, the merit of not throwing the baby (of control of arbitrary administration) away with the bath water (of aberrant examples where dictatorial powers invested by constitutions of the one or few, permit the tail of execution to wag the dog of legislation and even, sometimes, of adjudication).

Sir Ivor Jennings's suggestion of a democratic basis for a modern "rule of law" coupled with the authoritative support of the International Commission of Jurists (especially in clause 1 of their "Law of Lagos," 1961),

---

[105a] Cf., Manin (*supra*).

may, when juxtaposed against Professor Ewelukwa's modernist contributions (inviting a legitimate foundation for all governmental authority), be characterized as the most important expansion of the concept pointing to the future.

Other attempts towards expansion of the notion of the rule of law have been made and it is possible to classify Dicey's contribution in that genre. For more than one century since its first publication in 1885, Professor Albert Venn Dicey's formulation (in his *Introduction to the Study of the Law of the Constitution)*, has been the first word on the subject. Not many years ago, it would have been considered most disrespectful on our part to consign consideration of this magisterial contribution to the concluding sections of the discussion. But those days are no more. The gradual demystification of Dicey's version of the theory commenced with a not so gradual assault on its factual foundations launched by no less a person than Sir Ivor Jennings.[105] However, this did not prevent consideration of Dicey's theory by others, even if critical.[106] It was, however, with de Smith's entirely dismissive attitude that Dicey's theory of the rule of law fell to the nadir of its dignity: "Dicey saw the rule of law," de Smith's book proclaims,

---

[105] Sir Ivor Jennings, *The Law and the Constitution*, 5th ed., *op. cit.*, chapt. II, s.1 (42 to 62) and esp. Appdx. II (305 to 317): "Dicey's Theory of the Rule of Law."
[106] A more sympathetic critique is found in the "Introduction" by E.C.S. Wade in A.V. Dicey, *An Introduction to the Study of the Law of the Constitution*, 10th ed., *op. cit.*, at xcvi-cli (96 to 151); and O. Hood Phillips and Paul Jackson, 6th ed., *op. cit.* at 16-18, 35-40, but esp. at 36, fn. 88 citing E.C.S. Wade (*supra*).

"as a central feature of the British constitution."[107] Continuing, de Smith adds,

> His ideas, rooted in whiggish libertarianism, were very influential for two generations...

but today,

> They no longer warrant detailed analysis.[107]

With the sort of destructive criticism leveled by Jennings on Dicey's "rule of law," we are tempted to adopt de Smith's attitude and entirely ignore any detailed consideration of that author. However, we shall not. The seminal nature of the three postulations and the immense originality of the ideas,[108] no matter how factually inadmissible, impose upon the new commentator, at least one or two lines in homage. We propose to give this homage by an extensive quotation of Dicey's three postulates of the rule of law. These are rendered verbatim at pages 305 and 306 of Sir Ivor Jennings's extended critique entitled: "Dicey's Theory of the Rule of Law."[109]

> That `rule of law' which forms a fundamental principle of the constitution ... has three meanings, or may be regarded from three different points of view.

---

[107] Harry Street and Rodney Brazier, eds., *de Smith's Constitutional and Administrative Law, op. cit.* at 30.
[108] But see the argument that Dicey's formulation was not original but borrowed from the book by W.E. Hearn on *The Government of England* (1867). See for this, H.W. Arndt, "The Origins of Dicey's Concept of `The Rule of Law' " (1957) 31 A.L.J. 117. Cited in O. Hood Phillips, 6th ed., *op. cit.*, 36 at fn. 87.
[109] Appdx. II in Jennings, *The Law and The Constitution, op. cit.*

It means, in the first place, the absolute supremacy or predominance of regular law as opposed to the influence of arbitrary power, and excludes the existence of arbitrariness, of prerogative, or even of wide discretionary authority on the part of the Government. Englishmen are ruled by the law, and by the law alone; a man may, with us be punished for a breach of the law, but he can be punished for nothing else.

It means again, equality before the law, or the equal subjection of all classes to the ordinary law of the land administered by the ordinary law courts; the `rule of law' in this sense excludes the idea of any exemption of officials or others from the duty of obedience to the law which governs other citizens or from the jurisdiction of the ordinary tribunals; there can be with us nothing really corresponding to the `administrative law' *(droit administratif)* or the `administrative tribunals' *(tribunaux administratifs)* of France. The notion which lies at the bottom of the `administrative law' known to foreign countries is that affairs or disputes in which the Government or its servants are concerned are beyond the sphere of the civil courts and must be dealt with by special and more or less official bodies. The idea is utterly unknown to the law of England, and indeed is fundamentally inconsistent with our traditions and customs.

The `rule of law', lastly, may be used as a formula for expressing the fact that with us the law of the constitution, the rules which in foreign countries naturally form part of the constitutional code, are not the source, but the consequence of the rights of individuals, as defined and enforced by the courts; that, in short, the principles of private law have, with us, been by the action of the courts and Parliament so extended as to determine the position of the Crown and of its servants; thus the constitution is the result of the ordinary law of the land."[110]

From Jennings, Wade and de Smith, down to Hood Phillips and Ewelukwa, it has been common ground that there is error in the factual premises for at least the first two postulates. On the first, it is shown that (even in England for which Dicey was concerned) the very essence of modern government has increasingly involved conferment of discretionary powers on the executive. In addition, apart from the Crown's very "wide discretionary powers," there is much delegation of legislative and quasi-judicial authority.

On the second postulate, it is shown that `equality before the law, or the equal subjection of all classes to the ordinary law … administered by the ordinary law courts' involves another misplaced reliance on non-factual premises. The king could not be tried in his personal status in any ordinary court (except, perhaps at the House of Lords after the special procedure of impeachment by the

---

[110] Prof. A.V. Dicey, *Law of the Constitution*, 9th ed., Chapt. IV, at 198 and 199 (as cited by Sir Ivor Jennings, *The Law and The Constitution*, 5th ed., *op. cit.*, 305 and 306 esp. at 305, fns. 1 and 3).

House of Commons). Immunity was granted to "special classes" of persons, which was not extended to "all classes." For example, foreign heads of state and diplomats could not be impleaded in the ordinary courts (and indeed, in any other special courts for that matter).[110a] Certain powers were granted to officials such as the police which powers were not readily available to ordinary citizens.

Jennings's response to Dicey's second postulate is a model of ironic witticism: "By 'equality,' of course, he does not mean equality."[111] As to the contrast with *droit administratif,* Ewelukwa supplies an apology.[112] He explains that in a later edition of the work, Dicey (in 1914) admitted that he misunderstood the true nature and role of that institution as it operated on the continent,

---

[110a] A landmark decision of the British House of Lords seems to have changed the position. See, *Regina v. Bartle and the C.O.P. for the Metropolis and ors., Ex parte Pinochet* of 24 March, 1999. Peggy Hernandez of *The Boston Globe* Newspaper of 25/3/99 (which I downloaded from http://www.boston.co.../Court_strips_Pinochet_immunity_let s_3_of_27_charges_stand+.shtm) reports that in stripping "away General Augustus Pinochet's diplomatic immunity from arrest," this was "the first time in modern British history that a foreign head of state has been denied court protection from prosecution." The High Court had adopted the traditional view and granted immunity on 28/10/98. On 25/11/98, the Lords by 3 to 2, overruled this orthodoxy. However, because of Lord Hoffman's links with Amnesty International, an interested party, the Lords on 17/12/98, nullified their 3-2 decision and constituted a larger panel for rehearing of the appeal. It was here that 3 of the 30 charges were held to exclude immunity since they were allegedly perpetrated after 23/9/89 when all the 3 concerned states had signed the International Convention against Torture.

[111] Sir Ivor Jennings, *Ibid.,* 311.

[112] Ewelukwa, *loc. cit.,* 4.

especially in France. Dicey is said to also regret his failure, on the equality question, to recognize the massive number of existing exceptions even at the time he first wrote in 1885. As Jennings, so, Ewelukwa. The criticism on the contrast of Administrative law is that the *droit administratif:*

> ...Served, not a shield to protect officials from liability to claims by private citizens, but as a means of ensuring that private claims are considered by experts [113] ...

Jennings goes so far as to suggest that there is no real difference in nature between the "ordinary law courts" and the "tribunaux administratifs":

> Administrative courts are as ordinary as the civil courts. There is no more reason for calling them extraordinary than there is for calling the criminal courts extraordinary. Also, they are just as much official as the civil courts, and no more. [114]

As to the third postulate, we are not at all sure that the vociferous assault mounted by Jennings upon its ramparts has been successful. Hood Phillips notes Dicey's ethnocentric analysis and it is true that it has been a study in very localized jurisprudence. However, this is not a matter he denies. He makes clear his scope of enquiry at the earliest stages of

---

[113] Ewelukwa, *Ibid.* Jennings, *op. cit.* at 312 and 313: "... the purpose of droit administratif ... is not to exclude public officers from liability ... but to determine the power and duties of public authorities and to prevent them from exceeding or abusing their powers."
[114] Jennings, *Ibid.* at 313.

the analysis and admits that the rule of law, of which he comments, is that contained in the English constitution. We consider this the proper background for a meaningful and fair evaluation of Dicey's third postulate.

In our reading,[114a] Dicey is trying here to emphasize what he considers a significant peculiarity of the English constitution. His point, misunderstood especially by Jennings, is that while written constitutions enumerate and protect specified individual rights as against the government, in England there is no such enumeration. The courts require no "codes, pandects, decretals of Popes" etc., before embarking on liberty-sensitive restriction of governmental powers in favour of the individual. In other words, when it is said in England that it is against the law of the constitution to tax an individual without the consent of Parliament, what is actually being conveyed is that this protection of the citizen from arbitrary taxation is not derived from some conscious position of legislation but, rather, it is a manifestation, through court declaration, of what inherently, has always been the right of an Englishman: not to suffer impositions upon his property except by his consent obtained directly or through his representatives. That right, expressed as a law of the constitution, is thus the consequence of reality: that is, the inherent right of the individual simply concretized by court determination, declaration and enforcement.

[114a] David Yardley's mostly sympathetic review of Dicey's rule of law expresses the same sentiment. See, D.C.M. Yardley, *Introduction to British Constitutional Law*, sixth ed., (London: Butterworths, 1984) Chapt. 5, 69 to 74 esp. at 73: "the third branch of Dicey's rule is largely true …."

In other words, "rule of law" in England is a useful formula to express what, rightly or wrongly, Dicey considers the more valuable system of rights available to the English. He clearly believes that when individual rights are conferred by the laws of a (written) constitution, it follows, as perceptively noted by Ewelukwa, that: "If the constitution is abrogated or overthrown (as was the case in Nigeria), the rights would automatically go with it."[115] But in England, because the courts declare individual rights without relying on any special "law of the constitution" (mostly codified in other jurisdictions), it is the case that these rights are recognized as remaining; notwithstanding any change of government or of the constitution. That is the explanation for Sir Ivor to enable him now to "Understand how it is correct to say that the rules are the consequence of the rights of individuals and not their source."[116]

Again, it may be observed that the third postulate, which is mostly descriptive in tone, stands out from the previous two, which are preponderantly, prescriptive. It expresses most poignantly, why the executive branch is, by itself, not permitted to finally interpret and assess the nation's laws. A law is not such until it has been tested by the courts and fashioned, as it were, to suit the English tradition of respect for liberty and other rights of the individual.

Because of the restricted scope of Dicey's analysis, it is of little use outside the British jurisdictions. Even within England, its maxims, except for the third, have been found

---

[115] Prof. D.I.O. Ewelukwa, *loc. cit.*, 3.
[116] Sir Ivor Jennings, *op. cit.*, 314.

unjustifiable by facts on the ground. It is a bit surprising that this theory has survived so long. If truth be told, it is a theory whose value is spent.

The future lies with such wider analyses as are represented in the "rule of law" by Jennings and by Ewelukwa. Even if we consider as too pessimistic, the view expressed by Ewelukwa that the rule of law: "is impossible of realization; it has never been achieved and may never be achieved by any human society ...,"[117] we may yet see his point that it "Is in the nature of a high tension wire"[117] stepped down for domestic use by the instrument of written constitutions (of the fourth definitional model of our earlier explanations).[118]

Modern theories of the rule of law increasingly find expression in the written constitution. In most of these, it seems an article of accepted faith that a full realization of the rule-of-law-ideal is almost inseparably tied to the sub-concepts of separation of powers, checks and balances, constitutionalism, the independence of the judiciary, etc. (all to the purpose of achieving limited government and, thus, protection and promotion of the rights of the individual citizen).

It seems, then, appropriate to now proceed with an examination of some of these sub-concepts. The first that we propose to consider is the doctrine of separation of powers along with the related notion of checks and balances. This area particularly excites us, not least, for the special insight we claim regarding the

---

[117] Ewelukwa, *loc. cit.* at 19
[118] *Supra*, chapt. 3.

discovery of what we think is a sustainable distinction between the idea of "checks" from those of "balances."

SEPARATION OF POWERS AND THE NOTION OF CHECKS AND BALANCES.

The semantic approach adopted for analysis of the "rule of law," has proved itself a very useful tool of interpretation. On the strength of its previous performance, it is here again, called in aid for the interpretation of the term "separation of powers."

THE THREE TYPES OF SEPARATION.

Adopting this approach, it will be seen that separation of powers has not one but three plausible uses. In the first place, it could refer simply to the analytical breakdown of power into constituent units all based on type (regardless of the fact that a single individual or body of individuals retains the actual use of it all). Secondly, it could mean the retention of the corporate nature of power while only distinguishing the various functionaries called upon to exercise it. Finally, it may mean both the analytical breakdown of power according to its various manifestations as well as apportionment of each distinct type of power to different functionaries, whether individual or corporate.

The trend of professional opinion has exhibited a bias for the third use. The consequent neglect of the first has led, under this concept, to a disregard of certain "sultanistic" constitutions such as that of Bahrain, which in its section 32, sub-section a, proclaims that:

> Legislative power shall be vested in the Emir and the National Assembly in accordance with the constitution and the Executive power shall be vested in the Emir, the Cabinet and Ministers. Judicial decrees shall be passed in the name of the Emir, all in accordance with the constitution.[119]

The various military dictatorships Nigeria has had to endure since 16 January 1966, would present an almost equally apt illustration. The crudest, General Sani Abacha's barbaric tyranny, divinely cut short on 8 June, 1998, is stark in its example but it would seem that, as for the rest, it never fully achieved its totalitarian aim as a result of the, at least, formal independence retained by the Nigerian Judiciary. However, this remains debatable.

By Abacha's constitution,[120] the previous separation of governmental powers (into the legislative, executive and judicial) achieved by the 1979 Constitution,[121] was nullified. In its place, section 6, sub-section (6), when read along with the rest of the 1993 military constitution, effectively invested on General Abacha, as Head of State and Commander-in-Chief

---

[119] See, also ss. 33 to 40 of the said 1973 Constitution of Bahrain. See further, Jan-Erik Lane, *op. cit.* at 120.

[120] See Jinadu, J., in the unreported case of *J.O. Esezoobo v. Provisional Ruling Council and ors.* (FHC/L/640/95) in Human Rights Newsletter [1998] Jan. – Mar., 18. Constitution (Suspension and Modification) Decree No. 107 of 1993.

[121] S. 4 (legislative power to the National Assembly and to the States Assemblies); s. 5 (executive power to the President and States Governors); and s. 6 (judicial power to the federal and states courts enumerated thereunder).

of the Armed Forces, the entirety of Nigeria's sovereign powers. The sub-section reads thus:

6. ...

(6) *The powers vested in the President* of the Federal Republic of Nigeria, *the Federal Military Government, or the Provisional Ruling Council,* as the case may be, specified in the sections of the Constitution of the Federal Republic of Nigeria 1979, as amended by this Decree ... shall vest in the Head of State, Commander-in-Chief of the Armed Forces.[122]

The amplitude and plenitude of powers conferred by this sub-section is not readily appreciated until one is appraised of what is involved in "the powers ... vested in the Federal Military Government..."

The very first words of this military constitution implicitly convey our meaning:

THE FEDERAL MILITARY GOVERNMENT hereby decrees as follows: -

1. (1) The Constitution of the Federal Republic of Nigeria, 1979, as suspended by the Constitution of the Federal Republic of Nigeria (Suspension) Decree 1993, is hereby restored and amended as set out in this Decree.

(2) ...

---

[122] s. 6(6) of Decree 107 of 1993. See, *supra*, fn. 120. Both emphases are mine to demonstrate the vastness of power conferred by this provision which was craftily tucked away in an obscure sub-section. we must admit however that the schedule 3 powers (of the Pres., the FMG, and PRC) referred to in this s. 6(6) are not that monstrous unless the whole context of the Decree is considered.

> (3) *Subject to this and any other Decree* ... the
> provisions of the said constitution which are not suspended by subsection (2) of this section shall have effect subject to the modifications specified in the second schedule to this Decree."[123]

The unarticulated major premise here is blunt: the Federal Military Government (FMG) does not only, as provided in section 2, subsection (1),

> ... Have the power to make laws for the peace, order and good government of Nigeria or any part thereof with respect to any matter whatsoever"[124]

but, even more, it has constituent power to make and unmake constitutions for the Nigerian State.[125] This constituent power, like the ordinary legislative powers of the FMG, shall be exercised by the simple expedient of:

> ... Decrees signed by the Head of State, Commander-in-Chief of the Armed Forces.[126]

When any Decree is made, it has the capacity of modifying or withdrawing the material part of judicial power previously vested on the Nigerian courts. Such a decree has the competence of sharing or transferring judicial powers of the federation and/or of the

---

[123] Decree 107 of 1993. My emphasis.
[124] *Ibid.*
[125] See, *Ibid.*, 2nd Schd., pt. B, s. 1: "... as amended by ... any ... Decree."
[126] *Ibid.* at s. 3(1). An attempt was made by the Fed. Att. Gen. to question some ten Decrees which had court-ouster provisions. His ground was that the PRC of which he was a member had never passed (nor even considered) any of them before promulgation. The Nigerian Court of Appeal in *Guardian Newspapers Ltd. v. Att. Gen. (Fedn.)* (1995) 5 NWLR (pt. 398) 703, Rejected this argument.

various constituent Nigerian States to any
person or body of persons other than the
"courts established for the federation"[127] or
"for a state."[128] The Head of State can
logically, make this transfer even to
himself.[129]

In sum, apart from the general latitude of
section 6, subsection (6) above, the military
constitution of 1993 seems, in effect, to
confer the sovereign powers of the nation on
General Sani Abacha as Head of State.
Particularly, it does so expressly by section
3, subsection (1) (for legislative powers) and
section 6, subsection (1) (for executive

---

[127] See, s. 6(1) of the of the 1979 Constitution.

[128] See, s. 6(2), *Ibid.*

[129] Kayode Eso, J.S.C., has recognized this point both in
his judicial and juristic capacities. He says, in *The
Military Gov., Ondo State v. Adewunmi* [1988] All N.L.R.
274 at 289, that: "There is no doubt that the
legislature cum the executive (now merged under one
under the militia) [sic] could enact laws which could
deprive the courts of jurisdiction." In *Gov. of Lagos
State v. Ojukwu* (1986) 1 NWLR (pt. 18) 621, he admits
that a total abolition of the courts was even possible
in favour of granting judicial powers to the exec./leg.
(military) but adds however that until this is done, the
military should obey court orders and conform with "the
rule of law." In his non-judicial writings, he has
expressed similar views. See, for e.g., Kayode Eso, *The
Mystery Gunman* (Ibadan: Spectrum, 1996) at 181: "Once
the tyrant leaves the "Rule of Law" to operate, he must,
per necessitate, submit to that rule. His only position
is to abolish the judiciary, but he has never summoned
up sufficient courage so to do." Chief F.R.A. Williams,
S.A.N., is of a similar sentiment as evidenced by
numerous oral and written Presentations. See, esp., his,
"The Nigerian Judiciary and Military Government" (1995)
J.N.L., vol. 2, no. 2, 1 to 30. I have documented these
in R.A.C.E. Achara, *Meta-Constitutional Conceptions:
Subjective Legitimacy in the Jurisprudence of June 12*,
op. cit. 65, fn. 93.

powers). The general investment of total power by the various sections will suggest that the particular allotments into executive and legislative jurisdictions, is of merely analytical, but not substantive, consequence. The Head of State is invested with "ultimate" power. In exercising this power, he, or his delegates and subordinates, may be seen from different spectacles. When he makes law, section 3(1) sees him through legislative spectacles. When he implements the laws he has made, he is observed with the aid of executive glasses. In the ultimate interpretation of laws however, the available sunshades of assessment tend to blur the vision of analysis.

Formally, the judicial power conferred on the courts by section 6 of the 1979 Constitution, survived. Substantively, however, the integrity of the courts' hitherto,[130] exclusive province did not fare as well under the military. Yet, it is only regarding the judicial function that questions still arise debating the totalitarian pretensions of the military Head of State (under Decree 107 of 1993). Even though Justice Eso of the Supreme Court has maintained that obedience is due from the military to court orders unless judicial powers presently invested in the courts are revoked, this has not stopped the prevalent phenomenon of disobedience to court orders. In *M.K.O. Abiola v. The Federal Republic of Nigeria*[131] for instance, Chief Abiola had appealed the refusal of his application for bail by Mustapher, J., at the Federal High

---

[130] I refer here to the period before 1 January, 1984, when the 1979 Constitution held undeniable and unmodified sway.

[131] (1995) 1 NWLR [9 January, 1995, edition] 155.

Court. The Court of Appeal granted the bail but the military government refused to release Abiola. It is a reflection of the feeling of total hopelessness that transfixed the judges of the Court of Appeal that, weeks into this disobedience, they, instead of committing the Attorney General for contempt, rather, granted him a stay of execution of the bail order.

The courts mouthed sanguine opinions of independence due to the non-repeal of their exclusive judicial powers under the 1979 Constitution. Nevertheless, it is true to say that substantively, most of the judges had been cowed to such a point that judicial power had, effectively, been re-transferred to the Military Head of State. This sweeping claim may not be apparent except to those constantly at the courts especially during the Abacha tyranny. Before a government defence counsel even introduces himself to the court, the lawyer for the other side is already faced with a belligerent request from the judge to satisfy him that jurisdiction exists to entertain such a claim against the Federal Military Government and/or any of its agencies (including, even, the police). No answer is normally sufficient to dissuade the judge from striking out the suit for want of jurisdiction or for any other technical point that, no matter how unmaintenable, fortunately for the harried judge, presents itself.

The "rule of commonsense" which Publius asserts in the Federalist Papers to be the "rule of legal interpretation,"[132] is exchanged

---

[132] Publius (Alexander Hamilton) "Federalist No. 83" in *The Federalist Papers, op. cit.* at 462: "The rules of legal interpretation are rules of commonsense, adopted by the courts in the construction of the laws." (Emphasis in the original.)

in fright in the course of the judge's flight to rules of palpable nonsense. A rule of commonsense that judges have applied for ages is the one that legally interprets legislation in such a way that where there is ambiguity or the consequence of total denial of access to judicial interpretation of a disputed question, the ordinary jurisdiction of the courts or, at least, of the superior courts, would be retained. But in Nigeria under the Abacha tyranny (and a bit less so, under the Babangida and Buhari dictatorships), the trend has been an unthinking tendency in most courts to lean in favour of denying a remedy. Alternatively, the courts would accept the consequence of lack of forum, rather than the commonsense position accepted since Lord Coke in the reign of that pernicious Stuart, James 1.

Quite apart from the refusal to obey court orders, the Federal Military Government has by other direct and indirect methods attempted to divest the ordinary courts of judicial power (in favour of the Head of State or his delegates). It has directly ousted the jurisdiction of ordinary courts and transferred these to military and other tribunals set up by the Head of State (to whom final appeals would usually lie). It is one of such military tribunals, chaired by a civilian, which controversially, convicted Ken Saro Wiwa of four murders committed by a mob when Ken was already in Abacha's gulag. The Provisional Ruling Council (PRC) under the dictatorial chairmanship of the Head of State, General Sani Abacha, was made the ultimate court of appeal from this tribunal. In keeping with the perceived bias of the Head of State against this minority-rights crusader, the so-called conviction was confirmed in less than ten days.

By this unusual speed, the FMG implemented the "judicial murder" of Mr. Wiwa and eight of his Ogoni kinsmen on 10 November 1995. It was highly unlikely that the PRC could have read the voluminous, records of proceedings before confirming the sentences.

The enactment of *ad hominem* decrees is another method used by the military to divest the courts of jurisdiction. Such decrees punish named persons or corporations and thus by-pass judicial enquiry that would have fairly determined whether, in fact, the named individuals or groups have broken any laws. In general, the appellate courts have displayed a history of gallant resistance to this particular method of, as it were, transferring judicial powers of the courts to the soldier-legislators of the country. Sir Adetokunbo Ademola, C.J.N., bravely stood with his four brother judges of the Supreme Court against an attempt at this sort of imposition in the case of *Lakanmi and anor. v. Att. Gen. (West) and ors*[133]. More recently, Justice Pats-Acholonu, with the unanimous support of his two brother judges at the Lagos Division of the Court of Appeal, similarly struck-down the Abacha decrees of 1994 which, without any judicial trial, purportedly closed-down the Guardian, Concord and Punch (print) media houses on some unsubstantiated and obviously trumped-up complaints of gun-running.

It is regrettable that some jurists, rather than encourage this bravery, have sought to make academic capital out of it: lashing out

---

[133] [1971] 1 U.I.L.R. 201; (1974) E.C.S.L.R. 713. See also the full report in D.O. Aihe and P.A.O. Oluyede, *Cases and Materials on Constitutional Law in Nigeria* (Oxford: O.U.P. and University Press Ltd., Ibadan, 1979) at 44 to 64.

in gleeful ridicule that the military government has effectively overturned the decisions by the "Federal Military Government (Supremacy and Enforcement of Powers) Decree" of 1970,[134] in respect of *Lakanmi*. And, by a total neglect of, and a contemptuous refusal to obey, the clear directions to unseal the closed premises of Guardian Newspapers, that the executive has done the same in respect of the *Guardian case*. To make blatant, the already ignoble contempt, Abacha, rather than obey the Court of Appeal, made another decree some weeks later de-proscribing the Guardian Newspapers before ordering his soldiers to withdraw therefrom. In spite of some contrary juristic opinion, we are satisfied that *Lakanmi* remains good law. Since Decree 28 of 1970 is itself *ad hominem*, it would, by the same reasoning in *Lakanmi* (which it tried to nullify), be deemed null and void and therefore incapable of achieving its object. Until another Supreme Court decision confirms Decree 28 of 1970 to be good law, it may be seen as legally, impotent.[135]

So much for the digression. We have, by this extended narrative, only tried to buttress the view set out earlier. Although there is a specific separation of governmental functions

---

[134] Decree No. 28 of 1970 passed barely 9 days after the *Lakanmi* decision and purportedly abrogating it.
[135] Consider for e.g. Publius (James Madison), "Federalist No. 37" in *The Federalist Papers, op. cit.* at 245: All new laws … are considered as more or less obscure and equivocal, until their meaning be liquidated and ascertained by a series of particular discussions and adjudications." Various J.S.C.s have made comments that imply the effectiveness of the *Lakanmi* abrogation. These are mere *obiter dicta*. They must be considered as ineffective unless the issue directly arises in a future case.

in the Nigerian military Constitution of 1993, it is yet the case that all these, effectively, are invested in one functionary (the Head of State). He may exercise all of it either directly himself or indirectly by his delegates or agents. In this, even the ordinary courts constitute, in effect, part of his delegates.

Under this first interpretational approach to the concept of separation of powers, the English parliament appears to present a similar model. However, we shall argue later in this work that they are poles apart. Even though power is popularly said to aggregate in one body known as Parliament (consisting of the three estates of (Queen) King,[135a] Lords and Commons), we argue that this British institution is, not one but, several mutually checking and balancing institutions.

The second plausible interpretation of "separation of powers" relates to the distinction between functionaries rather than functions of government. But here, political history presents us with hardly any apt examples. Under this approach, the concept of separation has nothing to do with any demarcations in the nature of sovereign power. Power remains whole but those to exercise it may be separated. For an example, we are forced back to ancient Rome and with Alexander Hamilton as guide,[136] we may point to the "Comitia Centuriata" and "Comitia Tributa." These two ultimate, yet separate, legislative

---

[135a] "… The monarch who heads the government, also in effect forms the `third House of parliament' … ": Prof. D.C.M. Yardley, *Introduction to British Constitutional Law* (London: Butterworths, 1984) 77.

[136] "Federalist No. 34," *The Federalist Papers, Ibid.* at 226 and 227.

authorities of the Roman Republic, mutually had:

> Power to *annul* or *repeal* the acts of the other … and yet these two legislatures coexisted for ages, and the Roman republic attained to pinnacles of human greatness.[137]

There is a sense in which the defunct communist regime of the Soviet Union may be seen as falling under this class. Comrade Gennady has shown how the Soviets of People's Deputies is constitutionally invested with all sorts of powers without discrimination (regardless of the fact that the Politburo and various other party and state agencies seem also vested with the same competences):

> … The Soviets of People's Deputies not only adopt laws and take decisions, but also help implement them and monitor their application in practice…"[138]

Power (the function) is thus not separated. Rather, the power-user (the functionary) is. The power wielder is separated into different bodies: the Politburo, the Presidium, the Central Working Committee of the Communist Party, the Secretary-General of the Party, the Soviets of People's Deputies, etc.

A similar point can be made with reference to the modern Russian Republic. Although it has a Duma, which principally makes laws, its executive President is constitutionally enabled also to make Decrees. The current French Republic where both the National Assembly and the French President are competent to make laws achieves a similar diarchic separation of

---

[137] *Ibid.* (The emphases are supplied in the original).
[138] Gennady Belov, *What is the State?* (Moscow: Progress Publishers, 1986) at 86.

functionaries. The analogy in these diarchic examples cannot, however, be stretched too far. While there are fields of concurrent competence, nevertheless, the Russian and French constitutions are clearly committed to a separation both in functions as well as in functionaries.

The same caveat seems true of the British Parliament. Although it seems to concentrate all powers in Parliament while distinguishing only as between particular functionaries that may exercise any, some, or all types of sovereign power, it may yet be seen to distinguish (since 1998 at least) between the judicial function and the others[138a]. The Crown and Cabinet have executive functions (even if some or all of the members are a minuscule part of the legislature). The House of Lords and courts subordinate to it have judicial powers (this excludes the Commons except, maybe, at the "High Court of Parliament" during impeachment trials of the King or Queen). The Parliament has supreme legislative powers and sitting as such body, it is immaterial that the Prime Minister and his cabinet are present. When present, they contribute as executives but make laws only in their individual capacities as legislators.[138b]

The same reasoning applies to the Lord Chancellor's participation in law making as well as in execution of laws. Even though he is the highest judicial personnel when sitting in

---

[138a] In s. 6(4) of the British Human Rights Act, cap. 42, of 9 November, 1998: ' … "Parliament" does not include the House of Lords in its judicial capacity'.
[138b] To this effect, Prof. Yardley reiterates that: "… the common usage of `Parliament' and `government' as interchangeable terms … is of course incorrect." See, D.C.M. Yardley, *op. cit.* at 77.

the Judicial Division of the House of Lords, he is, when on the Woolsack, no longer a judge but Speaker of the upper legislative house. At the Cabinet, he is neither a judge nor a legislator but sits in his capacity as Minister of the Crown. All this may appear a bit perplexing. The point to be stressed, however, is that the United Kingdom of Great Britain and Northern Ireland,[139] as well as the modern Republics of Russia and France, although susceptible of categorization under this second interpretational regime, are, nevertheless, *sui generis*. They demarcate functionaries but do not, in practice, fail to also separate the nature of available state functions. The British system symbolizes what political scientists since Aristotle have referred to as a mixed government or a mixed constitution. Here, powers of the state are balanced-out by being allocated, irrespective of nature, to the three great estates (in most feudal European societies) of the king, the nobles and the masses. Unless properly mixed, it was thought that Monarchy (for kingly rule) would degenerate to Tyranny; Aristocracy (for nobles), to Oligarchy; and Democracy (for the masses), to Mobocracy.

If separation of powers is read along the lines of the second interpretation we have offered above, it would mean that in Ancient Rome of the *Comitia Centuriata* and *Comitia Tributa*, regardless of the non-demarcation of

---

[139] The reader will observe that I sometimes conflate this full name of the state with "Britain" and, sometimes, even with the less accurate "England." I do so sometimes for brevity and also I do it sometimes for the sheer fact that this is how it is, in fact, popularly understood: as synonyms reflecting the dominance of the English in the Union.

(legislative, executive and judicial) functions, "separation of powers" had been achieved. Clearly, this is not what most jurists and political scientists would regard today as true separation of powers.[140] To achieve the "ideal," a constitution would be expected both to divide the sovereign powers (whether legislative, executive and judicial or whatever else), as well as assign these to independent, separate, functionaries. With this sort of understanding of separation of powers, none of the polities falling under the first two interpretational regimes (above) would qualify. It is this third interpretation of "separation of powers" that John Locke is credited with enunciating and Baron Charles de Montesquieu is credited with expanding and popularizing.[140a]

At the time he published the *Two Treatises of Civil Government*,[141] John Locke, like most of his liberty-conscious co-inhabitants of the British Isles, was experiencing the one or two years of heady pride arising from the Glorious

---

[140] "Totalitarian social systems recognize the divisions between legislative, executive and judicial branches of government only pro-forma": Adam Podgorecki, "Totalitarian Law: Basic Concepts and Issues," Chapt. 1 in Adam Podgorecki and Vittorio Olgiati, eds., *Totalitarian and Post-Totalitarian Law* (England: Dartmouth Publishing Coy. Ltd. for the Onati International Institute for the Sociology of Law, 1996) at 17 and 18.

[140a] It is even traced as far back as Aristotle. See Harry Street and Rodney Brazier eds., *Constitutional and Administrative Law de Smith, op. cit.* at 31. See also D.C.M. Yardley, *op. cit.* at 75.

[141] This was published in 1690. See, John Locke, *Two Treatises of Civil Government* (London: Everyman's library, 1962). Cited in Jan-Erik Lane, *op. cit.* at 37 and 275.

Revolution of 1688 and 1689.[141a] His elitist roots could not exclude him from the exultation resulting from seeing the English people's representatives dictate terms of rulership to the new monarchs, William of Orange and his wife, Mary. Like most liberal writers of his time, he felt unconsciously compelled to offer a philosophical justification for what had happened. And in this, he relied principally on the social contract theory of the state to show that:

> Men being, as has been said, by nature all free, equal, and independent, no one can be put out of this estate and subjected to the political power of another without his own consent, which is done by agreeing with other men, to join and unite into a community for their comfortable, safe, and peaceable living, one amongst [sic, "with"] another, in a secure enjoyment of their properties, and a greater security against any that are not of it ...[142]

If this power conferred voluntarily upon the government is abused, he wrote, the "supreme power" simple "reverts" back to society, and the:

> People have the right to act as supreme and continue the legislative in themselves or place it in a new form, or new hands, as they think good.[143]

[141a] See, C. Ogwurike, *Concept of Law in English-Speaking Africa* (New York: NOK Publishers, 1979) at 102: "It has been said that Locke's rejection of the absolutism of sovereign power ... made him a champion of the 1688 revolution in England."

[142] John Locke, *Ibid.* at 164. See Jan-Erik Lane, *Ibid.* at 37 [my square brackets].

[143] Locke, *Ibid.* at 242. See Lane, *Ibid.*, at 38.

Implicitly therefore, Locke reasons, even though there was no lawful king available to validate the Bill of Rights and, later, the Act of Settlement, these were, nevertheless, objectively legitimated by the more fundamental consent of the people. They had withdrawn supreme power from the erstwhile, legal, regime symbolized by the Stuart Kings to "place it in a new form, or new hands" in the Convention Parliament.

Locke, as the foregoing demonstrates, was not principally concerned with separation of powers but with elaborating principles of government that explain and justify mandates placed by ordinary citizens in the hands of rulers. In this elaboration of constitutional principles, he found it incidentally expedient to propose the sort of distribution and operationalization of state power, which would, for the people, ensure security and avoid tyranny and impositions; and for the government, prevent rebellion and overthrow.

It is in this context then, that Locke proffers the thesis that governmental power involves three functions: (a) legislative, (b) executive, and (c) federative. The legislative is the law-making power; the executive concerns power over internal administration of domestic questions; and the federative is the power relating to external affairs and the law of nations. It will include power to declare war and sue for peace; to send and receive diplomats; to conclude treaties; etc. To ensure security of the state, Locke proposes the conjunction of executive and federative powers in the hands of a single functionary, for otherwise:

> Both of them requiring the forces of the society … the force of the public would be under different commands.[144]

This, he believes, would weaken security both in the state and in its constituent populace.

Separation, he says, should however take place as between the functionaries who hold the legislative power and those he recommends should conjoin both federative and executive powers. Since it is necessary to leave a lot of discretion in the executive functionary, the liberty of the citizen is best protected when a different individual or body of individuals exercises legislative power (as shown in the balancing actions of the Convention Parliament against the excesses of James II). From this, he is able to conclude that: "In all moderated monarchies and well-framed governments,"[145] it is easy to observe and approve that: "the legislative and executive powers are in distinct hands."[145]

From the above, some commentators have remarked that Locke's theory does not include judicial power[146]. We are not at all sure that this is an entirely valuable observation. Admittedly, Locke was not explicit. But from what is said some 58 years later by Montesquieu, it is plausible to argue that by "executive," Locke includes both normal administration as well as the judicial function. Baron Charles de Montesquieu's *L'Esprit des Lois*[147] ("The Spirit of the Laws")

---

[144] Locke, *Ibid.*, 192. See also Lane, *Ibid.*

[145] Locke, *Ibid.*, 199. See also, Lane, *Ibid.*

[146] See for instance, Lane, *Ibid.* at 39.

[147] Baron C. de S. Montesquieu, *The Spirit of the Laws* (1748; New York: Cambridge University Press, 1989) first published in France in 1748 under its French title. Cited by Lane, *op. cit.* at 37 and 276.

presents the most explicit representation of the third interpretational regime. He divides sovereign power into three compartments.

> In each state there are three sorts of powers, legislative power, executive power over things depending on the right of nations, and executive power over the things depending on civil right"[148].

He contends that for each power, there should be a distinct functionary to avoid investing, at the same time, more than one type of function/power on the very same individual or corporate functionary.

Montesquieu's formulation is predicated upon different concerns from Locke's. His, bears on the problem of overwhelming governmental power vis-à-vis the liberty-interests of individual citizens. For him, to allow the executive power, which by nature is already overwhelming, to be joined in the same functionary as exercises legislative authority would be an invitation to abuse. However, to add judicial power to this political hotchpotch would be a sure recipe for liberty-destruction. The wordings of earlier translations[149] are usually more picturesque than current renditions:

> Political liberty is to be found *only* when there is no abuse of power. But constant experience shows us that every man invested with power is liable to abuse it, and to carry his authority as far as it will go … To prevent this abuse it is necessary from the nature of things that

[148] Montesquieu, *Ibid.* at 156. See Lane, *Ibid.*, 39.

[149] See for e.g., Baron Charles de Montesquieu, *The Spirit of the Laws*, Book II, T. Nugent, transl. (New York: Hafner Publishing Co., 1949). Cited in E. Michael Joye and K. Igweike, op. cit. at 116 and 370.

one power should be a check[150] on another ... There would be an end of everything if the same person or body, whether of the nobles or of the people, was to exercise *all* three powers"[151].

Now, it would appear, Montesquieu's view seems fairly manifest. He wants an entire separation of functions and each of the separated functions is to be assigned to a distinct, independent, functionary. But his categorization of the functions seems, like Locke's, to have left out the judicial power. His "executive power over things depending on the right of nations" seems congruent with Locke's "federative" powers of a state while his "executive power over the things depending on civil right," obviously refers to Locke's "executive" power, simpliciter.

Our argument is that executive power (for Locke) and internal executive power (for Montesquieu) both refer, in the language of the 17th and 18th Centuries (when they respectively wrote), to the same idea: the power of administration of laws by direct implementation (what we now call executive power) or by interpretation and declaration (what we now call judicial power). In this respect, Locke and Montesquieu both appreciated the analytical difference in the functions but only Montesquieu required a separate functionary to exercise the judicial aspect of executive powers. He, alone of the two, was explicit that:

---

[150] I shall show later that what he meant to say was "balance" not "check."

[151] See fn. 149 (*supra*) Joye and Igweike, *Ibid.* at 116. (Our emphases.)

> All would be lost if the same man or the same body of principal men, either of nobles or of the people, exercised these three powers, that of making the laws, that of executing public resolutions, and *that of judging the crimes or disputes of individuals ...*"[152a].

The North American colonies were the chief disciples of Montesquieu's more extreme separation theory. Varying in degrees of compliance, none was yet able to achieve a total demarcation in the sense of having any function exclusively performed by one (individual or corporate) functionary. This was even less so under the Articles of Confederation of 1781 when the thirteen colonies chose to come together under one constitution five years after their declaration of independence from Britain in 1776. Fiercely jealous of freshly acquired independence, each of the colonies was rather suspicious of any symbol of kingship or sole executive power.[153] Therefore, they concentrated power in the various state legislatures, which, despite formal demarcation, effectively sought to acquire all power (executive and judicial) to themselves. In fact, this was the principal reason for the constitution review, which resulted in the current, federal, constitution of the United States of America, 1787[154].

[152a] See fn. 147 (supra). Montesquieu, *Ibid.* at 157. Jan-Erik Lane, *Ibid.* at 39. (Our emphasis.)

[153] See for eg., Rodee, Anderson, Christol and Greene, *op. cit.* at 139: "The state governor was reduced to virtual impotence; in most states ..."

[154] This 2nd constitution of the U.S.A. was prepared in 1787 but took effect only on 4 March, 1789, when the required 9th of the thirteen states ratified the draft.

Montesquieu's strict demarcations have been criticized as practically unworkable. However, there is no evidence of any failed attempt at implementation. The criticism is based on speculation and, without much critical thinking, it would appear to have some weight. If a detached analysis were made of the British constitution, Montesquieu would, perhaps, be found less mistaken than his numerous critics who simply mouth the censure of ancestors.

Since Hood Phillips's censure (in the first edition of his very educative book) that Montesquieu's elaboration of Locke's doctrine of separation, was based on an "imperfect understanding of the eighteenth-century English Constitution,"[155] whoops of uncritical echoes have resounded from the juristic posterity of this constitutional tradition. In Nigeria, Messrs Iluyomade and Eka repeat the unmerited criticism.[156] Having, apparently, copied the relevant provisions of this topic (almost verbatim) from the last mentioned work (or

---

[155] (1st ed., 1952). See also the same sentiment in the 6th ed., O. Hood Phillips and Paul Jackson, *op. cit.* at 14.

[156] B.O. Iluyomade and B.U. Eka, *Cases and Materials on Administrative Law in Nigeria* (Ile Ife, Nigeria: Univ. of Ife Press, 1980) at 5. The "Preface" at p. vi, acknowledges the "practical assistance" of "Dr. D.O. Aihe" suggesting, with the earlier date of publication of the version by Aihe and Oluyede, that theirs is the original. However, the same acknowledgement goes on to show that Aihe saw the initial drafts by Iluyomade and Eka in 1970, i.e., nine years before he and Oluyede published their almost verbatim reproduction of the topics of "Rule of Law" and "Separation of Powers" in the present book. This is very remarkable but is no less annoying to a purchaser of these identical books.

vice-versa), Aihe and Oluyede[157] also could not avoid the unjustified attachment to Hood Phillips.

Right from his original in 1971 down to his editors' fifth edition, reprint of 1987,[158] Professor Stanley de Smith has joined in the attacks. He describes Montesquieu's separation of powers as:

> Based on an analysis of the English Constitution of the early eighteenth century, *but an idealized rather that a real English Constitution.*[159]

It has become conventional to endorse this sort of attack and it will be observed that most writers who indulge in it make no attempt at justifying the conclusion with evidence, reasons or other proof. However, not every constitutional jurist has participated in the public lynching. Although Yardley does make similar allegations, he, at least, offers a mild apology:

> … Montesquieu was mainly concerned to warn against the dangers of monopoly of power, and he may therefore have been less mistaken than is sometimes asserted.[160]

Professor Jan-Erik Lane happily makes no criticism of Montesquieu on this point and some passages of his very illuminating treatise of law and politics could even be used as an endorsement. When read against our common knowledge of the working of the constitutional monarchy in Britain, it would appear that

---

[157] D.O. Aihe and P.A. Oluyede, *Cases and Materials on Constitutional Law in Nigeria* (Oxford: O.U.P. in association with U.P.L. of Ibadan, 1979) at 19.
[158] Street and Brazier, eds., *op. cit.* at 31.
[159] *Ibid.* (Emphasis is mine).
[160] D.C.M. Yardley, *op. cit.*, at 75, fn. 2.

Montesquieu is vindicated by passages such as the following:

> Actually, complete separation of powers is only to be found … in a constitutional monarchy where the king still has executive powers."[161]

There ought to be a distinction between a specific repository of a particular power and an individual member of that body. We submit that separation is retained even though an individual member of the specified class also serves as member of another body invested with analytically different governmental functions. But if the very same members of a particular body exercise at the same time two or more governmental functions, Montesquieu's separation is not achieved.

From this standpoint, it is plausible to urge that the British constitution is an appropriate model for Montesquieu's separation thesis. The three functions of government are quite evidently entrusted to, and exercised by, three different bodies of functionaries. Legislative power is entrusted to the (King or) Queen in Parliament (not to the constituent parts of that institution) and it is immaterial that any person participates who, individually, has executive functions, for example, the Prime Minister; or, has judicial competence, for example, the Lord Chancellor. It would be different if the same King or Queen and Cabinet also constitute the total membership of what we have described as "the King in Parliament." Or, if the same Lord Chancellor, Lords of Appeal in Ordinary, as well as the entire body of judges of the superior and inferior courts and

---

[161] Jan-Erik Lane, *op. cit.*, at 129.

tribunals, was to constitute the membership of the said "King in Parliament."

Similarly, the executive power as well as the executive functionaries are obviously separated from the other governmental functions and functionaries. The King in Council with the mandatory advice of 'the Ministry' (Cabinet of Ministers) is invested with the executive powers of the United Kingdom. This separation is not adversely affected merely because the King (or Queen) and some of his Privy Councillors and Ministers, also, individually, partake of the legislative function[161a]. As Attorney General, Sir Frank Soskice remained part of the executive ministry despite the loss of his parliamentary seat in the general elections of 1950. Mr. Gordon Walker, as Foreign Minister, remained part of the executive although he had lost his entitlement to remain a legislator after the elections of 1964. These examples[162] demonstrate that membership of the executive in England is not an automatic ticket for the legislature. Effectively therefore, they are two different corporate bodies being, as they are, distinct from their individual memberships.

To be thorough, we are to say too, that the judicial power in England is invested not just in the judicial division of the House of Lords, but that it spreads down to the High Court judges, County Court judges, etc., as

---

[161a] The point is made more apparent by Sir Ivor's remark that the Parliament, *qua* Parliament, cannot give a direct order to a policeman or even to the most junior civil servant. It will make laws and these orders will be carried out by Ministers and other members of the executive who the Parliament would hold accountable for satisfactory and faithful implementation.

[162] See for these, Yardley, *op. cit.* at 77.

well as to the various lay and stipendiary Magistrates, Recorders, Chairpersons and members of judicial tribunals, etc. It follows from the foregoing, that a few Law Lords' membership of the legislature cannot be so fundamental an inroad as would warrant a denial that the constitution operated at Westminster reflects Montesquieu's ideas about the separation of governmental powers. It may be recommended that more separation be effected to restrict individual functionaries each to only one governmental function; but certainly, it would be non-factual to maintain that there is no separation as between the corporate functionaries to whom the three functions are differently allocated.

To facilitate the sort of separation where not only the institution but also the individual members thereof are precluded functions in other than their own specified governmental areas, there have been various constitutional modifications of Montesquieu's original model. The general trend of thought seems to credit the United States of America with the closest link to that supposed ideal. In the first three articles of its constitution of 1787 (which commenced operation in 1789), the federal legislative power is given to the Congress consisting of a Senate and a House of Representatives. Neither the President nor his cabinet nor the judges are permitted to be members of either House of Congress. There are, however, two important caveats to be entered here. The Vice-President presides ex-officio at the Senate. During impeachment trials of the President by the Senate (such as was going on up to February, 1999, against President William Jefferson Clinton of the United States), the Vice-President gives way to the Chief Justice of the Supreme Court to preside. We are not entirely sure that these two points serve as "real" exceptions to the rule that an executive or a judicial functionary is not allowed membership of the U.S. legislature. The Vice-President and the Chief Justice merely "preside," they are not members[162a] who make law.

An analogy can be drawn with such formal functionaries as the legislative Clerk. Under the 1999 Constitution of Nigeria, for example, the Clerk of the National Assembly is a constitutionally and statutorily entrenched "fixture" with influence and powers, sometimes, exceeding those of individual, elected, members. In spite of all this, it would be wrong to regard the Clerk as a member of the National Assembly.

The federal executive power of the United States of America is vested in the President. Strictly, neither he nor any of his appointed ministers is, for tenure of office, responsible to the Congress. The federal judicial power vests in the Supreme Court and courts subordinate to it. No legislator and no member of the executive is permitted, while retaining any such office, to become a judge of the Supreme Court. It must be pointed out however that after an impeachment by the House of Representatives, the Senate transforms, for the purposes of trying the Article of Impeachment

---

[162a] See, art. 1, s. 3. The Vice-President has a vote only in the event of a tie at the Senate. Conviction at the Senate is based on a fixed two-thirds majority of senators present. There is thus, no possibility of a tie at an impeachment hearing in which the Chief Justice presides (for the president's impeachment) or where the Vice-President presides (for other officials of the United States such as Federal judges).

against the President, into a "court"[163] of exclusive and ultimate jurisdiction. Chief Justice William Rehnquist's ruling during President Clinton's post-impeachment trial at the U.S. Senate may leave room for further controversy.

In saying that the Senator was right in objecting to being called a juror, he did not go further to explicitly say that the concerned Senators were, instead, judges. He merely ruled that the Senate, in those hearings, resembled more a court than it did a jury. If the Senate equals a court in such proceedings, it cannot merely resemble it. You cannot resemble yourself. You are either yourself or another person or thing. It may therefore be argued that even for impeachment proceedings, the Senate is no court but, *sui generis*, exercising a specially designated function,[164] which is, by the constitutional assignment to it, not quite a judicial but legislative function (*ad hominem*).[164] Alternatively, it is a specially composed court different from the bi-cameral composition of the United States' legislature.

---

[163] In fact, on the second day of the impeachment trial of Pres. Clinton, (the cable television "BBC World" was relayed live at 5.06p.m. of 15 January 1999, Washington time or 11.06p.m. Nigerian time), Senator Tom Harkin of Iowa objected to the House Managers' continued reference to the senators as jurors. Chief Justice William Rehnquist immediately upheld this objection in two sentences holding that the Senate was not a jury but more in the nature of a court for the purposes of the impeachment hearings.

[164] Art. 1, section 3: "… The Senate shall have sole power to try all impeachments. When sitting for that purpose, they shall be on Oath or Affirmative. When the President of the United States is tried, the Chief Justice shall preside; And no person shall be convicted without the concurrence of two-thirds of the members present …"

Whatever the proper answer to this controversial question, the important point demonstrated is the extent of separation of powers achieved by the United States' constitution even to the level of individual members of governmental institutions. The 1999 Constitution of Nigeria borrows from the United States and similarly separates functions and individual functionaries. In section 4, legislative power at the federal level is given to the bi-cameral National Assembly while state legislative power is invested in the various unicameral Houses of Assembly at the states. Section 5 confers federal executive power on the President but this is expressly made subject to any contrary provisions of the self-same constitution. Similarly, at the state level, it confers executive powers on the Governor subject to the constitution. Finally, in section 6, federal and state judicial powers are respectively conferred upon the federal and state courts, therein enumerated or later to be established by legislation. The detailed provisions in Chapter VII of the constitution, render dubious the distinction between federal and state competences of certain courts especially, federal appeal courts.

This then is what Locke and Montesquieu meant by separation of powers. In modern times, it is sometimes suggested that separation of powers can be made to refer even to the division between central and fringe authorities in a federal constitutional setting. In this regard, separation of powers is said to be both horizontal as well as vertical.

It is horizontal separation of powers when, like Aniagolu, J.S.C.,[165] we refer to the separation of the functionaries of the

"Three great departments of state"[166]

which are,

"Independent, equal and co-ordinate."[166]

It is, however, a vertical separation (for analytical clarity, more usually described as vertical division) when we refer to the demarcation in a federal constitution between the central government and the federating units thereto.

Vertical separation is usually between two spheres: the centre and the states. Nevertheless, it may further be divisible to three or more spheres by adding more grassroots units such as the local government. In Nigeria, local governments did not normally have an autonomous constitutional existence. All the constitution did was to authorize states to create them and, by law, to regulate their operations. In this circumstance, legislation by local councils was necessarily tied, in subordination, to the relevant, enabling, state law. Departure from its provisions would be nullified as ultra vires.

Section 7 of the 1979 Constitution (and the Fourth schedule thereof) guaranteed the system of local government in Nigeria but not until General Babangida's Decrees of 1989 and 1991, did a full-scale, autonomic, third-tier

---

[165] In *Paul I. Unongo v. Aper Aku* [1983] 9 S.C. 126.

[166] *Ibid.* Quoted by T.A. Oyeyipo, "Enhancing the Efficacy and the Independence of the Judiciary in the Third Republic" in I.A. Umezulike, ed., *Towards the Stability of the Third Republic* (Enugu: F.D.P. for the Fed. Min. of Justice, Lagos, Nigeria, 1993) 17 at 26 with citation supplied by Justice Nnaemeka-Agu, at 60, n. 19.

of government, have effective, formal and substantive grounding in Nigeria[167].

To analyze how the constitutional doctrine of separation of powers has fared in promoting liberty-sensitive governments, it is important to discuss the various emendations to that theory by future practitioners of Montesquieu's theoretical construct. The most important modification of the original idea held by Montesquieu is the notion that the division of functions and functionaries should not be too rigidly implemented as by watertight compartments. By this notion, certain functions of a class are given to functionaries of a separate category. And sometimes, without permitting the exercise of a certain function by functionaries of a different category, the constitution nevertheless gives out power of the negative to contain the otherwise free rein, which ordinarily should have resided in the given functionary whose peculiar function is in question. This is a sub-concept under the doctrine of separation of powers commonly referred to as the notion of checks and balances.

CHECKS AND BALANCES.

First of all, we need not fall into the pit which confuses "checks" with "balances." This is the bane of all previous thinkers on this subject who use the terms interchangeably. Given the synonymic relationship between the two, however, this tendency is not sufficient to invite any great censure to the practice. We

---

[167] See the Local Government (Basic Constitutional and Transitional Provisions) Decree No. 15 of 1989 as amended (with more detailed powers) by the Local Government (Basic Constitutional and Transitional Provisions) (Amendment No. 3) Decree No. 23 of 1991.

only suggest here that distinction between the two would more eloquently convey our meaning and facilitate understanding. Here, again, our semantic or syntactic methodology may yet prove more useful than tenacious adherence to flatulent axioms, which are based only on historical authority and traditional usage. We should read the phrase as a whole to get its real meaning. Then, single words, individually.

Clarity of thought manifests when "checks" are made to refer, in this sub-concept, only to constitutional powers of the negative held by other branches over the field, ordinarily, the province of a specific arm of government. In this regard, "balances" simply signify the separation of functions between the various governmental functionaries. It refers to the specific areas granted to each functionary (or branch of government) beyond which, intrusion into the area of another functionary (or arm of government) will necessarily result and, probably, be resisted and/or repelled. Each functionary, in order to guard her own domain, necessarily, by even the mere exercise of her designated function, fills any void and blocks most or all vacuums which any other ambitious functionary could have invaded. This is a balancing phenomenon. In the nature of things, power is ever grasping of more control and if there is no countervailing power to restrict its trespasses, there is danger of totalitarianism[167a] and thus, diminution in the liberty-rights of individuals.

[167a] See Bernard Bailyn, *op. cit.* at 56 and 57, esp. fn. 3: "power is like avarice, its desire increases by gratification" (citing the Newport Mercury of 30 July, 1764). At 56, he quotes many pamphleteers who describe power amongst others, as having an "encroaching nature"

James Madison has brilliantly portrayed this fear. In his characteristic lucidity, he states the underlying premise thus:

> What is government itself but the greatest of all reflections on human nature? If men were angels no government would be necessary."[168]

Not being angels, government becomes necessary in the community of men, women and children. So, he notes, "ambition must be made to counteract ambition."[168a] For there must be, he concludes, a

> Policy of supplying, by opposite and rival interests, the defect of better motives.[168a]

Alexander Hamilton, the principal brain behind the collaboration of himself, James Madison and John Jay, under the pseudonym of "Publius," for the publication of the Federalist Papers (eight-five essays in defence of the draft, American constitution then about to be debated at the New York State ratifying convention), has shown that "balances" can be achieved not only under a horizontal, but also a vertical, separation of powers.

---

and "if at first it meets with no control [it] creeps by degrees and quick subdues the whole."

[168] Publius (Madison), "Federalist No. 51" in *The Federalist Papers, loc. cit.* at 53. Thomas Paine expresses very similar sentiments in his, *Common Sense* (of 1776): "Government, like dress, is the badge of lost innocence; the palaces of kings are built on the ruins of the bowers of paradise." Cited by Isaac Kramnick, "Editor's Introduction," *The Federalist Papers, Ibid.* at 23. I may add in response to Madison, that even if men and women were angels, they would still require government: angels, like Lucifer, sometimes entertain un-angelic thoughts.

[168a] "Federalist No. 15," *Ibid.*

Explaining the merits of division of powers between the federal and the state government, he sought to show that this would guard better, the liberty of the citizen. Any attempt to form a dictatorship by the federal government would be curtailed by the states. These would assert the sanctity of their exclusive areas of competence against any federal encroachments. On the other hand, the federal government is unlikely to stand aloof if any powerful state government attempts to trespass into the province of another state. In fact, the constitutionally, entrenched rights of individual citizens would ensure that when disputes of this sort arise, even if the contending parties was to be equally matched, the support of the populace would tip the scale against that government which seeks to prevent the hitherto accepted constitutional limits on power. Hamilton's own words will best reflect our meaning:

> Power being almost always the rival of power, the general government will at all times stand ready to *check* the usurpations of the state governments, and these will have the same disposition towards the general government. The people by throwing themselves into either scale, will infallibly make it preponderate. If their rights are invaded by either, they can make use of the other as the instrument of redress.[169]

The traditional excuse for the introduction of checks and balances is that

---

[169] Publius (Hamilton), "Federalist No. 28," in *The Federalist Papers, loc. cit.* at 206. The emphasis is mine to underscore the erroneous, but conventional, use of "check" to signify "balance" and vice-versa.

strict separation is impracticable. As has been stated earlier, there is no demonstrable reason why government cannot be carried on under such a scenario. There is no evidence of a failed attempt, it is true, but conventional wisdom here, seems quite sensible. Apart from the perceived unworkability of strict separation, there is a more cogent basis for the introduction of "checks and balances" to the original concept of separation of powers. Madison, in *The Federalist Papers*,[170] has identified this in his contention that even if it was possible to get operators who could act strictly and yet smoothly within their separate fields of authority, that nevertheless, the difficulty (and almost impossibility) of definitively demarcating the precise boundaries and scope of each of the three accepted arms of government,[170a] would inherently and necessarily call for their inter-mingling and inter-dependence. This is because:

> Experience has instructed us that no skill in the science of government has yet been able to discriminate and define, with sufficient certainty, its three great provinces – the legislative, executive and judiciary [sic]; or even the privileges and powers of the different legislative branches ...[171]

This problem of definition has been reflected by evaluations of some constitutional

---

[170] See *op. cit.*, "Federalist No. 38," esp. at 244 and 245.

[170a] The Privy Council in *Liyanage v. R.* [1967] A.C. 259 at 289 to 290 says that "their Lordships do not find it necessary to attempt the almost impossible task of tracing where the line is to be drawn ..." between legislative and judicial functions.

[171] *Ibid.* at 244. Square brackets and word therein, mine.

scholars. Professor Mike Ikhariale has, for example, classified the investigatory powers of the legislature under section 86, sub-section (1), of the (still-born) 1989 Constitution of the Federal Republic of Nigeria, as:

> One of the most visible *non-legislative functions* of the National Assembly"[172].

This evaluation is not likely to meet with uncritical or unanimous approbation. Many could plausibly argue that investigation, for the making of laws or for checking already made laws in order to make corrections, or to assess the level of successful implementation, is a function that is part, and inextricably wrapped up in the process, of law making or legislation.

Again, Honourable Justice Uche Omo[173] has made the highly debatable assertion that the executive branch "holds the purse strings." Many people would honestly and credibly ascribe that function to the legislature without whose enabling "Appropriation Acts," funds may not legally be withdrawn or expended from the treasuries of most countries. It is a good excuse to offer on behalf of his Lordship, that military-Nigeria from whence he wrote, incorporated in the same Chief executive, the full powers normally to have resided in a separate legislative assembly.

---

[172] Mike Ikhariale, "Constitutionalism and the Third Republic" in I.A. Umezulike, ed. *Democracy Beyond the Third Republic*, vol. 14 (Nigeria: Fourth Dimension Publishers for the Federal Ministry of Justice, 1993) 168 at 175 (the emphasis is mine).

[173] See his, "Separation of Powers: Managing the Legislative, Judicial and Executive Relationships in a Democratic Polity" in I.A. Umezulike, ed. *Democracy Beyond the Third Republic*, *Ibid.*, 1 at 6.

Despite all these, however, there is no infallible test by which criticism can be made against the two earlier assessments quoted above. Apart from the general understanding that the legislature makes laws, the judiciary interprets and declares these laws, while the executive administers them, the delimitation of the specific, detailed, functions within the above general categorization, remains hazy and vulnerable to individual, subjective, evaluation. This problem of demarcation also embarrasses analysis at the level where we try to isolate "checks" from "balances." Let us, then, attend some examples to illustrate the point.

BALANCES.

Examples of balances will be found in the strict conferment of parts only of sovereign power on each of the departments of government. They consist also of those powers distributed specifically between states and the central government. Absolute power is restrained by each resisting or, as it were, balancing out the encroachment of the other beyond allotted terrains.

More specifically, the fight by courts against *ad hominem* legislation is an example of judicial authority balancing the weight of otherwise, apparent, legislative power.[173a]

[173a] See, Lords Guest and Devlin in *United Engineering Workers' Union v. Devanayagam* [1967] 3 W.L.R. 461, esp. at 479 where this Privy Council minority held that: "Judicial power is a concept that is capable of clear delineation … It has to be, since it is the basis of a constitutional requirement and legislation which falls on the wrong side of the line can be completely avoided." Although the following discussion will show that judicial power has still not been clearly

Ordinarily, it would be supposed that the legislature is entitled to make all laws; including even those specifically directed or targeted at named individuals. In many cases however, the judiciary has asserted its own adjudicatory powers to hold that these special laws, being judicial in nature, are, strictly, non-demonstrative of the exercise of true legislative power. In such cases, they have been termed "legislative judgements."[174] And, as far as the legislature, which purports to deliver such judgment, is not constitutionally entrusted with judicial power, the exercise is nullified and avoided by the courts.

In the case of *United States v. Lovett* for instance, Black, J., of the U.S. Supreme Court had this to say (before striking down a similar such legislative sentence by the Congress):

> Those who wrote our constitution well knew the danger in special legislative acts which take away the life, liberty, or property of particular named persons … they intended to safeguard the people of this country from punishment without trial by duly constituted courts … legislative trials and punishments were too dangerous to liberty to exist in the nation of free men ... and so they proscribed bills of attainder."[175]

---

delineated, yet, my point has been made as to the power to nullify *ad hominem* legislation.

[174] See Chase, J., of the U.S. Supreme Court in *Calder v. Bull* (1798) 3 Dallas 386: "These acts were legislative judgments; and an exercise of judicial power." Quoted in *Lakanmi v. A.G. (West)* [1971] 1 U.I.L.R. 201 (fully reported by Iluyomade and Eka, *op. cit.*, at 5 to 18, esp. at 16.

[175] 328 U.S. 303 at 318 (1945) (also, 90 L. ed. 1,252 at 2,260. Cited by B.O. Nwabueze, *Ideas and Facts in*

In Ceylon (now Sri Lanka), the same principle has been adopted. Even without a clear, exclusive, allotment of "judicial powers" to the normal courts, the Privy Council has held in *Liyanage v. R.*,[176] that that jurisdiction must be implied in order to counter-balance any legislative condemnations of particular persons (when there has not been the benefit of protective processes of normal court trial).

Interestingly, the Adetokunbo Ademola Supreme Court has given, perhaps, the most definitive expression of this balancing power in Nigeria. In the famous, but mostly maligned, case of *E.O. Lakanmi and Kikelomo Ola v. Attorney-General (Western State) and ors.*,[177] the unanimous opinion of the court was that:

> These principles are absolutely fundamental and must be recognized. It is to define the powers of the legislature that constitutions are written and the purpose is that such powers that are left with the legislature be limited, and that the remainder be vested in the courts"[177].

The court however acknowledged

> The fact that not all enactments of this nature are judicial legislation"[178]

and thereby distinguished the Ceylonese case of *Kariapper v. Wijesinha*:[179]

Constitution Making, op. cit., at 191, fn. 1). See too, (1946) 66 Supreme Court Reports 1,073 at 1,079.

[176] [1967] A.C. 259.

[177] [1971] 1 U.I.L.R. 201. See fn. 174 (supra) (at 15 of Iluyomade and Eka).

[178] Iluyomade and Eka, *Ibid.* at 17. See also, *Liyanage v. R. (supra)* at 289 to 290 for the same sentiments by the Privy Council.

[179] [1968] A.C. 717; [1967] 3 All E.R. 485.

The reasoning in the case was that the Act was not a judicial [sic, legislative] usurpation for reasons stated in the judgment. Decree No. 43 of 1968 was not in the form of an alteration of any existing law but it was clearly a legislative sentence and the Decree was spent on the persons named in the schedule ... *section 3(1) of Decree No. 1 of 1966 does not envisage the performance of legislative functions as a weapon for exercise of judicial powers.*[180]

Although the Federal Military Government of Nigeria purported, some nine days after this judgment, to nullify it,[181] it is yet gratifying to note that the Court of Appeal, in a leading judgment delivered by Pats-Acholonu, J.C.A., re-affirmed the same principle twenty-five years later.[182] In yet another act of balancing, this time, against the executive, the Supreme Court has held[182a] that only courts and judicial tribunals should try criminal allegations.

Another illustration of power balancing power may be gleaned from the courts' refusal to be drawn into matters considered internal to the legislative branch. This comes under the principle of "self-restraint" developed by the courts[183]. It is considered in-depth in the

---

[180] *Ibid.* The square brackets, word therein, as well as the emphasis at the tail-end of the quotation, are mine.
[181] The Federal Military Government (Supremacy and Enforcement of Powers) Decree No. 28 of 1970.
[182] *Guardian Newspapers v. Att. Gen. (Fedn).* (1995) 5 N.W.L.R. (pt. 398) 703 (*supra*).
[182a] See, *Garba v. University of Maiduguri* (1986) 1 N.W.L.R. (pt. 18) 1.
[183] There is a particularly brilliant discussion of judicial power which touches on this matter. See, B.O. Nwabueze, "The Independence and Separateness of Judicial

numerous publications, especially in the United States, under the topic: "political questions." For our present purposes, Adefarasin, C.J.'s opinion in *Senator B.C. Okwu v. Senator (Dr.) Joseph Wayas*, sufficiently instructs us that:

> ...This court (and if I may so, any court in Nigeria) cannot interfere in the internal proceedings of the legislature. Any such interference would amount to an arm of the Government (on [sic] this case the judiciary) imposing its control in the house of another who is master there" [183a].

The above opinion of the then Chief Judge of the Lagos State High Court is a correct statement of principles in regard to maintaining balance but, in its application to the facts of the present case, it is, in our submission, a quite unfortunate conclusion. Senator Okwu had challenged the action of the defendant (President of the Nigerian Senate), which had been taken contrary to the Standing Orders made under the 1979 Constitution by the very same Senate to guide its proceedings. The justification of this attitude is borrowed from the *Rule in Foss v. Harbottle*. The minority is prevented from judicial invalidation of an irregularity, which the majority can ratify. It would have been right for Adefarasin, C.J., to adopt the present attitude if Senator Okwu had been challenging, perhaps, an amendment of those standing orders made to ratify the earlier breach for which he was complaining. It is a quite different thing, in a constitutional government (in spite of the same erroneous practice in the United States), to decline

---

Power" in *Judicialism in Commonwealth Africa, op. cit.,* Chapt. VIII, 191 to 211.
[183a] [1981] 2 N.C.L.R. 522.

jurisdiction over the procedural effect of subsisting laws and sub-laws clearly and constitutionally made. Would the courts prefer aggrieved senators to resort to violence? What if the Senate President had deliberately breached the standing orders in spite of opposition from a majority of the senators? How can the court find that the breach has been ratified or is supported by the majority unless it, at least, enquires into the matter?

To maintain balance also, the courts have held that the legislature is not to grant judicial powers to the executive; nor, without provision for supervision, permitted to delegate its legislative powers to that organ of government. For this, the case of *Balogun v. Attorney General of Lagos State*[184] is particularly apt.

Here, the Lagos State House of Assembly had enacted a law[185] in which the state government was empowered:

(a) To define the territorial limits of a local government area (but the House of Assembly did not set down the standards upon which the governor was to exercise this power).

(b) To determine any dispute that may arise as to whether any person had become President or nominated member of the said Council. In addition, whether a person had been duly elected or her seat had become vacant.

The High Court *held* that: "(a)" is legislative and the executive could not, under "the doctrine of separation of powers"[186] in the 1979 Constitution, exercise same except under a limitation of a prescribed standard. As for

---

[184] [1981] 1 N.C.L.R. 31.
[185] Lagos State Local Government Law, 1980.
[186] In other words, under "the idea of balances."

"(b)," despite the regulations made under section 20 of that law to guide the governor in his decisions, this was still a judicial function from which the executive was absolutely prohibited. Section 6 of the 1979 Constitution vested judicial powers in the country only on the courts recognized or enumerated therein.

The "(b)" part of the decision seems to us, wrong. Administrative adjudication is legitimate as far as the superior courts of record retain supervisory jurisdiction. Section 6 (4) (a) and sections (6) (5) (j) and (k) of the 1979 as well as the current 1999 Constitutions are quite clear on this. Sections 33 (2) and 36 (2) of the 1979 and 1999 constitutions are respectively also in point.

Still on the subject of "balances," the courts have ruled against the usurpation of executive functions by the legislature. In *Governor of Kaduna State v. Kaduna House of Assembly*,[187] the defendant by law conferred certain executive functions on the Local Government Commission. The governor challenged this. The court agreed with the principle that the legislature could not validly legislate away executive functions to other branches but validated the instant law on the basis that the said "Local Government Commission" was part of the executive department itself. The court would have nullified the power-conferment if it had been to a non-executive functionary. This misses the point. If the allocation is autonomous, it necessarily derogates from the plenitude of total executive power allotted by section 5 of the constitution to the Governor. If the Local Government Commission were to

---

[187] [1981] 2 N.C.L.R. 444.

exercise the allotted power under the general or specific ambit of the governor's executive authority, the court's reasoning would have been more convincing.

A very interesting instance of the fierce battle waged by the least dangerous branch (the judiciary) against the natural encroachments of what Madison considers to be the most dangerous one (the legislature), is the case of *Ekeocha v. Civil Service Commission for Imo State*[188]. In this case, it was held unconstitutional for the legislature to purport to interpret and decide on the constitutional existence of the Civil Service Commission. The court was of the firm opinion that any such interpretation was a peculiarly judicial function only to be performed by the judiciary – and not by the legislature (even if some very erudite lawyers constitute the cream of that legislature's membership)[189].

The checking function is analytically different from the balancing one. There is a sense in which it would be right to say that separation of powers has consequences only for balances. If you want checking to take place under the government set up by a particular constitution, then, you must not stop at separation. New devices must be employed. You must break down the watertight compartments of separation and place powers of the negative in

---

[188] [1981] 1 N.C.L.R. 154. It is with gratitude that I pause here, to acknowledge my debt, for many of the cases cited in this part of the discourse, to Dr. [now, Prof.] B. Obinna Okere, "Essential Principles of Separation of Powers and their Place and Importance in the Nigerian Administrative Process," (Lecture Mimeographs), Faculty of Law, University of Nigeria, Enugu Campus, N.D.) esp. at 2 and 3.

[189] Brackets and words therein, supplied by me.

arms different from those entrusted the particular functions. In other words, strict separation is mutually antagonistic to the checking function. If in any field there is a check, strictly then, there is no complete separation in that province of power.

CHECKS.

The powers of the negative that we ascribe to the checking function require further explanation. There is a possibility of its confusion with another type of obstructionist power invested in one branch over the field of another. However, that type is not a check but a peculiar type of balance. This type arises due to difficulty in determining, with any reasonable exactitude, all the possible powers that are executive, as distinguished from all that are judicial, and all that are legislative by nature.

The check comes only in one form. It must relate to a function, which the checking power is, itself, not authorized to exercise. The negating power arises when the lawful authority has concluded its work but is constrained to seek approval of the holder of the power of the negative if the concluded function is to have legal effect. A generalized type of check is the power granted to the legislature (not to exercise the President's executive powers themselves, but if we do not want him to perform it in a way we do not like,) to impeach and remove him from office. A particularized example is such as authorizes the president to check the legislature, not by making the laws himself, but by blocking those made in the lawful exercise of legislative power. This is achieved by simply entering a veto on, otherwise, constitutionally enacted laws. The judiciary's power of judicial review of legislation is also a check. With it, duly enacted laws by the legislature may be struck-down (with no claim on the part of the court that it is entitled by itself, to make such laws). The power to cancel returns of elections of even the chief executive of the country is a clear check of the executive power of the electoral authorities even though the court does not claim to be a returning officer.

The twilight zone is, however in the areas we alluded to, which because of difficulty in determining their particular province, makes it difficult to say whether the holder of the power of obstruction is merely exercising a balancing function inherent in its nature, or, a checking one, outside the essence of its character.

To illustrate, we may return to the legislative power of investigation[190]. Confusion of thought may easily present itself in this area. In her "Legislative Investigation under the Nigerian Constitution," Dr. (Mrs.) B.A. Susu[191] refers to *Adikwu v. Federal House of Representatives*[192] to claim, quoting A.L.A.L. Balogun, J., that the legislative power to investigate, is a "balancing process." She seems, to me, right. However, there is a legitimate belief that the power of investigation is executive or judicial in nature and since in this instance it is exercised by the legislature, it is a power in

---

[190] See, s. 82 of the 1979 Constitution and also ss. 86 and 126 of the moribund 1989 Constitution. See currently, ss. 88 and 128 of the 1999 Constitution of 5 May, 1999, with effect from 29 May 1999.
[191] In I.A. Umezulike, ed. *Towards the Stability of the Third Republic, op. cit.,* 86 at 94.
[192] [1982] 3 N.C.L.R. 394 at 407.

the terrain of another body and thus, a check on the full exercise of executive or judicial powers. Our answer is that even if judicial in nature, it is, nevertheless, not necessarily a checking power. The constitution has specifically conferred that facilitative function upon the legislature. It now becomes a peculiar, constitutional, power within the legislative terrain and will be protected just like any other legislative power within the balancing network of functions which the other arms would be repelled from encroaching upon.

Similar to the investigating power is, in this hazy area, such power as is sometimes given to a Chief Judge to make rules of court[193]. This area should include the power of the executive (with the assistance of the legislature) to appoint judges. If judges become too extremist in their opposition to an existing executive, which has the support of the legislature, the executive and legislature may simply appoint judges of a different disposition to water-down the majority currently retained by the disagreeable judges[194]. This, semble, would amount to a balancing act. Impeaching the judges would seem, however, to constitute a special form of the balancing process. The impeachment and trial on the floor of the relevant legislative house would normally have been an adjudicatory

---

[193] See, for e.g., s. 42 (3) of the 1979 Constitution and the Fundamental Rights (Enforcement Procedure) Rules of 1979 made thereunder. The 1999 counterpart is s. 46 (3) and by its s. 315 (4) (b), when read with s. 315 (1), the Rules of 1979 made by the Chief Justice of Nigeria are retained currently as "existing law."

[194] As was done by the conservative Republicans to water down the libertarian majority of the Earl Warren Supreme Court.

process. But now, it will vest constitutionally in a body other than the courts. Remarkably, as between the executive and the legislature, the legislative power of the negative over the executive function of hiring and firing of (unelected) judges, is a clear check - not simply a balance.

The examples can be multiplied. Admittedly, there are areas it is difficult to say with certitude that a particular function is a check rather than a balance or vice-versa.[194a] This, however, ought not dissuade us from the very important task of continually trying to achieve devices for analytical precision in these matters. In tying down the semantic methodology to the principle of separation and the notion of checks and balances, five remarkable points, which may be rendered in a somewhat mathematical formulation, arise.

If we separate the function but not the functionary, the result would be a cosmetic balance (but in reality there would neither be a check nor any balance).

If we separate the functionaries and assign specific tasks to each but if we do not analyze the nature of power into different compartments; the result will be the mutual

---

[194a] The requirement in some constitutions for legislative enactment and, thus, domestic incorporation of treaties made by the executive with foreign countries is illustrative (see for eg., s. 12 of the 1999 Constitution of Nigeria as well as s. 3 of the Treaties (Making Procedure, ETC) Decree No. 16 of 1993). Lord Atkin in *Att. Gen. for Canada v. Att. Gen. for Ontario* [1937] A.C. 326, says that the making of treaties is an executive function by nature. This would make legislative incorporation a check. However, it would be a special balance on the part of the President if it was seen as an essentially legislative function.

balancing of powers (based only on the delineated terrain).

If we separate the functionaries but concentrate all powers (without any division) on each (as was the case for the Roman *"Comitia Centuriata* and *"Comitia tributa"*), the result would, again, be a mutual balancing of powers (based on personal charisma but not on any designated spheres of constitutional authority).

If we separate both the functions as well as the functionaries and restrict each functionary to a designated sphere of exclusive control, the result would be the balancing of powers, but no checks.

If we separate both functions and functionaries allotting only a single type of function to each functionary; and if we permit functionaries of one class the authority to obstruct or delay the effectuation of decisions by the functionary upon whom that particular function is assigned or deemed by nature to inhere, the result would now be, both a mutual balancing of powers as well as a discretionary ability to check the exercise of authority by a different functionary.

From the above, it will be seen that the idea of balance will almost always arise except in totalitarian dictatorships where not only is power not dissipated constitutionally to separate functionaries but also, where it is analytically not conceived as separate. *However, checks will arise only where there is a distinction in functions as well as in functionaries and there is power of interference.* With this background, we may conveniently now discuss that part of separation, which deals with the vertical rather than the horizontal sphere of governmental functions.

FEDERALISM.

The notion of checks and balances has application both in respect of horizontal as well as vertical separation. In polities where federalism has taken root, enumerated powers in the legislative lists determine balance. If, for the federal government, the enumeration is in the exclusive (and designated parts of the concurrent) list, it means, *expressio unius est exclusio alterius*, that the residual powers which are not enumerated, will result to the state governments. This was the case under the 1960, 1963 and 1979 Nigerian Constitutions (including the never-used 1989 and 1995 versions). Federal intrusion in areas not enumerated (or otherwise constitutionally authorized), would in these circumstances, naturally be repulsed by the states to which those powers result. This amounts to a vertical balancing of powers.

Sometimes the federal government is, for example, deemed entitled to deal with certain matters such as the creation of new states. If the state governments are also given power to accept or reject such proposals, this obstructionist authority in the states is a check. In section 8 of the 1999 Constitution for example, it is provided in sub-section (1) that:

> *An Act of the National Assembly for the purpose of creating a new state shall only be passed if -*
> (a) ...
> (b) ...

(c)   the result of the *referendum*[195] is then *approved by a simple majority of all the states of the federation* supported by a simple majority of members of the Houses of Assembly; and

(d)   ...[195]

This is a good example of a vertical check. The state governments are empowered here to control the federal legislature, which, by an Act of the National Assembly, is otherwise the competent authority to create new states[196]. From this and what has been said in the discussion of unitary and federal constitutions, it may well be correct to say that federalism is a specialized instantiation of the abstract conceptions of separation as well as those of checks and balances.

Similar short shrift may be given to the other liberty-sensitive constitutional concepts, which we have highlighted at the start of this section of the chapter. Once a full and extensive discussion is made of the controlling idea of the "rule of law" as well as separation and checks, the rest fall into

---

[195] My emphases. In the 1979 Constitution, para. (c) speaks of "resolution" not "referendum."

[196] Confusion arises when it is suggested that states creation is not necessarily a federal preserve: the power to participate is equally given to both the centre and the fringes and each merely balances the other's specifically conferred constitutional authority to contribute. Plausible as this may seem, the better view is that state creation is naturally the province of the national, not the state, authorities as further demonstrated by the fact that it is enacted by a federal "Act" not a state "Law." States merely give approval. Either way, I claim enhanced clarity by the analytical devices proposed here.

place. Federalism is merely a vertical separation of powers with incidents of checks and balances. Federalism is a useful, but not a necessary, content of a constitution (even of the liberty-sensitive type). The successful unitary model practised at Westminster demonstrates this. On this basis, we feel able to give very brief treatment to "constitutionalism" and the so-called doctrine of "parliamentary sovereignty" as contra-distinguished by the idea of the "supremacy of the constitution." All these involve "limited government." We shall close by calling attention to the fact that the above need not be contained in a constitution. If they are, the product will likely be a progressive, popular, liberty-sensitive, constitution. But a dictator who wants a constitution will probably have no use for such power-constricting devices.

Whether it is the constitution of the people or a constitution framed to benefit a tyrant however, there appears to be certain provisions, which must be in any constitution (whether expressed or merely implied). For example, there can be no constitution, which does not (in writing or otherwise) provide for citizenship/membership qualification. However, let us first conclude the discussion on liberty-sensitive constitutional concepts. We shall deal very briefly with only three more: "constitutionalism," "supremacy of the constitution" and "limited government."

CONSTITUTIONALISM.

This high falutin word merely implies an authority or force superior to the government in any given polity. Unless this is so, the lawmaker can simply legislate that it is no longer bound by previously prescribed fetters (such as fundamental rights) entrenched in the constitution on behalf of the individual. The idea of constitutionalism imports the limitation of, otherwise, sovereign powers of government and this is why Professor Jan-Erik Lane is able to write that: "Constitutionalism implies that there are institutions constraining the exercise of state powers ..."[197].

Constitutionalism as a concept of limited government is of relatively recent origin. The idea was gradually shaped by tentative statements nibbling at the previously ascendant notion of the absolute sovereignty of the legislative authority – whether, the one-person ruler (who aggregates both administrative and legislative functions to herself) or, especially in feudal, occidental practice, a group of powerful advisers in conjunction with the individual ruler.[198]

---

[197] Jan-Erik Lane, *op. cit.*, 53.

[198] Because of the volume of work, the king's top servants sat in council with him to deal with state matters. As matters became more complex, he allowed them (as his court) to sit separately in specialized committees which later grew into courts of law, etc. In England, the highest such court was the one where the representatives of even the commons were summoned to seek redress from the king in exchange for raising taxes. This was the "High Court of Parliament." It gradually grew so assertive that it now insisted on being consulted before any taxation, and later, for any matter whatsoever. After the Glorious Revolution of 1688 and 1689, it even succeeded to ensure that any act of the king or queen must be based on the advice received by the person who commands majority support in the lower house called the "Commons." See for e.g., Prof. Lane, *Ibid.* 24 and esp. at 25 (for a similar historical reconstruction): "A court was also set up to give the king advice, whether he wanted it or not."

In *Dr. Bonham's case*,[199] for example, Lord Coke, C.J., stated (although obiter)[199] that an Act of Parliament was null and void if against the constitution; and the courts would so declare. In saying this, however, he only meant that the courts would interpret legislation as if all was predicated on reason. All statutes would be deemed implicitly to contain the principles of liberty associated with the common law of the realm. Under Coke's conception, the common law is the reason-filled English constitution. Statutes will be deemed congruent with this constitution except, otherwise, expressly stated. An expressly, unreasonable statute would then amount to a constitutional amendment.

To the chagrin of Thomas Hutchinson, C.J., in the *Writs of Assistance Case* of February 1761,[200] James Otis had, before the highest court of the Massachusetts Bay Colony, convincingly argued that an Act of Parliament "against the constitution is void"[201]. Relying on Coke, he goes even further to say it is the duty of the courts to "pass such acts into disuse." This is because, the "reason of the common law [would] control an act of Parliament"[201]. Quoting the Swiss theorist, Emmerich de Vattel, Otis wonders whether the power of legislators could extend to

---

[199] (1610) 8 Co. Rep. 114. See Bailyn, *op. cit.* at 177; Hood Phillips, 6th ed., *op. cit.* at 49; and see also, T.F.T. Plucknett, "Bonham's Case and Judicial Review" (1926) 40 Harv. Law Rev., 30; S.E. Thorne, "Dr. Bonham's Case" (1938) 54 L.Q.R. 543. Cited by O. Hood Phillips and P. Jackson, *op. cit.* at 49, fn. 33.
[200] See, A.J. Langguth, *op. cit.* esp. at 22 and 23.
[201] Quoted by Bailyn, *op. cit.* esp. at 176 [square brackets and word therein, mine].

fundamental law. His eventual answer is in the negative because:

> The constitution of the state ought to be fixed; and since that was first established by the nation, which afterwards trusted certain persons with the legislative power, the fundamental laws are excepted from their commission."[202]

[handwritten: Cts don't annul statutes — they declare them as unconstitutional or otherwise]

In later writings, Otis appears confused. He fails to follow the argument to its logical conclusion. His problem stems from rationalizing this novel principle with that of Parliamentary sovereignty. He asserts Parliamentary sovereignty even when courts may annul statutes. It was, he argued, the supreme executive (i.e. the courts), in the very same sovereign parliament (i.e., the legislature), that would make the correction. In other words, parliament itself would annul parliament's errors. *[handwritten: — Yes, in UK]*

This, admittedly, is quite a stretch. Professor Bernard Bailyn's sardonic stricture is therefore very much in order. He criticizes Otis for:

> Quoting Coke together with Vattel without grasping the implications of their conjunction."[203]

From his earlier postulates, Otis should have reached the inevitable conclusion. If statutes are susceptible to judicial annulment, then, parliament is not sovereign. If anything, it is that higher, more important or fundamental law

---

[202] *Ibid.* at 178.
[203] *Ibid.*, 180.

(the constitution), which should rightly be considered supreme.

Years before independence, others carried the argument to its limits. With the materials available to Otis, they were able to rationalize, perhaps for the very first time in the history of government, that a constitution, especially a written one, made by authority of the people in their mass, is not only superior to the legislature, but is the creator of the entire government of which the legislature is only part. This new conception of a constitution as something anterior to the legislature and superior to the entire government is what is now known as "constitutionalism." Since it claims that governmental powers are limited by prior dictates of the constitution, it applies only in those states where, conceptually, the "constitution" is separable from the capricious and mutable wills of those currently wielding governmental powers.

It is the conceptual springboard for entrenchment of laws of the constitution that protect individuals against over-bearing state power. These rights usually include what are known as fundamental human rights. These may include the rights to life, to liberty, to property, to free speech, association, religion, etc.[204] These rights are subject of vast academic literature and copious practical jurisprudence. They have sometimes been classified in virtue of temporal priority into:

---

[204] See for e.g., Chapt. 4 of the 1999 Constitution esp. ss. 33 to 44 including the claw-back provision that generally derogates from the plenitude of most such rights at s. 45. Their enforcement is facilitated by s. 46.

first-, second- and third-generation rights.[205] Joy Ezeilo has even documented attempts to create fourth-generation rights. However, her: "Fourth-generation rights dealing with environmental issues,"[206] seem to be the same as Geoffrey Robertson's third-generation rights and, generally, seem congruent with his scheme of three generations of rights. His most recent edition of *Freedom, the Individual and the Law*,[207] which was originally written by Professor Harry Street under commission of Penguin Books in 1963, is entirely devoted to "The first generation of civil and political freedoms ..."[207] But he acknowledges two other generations of rights:

> "second-generation" rights to housing and health and education and social security and other such concerns...[208]

and, he adds also, the

> "third-generation" rights to a protected environment.[208]

Large volumes of books can be written on many of the fundamental human rights[208a] and

---

[205] See, Hon. Justice C.C. Nweze and G.C. Nnamani, *Justice Phillip Nnaemeka-Agu: Imprints on Law and Jurisprudence* (Enugu: F.D.P., 1996) esp. at 67, fn. 50.

[206] Joy Ezeilo, "The Influence of International Human Rights Law on African Municipal Legal Systems" (1994–1997) 6 Nig. J.R. 50, esp. at 53, fn. 9.

[207] Geoffrey Robertson, Q.C., 7th edition, *Freedom, The Individual and the Law* (England: Penguin Books, 1993) esp. at xi.

[208] *Ibid.*

[208a] Prof. Niki Tobi, J.C.A. [now, JSC], takes exception to this designation. In his Justice A.B.N. Obayi lecture, "The Judiciary in a Democracy" given on 29 May, 1996, at Hotel Presidential Enugu, his Lordship insists it should either be "human rights" or "fundamental rights" but never "fundamental human rights." See p. 27 of the published lecture. He says it is tautologous.

full explication of any is beyond the scope of the present work. It is only useful to add that much of the credit for these sorts of rights should go to the Americans for their Bill of Rights: the first ten amendments, in 1789, to the United States' constitution. There are, no doubt, earlier precedents such as the Magna Carta of 1215 and the English Bill of Rights of 1689. However, there are fundamental departures in their starting points. While the one or few in power made the English charters of 1215 and 1689, respectively, the American charter of 1789 was made by the people as a command to the one or few it was to set-up in power. Madison's statement of the distinction is always the most poignant:

> In Europe, charters of liberty have been granted by power. America has set the example, and France has followed it, of charters of power granted by liberty ...[209]

As credit for the seminal idea lies with the Americans, so must the modern spreading be attributable to the United Nations (through Mrs. Eleanor Roosevelt's Committee). On 10 December 1948, the member states of the United Nations passed, with not a single objector, the Roosevelt Committee's, draft Universal Declaration of Human Rights (UDHR). Most entrenched human rights are "first-generation" and deal with political and civil rights. The economic, social and cultural rights get some mention but are mostly declared in hortatory rather than mandatory terms as "Fundamental Objectives and Directive Principles of State Policy," which states should strive for but are

---

[209] James Madison made this statement in 1792 and he is quoted by Prof. Bernard Bailyn, *op. cit.* at 55.

not legally bound to execute in favour of individuals.

Although Ezeilo considers "3rd and 4th generation rights[210] as still nebulous and not yet crystallized"[210], this conclusion is tempered by the African Charter on Human and People's Rights[211], which declares that:

> 1. All peoples shall have the right to their economic, social and cultural development with due regard to their freedom and identity and in the equal enjoyment of the common heritage of mankind.
>
> 2. States shall have the duty, individually or collectively, to ensure the exercise of *the right to development*
> [212]
> ...

Much as we see no reason to be drawn into the intellectually riveting, but practically diverting, debates of natural and international lawyers concerning hortatory, non-legislative, "rights," it is helpful to emphasize Obiora Okafor's illuminating contribution. Although he has not deigned to classify it in terms of generation, he has made the point that consequence rather than nomenclature is central. "...The essence and utility of law," he writes,

---

[210] Ezeilo, *loc. cit.* (fn. 206, *supra*) at 53, fn. 9.

[211] Incorporated after ratification by Nigeria as the African Charter on Human and People's Rights (Ratification) Act, cap. 10, L.F.N., 1990.

[212] Art. 22 of the charter. The emphasis on "the right to development" is mine. See further, Obiora C. Okafor, "The Status and Effect of the Right to Development in Contemporary International Law ...." *loc. cit.*, 865 esp. at 873.

is not really the formality of its status but its functional operation as law.[213]

Considering that the Vienna Declaration and Program of Action of 1993, affirmed, in the United Nations World Conference on Human Rights of that year, that the right to development is a: "Universal and inalienable right and an integral part of fundamental human rights,"[214] and, considering its unanimous adoption by 171 states including the United States (which was formerly the most significant opponent of this type of right as a solidarity one), it is difficult to agree with the previously ascendant view as expressed by Ezeilo. Although the Vienna Declaration does not count as law in the formal sense, Okafor's argument of its meta-legal force is a rather compelling one.

In its application to the legislative aspect of sovereign powers, constitutionalism has given rise to the interesting debate concerning the supremacy of the constitution as against the supposed sovereignty of Parliament.

SUPREMACY VERSUS SOVEREIGNTY.

It is obvious that continued reference to the sovereignty of parliament in situations where there is in existence a supreme constitution separate from it, is an aberration only explainable by the scholastic tradition of mystical attachment to terms that have lost their currency. An arm of government cannot properly or meaningfully be described as sovereign when its power is subservient to the rules of another entity. This is so or else,

---

[213] *Ibid.* at 878.
[214] Quoted *Ibid.*

the word "sovereignty" requires re-definition as no longer a reference to *summa potestatis.*

Sovereignty of parliament exists only when the legislature, itself, constitutes the constitution as under the first definitional approach discussed (supra) in Chapter 3. Where the constitution is the sort under the fourth (or even the second) definitional approach to the meaning of constitution, it is anterior and superior to all the other arms of government. In this way, it is supreme – merely delegating bits and pieces of sovereign state-power to particular arms of government including the legislature itself. Since these delegated powers are necessarily restricted, *ex-definitione*, it follows that any extravagation by the legislature can be constrained by the constitution; usually, through the courts. In the battle for supremacy, parliaments have sometimes even under written constitutions sought to assert sovereignty. However, in modern times, such challenges have usually failed.

In *Bribery Commissioners v. Ranasinghe*,[215] the Privy Council rejected the argument that a palpable, non-adherence to constitutional, law-making procedure could be saved by the simple expedient of producing the Speaker's certificate (of proper passage of such law). The argument usually made in England, that a mere procedural defect cannot annul the clear will of a sovereign Parliament,[216] was held to be applicable only where there is no supreme constitution deciding otherwise. A better way

---

[215] [1965] A.C. 172.

[216] Sir Ivor Jennings traces the English tradition in his, *The Law and the Constitution, op. cit.* at 137 to 192, esp. at 139 to 156.

of saying this is that the parliamentary power in such polity is, itself, constitutional. In fact, Sir Ivor explains that the English practice is not even based, as such, on the alleged sovereignty of parliament. It is rather based on the historical reason that the king (or queen) in parliament is the highest court of the land; higher, even than the judicial division of the House of Lords and higher than the King in Council (which since 1641, has no jurisdiction except outside England)[217]. Because it is a court of record, the Parliament Roll which is its record and contains all the enrolled "Acts" of Parliament, cannot, just as for other such records, be challenged by extraneous oral or written evidence, except for "error on its face."[218]

Nevertheless, in places where there is a written, supreme constitution, the courts have implied or enforced express provisions curtailing the plenitude of legislative power by reference to procedural limitations. In *Attorney-General (Bendel) v. Attorney-General (Federation)*,[219] the Nigerian Supreme Court annulled a money bill purportedly passed by the National Assembly through its "joint" finance committee without the bill having come back to the full Assembly for confirmation, contrary to the procedure laid down by the 1979 Constitution.

Perhaps, the most interesting demystification of the alleged "sovereignty" of

---

[217] *Ibid.*, 138.

[218] *Ibid.* 139. Various cases have been cited to support the general argument. See for e.g., *Case of Shipmoney* (1637) 3 St. Tr. 825; *The Prince's Case* (1606) 8 Co. Rep. 1a., *Ellen Street Estates v. Min. of Health*, [1934] 1 K.B. 590; etc.

[219] [1981] All N.L.R. 85 (Judgment from 110 to 292).

parliament happened in the Union of South Africa. The Union constitution of 1909 required a special (two-thirds) majority of both houses in a joint sitting before the section, which entrenched the franchise rights of certain blacks and colored voters could be amended. It also required an identical majority for any amendment of the section that entrenched this race-protector clause. In 1936, Parliament amended the franchise provision peripherally but using the requisite procedure. A native (black) voter challenged the amendment contending that ever since the Statute of Westminster, 1931, the Union Parliament could only act bi-camerally and thus, the amendment effected in a joint sitting was ultra-vires.

The Appellate Division of the South African Supreme Court accepted the government's response that, in fact, the Statute of Westminster had rather invested the Parliament with Supreme and unlimited sovereignty equal to that of the British Parliament and, thus, the courts were incompetent to question a duly promulgated and enrolled Act. In a rather rude ejaculation, the court declaimed that:

> It is obviously senseless to speak of an Act of a sovereign law-making body as ultra vires.[220]

About 14 years later, the government passed, by a simple majority of each House (sitting separately), another amendment to the entrenched franchise provision[221]. A colored (mulatto) voter named Harris challenged this

---

[220] *Ndlwana v. Hofmeyr* [1937] A.D. 229 at 237. See further, B.O. Nwabueze, "Judicial Review and Democratic Government," Chapt. X. in *Judicialism in Commonwealth Africa, op. cit.* 229 to 246, esp. at 236, *et. seq.*
[221] The Separate Representation of Voters Act, 1951.

breach and went further to request an overruling of the court's previous decision in *Ndlwana*. This time, the court agreed that the Act was ultra vires the constitution for to hold otherwise would be to allow the legislature:

> To deprive by a bare majority in each House sitting separately … rights which was solemnly safeguarded in the constitution of the country … previous decision was wrong …[222]

The government felt affronted and took a drastic step. By a bare majority (because it did not have the support of up to the requisite two-thirds of all members of both Houses of Parliament), it passed the "High Court of Parliament Act, 1952" and constituted the Parliament into the Highest court of the land with jurisdiction, solely to be activated by a Minister, to overrule any decision of the Supreme Court if it invalidated or denied the legal effect of any Act of Parliament.

Harris went back to court and this High Court of Parliament Act was, itself, also declared unconstitutional and void because, in substance, it would enable the parliament by different name, to amend the entrenched constitutional provisions other than as specified by the constitution[223]. Further, it held that the Act was void, amongst other things, for constituting an attempt to block individual access to judicial remedy (having restricted access only to a Minister). The court rejected the ingenious argument that so

---

[222] See, per Centlivres, C.J., *Harris v. Minister of the Interior* 1952 (2) S.A. 428 at 472.
[223] *Min. of Interior v. Harris* 1952 (4) S.A. 769.

long as no amendment was made to the entrenched provision itself, parliament was competent to make laws to reshape the hierarchy of courts by creating a new one such as the High Court of Parliament with final appellate powers. The view of Centlivres, C.J., was that although Parliament had such powers, nevertheless, it could not exercise it in such a way as to render the protection in the entrenched sections, meaningless:

> ... the authors of the constitution intended that those rights should be enforceable by the courts of law. They could never have intended to confer a right without a remedy. The remedy is indeed, part and parcel of the right.[224]

It was only after the Parliament in 1953 passed the Senate Act to pack the Senate with more members supportive of the ruling party, could the government muster the requisite two-thirds majority in a joint sitting of both Houses. The Parliament, with this special majority at a joint sitting, then proceeded to enact the "South Africa Act Amendment Act of 1956," which validated the nullified Act of 1951 to destroy the entrenched right of franchise for colored voters. Collins, a colored voter from the Cape of Good Hope, mounted a challenge but this time the court accepted the alteration.[225]

All these cases demonstrate supremacy of certain constitutions and, therefore, the absence of real "sovereignty" in parliaments

---

[224] *Ibid.*, 780 to 781.

[225] *Collins v. Minister of the Interior* 1957 (1) S.A. 428. This was by a ten-to-one decision of the court which had also been packed with more judges by the government majority in parliament.

where such constitutions exist. But it is noteworthy that even in the United Kingdom, as Sir Ivor Jennings has so convincingly argued, it is not entirely correct to say that "Parliament is Sovereign." Various institutions and ideas, including the European Union (through the European Court on Human rights), the common law, the laws of nature, commonsense, etc., all restrict parliamentary power. This takes us to the last sub-concept to be discussed at this stage.

LIMITED GOVERNMENT.

Any government that may have its will unenforced as a result of being tested and found wanting against a particular, predetermined, standard outside itself, is a limited government.

Limitation can come various ways. These include the two principal limitations: those imposed by the interpretive jurisdiction of the courts (so well used by Lord Coke, C.J.)[226] as well as those imposed by a written constitution (usually through the instrumentalities of separation of powers, judicial independence, federalism, checks, etc). Sometimes, it is clearly stated that a written constitution is supreme. Section 1 (1) of the [1979] 1993 Constitution of Nigeria provides, for example, that:

> This constitution *as amended by the Constitution (Suspension and Modification) Decree 1993 or any other Decree* is supreme and its provisions shall have binding

---

[226] See, for e.g., *Prohibitions del Roy* (1607) 12 Co. Rep. 63 (to King James 1, that the king cannot intervene in legal proceedings but must "speak his judgements" only through the mouths of his learned judges of the realm).

force on all authorities and persons throughout the Federal Republic of Nigeria.[227]

However, even when it does not so provide, it has usually been implied. Bold judges have often interpreted the mere existence of a written constitution as implying its supremacy. Chief Justice John Marshall of the United States' Supreme Court blazed this trail in the seminal judicial review case of *Marbury v. Madison*[228]. This has been brilliantly followed by various decisions from diverse jurisdictions. The Privy Council decision in *Liyanage v. R*[229] is in this genre.

For the purpose of effective and energetic governance, it is no doubt expedient to have an uninhibited government. However, the danger associated with giving absolute power to an individual or body of individuals is so great that a supreme, government- limiting, constitution with the slowness and weakness it necessarily imposes, remains preferable. Professor Charles McIlwain in his *Constitutionalism: Ancient and Modern* (1940),[230] has perceptively warned, and we agree, that limited government or

Constitutionalism suffers from the defects inherent in its own merits. Because it cannot do some evil it is precluded from doing some good. Shall we , then, forgo the good to prevent the evil, or shall we submit to the evil to secure the good? …

---

[227] The words I have emphasized have been inserted to the original by pt. B., s. 1 of Decree No. 107 of 1993.
[228] (1803) 1 Cranch. 137.
[229] *Supra.*
[230] Quoted by B.O. Nwabueze, *Ideas and Facts in Constitution Making, op. cit.* at 61.

it is amazing, and to many of us very alarming, to consider to what insufferable barbarities nation after nation today is showing a willingness to submit, for the recompense it thinks it is getting or hopes to get from an arbitrary government.[230]

To conclude this chapter, we should like to re-emphasize the point we advanced at the very beginning, that is, that in the theory of contents of constitutions, we must not confuse felicity for necessity. Just as the classificatory dualisms are merely to facilitate analysis of already existing constitutions, constitutional concepts merely suggest to us what, when contained in a constitution, may probably improve its object of liberty for the people, or naked power for its rulers. This means that the liberty-sensitive contents are only desirable but are not necessary for the existence of a constitution. They should be striven for and not merely imagined to exist; waiting for an apathetic citizenry to cuddle.

But as there are selectable liberty-sensitive or power-oriented variants of possible contents of a constitution, we suspect that there are neutral contents which must exist in every constitution whether expressly or by implication; regardless of whether or not the constitution in question is power-oriented or liberty-sensitive. Amongst these other sorts of content are, provisions on the location of sovereign power (regardless of how ethically or unconscionably exercised); on citizenship; and on the latent and patent provisions for evolutionary, devolutionary, and/or revolutionary change of the constitution.

We shall deal with the theory of change in the next chapter to examine how constitutions get sick or old and how they are resuscitated or die. Death can be by natural causes or the constitution will exit by violent means; by accidental crashes or at the hands of armed gangs.

5.   The Theory of Change.

Principles of constitutional dynamics and inertia are usually discussed in Nigerian jurisprudence under the title: "Legal Consequences of the Change of Government by Extra-Constitutional Means." There is a certain sort of denial and avoidance underlying this somewhat misleading heading. There is a latent refusal to admit that effective government implies the existence of a justifying constitution. In this chapter, we shall attempt to isolate the limitedness of scope caused by this fallacious foundation. In trying to rectify the title, we shall offer what we hope will be sufficient material for re-evaluating the current philosophical bases for teaching and understanding the legal consequences, which arise from any sort of constitutional change whatsoever.

The change of a constitution or of part of a constitution may be analyzed under three broad scenarios. In the first, the existing constitution may authorize its own change by means of stated, achievable, procedures. Alternatively, if the constitution has failed expressly to advert to the change required, the omission is, by the interpretive jurisdiction of the courts, implied into it. The second scenario is when there is transfer or transmission of the entire powers of government as well as for constitution making to another authority. The new authority may continue under the constitutional provisions inherited. But it has latent or implicit competence to change it (with or without reference to the procedure stipulated by the previous wielder of constituent power). The third scenario is when either expressly or by the sheer incompatibility of certain types of change to the extant constitution, the sort of transformation that is forbidden during its continuance is, nevertheless, effected.

The first scenario is what Professor H.L.A. Hart has described in his "Self-Referring Laws." It also embraces the doctrine of "necessity" of which Professor B.O. Nwabueze is so manifestly fond. The second is devolutionary change and the third is change that most constitutional jurists, especially in the Nigerian academia, would refer to as "extra-constitutional." Logically speaking, "extra-constitutional" change of government is a quite incomprehensible conceptual construction. If the constitution that forbids the change is still valid and subsisting, the change is simply unconstitutional rather than extra-constitutional. It is illegal and not effective[1]. If, however, the pre-existing

---

[1] An example is the successful secession of the "Republic of Biafra" for some 30 months. Factually, there was an effective change of the Eastern Regional government into the government of Biafra by means not stipulated nor acceptable under the prevailing military constitution, to wit, Constitution (Suspension and Modification) Decree No. 1 of 1966. But because Decree No. 1 of 1966 survived throughout the period of this rebellion, immediately it regained control of the rebel enclave, the legal regime, laws, courts, etc., of the Republic of Biafra was nullified and avoided as being totally unconstitutional. See the Supreme Court decisions which even discountenanced the attempt by the Administrator of East Central State by Edict to validate some judicial decisions from the rebel enclave: *Ifegbu v. Ukaefi* (1971) 1 E.C.S.L.R. 184; *Akpati v. Obiechina (Odua of Akiri)* (suit no. SC. 138/1971) (see relevant commentary in Sunday Renaissance of 4 March, 1973) etc. I am grateful to Prof. Gaius Ezejiofor, S.A.N., for these

constitution has effectively been destroyed by the phenomenological fact of unauthorized change, it becomes naive and illogical to judge this change against the dictates of the now dead constitution. The only constitution upon which legality or illegality, constitutionality or unconstitutionality, can now be sensibly tested is the current, "prevailing, effective, framework of government" that has now been ushered in. When judged by this new constitution (written or unwritten), the so-called 'extra-constitutional change' is, rather, the very first exercise of constituent power by the new regime. In this sense, it is a change effected by constitutional, rather than, "unconstitutional" (or even "extra-constitutional") means. The change is constitutional according to the effective, subsisting, validated, new order.

This interpretive model is, by no means, uncontroversial. It is important, therefore, to give an account of the more commonly held views, which appear to us to be quite uncoordinated, confused, confusing, irrational and contradictory. Before this, one vital observation must be made. The fundamental basis for the opposing perspectives has to be understood. The traditional treatment of the topic proceeds on the premise that change factually occurs in any of the three scenarios. Our thesis has a different departure point. It acknowledges the factual differences in the analytical nature of the various scenarios but accepts "true" change as occurring only in the third (or last) one. Change occurs in the

---

references. See his, "Constitutionality of the Judicial Acts (Validation) Edict (E.C.S.)" (1976) 1 Nig. J.R. at 1 and 2, fns. 7 and 8.

second only if the old constitution is deliberately, thereafter, altered contrary to its own express stipulations.

Permissible 'change' under a pre-existing (but yet extant) constitution may be evolutionary or devolutionary. Real change — the sort not envisaged by, or more appropriately speaking, the sort not acceptable to, the overthrown constitution, is neither evolutionary nor devolutionary. It is, rather, revolutionary in nature. This is the aspect of the constitutional theory of change with which much of the literature is pre-occupied. It is only a third of the large vista of knowledge unwittingly disregarded by the continued Nigerian practice of limiting the study to "extra-constitutional" change.[2] We propose now to trace the outlines of our three-tier conceptual framework. We start with evolutionary change, touch on the devolutionary kind, before ending the examination with the most controversial and most disproportionately stressed type of constitutional change, that is, the revolutionary sort.

EVOLUTIONARY CHANGE.

In a manner of speaking, evolutionary "change" is really no change at all. Evolutionary change refers to modification effected according to the pre-ordained procedure stipulated by the constitution that is purportedly changed. One may argue that whenever modification has been effected in the

_____

[2] The National Universities Commission (NUC) is the regulatory body for all Nigerian Universities (whether private, state or federal). The NUC inspired curriculum for 1st semester Constitutional Law specifies the topic in this way and this probably explains why there is such uniform error in the Nigerian academy.

erstwhile constitution, change has taken place such that it becomes futile to maintain the present sort of argument we now offer. This would be a valid criticism if the discourse were to be conducted on the superficial, rather than the ontological or foundational, plane of reasoning.

On the face of it, and apparently, there is change. There is change because, for example, in accordance with Decree 107 of 1993, which provides for amendment by any future decree, General Sani Abacha was entitled to change the composition of the Provisional Ruling Council (PRC) to exclude its four civilian members. On the face of it, by this exclusion, Decree 107 (the constitution) has been changed. By this (apparent) modification, the PRC that used to have a mixed composition of military and civilian personnel, now only has a completely military membership. Superficially, therefore, change has been effected.

Professor Alf Ross[3] describes this superficial conclusion (although imperfectly), as an "alegal" phenomenon in the nature of metaphysical and "magical" logic rather than based on practical and real reasoning. His point is this. Since the so-called change of factual circumstance was *effected* and validated *by the pre-existent constitution through its amendment provisions*, it follows logically that, in real terms, the pre-existent constitutional regime is thereby still in place. By allowing for amendment, which could authorize re-composition of the PRC, that

---

[3] See fns. 83 to 91 and text, *et seq.* at Chapt. 3 (*supra*) as well as fn. 27 of Chapt. 2 (*supra*) including Prof. H.L.A. Hart's attempt at rapprochement.

constitution (Decree 107) could, from the onset, be said to have foreordained the change. After a period, we may then suppose, the constitution accepts that civilians in the PRC could be ejected therefrom. In other words, this apparent modification of the constitution is merely a crystallization of what it has always been.

To properly appreciate the point, one has to discard the prevalent notion of what the term "constitution" means. It is, as we have pointed out elsewhere,[4] not merely the official document designated as such in any particular polity (as is the popular case nowadays). Rather, it is the effective framework of government existing at any given *punctum temporis* within the relevant polity under consideration. It may, indeed, correspond with the document popularly recognized as such, for example, as is substantially the case in the United States of America. However, it is more often the case that there is absence of congruence between the material popularly so-called and the abstract phenomenon which, in truth, actually is so.

When Dr. Olu Onagoruwa called a press conference, in late 1994, to denounce as illegitimate, some ten decrees that contained court-ouster-clauses, as the Federal Attorney General, he was an important civilian member of the PRC[5]. He and the other civilian members of

---

[4] R.A.C.E. Achara, *Meta-Constitutional Conceptions: Subjective Legitimacy in the Jurisprudence of June 12*, *op. cit.*, R.A.C.E. Achara, "Textual Fetishism and the Ambiguities of Constitutional Definition," *loc. cit.*

[5] See, s. 8 (2) (h) of the Constitution (Suspension and Modification) Decree No. 107 of 1993: "The Provisional Ruling Council shall consist of … (h) the Attorney-General of the Federation …" But see, A.B. Wali, J.S.C.,

the PRC were, thus, entitled to be present during the deliberations of the PRC at which:

Constitutional matters, including amendments of the constitution of the Federal Republic of Nigeria 1979 ..."[6]

were to be deliberated upon and determined. Surely, the excision of paragraphs (h) (i) (j) and (k) of section 8, subsection (2) of Decree 107 (which provide for civilian membership of the PRC), is a "constitutional matter" within the jurisdiction of the PRC. It is not the sole prerogative of General Sani Abacha to so decide (if the mere text of Decree 107 was the sole proof of what the constitution in Nigeria was, at that time). Even in the deliberations to exclude them, the civilians should have been invited to participate. In fact, we were not. Actually, 'the rubber-stamp' military members of the PRC were, themselves, not even privy to this unilateral decision of General Abacha. They probably heard it over the news media same as other Nigerians. The question that arises then, is this: "In the absence of express constitutional authority to recompose the PRC, was General Sani Abacha's unilateral but *effective* decision in this direction, constitutionally valid? In other words, had the pre-existing provisions of section 8(2) (h) to (k) of the 1993 military constitution been validly changed?" Again, we would say "yes." Just as no pre-existing constitutional

---

in *A.G. (Fedn.) v. Guardian Newspapers* [1999] 5 S.C.N.J. 324 at 387: "The ... Attorney-General ... is not a member of the ..." [PRC]. This unfortunately misleads. At the [non-relevant] time of the judgement on 28 May, 1999, the A.G. "is" not a member of the PRC. But he "was" surely so at the time of the press conference.

[6] *Ibid.*, at s. 10 (1) (b).

provision authorized his making of Decree 107, so is it unnecessary, in respect of such evolutionary change, for Abacha to obtain prior express authorization. The authority to amend is by the doctrine of necessity built into the unwritten constitution of force by which Abacha's administration is truly powered. Decree 107 of 1993 is merely the expressed and highly flexible portion of this abstract constitution.

Evolutionary change is most starkly demonstrated by the constitutional alterations effected in Nigeria under colonial domination. The Orders-in-Council and Letters Patent, etc.[7] that gave birth to the so-called Lugard's Constitution of 1914 was issued under no pre-existing Nigerian constitution. The simple reason being that prior to this time,[8] there was no single state-entity known as Nigeria. Amalgamation of the Colony and Protectorate of Southern Nigeria with the Protectorate of Northern Nigeria was accomplished under the constitution of 1914. The consequent creation of the Colony and Protectorate of Nigeria was the progenitor of the corporate state-entity, which has metamorphosed through several shapes

---

[7] Ewelukwa identifies them as six: Letters Patent of 29 November, 1913, Royal Instructions of same date, the Nigerian Protectorate Order in Council, 1913, The Colony of Nigeria Boundaries Order in Council, The Nigeria Council Order in Council and the Royal Instructions to the Protectorate dated 19 November, 1913. See, Ewelukwa *op. cit.*, at 99. The Nigeria (Privy Council, Appeals) Order in Council of 1917 seems to refer to the 5th as the "Nigeria Order in Council, 1913." This constitutional document made on 22 November, 1913, and amended on 10 August, 1914, set up the first deliberative/partially-legislative organ for Nigeria known as the "Nigeria Council."

[8] 1 January 1914.

and nomenclature to its present appellation in 1999 as the Federal Republic of Nigeria[9].

But that is not the significant point we wish here to highlight. Strictly speaking, "Lugard's Constitution of 1914," remained unchanged despite its ostensible modifications by "Clifford's Constitution of 1922," Richard's of 1946, Macpherson's of 1951, "Lyttleton's Constitution of 1954" up to and including Governor Robertson's "Independence Constitution of 1960." This conclusion derives from the fact that each successive "constitution" was brought about under the amendment authority of the previous one as well as the implied constitutional authority of the Westminster Parliament to overrule its or the Crown's previous legislative positions. This is why Walter Bagehot's writing as far back as 1867[9a] must retain its picturesque poignancy and piquant purity to the inverted effect that:

> An ancient and ever-altering constitution is like an old man who still wears with attached fondness clothes in the fashion of his youth; what you see of him is the same; what you do not see is wholly altered.[10]

---

[9] See, the instructive maps indicating the changing boundaries of Nigeria since 1955 by Martin Dent, "Federalism in Africa, with special reference to Nigeria" in Murray Forsyth, ed., *Federalism and Nationalism* (Leicester and London: Leicester University Press, 1989) at 171.

[9a] Walter Bagehot, *The English Constitution* (1867; Oxford: Oxford University Press, 1928) 1.

[10] *Ibid.*, quoted in Geoffrey Marshall and Graeme C. Moodie, *Some Problems of the Constitution*, in Prof. W.A. Robson, series ed., *Politics* (London: Hutchinson & Co. (Publishers) Ltd., 1959 and 1961) at 13.

Since 1843, at least, the Westminster Parliament has sought and in fact achieved control of the Crown's prerogative to directly rule its empire beyond the seas. This has been done mainly through the instrumentality of various "Foreign Jurisdiction Acts"[11]. The Foreign Jurisdiction Acts of 1890 and 1913 were, by virtue of currency, the relevant ones applicable to Nigeria as statutes of general application in force by 1 January 1900, and later, by local adaptation[12].

The Foreign Jurisdiction Act recognizes the peculiar manner by which the Crown legislates for these foreign possessions and dependencies but insists that where an Act of Parliament covers the same field, the legislative instruments of the Crown must yield, to the extent of their inconsistency (but not otherwise), to the relevant Act of Parliament[13]. However, the Crown also gained. Although subjected to the Parliament, in other respects, its instruments of foreign governance was promoted in status to the level of Acts of Parliament:

> Every Order in Council made in pursuance of this Act shall be laid before both Houses of Parliament forthwith after it is made, if Parliament be then in session, and if not, forthwith after the commencement of the then next session of

---

[11] F.J.A. of 1843 (as amended in 1865 and 1866), F.J.A. of 1875 and of 1878 as well as that of 1890 (as amended in 1913).

[12] See, 53 & 54 vict. c. 37 in Donald Kingdon, Att. Gen. of Nig., *The Laws of Nigeria vol. IV of 1923* (Lagos: Government Printer, 1923). See also, "The British Settlements Act, 1887" 50 & 51 Vict. c. 54, *Ibid.* at 104 to 106.

[13] S. 12 (1) of the F.J.A., 1890.

Parliament, *and shall have effect as if it was enacted in this Act.*[14]

Acting under the Foreign Jurisdiction Acts, the King or Queen in Council is empowered to:

...revoke or vary any Order in council made in pursuance of this Act.[15]

Therefore, even if no amendment provisions were contained in the Orders in Council, Letters Patent and/or Royal Instructions by which the Crown (and its Privy Council) imposes constitutions for Nigeria, nevertheless, it would remain within the Crown's competence to effect such change relying on the omnibus authorization provided by the Foreign Jurisdiction Acts of 1890 and 1913.

However, the Crown has not left the matter only to implication. It has gone one step further and embedded its amendment authority in each of the constitutions it has made during its colonial rule of Nigeria. For example, "The Nigeria (Legislative Council) Order in Council of 1922"[16] has made it clear that as respects the old "Lugard's Constitution" of 1914:

From the date of coming into operation of this Order the above recited Orders in Council, dated the Twenty-second day of November, 1913, and the Tenth day of August, 1914, shall be revoked, without prejudice to anything lawfully done thereunder, and thereupon the Nigeria Council shall cease to exist.[17]

---

[14] See, s. 11 *Ibid.* (the emphasis is mine)
[15] *Ibid.*, at s. 10.
[16] As amended by Ordinances for the Protectorate of Nigeria Royal Order in Council Gazette of 16 May 1928.
[17] Ord. XXXIX (39), *Ibid.*

After effectively killing its predecessor, the new constitution (popularly known as Governor "Clifford's Constitution") delivers the murder weapon to the maker of its successor-constitution:

His Majesty may from time to time revoke, alter, add to, or amend this order ..."[18]

The King in Council therefore made Richard's Constitution of 1946 under the "self-referring" authority of its predecessor of 1922.

A very interesting example of the evolutionary model is "The Nigeria (Constitution) Order in Council, 1951."[19] Made by the "The King's Most Excellent Majesty in Council" sitting "at the court at Windsor" Palace on "the 29th day of June, 1951," the preamble recites with almost disdainful arrogance the facility by which the British monarch, thousands of kilometers away from Nigeria, could simply change the pre-existent constitution with no other formality than the flourish of a pen-stroke in the presence of his attendants of the Privy Council:

Whereas by the Nigeria (Legislative Council) Orders in Council, 1946 to 1949, there is established a legislative council in and for the Colony and Protectorate of Nigeria, and the Cameroons under United Kingdom trusteeship (which territories are hereinafter together referred to as "Nigeria"):

... ...

---

[18] Ord. XL (40), *Ibid.*
[19] Popularly called "Macpherson's Constitution" of 1951.

And whereas *it is expedient to make other provision for the matters aforesaid and generally for the government of Nigeria:*
Now, therefore, His Majesty, by virtue and in exercise of the powers in that behalf by the Foreign Jurisdiction Act, 1890 ... or otherwise in His Majesty vested, is pleased, by and with the advice of His Privy Council, to order, and it is hereby ordered, as follows.[20]

In rehearsing the authority for the constitution of 1951, the King in (Privy) Council made it clear that his constituent power is not to be taken as fettered by any powers therein granted:
His Majesty hereby reserves to Himself, His Heirs and successors power, with the advice of His or Their Privy Council to amend, add to or revoke this Order as to Him or Them shall seem fit.
(2) Nothing in this Order shall affect the power of His Majesty in Council to make laws from time to time for the peace, order and good government of Nigeria.[21]

In fact, not very long after the operationalization of this constitution, the King's "Heirs and Successors" felt called upon to, again, exercise the power of evolutionary change. The result was the 1954 Constitution, which was named after a Secretary of State (Lyttleton) in a capricious departure from the puerile pastime (at the Colonial and Foreign Offices) of nicknaming Nigerian "constitutions"

---

[20] *Ibid.*, the preambles (the emphasis is mine).
[21] See, Ord. 13, *Ibid.*

after British Colonial Governors. This process continued even up to the 1960 (Independence) Constitution[22]. It should have stopped then. At the transfer of not just governmental but also constituent power, the provisions of an old constitution apply only at the sufferance of the new regime emplaced. The new regime may comply with requirements precedent to amendment as specified by the inherited constitution. However, it is not so bound.

The colonialists failed to appreciate this principle of commonsense and thus enacted in the first schedule to the said Independence Constitution, that:

6. Nothing in this Act shall confer on any such legislatures as aforesaid[23] any power to repeal, amend or modify the constitutional provisions otherwise than in such manner as may be provided for in these provisions.

In this paragraph, the expression "the constitutional provisions" means this Act, any Order in Council made before the appointed day which revokes the Nigeria (Constitution) Orders in Council, 1954 to 1960, and any law, or instrument made under a law, of any such legislature as aforesaid made on or after that day which amends, modifies, re-enacts with or without amendment or modification, or makes different provision in lieu of any of the provisions of this Act, that Order

---

[22] The Nigeria Independence Act, 1960 (made on 29 July, 1960, but by s. 1 thereof, made to commence on 1 October, 1960).

[23] Referring, i.e. to the "sovereign" Parliament created for Nigeria as from 1 October, 1960, as well as those legislatures created for the regions.

in Council or any such law or instrument previously made.[24]

The Republican Constitution of 1963 clearly put paid to this petulant attempt by the British government to "rule" Nigeria "from the grave." Deliberately, and without reference to the Governor-General (as required by the 1960 Constitution), amendment was nevertheless made. This was effected by the signature of the, previously non-existent, "President" of Nigeria (whose name was entrenched[25] even before he signed[26] and gave life to the new constitution). We shall pause here and delay further discussion until our treatment of devolutionary change. It only remains to point out that after the devolutionary break in continuity of the 1963 Republican Constitution, the next phase of evolutionary constitutions ostensibly commenced on 1 August, 1966, when Gowon, allegedly on appointment by the pre-existing Supreme Military Council (SMC), purported to take over from Ironsi. This was, purportedly, under Ironsi's constitution of January 1966.[27]

The sociological proofs, give the lie to this claim. The change was rather revolutionary than evolutionary. As Ojukwu, military governor of the eastern group of provinces and member of

---

[24] Quoted from D.I.O. Ewelukwa, *Historical Introduction to Nigerian Constitution*, *op. cit.*, at 183 to 189, esp. at 188/189.

[25] Under s. 157 (1) of the (draft) 1963 Constitution.

[26] The President's assent was required by s. 62 (1) of the 1963 Constitution to validate Acts of Parliament (including, thus, the constitution itself). See, generally T.O. Elias, *Judicial Process in the Newer Commonwealth*, *op. cit.* at 139.

[27] Constitution (Suspension and Modification) Decree No. 1 of 1966.

the SMC, had insisted, Gowon was part of the coup d' etat that saw the death of Ironsi and no SMC had sat to appoint him as claimed. Continued use of the 1966 "Ironsi" constitution was, therefore, of peculiar constitutional import. Although the content was identical, its validating force was radically different. It was new wine but in the very same old and drab bottle.

The next stage of evolutionary re-continuation took place, in Nigerian constitutional history, when General Obasanjo was selected by his colleagues in the SMC to replace the assassinated head of state in February of 1976. There was a reasonably clear provision in the pre-existent military constitution[28] regarding competence to appoint the Head of the Federal Military Government. In section 8, subsection (d), the function of the SMC is shown to include:

> exclusive responsibility for the appointment of the Head of the Federal Military Government ...[29]

At the death of General Murtala Mohammed, his colleagues at the SMC were clearly empowered under section 6, sub-section (7)[30] to proceed to appoint a new helmsman. As required by the said 1975 constitution, Obasanjo presided in the "absence" of Mohammed and under the "rule of procedure" made by themselves as permitted by paragraph (b) of sub-section (7) aforesaid, the SMC exercised its exclusive authority and appointed the former Chief of

---

[28] Constitution (Basic Provisions) Decree No. 32 of 1975.
[29] *Ibid.*
[30] *Ibid.*

Staff[31] as the new Head of State without adversely tampering with the extant constitution.

This 1975 constitution is second to the longest-lasting autochthonous Nigerian constitution[32]. By the evolutionary principle we have set out above, it is easy to conclude that in so far as the 1979 Constitution (which is merely a schedule to a decree)[33] was made under its auspices, it continued in effect until 31 December, 1983, when General Buhari and his unsmiling confederates struck and forcefully emplaced a different constitution upon Nigeria[34]. This tenure from 29 July, 1975, up to 31 December, 1983, is five months less than Gowon's but surely surpasses Babangida's eight year-old constitution of 1985[35] as well as General Abacha's of 1993.

Even though General Abubakar claims to continue under the Abacha constitution of 1993, it is difficult to see how he can avoid the applicability of Kelsen's theory of discontinuity regarding his accession to office after Abacha's death. Decree 107 did not give responsibility for appointment of a new head of the Federal Military Government to anybody. Abacha, its author, did not contemplate the limits of mortality. Abubakar, again, was not the most senior military officer in the PRC at

---

[31] General Obasanjo.
[32] The very first being Gowon's 9 year-old, refurbished, Ironsi, constitution.
[33] The Constitution of the Federal Republic of Nigeria (Enactment) Decree No. 25 of 1978 (as variously amended by Decrees 26 of 1978; 104 and 105, of 1979).
[34] The Constitution (Suspension and Modification) Decree No. 1 of 1984.
[35] Constitution (Suspension and Modification) (Amendment) Decree No. 17 of 1985.

the time. General Useni was his senior in rank, age and experience.

Assumption of this authority by the PRC can be rationalized but it is rendered doubly dubious by the fact that the immediately preceding constitution of 1985 by Babangida, specifically altered the 1984 constitution (of Buhari) in order to include for the AFRC:[36]

> (d) exclusive responsibility for the appointment of the President, Commander-in-Chief of the Armed Forces ..."

Expressio unius personae est exclusio alterius. The very fact that Abacha carefully excised this provision when making Decree 107 leads to the conclusion that the 1993 Constitution was made mutually antagonistic with any power to appoint a Head of State other than Abacha. To make such appointment, therefore, one must first overthrow the old constitution with a new one. Decree 107 of 1993 was, by this reasoning, destroyed on 9 June 1998, when Abubakar was selected the new Head of State.[37] The text of Decree 107 has been, as it were, resuscitated by the 1998 unwritten constitution of Abubakar, billed to devolve power to a new civilian regime on 29 May 1999. This account does not carry much conviction. Having regard to the peculiarly, smooth transition, it rings a bit hollow. The better view is to import the doctrine of necessity. Necessity would imply into Abacha's constitution, a power in the PRC to do what they did (after that tyrant's demise without any express procedure for installing a replacement).

---

[36] Armed Forces Ruling Council (AFRC), the ultimate military authority in 1985 corresponding with the previous SMC and to the later PRC of the other Nigerian military regimes.

[37] A day after Gen. Abacha's death.

There are hardly any litigations concerning evolutionary change. This is not surprising. The holder(s) of constituent power remain substantially the same. However, a remarkable rejection of a claim to evolutionary succession was recorded by the decision in *Bashorun M.K.O. Abiola and anor. v. National Electoral Commission and anor*[38]. The questionable reasoning upon which the judgment is based, only marginally impugns the impressive and courageous use by Dolapo Akinsanya, J., of the hermeneutic jurisdiction of the courts. With this interpretive jurisdiction, Her Ladyship sought teleologically to arrive at a fair decision (regardless of legalistic obstacles placed by tyranny on the paths of justice).

General Ibrahim Badamasi Babangida (IBB) had promised to devolve constituent power to civilians by 27 August 1985. Chief Abiola won the Presidential election of 12 June 1993, instituted towards this object. IBB annulled the election by Decree No. 39 of 22 June 1993. Massive protests, local and international, put upon him unprecedented pressure to transfer power on the pre-ordained date. He signed Decree No. 61 of 1993[39] on 26 August 1993, with the intention of installing an unelected civilian government in the interim period until 1 April 1994, when a new election should have been conducted.

---

[38] Suit No: M/573/93 of 10 November, 1993, certified true copy (CTC) of the (unreported) judgment of the Lagos High Court is published by the Federal Ministry of Information and Culture in June 12 and the Future of Nigerian Democracy (Lagos: Fed. Ministry of Information and Culture, 1996) at 192 to 215.

[39] Interim Government (Basic Constitutional Provisions) Decree No. 61 of 1993.

Bashorun Abiola and his running mate challenged this "interim" constitution and Justice Dolapo Akinsanya of the Lagos High Court agreed with them that it was void. The main reasoning for its invalidity was stated to be IBB's loss of power to sign decrees by virtue of Decree No. 59 of same date, which purportedly, took effect by midnight of 25 August, 1993, therefore, preceding the signing of Decree 61 on 26 August, 1993. This is nonsense, of course. The justification for saying that Decree 59 took effect by the end of the preceding day[40] necessarily must show also that Decree 61 commenced the very same time.

In any event, *Abiola's case* may stand as a judicially truncated attempt at evolutionary change. The interim government was judicially declared unconstitutional, null and void. One week later, barely 75 days after Babangida's pretended devolution to Shonekan of (actually) evolutionary powers, a real change occurred. Abacha forcefully took over on 17 November 1993. Of course, we may safely ignore Abacha's claim of a merely evolutionary transfer of powers by virtue of Chief Shonekan's, allegedly, "voluntary" resignation. No perspicacious observer was fooled. Shonekan did not jump, obviously, he was pushed!

DEVOLUTIONARY CHANGE.

The judiciary has also had something to say about the nature of that constitutional "change," which took place on 16 January 1966. While General Gowon's successor government, in

---

[40] I.e., midnight of 25 August 1993. S. 2(3) of the Interpretation Act of 1964 says that "where an Enactment is expressed to come into force on a particular day, it shall be construed as coming into force immediately on the expiration of the previous day."

place at the time of the decision, contended that it and Ironsi's was revolutionary, the applicants who became appellants at the Supreme Court, although not using our exact terminology, claimed the change to be merely of the "evolutionary" kind. Chief Rotimi Williams, for the appellants, contended at the Supreme Court that power was voluntarily transferred by the constitutional government; not taken by the unelected military. Adetokunbo Ademola, C.J.N., who read the Supreme Court judgment in *Lakanmi*,[41] noted the unique nature of the facts.[42]

On 15 January 1966, at the onset of the coup d' etat led by Major Kaduna Nzeogwu, the Nigerian Prime Minister, Balewa, was missing and presumed dead. The President, Azikiwe, was abroad. The acting President, Nwafor Orizu, in consultation with the rump of the Prime Minister's Cabinet, invited the General Officer Commanding the Nigerian Army, Major-General Aguiyi-Ironsi, to take over power in order to more effectively bring his mutinous troops to order. The invitation was given on 16 January 1966, and the same night, General Aguiyi-Ironsi proclaimed himself "Supreme Commander;" instituting what he described as the "Federal Military Government" (with unlimited jurisdiction to rule the country by decrees).

In his epoch-making "acceptance" speech, Aguiyi-Ironsi seemed to go beyond his brief. He "accepted" the abdicated power not under the

---

[41] *E.O. Lakanmi and Kikelomo Ola v. The Att. Gen. (West)* S.C. 58/69 of 24 April, 1970 [1971] 1 U.I.L.R. (pt. I) 201 to 223.

[42] *Supra* at 215: "It is no gainsay that what happened in Nigeria in January 1966 is unprecedented in history. Never before, as far as I am aware, has a civilian government invited an army take-over ..."

extant 1963 Constitution, but under a fresh framework of his own machination, which merely incorporated parts of the 1963 Constitution deemed by him expedient:

> The Government of the Federation of Nigeria *having ceased to function*, the Nigerian Armed Forces have been invited to form an *interim* military Government for *the purpose of maintaining law and order and of maintaining essential services ...*"[43].

Nevertheless, he went off at a tangent to the effect that:

> This invitation has been accepted, and I General J.T.U. Aguiyi-Ironsi, the General Officer Commanding the Nigerian Army, have formally been *invested with authority as Head of the Federal Military Government*, and Supreme Commander of the Nigerian Forces.[43]

There appears, at least, some misapprehension of what was agreed. While the civilian government thought it was transferring interim power under an implied constitutional amendment occasioned by grave political necessity, General Ironsi accepted this power deliberately or under a misapprehension that it was devolutionary authority which he could, therefore, exercise contrary to any pre-existent procedural limitations enjoined by the erstwhile constitution.

The Supreme Court made a correct finding. The phenomenon of 16 January 1966 was of a novel sort. Elected civilians *voluntarily*

---

[43] Govt. Notice No. 148 of 1966, Nigerian Gazette, Lagos, 26 Jan., 1966, at 103. Quoted by Okay Achike, *Groundwork of Military Law and Military Rule in Nigeria* (Enugu: Fourth Dimension Publishers, 1978 and 1980) at 98 (Emphases, mine).

handed power to an unelected military leader. Professor Okay Achike[43a] denies the correctness of this finding. He submits the handover was precipitated by violence and satisfies the definitional requirements for a revolutionary change[44]. He adds, however, that:

> The hand-over of sovereignty by the president to the armed forces under the doctrine of necessity was permissible and supportable.[45]

The Attorney General for the Western Region of Nigeria, respondent in the appeal, was of a similar sentiment. He considered the change a revolutionary one and was confirmed in this view by the Supremacy Decree of 1970.[46]

With due respect, all three, were wrong. Although the court was right that the transfer was voluntary, it failed to take into account the difference between a voluntary transfer of merely government al power[46a] and one where the transferee accepts not just governmental, but also, constituent, power. The first is evolutionary, the second involves devolution. The first restricts the transferee to laid down constitutional limits in the extant constitution upon which transfer is made; the second, expressly or impliedly, acknowledges that the power-transferee, immediately upon

---

[43a] Later, Justice Okay Achike of the Supreme Court of Nigeria.

[44] Okay Achike, *op. cit.*, at 118 and 119.

[45] *Ibid.*, 119.

[46] See, preamble to the Federal Military Government (Supremacy and Enforcement of Powers) Decree No. 28 of 1970.

[46a] E.g., where a tired president hands over to the vice-president, or a constitutional monarch transfers power to her only son in order to retire.

transfer, acquires competence to continue within the framework of the old order or to ignore the pre-existing constitution in preference for a new one.

This is the point they all have missed. Another point missed by all except Professor Achike, is one arising from the peculiar facts of *Lakanmi*. Under the doctrine of necessity implied in every constitution, the court legalized the, otherwise unconstitutional, transfer of power. The principle is clear enough. Achike explains that "necessity may excuse an act which is otherwise unlawful."[47] The Supreme Court, through Ademola, C.J.N., relied on this principle to contend that:

> … It is wrong to expect that constitutions must make provisions for all emergencies.[48]

Rather, since:

> No constitution can anticipate all the different forms of phenomena which may beset a nation …[48]

in a case of emergency, the executive authority vested in the president, could be exercised by him:

> In the best interest of the country, acting under the doctrine of necessity[48]

Our point is this. Although quite correct in its statement of the principle of necessity, the Supreme Court sorely overlooked the vital issue of which person or authority, on this particular occasion, was competent to exercise it.

In *Phillip v. Eyre*[49], Willes, J., of the English Supreme Court of judicature, held that

---

[47] Okay Achike, *op. cit.*, 114.
[48] *Lakanmi's case (supra)*. Constitution, in this context, seems restricted only to the written kind.
[49] [1871] 6 L.R.Q.B. 16. Cited by Achike, *op. cit.*

the executive (a "Colonial" Governor) was the competent authority to put down an insurrection not anticipated by the constitution. But in *Attorney General for the Republic v. Mustafa Ibrahim of Kyrenia and ors.*,[50] the Supreme Court of Cyprus recognized this competence not in the executive, but in the legislative branch of government.

In *Lakanmi*, no one considered this matter. But they should have. Under the constitutional setting operative at the time, was such power as claimed by the (acting) President not one, which, if at all, should have been exercised by Parliament?[51] The absence of the Prime Minister, at least, would then not have occasioned the unnecessary disputation it aroused. Besides this, we are not as confident as the Supreme Court or, for that matter, Achike, in concluding that there was sufficient necessity to justify this very unorthodox course of conduct by the weak-kneed civilian politicians Nigeria was unfortunately saddled with in January 1966. There was absolutely no reason (except unwarranted notions of self-preservation) for the civilians to abdicate power to the military rather than simply *directing* them to crush the rebellion.

Achike's mistake lies, with the greatest respect, in his application of the theory of necessity to the events of the 15th rather than the 16th day of January 1966. On the 15th,

---

[50] [1964] Cyprus Law Reports 195.

[51] I contend that Parliament was the proper authority under the sort of regionalized and Parliamentary constitution Nigeria was then run. Prof. Achike adverted to this issue but unfortunately, failed to follow it through: "the question is not ... whether it is necessary to do it without the sanction of parliament." See, Achike, *op. cit.* 118.

Nzeogwu and his confederates had abducted the Prime Minister but loyal forces under Aguiyi-Ironsi retained substantial territorial control of the country (especially, the seat of the federal government in Lagos). The "extraordinary imminent emergency"[52], which was alleged to beset "the continued existence of the state"[52] was simply, therefore, just not there. Even if the uncertainties of sudden action of the 15th justified the level of cowardice exhibited by the civilian leaders, there was so much reassuring security in the presence of the loyal forces as to require, on the 16th, a little more intrepidity.

The foregoing analysis demonstrates how the *Lakanmi* case constitutes a singularly, complex constitutional problem. From their own viewpoint, while it may be accurate to say that the civilians effected by necessity a merely evolutionary modification of the 1963 Constitution, the military to which they handed power, saw the constitutional change in a devolutionary light. The military felt the civilians had transferred not just interim governmental powers but, also, under an entirely different *grundnorm* or constituent authority, power to make a new constitution if desired.

The analytical confusion was compounded by the immediate exercise of this constituent power. That same night of 16 January 1966, the military put a brake to the 1963 Constitution. Such parts of it that remained were, as shown by Decree 1 of 1966, merely dead letters energized afresh. In status therefore, the surviving portions was part of the military constitution then in place. It was as if Ironsi

---

[52] Achike, *Ibid.*, 118.

had extracted those portions of the 1963 Constitution, which he had not suspended or modified, and patiently copied them word for word in the new decree upon which the framework of his military government was expressed.[53]

Minute analysis should lead us to conclude that on 16 January 1966, a constitutionally bizarre phenomenon occurred. The incumbent administration voluntarily transferred governmental power in a way it thought was merely evolutionary. However, in the same transaction, the recipient accepted the constitutional modification in a totally different light. It took constituent power, which, in the circumstance, was not intended to be transferred along with governmental authority.

In taking what was not "voluntarily" given, the Ironsi acceptance could have amounted to a revolutionary act. The federal military government as well as Professors Achike, Elias and Ojo would then, have been right. However, they were wrong. The voluntary transfer of full governmental power (despite mental or other reservation for constituent authority) serves to attenuate the rough edges of forceful "revolution" into the middling hybrid of voluntary but misconceived "devolution."

This is not necessarily to say that 1966 presented an unprecedented constitutional occurrence. Apart from the space of three years which separated the autochthonous amendment of 1963 from the voluntary grant in October, 1960, there is little to distinguish the British

---

[53] I.e., The Constitution (Suspension and Modification) Decree No. 1 of 1966 (The first written military constitution of Nigeria).

grant of an independence constitution to Nigeria from the equally voluntary transfer of governmental power (within prescribed limits) to the military in 1966. As noted earlier in this chapter, the British had even expressly forbidden a change of the constitution except under the procedure they had pre-ordained in 1960.[54]

In 1963, despite acting for three years under the requirements of the 1960 Constitution, the new government deliberately disregarded it. This would ordinarily amount to a forceful divestment of constituent power without the agreement or volition of its previous holder. This might have amounted to revolutionary change; but the fact of voluntary transfer makes it incongruous to regard the change in revolutionary terms.

This is why, for analytical clarity, we have devised the concept of "devolutionary" constitutional change. In this, we have polished the vague term of "devolution," which in its more common usage signifies the autonomous, but not totally independent, hand-down of governmental responsibility to persons indigenous to a territory formerly governed by "foreigners." As Bentham[55] would, we have rather "fixed" the term than "expounded" it. It refers to a hand-down or handover by which a

---

[54] See, *supra*, text to fn. 24 or s. 6 of the 1st schd. to the 1960 Independence Constitution.

[55] See Jeremy Bentham, *Pannomial Fragments* in John Bowring, supt., *The Works of Jeremy Bentham* (Edinburgh, 1938-43) vol. VIII, at 247. Cited by H.L.A. Hart, *Essays on Bentham: Jurisprudence and Political Theory* (USA: Oxford University Press, 1982) 131 and 161. See also, R.A.C.E. Achara, *Meta-Constitutional Conceptions: Subjective Legitimacy in the Jurisprudence of June 12* (Enugu: Mike Lawrence Publishers, 1998) 35, fn. 54.

transferee government assumes constituent power from the merely governmental one originally allowed to it. It may assert this by an act of "unauthorized" but effective constitutional break.

REVOLUTIONARY CHANGE.

The most important attribute of evolutionary and devolutionary modification is the element of voluntary participation by the pre-existent holder of constituent power. Under evolution, (s)he retains constituent and governmental power. What appears a change is only apparent. Because it has already been authorized, the seeming modification is merely a self-reflexive expression of what the old constitution has always been. When, however, he transfer accepts not just the power to run government but, also, takes charge of the rules upon which this authority is to be determined, the original transfer itself will remain, nevertheless, voluntary and therefore, evdutionary[56]. This remains the case even where the transferee of constituent power exercises it in breach of the pre-stipulated procedural rules.

Unlike the previous two categories however, revolutionary change is characterized by effective appropriation of governmental and constituent authority by a new locus of power in forcible and direct opposition to the will

---

[56] The difference between mere governmental power and fully constituent authority seems analogous, in New Zealand, to "the Kawanatanga (government) ceded to the Crown by Art. 1" of The Treaty of Waitangi as opposed to "the tino rangatiratanga reserved to the chiefs by Art. 2." See Ian Brownlie, *Treaties and Indigenous Peoples* , F.M. Brookfield, ed. *The Robb Lectures* (New York, USA: Oxford Univ. Press. 1982) at 9, fn. 15.

of its previous holder. To determine the existence of revolutionary change, it is important first to isolate the erstwhile and current locations of constituent power. If a current holder of constituent power is found to have acquired it consistently with the previous, but apparently altered, state of legal affairs, no revolution has occurred regardless of what the textual evidence may be in theory. Let us give an example.

Logically, a part cannot be greater than the whole. Consequently, Babangida could not be greater than the Armed Forces Ruling Council (AFRC) of which he was only part. From 27 August 1989, up to 26 August 1993, however, Babangida unilaterally dissolved, re-composed and re-constituted the AFRC several times in circumstances that would have amounted to an undoubted coup d' etat if it had been by anyone else. In one instance, he created an entirely new ruling body called the National Defence and Security Council (NDSC) to supervise the also new but subordinate (civilian) executive body (the Transitional Council), set up, apparently, contrary to the pre-existent bodies specified by the 1985 constitution[57].

There were times when even the AFRC would be unilaterally dissolved by Babangida and not reconstituted for several days. Although all these took place contrary to the will of the AFRC, and although under the bare text of the 1985 constitution, the AFRC rather than Babangida was the wielder of constituent power,

---

[57] Constitution (Suspension and Modification) (Amendment) Decree No. 17 of 1985. The fact that a future decree was considered competent to override an earlier one, and seeing that IBB was solely invested with authority to sign (and make) decrees, it may credibly be argued that they were authorized by the said 1985 constitution.

the reality of the matter was different. Actually, at all material times, it was IBB, who solely wielded constituent power almost throughout his 8-year-tenure. Constitutional changes made during IBB's regime could therefore, not really be revolutionary unless effected contrary to his wishes by others.

Revolutionary change has a relatively stable definition. The *Shorter Oxford Dictionary* says that a revolution occurs when:

> There is an *overthrow* of an established government by those who was previously subject to it.[58]

Or, as Achike adds, still quoting the dictionary:

> Where there is a *forcible* substitution of a new ruler or form of government.[58]

This sort of definition has gained very influential judicial endorsement. In *State v. Dosso*,[59] Mohammed Munir, C.J., felt himself persuaded to concluded that:

> ... A change is, in law, a revolution if it annuls the constitution and the annulment is effective ... the revolution itself becomes a law-creating fact because thereafter its own legality is judged not by reference to the annulled constitution but by reference to its own success.[60]

Earlier in the same judgment, Munir, C.J. of the Supreme Court of Pakistan had been more explicit but less accurate in his analysis of what constitutes a revolution. He first explains, correctly in our submission, that:

---

[58] See, Achike, *op. cit.*, at 107, relying on the dictionary quotation by the Supreme Court in *Lakanmi's Case* (1971) 5 N.J.Q. at 151. (Emphases are mine.)
[59] [1958] P.L.D (S.C.) 633.
[60] *Ibid.* at 538–539.

> It sometimes happens … that a constitution and the national legal order under it are disrupted by *an abrupt political change not within the contemplation of the constitution.*[61]

"Any such change," he explains, "is called a revolution … " But, continuing, he confounds devolution with revolution:

> A revolution is generally associated with public tumult, mutiny, violence and bloodshed but from a juristic point of view the method by which and *the persons by whom a revolution is brought about is wholly immaterial.* The change may be attended by violence or it may be perfectly peaceful. It may take the form of a coup d' etat by a political adventurer or *it may be effected by persons already in public positions.* Equally irrelevant in law is the motive for a revolution, inasmuch as destruction of the constitutional structure may be prompted by a highly patriotic impulse or by the most sordid of ends.[62]

If this be the case, as supposed in *Uganda v. Commissioner of Prisons, Ex parte Matovu*[63] as well as in *Lakanmi*, then we lose the

---

[61] *Ibid.* My emphasis. "Constitution," here, must be taken as referring to the, now, dead one.

[62] *Ibid.*, my emphases. Extensively quoted by Achike, *op. cit.*, at 107 (and also at 108). I have underlined misleading portions of this, otherwise, unimpeachable dictum. A distinction must be drawn, although Munir, C.J., did not, between a revolutionary change and one which is merely devolutionary.

[63] [1966] E.A. 514.

opportunity of evading such incoherence as traditionally attends the conflation of voluntary and involuntary transfers of constituent authority. Application of identical terminology leads, sometimes, to absurd results. Separation, in our submission, opens new vistas of analytical rapprochement between the law in books and facts on the ground.

THE TWILIGHT ZONE.

Any problem of application is most likely to occur at the hybrid area between evolution and revolution. Consequential or evolutionary change of circumstance cannot really affect constituent authority. In addition, even where there is retention of the previous *modus operandi* for government, if the source of the current mode of operation is antagonistically opposed to the former, there is nonetheless, a change in real terms. This sort is revolutionary. When the facts bestraddle both evolutionary and revolutionary conditionalities however, it is difficult to apply the principles in the same way. This hybrid, which we call the devolutionary area, embodies all those circumstances where, although we see, for instance, the apparent retention of the source of constituent authority, we, nevertheless, have to admit the ludicrity of any suggestion that the consequential change effected, was ever contemplated under the previous constitution.

The dissolution of the Sudanese parliament is in this class. Nothing in the constitution could justify President El Bashir's action in this behalf when, in mid-December, 1999, to stave off the growing profile of his rival, Speaker Turabi, he declared a state of emergency and cordoned with troops, the parliament building. The President now rules almost alone but the power he exercises is not much different from what he was previously entitled to under the preexisting constitution. So, how should we constitutionally assess the action of December 1999? Was there a revolution by the president against himself? Alternatively, was there a mere evolutionary change since power has remained where it was, i.e., in the president?

In evolution, constituent power, i.e., the source of authority to make the constitution remains unchanged. Any future alteration is seen as a mere execution of what has originally been (patently of latently) authorized. Revolution is where the source of the previous constitution has been "overthrown" by a new constituent authority. This is so even where the new constituent authority chooses to retain the preexisting framework used for government. In devolution, however, the constituent authority is transferred in what, for lack of a more appropriate terminology, we should still call a "voluntary" process. However, the transfer is expressed, or implied to contain a limitation, substantive or procedural (mostly, procedural) to restrict the full exercise of this constituent power.

For example, the previous constitution may authorize a particular functionary to effect constitutional amendments provided he obtains the assent of a designated group or person. In this case, it would be difficult to assert, where that functionary unilaterally changes the constitution, that he has effected it in a revolutionary manner (in the strict connotative implications of that violence-impregnated terminology). It would, on the other hand, be most unconvincing to class such blatant disregard as evolutionary simply because the initial transfer of official authority was consensual and lacking in violence or force. It is this sort of hybrid that we refer to as devolution and unless it is called in aid, we submit that much of the theory of constitutional change will remain in analytical chaos.

The lack of discrimination between evolution, revolution and devolution, on one hand; as well as the conflation of revolutionary, evolutionary and devolutionary change on the other hand, appears to us, the principal reason why, for five centuries[64] at least, the legal consequences resulting from change of government by means not specifically or inferentially provided for by the, then, extant constitution, has continued to baffle political science and constitutional theory.

THE LEGAL CONSEQUENCE OF CHANGE.

Absolutely no extra-ordinary "legal" consequence attends the change of any constitution. This seems a startling conclusion but flickers down to a mere platitude when we consider the strict logic of the foregoing theoretical construct. This construct of thought, if we remember, excludes evolution and unexecuted devolution[65] from what may truly be

---

[64] Consider, *Bagot's Case* (1469) Y.B. 9 Edw. IV. Pasch., pl. 2. Cited by J.M. Finnis, "Revolutions and Continuity of Law," Chapt. III, A.W.B. Simpson, ed., *Oxford Essays in Jurisprudence* (2nd series), (Oxford: Oxford University Press, 1973 and 1978) 44 to 76, esp. at 46 and 47.

[65] By "unexecuted devolution," I refer to voluntary but restrictive transfer of constituent power, which although the transferee has implicit power to exercise in spite of the said restriction, he, nevertheless, applies according to the strict limitations of the

characterized as real constitutional change. To fully grasp the point, however, it is of the utmost importance that we should acutely understand the terms "legal" and "illegal."

It is by no means appropriate to assume, as many constitutional writers do that legality is a term that can independently stand away from the concept of a constitution. Contrary to the English jurisprudential tradition symbolized, amongst others, by Austin, Dicey, Wade and Bradley, an act cannot be unconstitutional and yet legal[66]. Rather, legality is hinged on constitutionality. An act is legal only when it is supported by the current constitution. It is illegal if the laws enacted within the authority of the extant constitutional order, forbid it.

Finnis may therefore, be seen as diving off from the wrong springboard when he joins "illegal" to the words: "change in the constitution"[67]. If it is illegal, it means the constitution which forbids and, thus, illegalizes the conduct is still effective and unchanged. If the constitution has been

---

previous grant. Before 1963, the constitutional devolution to the Nigerian nationalists in the 1960 Constitution remained an "unexecuted devolution" until it was "executed" as from 1 October, 1963, when there was a deliberate breach of the previously prescribed procedure for constitutional change.

[66] See for e.g., E.C.S. Wade and A.W. Bradley, *Constitutional and Administrative Law*, 10th ed. by A.W. Bradley with T. st. J.N. Bates and C.M.G. Himsworth (England: Longman Group U.K. Ltd., 1985 and 1986) at 25 (and also, para. 2 of 26): "Conduct may be unconstitutional without being illegal." I have criticized this view in my *Meta-Constitutional Conceptions…, op. cit.*, at 19 to 32.

[67] J.M. Finnis, "Revolutions and Continuity of Law," *loc. cit.* at 44: "this theory asserts that every illegal change in the constitution of a state is a revolution …"

destroyed, it means it has been changed by another one. Consequently, the now dead constitution cannot, sensibly, be used to judge legality or illegality any more. The change is, naturally, consistent with the new constitution, which it has automatically created. In the circumstances, it cannot but be legal. However, because this conclusion automatically follows every successful change of a constitution, the term "legal" becomes superfluous as a descriptive adjective for such change. In other words, when we correctly use the term "change" in relation to the subsistence of a constitution, we err if we precede it with the word "illegal." We also commit a *faux pas* even if we (correctly) describe the change by adding the word "legal." The first is an inanity; the second, a platitude.

When constituent power remains in the same location, a merely factual "change" of conditions will obviously be "legal" if done in accordance with the implied or expressed terms of that constitution[68]. Similar short shrift may

---

[68] Consider, for instance, the amendment which obliterates the exclusive, original jurisdiction given to the Supreme Court over disputes between states and between the federal government and states (under s. 212 of the 1979 Constitution). Decree 1 of 1984 in schd. 2 substituted a new s. 212 which merely says that "The Supreme Court shall have such original jurisdiction as may be conferred upon it by law." In *The Att. Gen. (Anambra State) and 13 ors. v. The Att. Gen. of the Fedn. and 16 ors.* (SC 140/1993) (of 23/7/93) reported as appendix "A" xiii of June 12 and the Future of Nigerian Democracy, loc. cit., 119 to 191; [1993] 7 S.C.N.J. (pt. II) 245 to 303; the evolutionary amendment to restore the former jurisdiction was held valid except to say that a yet future amendment postponed its operationalization under the 1989 Constitution (which in the end, never took off at all even for one day).

be given to the legal consequences of revolutionary and (executed) devolutionary changes of a constitution. They are legal by the very success and effectiveness of the new legal order created. But for historians and other academics that wish to amuse themselves with impractical diversions,[69] such a change is contrary to the old legal order and, when judged by that deceased constitution, is illegal.

A clearer but, sadly, unorthodox way of expressing all this is that legally, a constitution never permits of its own change. What appears to be thus is only reflexive of what the constitution has always been. Change, real change, implies the total death of the old constitution. In that state, it cannot any longer regulate anything. It decides no legal parameters and assigns no enforceable perimeters. In that situation, it does not change, it dies. The whole subject is thus predetermined, *ex definitione*. The methodology is teleological rather than empirical or even rationalistic. The very concept of constitution imports legality to itself. If it is not legal, it is not, properly speaking, a constitution.

The problem in this subject arises from the popular but misleading practice of confounding "legality" and "constitutionality"

Section 232 of the 1999 Constitution now actualizes this restoration.

[69] Consider, J.M. Finnis, "Revolution and Continuity of Law," *loc. cit.*, at 72, heavily relying on the brilliant analysis by Eric Voegelin, *The Nature of the Law* (unpublished paper available at the Institut fur Politische Wissenschaft, University of Munich): "... Analytical jurisprudence is intrinsically subalternated either to history or to ethics or to both and cannot be an independent discipline, with a viewpoint of its own."

with what is *sui generis*, that is, "legitimacy." This conflation of concepts has led to a seemingly intractable problem. This is the problem of determining the "legal" status of governments put in place contrary to the specifications of a previously predominating framework of government.

The theories of discontinuity and of effectiveness are among the principal constituents of this definitional paradigm that:

1. Every new constitution creates new laws. No old law survives a true constitutional substitution or change. The very fact of *independent* survival of laws made by a previous 'sovereign' indicates, *ex definitione*, that the pre-existent constitution remains unchanged and only evolutionary "change" has taken place (within a framework envisioned by the yet subsisting constitution). This is the theory of discontinuity of constitutions. It signifies that by the creation of a new constitution, the old one and the legal order *necessarily* tied to it, pass away. Its principal champion is the oft-quoted Kelsen[70] but traces of its bases can be located farther down in history, at least, up to Hobbes[71].

---

[70] See for e.g., Hans Kelsen, *General Theory of Law and State*, Anders Wedberg, transl., (Cambridge, Mass.: H.U.P., 1949) (20th century legal philosophy series, vol. 1) *passim*; Hans Kelsen, *The Pure Theory of Law*, Max Knight, *transl.*, (Berkeley: Univ. of Calif. Press, 1967) *passim*.

[71] See for instance, Thomas Hobbes, *Leviathan* (1651; London: Everyman's Library, 1965) at 141: "When long use obtained the authority of the law, it is not the Length of Time that maketh the Authority, but the will of the Sovereign Signified in his silence."

2. Only one constitution can subsist at any one time within a given political territory. And, in such polity, the test for determining which it is amongst the various versions (written and unwritten) competing for recognition is the criterion of effectiveness.

This is the theory of effectiveness whose major champion is, again, Professor Hans Kelsen. However, even plebeians and other common masses of citizens who would but think and reason out the basis of political power must have laid out its foundations centuries earlier.

Plato introduces us to Pindar[72] the poet and his follower, the brash, arrogant, youth, Callicles,[73] as partisans of this theory which is bluntly represented under the catchphrase: "might is right"[74].

To be contrasted with the theory of discontinuity and of effectiveness are those of continuity and validity. Continuity simply avers that, normally, revolutionary change only involves a destruction of what Finnis describes

---

[72] In the mouth of Plato's historical character called Callicles, Pindar is quoted to the effect that: "Law ... makes might to be right doing violence with highest hand..." See, Robert M. Hutchins, Ed.-in-Chief, *Great Books of the Western World*, vol. 7, Plato, "Gorgias" in *The Dialogues of Plato,* Benjamin Jowett, transl., (Chicago: William Benton of Encylopaedia Brit., Inc., 1952) 252 to 294, esp. at 272.

[73] *Ibid.,* per Callicles at 271: "It is just for the better to have more than the worse, the more powerful than the weaker ... justice consists in the superior ruling over and having more than the inferior ..."

[74] See, for instance, J.M. Eekelaar, "Principles of Revolutionary Legality," *loc. cit.,* at 40: "... Crudely, the principle states that might, once established, ipso iure becomes right."

as rules of competence[75]. In other words, the rest of the old legal system subsists by its former authority and not by permission of the new. The only laws that find foundation from the new political rulers are the new rules of competence because:

> ... Revolutions of all sorts, disturbing only rules of competence, need not be regarded as disturbing any other rules of the system, since all these other rules can be regarded as based on rules of identification which the revolution may leave quite unaffected ...[76]

In this wise,

> Repeal of the power-conferring law (rule of competence) by virtue of which a given rule was created *need* have no effect on the rule so created: the continuing and present validity of the rule, after its creation, rests on the general principle..."[77]

And therefore,

> In this sense, the power-conferring law can be said to be `existing' and `in

---

[75] J.M. Finnis, "Revolutions and Continuity of Law," Chapt. III in A.W.B. Simpson, ed. *Oxford Essays in Jurisprudence, op. cit.*, at 64, 48, 59 and esp. 63: "... There is a general principle of the practical and theoretical understanding of law which can be formulated as follows: a law once validly brought into being, in accordance with criteria of validity then in force, remains valid until either it expires according to its own terms or terms implied at its creation, or it is repealed in accordance with conditions of repeal in force ..."

[76] *Ibid.*, 59.

[77] See fn. 75 of this chapt. for the general principle that a rule once created remains valid until repealed in accordance with its original, energizing authority or by the new one (emphasis in the original).

force' even if it is no longer `existing'
or `in force' in its `forward-looking
aspect'...[77]

Deriving some impetus from this dubious
construct of thought, many natural lawyers
(jurists and judges) have developed the theory
of validity to contrast the common-sense theory
of effectiveness. But this has not been as
successful a venture as the Socratic rubbishing
of the older version (where might is rendered,
simply, as right).

As recorded by Plato, Socrates demolished
the foundations of the Calliclean principle
using his famous method of leading questions in
cross-examination. However, this was possible
only because the earlier crude version of the
theory of effectiveness, instead of confining
itself within the realms of law, extravagated
somewhat into that of morals. Might may
actually create law but this does not justify
the assertion that it, also, signifies the
"right." Might may be represented in the
fundamental sphere as law but, surely, to say
also that might is right, is an error not
defensible even by the most provocative
positivist. Hans Kelsen's theory may therefore
be seen as a more refined theory. It cuts out
the Calliclean input of "right" (or morality)
and scientifically restricts itself to the
observable and logically deducible fact-
conditions. From this, Kelsen comes to the yet
to be assailed conclusion that might (or
effectiveness), in the end, creates
constitutions which, in turn, determine laws.

The attempt by modern naturalists to
subvert Kelsen as Socrates did (Gorgias and)
Callicles has been quite obviously, a
monumental failure. The Kelsenian common sense

is too evident to be assailed by any examples of experience. It may be confounded and coloured by appeals to ethics and morality but, in the end, such tactics will mislead no meticulous researcher. By carefully excising the stupid equation of "might," by Pindar, with "right," the rug is pulled from the feet of Kelsen's would-be mental-assassins. Nevertheless, this has not prevented attacks.

John Finnis builds upon Raz[78] and ends up with a complex construct of thought, which identifies the possibility of different sources of law-validity in the same polity at the same time[79]. He says, from this, that most previous laws will continue after a revolution and this continuation will rest not upon the authority of the revolutionaries but from the earlier, but now, overthrown authorities[79]. The deduction as more fully drawn by Eekelaar is that if such an independent source of existence of certain laws can be proved, there is no evidence to unsettle the strong possibility that other such laws continue to exist, which owe their lives to sources independent of the new holders of constituent power[80]. Logically, such independent laws may provide for and justify the court, as mediator between society and government,[81] in

---

[78] Joseph Raz, *The Concept of a Legal System: An Introduction to the Theory of Legal System* (Oxford: Clarendon Press, 1970) esp. at 103 to 108. See also, the 2nd ed. (1980).
[79] J.M. Finnis "Revolutions and Continuity of Law," *loc. cit.*, at 52, 62, 64 and 65.
[80] J.M. Eekelaar, "Principles of Revolutionary Legality," *loc. cit.*, 37 and 38: "… there seems to be no a priori ground for excluding the possibility that other principles, too, might have survived … such principles do exist and can be applied even to override the enacted law of an effective legal system."
[81] *Ibid.*, 29.

holding some revolutionary changes to be illegal[80].

In our *Meta-Constitutional Conceptions: Subjective Legitimacy in the Jurisprudence of June 12,*[82] we have tried, in some detail, to reveal the foundational errors of this sort of moralizing thesis. The major enterprise of the positivist jurist is to clearly separate questions of law from those of ethics, morality and such-like extraneous matter. This does not make the positivist less hostile to wicked, vicious, laws; nor, less sensitive to the desirability of overthrowing by any means (including through judicial pronouncements), the obnoxious consequences that result from such laws or constitutions. What is however at stake is observatory fidelity (and even notions of academic independence). The researcher with a positivist attitude merely insists, like the international journalist, for example, that although President Slobodan Milosevic of Yugoslavia is a beastly bully whose genocidal ethnic-cleansing of Kosovo[83] is as reprehensible as the cowardly murder of Mrs. Kudirat Abiola by Abacha's military dictatorship, nevertheless, it must still be conceded that so long as he retains control of (the Serbian and indeed) the entire machinery of Yugoslavian law-making and government, the laws, bad laws, he makes over the territory which includes Kosovo, retain the status of laws.

---

[82] Cited, *op. cit.*, esp. at Chapts. 3, 4 and 5 thereof.

[83] In response, NATO forces launched a massive air bombardment of several days starting from 23 March, 1999, against Yugoslavia (esp. the Serbian Capital at Belgrade) to force a stop to this bully's antics against the ethnic Albanian majority of Kosovo (a Yugoslavian Province).

The matter, we must admit, is largely definitional; the problem, principally semantic. If we adopt what we submit is the most compelling view of the matter, it is easy to agree with Kelsen. Law is based on the constitution and this is dependent on a meta-legal grundnorm, of efficacy. Validity in this sense is tested objectively. From this efficacious *grundnorm*, the moral content of the resultant constitution and law is an entirely separate subject. It is a laudable project to denounce bad laws, bad governments and bad constitutions. It may well be that arguments such as those advanced by naturalists, aid vitally in this endeavour. Nevertheless, the distinction must be properly understood. While for analysis, effectiveness is the tool; for advocacy and censorship, validity may be key. It is wrong, however, to conflate the two. Absurdity results from analyses based on subjective validity; much as crude, unacceptable, cynicism manifests with change-advocacy that restricts itself to the theory of effectiveness. Naturalists must realize that nothing brings legal science to a more laughable level than insistence on the existence of high-sounding nonsense. What Bentham calls "nonsense on stilts." Chief Abiola's self-declaration as President of Nigeria[84] may have been justified as a subjectively legitimate pseudo-legislation made by the symbol of the oppressed Nigerian masses inviting rebellion against continued bondage. But as the subsequent events showed (from his provocative detention by General Abacha, up to his death on 7 July, 1998, moments before he

---

[84] On 11 June, 1994, nearly one year after IBB's nullification of his election of 12 June, 1993.

was billed to be released by General Abubakar), this auto-declaration lacked effectiveness and was, clearly, never ever law.

This may be contrasted with General Sani Abacha's declaration on 18 November 1993 that he had taken over the absolute rulership of Nigeria the previous day. Because this declaration was effective, it became law and was concretized in Decree 107 (his "constitution") as well as other subsequent decrees made by him and edicts and byelaws made thereunder by his delegates[85]. Abiola, though elected, was ineffective in fact. While Abacha, a known villain without any legitimate claims to office was effective and thus empowered.

Of course, the natural lawyers may still insist that their definition of law does not depend on effectiveness. If this be the case, there is no other common ground remaining for reconciliation. We can only shake our heads at such dogmatic stubbornness and reflect that they, like the Americans, may continue to call "rugby" by the term "football" with no attendant loss of sleep to FIFA and the millions of (real) football fans all over the rest of humanity (outside the U.S.A.).

CONCLUSION.

Confusion remains in the application of the foregoing principles. However, this need not be so. Mere legal knowledge needs to be supplemented with sociological/political input to serve any useful ends in this highly volatile area of practical philosophy. It is possible, for instance, to justify the

---

[85] Military "Administrators" at the state level and civilian "Sole Administrators" at the local government level, respectively.

(erroneous) validity and continuity theories by reference to Salmond's ingenious explanation that law is not necessarily always coincident with fact. Valerie Kerruish quotes Salmond, that:

> ... Even to [purely factual] questions the law will, on occasion supply predetermined and authoritative answers. The law does not scruple, if need be, to say that the fact must be deemed to be such and such, whether it be so in truth or not.[86]

But she adds, too that:

> Law's truths take precedence over others, in the end, by the use of physical coercion.[87]

Perhaps, it is upon Salmond that Finnis[88] is able to draw the compelling, but meretricious, conclusion that an effective government may nevertheless remain an illegal one. For this, he reminds us of the Lancastrian kings from Henry IV to Henry VI who had (allegedly) usurped[89] the English throne from the true line of succession. When in 1461, the Yorkist King, Edward IV, seized the throne and restored the line of succession, Finnis reports that from that time in 1461:

---

[86] From the 12th ed. of 1966 by Fitzgerald. See, Valerie Kerruish, *Jurisprudence as Ideology*, Maureen Cain and Carol Smart, series eds. *Sociology of Law and Crime* (New York: Routledge, 1991) 124.

[87] *Ibid.*, 126.

[88] J.M. Finnis, *loc. cit.*, 46 and 47, esp. at 46.

[89] It is difficult to rationalize the justification for this highly negative attribution. If there was a usurpation by the Lancastrians, was there not also a usurpation by the Yorkists? After all, what authorized their ruling line except, in the end, they not being elected, superior force?

> ... The Lancastrian Kings ... were officially
> regarded as usurpers ... "[88]

Eight years later, he continues, a question
arose as to the validity of the laws made by
[one of] the said usurpers, and it was, with
apparent success, submitted by counsel in that
case,[90] that:

> It is necessary that the Realm should have
> a king under whose authority laws will be
> held and upheld, and though [Henry VI]
> ...was in power by usurpation, any judicial
> act done by him and touching Royal
> jurisdiction would be valid, and will bind
> the rightful king when the latter returned
> to power.[91]

By this, Finnis attempts, but fails, to
show up the illegality of the "usurper's" law.
He fails to take heed of Valerie Kerruish's
caveat that "law's truths take precedence ... in
the end, by the use of ... coercion." If this
aspect had been considered, Finnis would surely
have seen that it was upon the coercive
effectiveness of Edward IV's accession that
"retrospective" validity was given to the,
actually, "current" law which made "illegal,"
on grounds of usurpation, the formerly "legal"
actions of the Lancastrians. At the time Henry
VI was in effective control, counsel in *Bagot's
case* could not have seriously offered such a
legal argument. In any case, Finnis's attempt
is botched even by the full import of the
submission of the previously mentioned counsel.
Even while denigrating Henry as a usurper, he,
nevertheless, submits, "apparently with

---

[90] *Bagot's case (supra)*
[91] See, Finnis, *loc. cit.*, 46 and 47, esp., fn. 7.

success,"[92] that necessity sufficiently engrafts the quality of validity (more properly, "legality") on acts of this clearly effective ruler.

Quite apart from effectiveness, it would be shortsighted to assume that the theory of continuity is the reason for which counsel submitted, and the court accepted, this argument. If the laws of Henry VI could legally continue by their own independent force, this submission of counsel in *Bagot's case* would never have been necessary and would not have arisen in the first place. The doctrine of necessity, in this context, was called in aid to signify the implied consent of Edward IV to the "revival" of Henry's law. It was almost like an appeal, in the best traditions of advocatorial logic, that the courts should, as it were, agree that the relevant law of Henry VI, which would long have died by the natural logic of revolutionary change, should be supposed to have been resuscitated under the authority of the new sovereign.

Austin, quoting Hobbes, expresses this very brilliantly:

> Even though it sprung directly from another foundation or source, it is a positive law, or law strictly so called, by the institution of that present sovereign in the character of political superior. Or (borrowing the language of Hobbes) `The legislator is he, not by whose authority the law was first made, but by whose authority it continues to be law'.[93]

---

[92] *Ibid.*, fn. 6.
[93] John Austin, *Lectures on Jurisprudence* (Glashytten inn Taanus: Auvermann, 1972) at 193. Quoted by Jan-Erik

The prevailing judicial attitude to this matter has been one with Kelsen's exposition. But there has been a respectable body of judicial decisions and dicta, which seem supportive of validity (and secondarily, continuity). However, even exponents of the theory of validity would, on occasion, be found to espouse effectiveness as a necessary condition for their own theory.

Widespread confusion remains. Some clarity may come from a realization, now unappreciated by most validity exponents, that if a court *successfully* denies the constitutionality and thus the legality of a serving government, this does not indicate a valid subversion of the "effectiveness" thesis. Rather, what it shows is that other forces competing for constituent power (the one, the few or the many), as reflected through the courts, have continued to battle the incoming regime; rendering it ineffective.

The courts successfully carried this out in Nigeria when on 10 November 1993, Mrs. Justice Dolapo Akinsanya, J., of the Lagos High Court, declared[94] Chief Ernest Shonekan's Interim Government and its enabling Constitution,[95] unconstitutional, illegal, null and void for being ultra-vires General Babangida (who constituted same). Seven days later, as a result of the almost total loss of

---

Lane, *Constitutions and Political Theory* (Manchester and New York: Manchester University Press, 1996) at 49.
[94] In *Bashorun M.K.O. Abiola and Amb. Babagana Kingibe v. National Electoral Commission and the Attorney-General of the Federation* (unreported Suit No: M/573/93) C.T.C. of Judgment published in *June 12 and the Future of Nigerian Democracy, loc. cit.*, esp. at 214 and 215.
[95] Interim Government (Basic Constitutional Provisions) Decree No. 61 of 1993.

authority by that government, General Abacha, its Defence Secretary, struck and, *vi et armis,* overthrew it. But the courts was not as successful when, in *Lakanmi's case,*[96] it was suggested, not even that the military government of January, 1966, was unconstitutional; but something much milder, that its legislative competence was limited by the preceding civilian constitution.

Scrupulous enquiry will reveal not two but three tendencies in the judicial domain all with a link to Kelsen. As Dr. Okere's analysis shows,[97] some decisions accept and apply Kelsen's efficacy principle and these include: *State v. Dosso,*[98] *Uganda v. Commissioner for Prisons, Ex parte Matovu,*[99] and *Attorney General of the Republic (of Cyprus) v. Ibrahim Mustafa of Kyrenia.*[100] To these, we may add the Nigerian, Federal High Court, case of *J.O.*

---

[96] *Supra.*

[97] B. Obinna Okere, *Sovereignty in National and International Law (A Theoretical and Functional Analysis)* (MS) (Gone to Press), Chapt. VII, 218 to 273, esp at 258 and 259.

[98] *Supra.*

[99] *Supra.* But also fully reported by the judge himself in: Sir Udo Udoma, *History and the Law of the Constitution of Nigeria* (Lagos, Ibadan...Oxford: Malthouse Press Ltd., 1994) 267 to 307. The reader of this book should not feel offended by the almost tactless immodesty of the author "who at such an early age ... had manifested sound knowledge ... of Constitutional Law ..." Similar patience must be extended in the shocking disavowal of his colleagues of the Supreme Court some 24 years after he had fully assented without demur to their joint decision in *Lakanmi.*

[100] [1964] Cyprus L. Rep., 195. Cited by B.O. Nwabueze, *Ideas and Facts in Constitution Making* (The Morohundiya Lectures, 1st Series) (Ibadan ... Lagos: Spectrum Books Ltd., 1993) 25, fn. 58.

Esezoobo v. Provisional Ruling Council and ors.,[101] where Jinadu, J., considers that:

> There is no doubt that there was a revolution in this country on 17th November, 1993 ... the revolutionary regime ... has successfully established itself as both *de facto* and *de jure* regime under its constitution which is Decree No. 107 of 1993 ...[101]

Okere classifies another stream of decisions, exemplified by *Lakanmi and anor. v. Attorney General, (West)*,[102] as indicating an acceptance of the principle but without properly applying it to the facts. We wonder whether the Privy Council decision in *Madzimbamuto v. Lardner-Burke*[103] should not also fall within this class? Eekelaar properly reports that their Lordships did not, in that case, uphold the legality of the Rhodesian revolutionary government:

> But this was only because it thought that the violated constitutional order might yet respond to the artificial respiration then being applied to it by the British Government.[104]

In other words, the theory of effectiveness was acceptable to their Lordships but, on the facts, they misconceived the situation on ground in Ian Smith's Rhodesia. They thought the Unilateral Declaration of Independence (UDI) was still battling for success and was, as yet, ineffective. The local judges perceived

---

[101] (Unreported Suit No: FHC/L/640/95). Reviewed by Olisa Agbakoba and Sam Amadi in *Human Rights Newsletter*, vol. 1, No. 2 [1998] Jan – March, 18 to 20 esp. at 19.
[102] *Supra.*
[103] *Supra.*
[104] J.M. Eekelaar, *loc. cit.*, 22 and 23.

the situation more correctly. The revolutionaries were in firm control.

The last batch of cases indicates a rejection of Kelsen. Amongst these, *Madzimbamuto*,[105] on appeal to the Privy Council, is given as one example. We have stated our reservations as to its exclusion from the second category. Others which have been included here are *Jilani v. Government of Punjab*,[106] where Yacoob Ali, J., bristling with naturalist indignation, thundered against Kelsen's effectiveness theory:

> However effective the government or usurper may be, it does not within the national legal order, acquire legitimacy unless the courts recognize the government as de jure;"[107]

There are also in this class such cases as: *Sallah v. Attorney General of Ghana*;[108] *Bhutto v. Chief of Staff, Pakistan Army*;[109] and *Mitchell v. D.P.P.*[110]

As for the Grenadine case of *Mitchell* so it seems to us is *Bhutto*. In that case, rather than an outright rejection of effectiveness,

---

[105] *Supra.*

[106] Pak. L.D. [1972] S.C. 139, cited by Livy Uzoukwu, *Grundnorm of Nigeria* (Lagos and Orlu: Greg Groupe and Friends..., 1991), at 56 fn. 59.

[107] See quoted in Okere, *op. cit.*, at 262. But see also Uwaifo, J.S.C., in *A.G. (Fedn) v. Guardian* [1999] 5 S.C.N.J. 324 quoting "Yaqub Alli, J."

[108] [1970] Const. S.C. 8/70 of 29 April, 1970. Discussed extensively in S.K. Date-Bah, "Jurisprudence's Day in Court in Ghana" (1971) I.C.L.Q. vol. 20, pt. 2, 4th series of April, 1971, 315 to 323. Also see, T.O. Elias, *Judicial Process in the Newer Commonwealth* (Lagos: Univ. of Lagos Press, 1990) at 108, 109 and 111, n. 52.

[109] Cited by Dr. B. Obinna Okere, *op. cit.*, esp. at 265/266

[110] [1986] L.R.C. (Const.) 35. Cited by Okere, *Ibid.* esp. at 245, 255, 257, 259 and 266 (quoting Haynes, P.).

the court seemed perpetually to attempt a reconciliation of validity with effectiveness:

> … Making effectiveness … the sole condition or criterion of its legality, it excludes from consideration sociological factors of morality and justice which contribute to the acceptance or effectiveness of the new legal order.[111]

In the same way, it will be seen that Haynes, P., does not deny the necessity for effectiveness but requires the ethical input of validity. At pages 71 and 72 of the law report, he proffers the, somewhat ambiguous, theory that:

> For a revolutionary government to achieve *de jure* status, that is to become internally a legal and legitimate government, the following conditions should exist …

That is to say, in Okere's summarization, that:

> (a) The revolution was successful, there being no other rival; (b) its rule was effective; (c) the conformity and obedience of the populace was not mere tacit submission due to coercion or force; and (d) it must not appear that the regime was oppressive and undemocratic.[112]

The first and second conditions are for effectiveness. The third and fourth are not really different. They both refer to the validity principle. The most curious observation, probably not even realized by Haynes, P., is that despite his obviously erroneous inclination towards validity, his formulation cannot, as presently presented, be

---

[111] *Bhutto's case* (*supra*, fn. 109).
[112] See, Okere, *op. cit.*, 266.

faulted in any logical way. As far as the dictum is predicated on an assertion that what is being determined is not just legality but also legitimacy ("a legal *and legitimate* government"), he is right. The government requires both ingredients of effectiveness (for legality) and validity (for subjective legitimacy).

The foregoing shows that a proper appreciation of the subject requires a title less inhibiting than that in the NUC syllabus. Justice is better done when we discuss the broad vistas of the theory of change than the narrow confines of "legal consequences of the change of government by extra-constitutional means." Constitutional change involves a spectrum transcending the ROYGBIV of mere governmental change. It is with change of government that much constitutional change manifests. However, this is not always the case. In executed devolution as represented by the 1963 Constitution, the same government remained although the constitution itself was changed in a manner not permitted by the previous one. Similarly, we can easily conceive of situations where the government changes while the constitution remains intact.[113] For

---

[113] It is here that sense can be made of the notion that the court can legitimately pronounce on the legality and constitutionality of governmental change. The Constitutional Court of the Republic of Mali in July, 1997, felt competent, thus, to annul the 1st round of legislative elections held that month and rescheduled it to 12 August, 1997: reported by C.N.N. (a cable television broadcaster) in its "Worldview" programme of 11.44pm (Nigerian time), Mon., 21 July, 1997. The Supreme Court of Ukraine has similarly annulled for massive voter fraud the presidential run-off election of 21/11/04 to Sunday, 26/12/04. See, the sub-text on CNN, "World News" 6.30PM Nigerian time, 26 December 2004.

example, under the 1979 Constitution, Chief C.C. Onoh was in 1983 returned as elected Governor of Anambra State to unseat the government of Chief Jim Nwobodo who, thus, lost the mandate he and his government enjoyed from the 1979 elections.

No extra-ordinary change takes place in law for any alterations, whether governmental or not; and, whether based on the constitution or not. If the supposed change is authorized or implicitly covered by the pre-existent constitution, the legal position remains the same. There is in truth, no constitutional change. The laws of the old constitution remain. If there is actual change of the old constitution, what it means is that only the new sovereign's will becomes the referent for judging legality and illegality. The old constitution dies like a dodo. In other words, legality is the legality of the new regime and its constitution. This constitution necessarily validates or, to be more precise, legalizes the killing of the old constitution and the substitution of the new government.

The only problem arises in the determination of when the new government or constitution actually succeeds and attains the criterion of effectiveness required to justify the Kelsenian construct of thought. This, however, should not bother the legal academic quite as much as it should worry the sociologist and the political scientist.

6.   The Theory of Preponderant Force.

In this chapter, we propose to summarize the current epistemological state of Nigeria Constitutional Law. Here, we attempt to tie up the discrepant pieces of doctrine into a consistent conceptual whole. The string for this will be our theory of preponderant force. So, what, it may be asked, is this principle of preponderant force?

The term "preponderant force" is just what its name suggests, that is, the force, which preponderates over (or outweighs) others. We use it here, in relation to government of human states and such-like societies. In this respect, it implies force that preponderates over other existing forces contending for constituent and governmental power within any given polity. The unarticulated major premise is, therefore, an existence of contending forces.

Given that a constitution is the prevailing, effective, framework of government, our claim is that the person(s) or group(s) in whom preponderant force inheres at any given punctum temporis within the relevant polity essentially, determines its creation, use and regeneration. To understand this more clearly, it is helpful to appreciate the idea of government. Government is necessarily associational. It is meaningless to talk of government in relation to just one person. To analyze human government, human nature is a necessary analytic device.

The central human nature relevant to government may well be the general tendency of individuals to seek intercourse based on their own terms or desires. In the welter of multiplied wills and desires, society qua society, necessarily has to choose. The "choice" by society is based on effectiveness. The "corporate" will is the one which is powered through in spite of some but in alliance with others. However, its existence and effectuation may conceal but not repeal those others antagonistic to it.

The "corporate" will is defined by time and space but its corporatist identity is a somewhat nebulous conception. Sometimes, the majority gladly adopts the will powered through. At other times, however, it is imposed despite disapproval. The former is the corporate will in both lexical and constitutional terms. The latter is the "corporate will" only in the artificial eyes of constitutional jurisprudence as well as domestic and international law. This may explain why, for example, the idiosyncratic excesses of a Saddam Hussein are attributed to the entire state of Iraq. This has led various times to severe economic and physical onslaught upon that unfortunate country affecting millions of innocent citizens. Yet, many of the victims are those deeply, but silently, opposed to Saddam's insensitive framework of government.

The analogy also holds true for Slobodan Milosevic and the Federal Republic of Yugoslavia. The NATO military bombardment, since March 1999, has occasioned grave damage and pathetic loss of lives despite the opposition of many of his own Serbian-Yugoslavs to Slobodan's murderous policy of ethnically cleansing the Albanian-Yugoslavs from Kosovo. The NATO bombings were designed to stop the ethnic cleansing at this province, hitherto dominated in population by the ethnic Albanians of Yugoslavia.

The opposition in Iraq; Vuk Draskovic and his defiant progressives in Serbian Yugoslavia; Chief Moshood Abiola in General Abacha's Nigeria; all these had their notions of how government in their respective countries should have been run. However, as long as preponderant force lay elsewhere, the framework each preferred, effective, perhaps, in the limited space of their homes, businesses and parties, could not, at the relevant times, be seen as the constitution in the larger space of their respective polities. This was because preponderant force lay elsewhere.

Constitutional Law cannot fully be taught or studied without appreciation of this underlying doctrine. While a politico-legal system consists of three planes,[1] a constitution should properly be seen as consisting of two: the macro and the micro planes. The first is the foundational one, which, as it were, gives the imprimatur or authority; and the second is the super-structural edifice that constitutes the actual, concrete, framework by which government is carried on. The principle of preponderant force is concerned with the more important sub-structural plane where the very authority (constituent power) to issue the lower-level framework of government, is located.

Lack of a clear appreciation of this discrimination has engendered much confusion of thought in the field of Constitutional Law. Nevertheless, a brief history of the written and unwritten constitutions of Nigeria since her amalgamation in 1914 will clearly

---

[1] See Table 1 at Chapt. 2 (*supra*).

demonstrate our point. The framework (usually documentary) is based on the preponderant force (constituent power) at the macro-level, which normally is unwritten. Both are inextricably interwoven. A written framework of government is an imponderable collection of very insignificant pieces of paper whenever the authority by which it is operated is supplanted by a new constituent power. It becomes, then, like any other document; commanding its almost sacred significance only when it is predicated on preponderant force.

The local chieftains of the various tribes now comprised in Nigeria had their own frameworks of government before British colonization in the latter part of the 19th Century. Those constitutions, unwritten constitutions, had substance when preponderant force resided in the local potentates. Immediately the superiority of English gun-powder was established over bare, native courage and prowess, these unwritten, "chiefly" constitutions were denuded of their supremacy and underlying force. Such structures as were retained became, in fact, merely part of the new imperialist constitution or framework of government for the relevant locale at the given point in time. This abiding power, based on the preponderant force of the British government, authorized and fuelled the, otherwise, worthless pieces of paper called the Lugard's Constitution of 1914, Clifford's of 1922, Richard's of 1946, Macpherson's of 1951, Lyttleton's of 1954 and the Robertson Independence constitution of 1960.

It was, ostensibly, only some months before 1 October 1963, that the political elite in Nigeria acquired constituent, as opposed to mere governmental, power. At the one-day-conference in which they realized this latent ability in themselves, they determined to defy the British-authorized 1960 Constitution with effect from 1 October 1963, and successfully did so. The Nigerian constitution thus depended, for the first time, on the authority of a local person or group. When thus the British lost constituent power, it would have been futile for any court or other authority to continue to recognize the 1960 Constitution.

After the abdication of 16 January 1966, but before the military constitution of General Aguiyi-Ironsi was made (with effect from 17 January, 1966), did the country exist in a constitutional vacuum? Even if it did (which is not conceded), what authorized Aguiyi-Ironsi to draw up that framework of government? It is the analytical discrimination between preponderant force and the actual framework of government thereafter authorized by it that most logically answers these questions. Otherwise, we become committed to inconsistent answers. With our traditional dogma as to the supremacy of the constitution, we may be compelled to accept the false doctrine that the Republican constitution of 1963 remained the supreme law in Nigeria. Alternatively, we may be led to the strange conclusion that no constitution existed between the abdication date and the actual date, weeks later, when the Constitution (Suspension and Modification) Decree No. 1 of 1966 was signed into law and promulgated. The American model of Constitutional Law teaches that laws are based on the constitution and not vice-versa. Could it then be, that for this interval of weeks, Nigeria was run without laws?

We think not. Contrary to the high sounding rhetoric of Thomas Paine, a legal system cannot exist without a constitution. In fact, more than one constitution cannot exist in a single legal system at any one time. Nevertheless, this is not to imply the absence of competing locations of power. The difference is that by definition, only the framework of government backed by preponderant force constitutes the "constitution." The others are just challengers. The one, which, from the turbulence of the unregulated political plane, supplants the current champion, will simply take over. This takeover retains its essential character whether or not the new framework adopted is the very same one used by the old authority.

This, in part, explains the constitutional position after the assassination of General Aguiyi-Ironsi on 29 July 1966. Even though General Gowon purported to resuscitate, and govern under, Aguiyi-Ironsi's first framework: Decree No. 1, the true position, nevertheless, was that that military constitution had become different. Its source of authority was no longer General Ironsi but General Gowon.

Gowon's constitution could not properly be said to have continued in operation immediately it became clear that Murtala Mohammed's junta had successfully acquired preponderant force. This remains so regardless of the fact that the written framework promulgated by General Mohammed was made weeks after the coup d' etat of 29 July 1975. All these demonstrate the inextricable, conceptual bond between the actual framework popularly called the constitution and the abstract political fact by which its authority is grounded. Until the written Decree No. 32 of 1975, Murtala governed under an unwritten constitution that simply ordained obedience to whatever is implied or expressed as the will of the Supreme Military Council.

Similarly, preponderant force explains the nature of the 1979 "civilian" constitution. However, the explanation here introduces a little more complexity. To be able, properly, to understand the correct constitutional position in this area, the traditional doctrines and long-ingrained orthodoxies have to be unlearnt or, at least, sidelined.

Because the macro and micro planes are intertwined, the identity of a constitutional framework must be read along with its foundational authority. Because the Murtala/Obasanjo regime wielded the preponderant force upon which the 1979 Constitution was made and operationalized, it follows that despite the Presidency of Alhaji Shehu Shagari under it, it yet remained the constitution of the military. However, although this conclusion would neatly follow our earlier stated premise, we are bound, nevertheless, to reveal a factual difficulty in this analysis.

It is difficult to deny that after Obasanjo's retirement and the military retreat to barracks, civilian politicians re-acquired constituent power. Thus, in this case, although retaining the Constitution of the Federal Republic of Nigeria 1979,[2] it was no longer the constitution of Obasanjo's military junta but truly those of the civilian politicians. Admittedly, it was possible that the 1979 Constitution could have remained a military constitution. This would have been the case if, like a "camouflage" constitution, it merely

---

[2] Actually, a mere schedule to the Constitution of the Federal Republic of Nigeria (Enactment) Decree No. 25 of 1978 as amended by Decrees 26, 104 and 105 of 1979.

gave formal power to the politicians when, in fact, Obasanjo and his confederates continued to exercise real power and control in spite of the published framework.

Weeks after General Buhari's coup d' etat of 31 December 1983, a new military constitution was made[3]. It was a refurbished version of Murtala's Decree No. 32 of 1975, which, itself, borrowed from Ironsi's Decree No. 1 of 1966. It would clearly be absurd to suggest that until Decree 1 of 1984 was published, the old 1979 Constitution remained. Indeed, even though when it was made long after the coup, it "resuscitated" the 1979 Constitution, our argument is that the 1979 Constitution (as originally made) was totally dead with no similarity to Jesus' Lazarus. The dead parts that were subsequently enforced were actually, in real terms, new provisions made as part of the constitution of 1984.

General Babangida's similar claim, after the palace-coup of 27 August 1985, is also flawed. He did not merely amend Decree 1 of 1984 but, by newly acquired preponderant force, created his own framework of government. This only incidentally, contained provisions almost identical with those of General Buhari whom he had overthrown.

Although Chief Ernest Shonekan took the title of Head of State and Commander-in-Chief of the (Nigerian) Armed Forces, it seems clear to any perceptive observer that he never acquired preponderant force in all of the 83 days Generals Babangida and Abacha propped him up under the camouflage, Interim Constitution

---

[3] Constitution (Suspension and Modification) Decree No. 1 of 1984 (with effect from 1 January, 1984.)

of 1993[4]. General Abacha, without the slightest whimper of resistance from Shonekan, simply took the preponderant force, which, for sometime earlier, had latently been seen to reside in him. This was on 17 November 1993, but it was not until many days later that he published the written framework for his own government[5]. Although Decree 107 purported to proceed with the unsuspended and modified provisions of the 1979 Constitution, the real position was that such parts as was used were, actually, inextricable portions not of the 1979, but of the 1993, constitution.

In so far as the General Abubakar regime was not clearly so authorized by Abacha's self-tailored constitution of 1993, it may be said that his accession to power on 9 June, 1998, signified a transfer of preponderant force to him. Therefore, although he adopted the pre-existing framework in Decree No. 107, totally without amendment, it may yet properly be asserted that the constitution became, in actuality, the new 1998 constitution of General Abdulsalami Abubakar. A different sociologist of law may, by the doctrine of necessity, plausibly contend that even though it is not specifically provided for in Decree 107, the general powers of the Provisional Ruling Council (PRC) to deal with constitutional matters justifies their appointment of General Abubakar as Abacha's replacement.

This second interpretation, which we favour, is not inconsistent with our doctrine of preponderant force. The PRC, the highest

---

[4] The Interim Government (Basic Constitutional Provisions) Decree No. 61 of 1993.
[5] The Constitution (Suspension and Modification) Decree No. 107 of 1993.

force, simply filled the vacuum. Necessity only seeks to show that the pre-existent constitution anticipated and, latently, authorized this transfer. In that case, it is merely an evolutionary amendment of the constitutional framework by the "same" or "descendant" authority, which first authorized it.

By the same logic, we may argue that the 1999 civilian-type constitution[6] remains a military constitution having been made under the authority of Abubakar's Decree 107. We do not reject this off-hand. The conclusion is plausible depending on sociological and political facts actually on the ground. If Abubakar, like Kagame [the then Vice-President of Rwanda], retains preponderant force but designates another person as the formal leader, then, the identity of the constitution will remain attached or imputed to his own.

At exactly 11.15a.m. of Saturday, 29 May 1999, General Olusegun Obasanjo took the requisite oaths of office as President of Nigeria under the 1999 Constitution. General Abubakar symbolically handed the instruments of office to him in a colourful ceremony. However, what we found most intriguing was the imperceptible but almost magical phenomenon, which occurred thereafter.

Abubakar and his military service chiefs arrived the Eagle Square venue of the handover at Abuja clearly still in retention of preponderant force. Only moments after the oaths and the symbolic handover by Abubakar, however, it seemed obvious to us that at that

---

[6] Schedule to the Constitution of the Federal Republic of Nigeria (Promulgation) Decree No. 24 of 5 May, 1999 (with effect from 29 May, 1999).

square, even if Abubakar had changed his mind, he could no longer enforce it. In the face of contradictory orders by him an Obasanjo to the soldiers who had previously, that morning, presented arms in loyalty to Abubakar, Obasanjo's order would, in our view, have been preferred. Such is the substantially, unscientific nature of this meta-physical concept.

It has many parallels with Kelsen's theory of effectiveness but we note one point of departure. This difference is essentially methodological. While his theory depends on a *grundnorm,* ours is, as it were, founded on what we may describe, for want of a better word, as a *"grundfact."* Although both *grundnorm* and *grundfact* consider the ultimate foundation of a legal system to be "effectiveness," his believes effectiveness a matter of norms, while ours considers effectiveness as clearly a matter of fact, which thereafter, energizes a system of norms.

We see the macro-plane of the constitution as the descriptive agency, which is not regulated by any norms but just happens. The micro-plane is the concrete framework that makes prescriptive, normative, stipulates, and "regulated" by the declarations of the wielder of preponderant force at the first plane.

If there is agreement as to the effectiveness of the proffered framework of government, it becomes the province of the court to interpret it between litigants even when the wielder of preponderant force is party on one of the sides. This appears to be the premise of Justice Kayode Eso's brilliant, and substantially consistent, standpoint.

In the *Military Governor of Ondo State v. Adewunmi,*[7] Eso, J.S.C., patiently explains:

> That the legislature cum the executive (now merged under one under the militia [sic] could enact laws which could deprive the court of jurisdiction.

But, he emphasizes especially in *Ojukwu's case,*[8] until this is done, they should submit to the rule of law, which is represented by the judicial powers invested in the courts. In his non-judicial writings, Honourable Kayode Eso has similarly expostulated that:

> Once the tyrant [the wielder of preponderant force] leaves the 'Rule of Law' to operate, he must *per necessitate,* submit to that rule. His only position is to abolish the judiciary, but he has never summoned up sufficient courage so to do.[9]

Chief Rotimi Williams seems of similar, but less strident, sentiment. He has made the point both as court advocate as well as text writer. In *Lakanmi's case*[10] of 1970 and the more recent *Guardian Newspapers, case*[11] of 1995, this most senior of the Senior Advocates of Nigeria has maintained that once made, the constitution binds even its maker until, otherwise, it is changed. The courts have generally agreed with him even if, sometimes, the military wielders of constituent power have not. Chief Williams seems to believe that, unless specifically altered, the instrument for identification of

---

[7] [1988] All N.L.R. 274 at 289.

[8] *Gov. of Lagos State v. Chief Odumegwu Ojukwu* (1986) 1 NWLR (pt. 18) 621.

[9] Kayode Eso, *The Mystery Gunman* (Ibadan: Spectrum, 1996) at 181 (Square brackets and words therein, mine).

[10] *Supra.*

[11] *Supra.*

the actual will of preponderant force is the judiciary. This will remain so regardless of whether or not the very maker of such constitution is also a party and finds the earlier view expressed therein as presently inconvenient[12].

The difficulty is not with a generally accepted framework. That is a matter for the orthodox courts and lawyers. The problem is with a disputed framework: where other competing framework(s) deny its supremacy. This is the province of the legal sociologist, political scientist and politician. The fitting methodology here is, necessarily, multi-disciplinary or inter-disciplinary in focus.

The framework contains prescriptive stipulates. However, its underlying authority is not determined beforehand by any posited rules. This authority is teleological and descriptive rather than normative or prescriptive. This presents problems for the undiscerning researcher. Because both the macro and micro planes are essentially intertwined, an undiscriminating investigator may find problems of Constitutional Law whose results may be ("is") descriptive in one sense and only ("ought") prescriptive in another. Like Hume, he may feel embarrassed by what he may, therefore, consider an unjustified conflation of different methodologies. Hume confesses himself "of a sudden"[13]:

---

[12] See for e.g. Chief F.R.A. Williams, S.A.N., "The Nigerian Judiciary and Military Governments" (1995) J.N.L. vol. 2, 1.
[13] David Hume, *A Treatise on Human Nature* (1777) excerpted in Lord Lloyd of Hampstead, *Introduction to Jurisprudence*, 4th ed. (London: Stevens & Sons, 1979) at 26.

> Surpriz'd to find, that instead of the
> usual copulations of propositions, *is* and
> *is not*,[13]

he meets with

> No proposition that is not connected with
> an *ought*, or an *ought not*.[13]

Unlike Hume, we do not find this a failure of analysis. Rather, we see it as a peculiar phenomenon; which, regardless of what may be the common nature of things (distinguishing the "is" from the "ought"), here, for the politico-legal system, successfully copulates both in a unique, singular, object. Sociologists may investigate to find how this strange occurrence can logically be; but that may not be a major worry of the jurist. The orthodox lawyer will recognize its existence and only be concerned as to how it affects the current methodologies for the identification of a legal system. From the *normative* laws and material constitution, he will trace it up to the *factual* point of constituent power.

Autopoiesis helps explain this strange copulation. It shows how it is possible to assert an autonomous understanding of legal and constitutional principles (the law *is* thus and so) while at the same time acknowledging that, sometimes, what is stated to be law under existing legal rules of recognition may, in *fact*, not be so. They may be the sort of dead letter identified by American realists and Scandinavian "law as fact" jurists.

The naturalists, through activist judges of that leaning, best exemplify the point. But sometimes, conservative judges, in the disguised power play between the arms of government, have even been known to subvert for ends of justice what is prescribed by constituent power. In matter of fact, therefore, law can be made no longer law! Just recently, the Enugu division of the Court of Appeal held, by a majority, that the constituent will reflected by the supremacy of decrees, was not to be so where strict application would deprive a litigant of vested rights through no fault of his.

In that case,[14] the appellant had lost his (local government) electoral petition at the trial tribunal. The applicable decree governing the elections provided for a maximum period of 30 days from filing within which the appeal must be heard and determined.[15]The appellant filed his papers within time and Niki Tobi, J.C.A., as the presiding justice of the Enugu Division, fixed hearing within the stipulated period.

Unfortunately for everybody, on the date fixed, justices of the Court of Appeal had to

---

[14] *Emesim v. Nwachukwu* (1999) 6 NWLR (pt. 606) 154. See to the contrary, the insistence of the Abuja Division of the self same Court of Appeal, that hearing cannot transcend the stipulated period under a similarly worded decree for presidential elections: *Falae v. Obasanjo* (1999) 6 NWLR (pt. 606) 285. The Enugu decision was in February while that of Abuja was in April, 1999 (per Mariam Mukhtar, J.C.A., delivering the leading ruling adopted unanimously by the five-Justice panel). For governorship elections, a similarly worded decree was construed by the five-member, Jos Division of the Court of Appeal (in March, 1999) as incapable of extension: *Jidda v. Kachallah and ors.* (1999) 4 NWLR (pt. 599) 426, per Pats-Acholonu, J.C.A. [now, JSC]: "While I sympathize ... with appellant ... Decree No. 3 of 1999, is meant to be interpreted strictly with regards to the time-frame allowed ..."

[15] See para. 2(2) of Schedule 5 of the Local Government (Basic Constitutional and Transitional Provisions) Decree No. 36 of 1998 (used for the chairmanship and councillorship elections of 5 December, 1998).

attend an important official assignment and the appeal had to be adjourned to the only remaining date within the 30 days stipulated. Professor B.O. Nwabueze (SAN) for the appellant moved on that date for a direction that the court could continue the hearing even thereafter. Senator N.N. Anah (S.A.N.) and Mr. D.O.C. Amaechina, respectively for the two sets of respondents, insisted on the statutory time limit.

In divergent rulings remarkable for an unusual "friendlessness," Niki Tobi, J.C.A. [now, JSC], denounced those who would permit injustice by sticking to the strict-letters of the time-bar; while Ubaezonu, J.C.A., condemned the "Kangaroo Court" which would dispense "sentimental," rather than legal, justice.[15a] Since the third judge in the panel agreed with Tobi, J.C.A., the appellant was allowed to proceed beyond the 30 days specifically prescribed by the then wielders of preponderant force.

[15a] In a very illuminating article, Endicott has suggested that judges can and should disagree with each other but never in disrespectful language. This, he contends, would be a breach of 'comity' and such rudeness would only make the offending judge to look 'absurd': Timothy Endicott, " 'International Meaning': Comity in Fundamental Rights Adjudication," *International Journal of Refugee Law*, vol. 13, no. 3, 2001, 280-292, esp. at 286-288. [Cited officially as: 13 IJRL (2001) 280-292. An e.g. of this sort of lack of comity is courteously attributed to Scalia, J., of the US Supreme Court [at 287]. In *PGA Tour, Inc. v. Martin*, 121 SCt 1879, US Or, 2001, 29 May 2001, at 1898, Justice Scalia's dissent "respectfully" [at 1898], describes parts of the majority decision as: "ridiculous" [at 1904] and "quite incredible" [at 1900]. He denounces the majority for asking an "incredibly silly question" [at 1903] and even expresses the view that the majority judgment "distorts...common sense" [at 1898].

Similarly, the Supreme Court, on Friday, 14 May 1999, ostensibly defied the will of the military wielders of Nigerian preponderant force. This was in another electoral appeal.[16] Abubakar Atiku selected the appellant, B. Haruna, to be his running mate at the gubernatorial elections of 9 January 1999, for Adamawa State. They were successful and returned as the Governor and Deputy-Governor elects pending 29 May 1999, when they would take the requisite oaths and assume office. Shortly thereafter, the Governor-elect accepted to run on General Obasanjo's presidential ticket for the national office of Vice-President. He had to renounce his gubernatorial victory and before the presidential primaries, he did.

The Independent National Electoral Commission (INEC) considered, in the circumstance, that fresh elections ought to be conducted and fixed a date for this. In response, the second appellant (joined by his party) took out a suit for a declaration that no vacancy existed as he, the deputy, should automatically take the place of the governor-elect. In the relevant electoral statute,[17] the closest provision dealing with the situation was contained in section 45, sub-section (1):

> The Deputy Governor shall hold office of Governor if the office of Governor becomes vacant by reason of death, resignation, impeachment, permanent incapacity or removal for any other reason.

---

[16] Reported in *The Guardian* Newspaper of 15 May, 1999, 1. The reasons for judgment were deferred and have now been reported as *Peoples Democratic Party and Boni Haruna v. I.N.E.C. and ors.* [1999] 7 S.C.N.J. 297 to 410.

[17] State Government (Basic Constitutional and Transitional Provisions) Decree No. 3 of 1999.

Nothing was said about vacancy at the stage when the Governor-elect and his deputy were yet to formally take office after the requisite swearing of Oaths.[18]

By the well-known doctrine of interpretation, *expressio unius est exclusio alterius,* it was clear that the specific mention of acceptable, transformation conditions should negate the implication appellant asserted. The trial court thought not and granted the declaration sought. The Court of Appeal (in lieu of the yet to be inaugurated Constitutional Court) overruled the trial court. INEC was enjoined to proceed with new elections. At the final appeal, which was filed at the Supreme Court, it was held by a slim majority of four against three that the second appellant was entitled to the reliefs he and his party sought.

Although these decisions seem to defy the framework emplaced by preponderant force, autopoiesis may provide a rationalization. The decree may be the formal manifestation of the will of the holders of preponderant force. However, implied in its provision for a judiciary is the principle that the will of the constituent authority is whatever, in the final analysis, a majority of the Supreme Court Justices says it is. The factual reality of an amorphous interpretive jurisdiction is thereby ingested into the system of formal legal rules and turned up into a form peculiarly normative and legal. Instead of opposing the legislative views of the military government with the

---

[18.] This lacuna is now supplied by s. 181 (and s. 136) of the 1999 Constitution. By this provision, Haruna as deputy to the Governor-elect would have automatically taken his place when he renounced his gubernatorial victory.

judicially discrepant one of the Supreme Court, an autopoietic methodology copulates them into a synthesis phrased in the normative language of law.

7. Conclusion.

SUMMARY.

Presumptuously perhaps, we have sought in this book to impose some order to currently chaotic constructs of constitutional jurisprudence. First, we deal with terms and concepts. We distinguish Constitutional Law from what it studies, that is, the constitution. In doing this, we try to highlight why. We show that otherwise, we lose the opportunity of, *inter alia*, observing the unique nature of Constitutional Law in relation to other legal subjects. Criminal Law, Contracts Law, Evidence Law, etc., systematize or symbolize the normative stipulates studied by those disciplines. However, Constitutional Law is peculiar. It deals with an object of study more factual than normative. While other laws only prescribe a certain course of conduct, the constitution consists of both a description of phenomena and a prescription of conduct. Constitutional Law is, therefore, called upon to describe not just norms, but what itself is essentially a description.

The principal merit of this distinction is the clarity it gives to analysis. We start aware that Constitutional Law is solely and entirely a didactic rather than legislative venture. With this background, it is easier to brush aside ethical distractions in the course of analysis. We study constitutions and identify without bias both the reprehensible and laudable ones. It is by so doing that we are better positioned to highlight the components that make the good praise-worthy and the bad condemnable. With the distinction between Constitutional Law and the constitution, we retain the ability to reserve censure and ethical considerations until such a time as we are able to deal with methods for acquiring and securing the good types.

Secondly, we have proposed a different approach to the study of constitutions. We try to show that the current methodology is unduly dependent on mere textual analysis. We contend that if this methodology were inadequate for lower level legal study (as we think it is), it is fundamentally inappropriate for a study of the "ultimate law" - the constitution.

If for the law of companies, for example, it is possible to excuse enquiry that is based only on text, this justification will probably stem from the fact that there is a clear law, which specifies what is required. But is this similarly logical for a course of study whose object is the constitution? The Company Code, in the first case, once authorized by the constitution, satisfies the requirements of the scholar and practitioner. All that is left is its application to particular facts. The matter is wholly different with the constitution. Even where it purports to be written, the immediate query would be "Who or what authorized that particular one"? "Why that one"? "Why not others"? If you say it is the constitution because the current legislature and the head of government formally authenticated it, the persistent question would still be: "On what basis? Who gave them this authority? Why they, not I"?

To claim that a particular document is the constitution only because it so asserts would overlook a few points of commonsense. Without a reflector, the eye cannot see itself.

Similarly, with no higher validating law, a constitution cannot fruitfully be identified based only on its content. The present system is confused mainly because of this failure of methodology. Besides, a constitution may not be written or may not be solely written.

For our part, we claim something additional. We contend that Constitutional Law must use other material in addition to the self-assertions of the constitution under examination. The methodology we urge is multi-disciplinary or following Evans's[1] distinction, "inter-disciplinary" or "cross-disciplinary" in focus. In this, we have explored Sociological Jurisprudence and gained insights from specialized areas as narrow as those of the Symbolic Interactionists in the field of Criminology. We have also drawn, gratefully, from the Sociology of Law and mostly zeroed-in on the novel organization of pre-existing thought now known as *autopoiesis* (as championed by Niklas Luhmann and Gunther Teubner). We agree with their view, similar to John Salmond's, that law is not always law unto itself. Sometimes, fact overthrows the formal norms of law. However, when this happens, it is

---

[1] G.R. Evans, *Calling Academia to Account* (Buckingham: The Society for Research into Higher Education (SRHE) & Open University Press, 1999) 169 esp. at 170: "There is a difference between multidisciplinary and interdisciplinary research. Assessing work which is merely multidisciplinary may be tackled by ensuring that representative expertise is available on, or to, the panels. That will not work for interdisciplinary work which is forging a new discipline. This is likely to be amongst the most truly original work; for that reason, it may be the hardest to `rate' by existing scales and criteria. Those who engage in it are likely to have had to overcome resistance in their institutions and to be persons of considerable intellectual courage ...."

open to the legal analyst to ingest the "aberrant" phenomenon into the legal system and turn it up in a form that can still be described as peculiarly legal. In other words, the fact of experience can be presented as prescriptive law, which is part of, anticipated in, and not inconsistent with, the existing legal system.

The third thing we have done is to study the current state of the subject. For model, we have adopted the NUC guideline for teaching Constitutional Law and we have tried to point out its logical and epistemological inadequacies. In the course of this examination, we have sometimes placed our methodology in counterpoise to demonstrate the superior results we claim will follow its adoption. Here, we get the opportunity to show in more detail why we say our present concepts seem to rule us rather than we, they. We show that contrary to current orthodoxies, Constitutional Law is a study rather than a rule. Also, that the constitution itself is what Constitutional Law studies but, unlike what most jurists think, it is not restricted to "the law of the constitution" but extends to conventions and other such quasi-prescriptive constitutional phenomena.

The unarticulated premise that defines a constitution by reference to requirements of given constitutional concepts is not rational. We scorch that heresy and borrow from Kelsen's "any kind of content might be law" to demonstrate that 'any kind of content can be constitution'. We, however, distinguish between good and bad contents of constitutions and censorially denounce the latter while applauding the former.

A very difficult part of Constitutional Law concerns how and when a constitution is changed and/or created. This is where there is the most amazing confusion. The current state of the subject is utterly confounded. The field is entirely chaotic. We concede the difficulty and propose a new conceptual framework for its solution. We demarcate the constitution into two planes: the macro-plane and the micro one. The macro-plane is where our doctrine of preponderant force plays itself out while the micro-plane is the inferior level where the actual framework of government (usually written) may be found. This is the fourth and final step we have taken in the course of this research. We use the first step to set the tone of discourse. In it, we advocate a wider stance for a more convincing and fuller study of Constitutional Law. In the second step, we explore the available extra materials and focus on one: *autopoiesis*, which is drawn from a teleological standpoint. With this background, we use *autopoiesis* at the third step, to examine the current state of the subject. In this, we highlight inadequacies and demonstrate availability of better alternatives. Having done these, our final step is to develop the doctrine of preponderant force in more detail. It is with this fourth step that we are able to draw general conclusions.

GENERAL CONCLUSIONS.

For convenience, we should wish, in this section, to distinguish the word 'conclusion' into two classes. There are direct findings drawn from particularized evidence. Moreover, there is the generalized deduction propounded as its consequence. This research reveals many minor findings. They have been highlighted in the body of the work. We are more concerned at this stage with the latter class of conclusions. These are the generalizations designed to point to the future and to sensitize action (for correction) or inaction (for stabilization).

From the various findings we have made in this research, we have come to the conclusion that the confused state of Nigerian constitutional knowledge and the resultant backwardness of its politico-legal system can be traced to the reversal of roles between the constitutional jurist and the mere practitioner in this field.

Constitutional Theory is the province of the academic jurist. It comprehends but transcends the practitioner's field of Constitutional Application. It is for the theorist to clearly grasp the problems, conceptualize alternative solutions and advance the isolated remedy. Practitioners appear only thereafter. Theirs is the mechanical, although occasionally creative, function of applying the general principles to particular circumstances. The first should precede the second. In Nigeria (and apparently, in other backward polities), the reverse is the case. The practitioner is left to flounder helplessly in the quicksand of uncoordinated precedents. Instead of supplying a unifying and controlling principle, the academic follows the choking lead of the troubled practitioner. All is consequent chaos. The roof is made to support the foundation.

Some of our conclusions have been designed to reverse this invidious order. We even claim some novel contributions. In the course of this eleven-year research, for instance, we have seen neither published nor unpublished material anticipating our discovery of a clear, systematic, differentiation between the constitution and Constitutional Law. Neither have we found a prior research distinction between the concept of checks as distinguished from the idea of balances. We have cleaned separation of powers and the rule of law of their obfuscating fogginess – at least to an extent not hitherto attempted (or considered worthwhile?). This research reveals that Kelsen's "rules of law in a descriptive sense" have consequences far more important than Martin Golding's "use/mention" explanation and even Hart's more sophisticated interpreter's interpretation. We are not even sure Kelsen himself would have gone beyond Hart's internal aspect of rules[1a] as developed further by Raz and MacCormick. We claim that so long as the legislator has a mediating organ between himself and enforcement of his law, so long is the product descriptive rather than normative. In this state of affairs, new devices for analysis become imperative.

It is not readily apparent that previous constitutional writers have understood or even considered the analytic discrimination of a constitution into two parts. In this book, there is a grandiose hope that it is an original contribution. Much of the confusion besetting this field finds root in too ready acceptance of age-reverenced orthodoxy. We are one with Paine that an old thing is not necessarily a good one:

[1a] H.L.A. Hart, *The Concept of Law*, 2nd ed. (Oxford: Clarendon Press, 1994) 56-57, 104 and 201. I am indebted to Prof. A.O. Obilade for this reference.

> The ragged relic and the antiquated
> precedent, the monk and the monarch will
> moulder together ...[2]

Discarding the currently chaotic state of the
subject, we have come to see that
constitutional change will only clearly be
understood when analyzed in three compartments.
Consequently, in this difficult field, we offer
the concepts of evolutionary, devolutionary and
revolutionary changes of a constitution. This
is new; and we claim it as an original
contribution in this hazy field of knowledge.

One thread that runs through is our
doctrine of preponderant force. It encapsulates
much of what we have already identified as new.
However, not all is new. Our intellectual debts
are many but principally owed to that awesome
intellectual of the 20th Century, Hans Kelsen.
Like a dwarf, we have climbed on his shoulders
and what we think new is merely our short head
protruding from his giant base.

But what has all this got to do with
anything practical? It is all too easy to adopt
Evans's haughty attitude and say that
intellectual insights need not have any
immediate practical values, for:

> On the foundations of true scholarship can
> be built ... something more rigorous ...
> involving conviction that it matters to
> extend knowledge about something even if
> the extension of knowledge has no
> perceptible application at any foreseeable
> time.[3]

---

[2] Thomas Paine, *Rights of Man*, *op. cit.*, 218 [see fn. 23
of Chapt. 3, *supra*].
[3] G.R. Evans, *Calling Academia to Account: Rights and
Responsibilities*, *op. cit.*, 9.

Happily, however, this research claims both intellectual as well as practical harvests.

The practical benefits mostly result from the copulation of conclusions. In resolving the June 12 problem, we have concluded that all law is dependent on the prevailing constitution. Therefore, the annulment decree was legal in so far as it was made within the rubric of Decree No. 17 of 1985 (the then extant constitution). We have however distinguished legality and constitutionality (on one hand) from subjective legitimacy (on the other hand). A copulation of these conclusions leads us to practical consequences for the political citizen. We are now well placed to see why the populace, which demands good laws, ought not rely solely on the goodwill of its governors. Since force is the ultimate determiner of law, people who want to ensure good laws must have a controlling hand in the military forces. Just because the mass of people in a large, modern, state cannot directly do so, does not mean we cannot ensure dissipation and separation of this all-important responsibility to agents with mutual rivalries. This is the major justification for democracy - real democracy. It is quite stupid to think that our new democracy is safe when, with the President's monopoly of force at the federal level, the people's representatives have control over no independent force whether at the state or in the centre[4]. The legislators

---

[4] This is the thrust of the orientation lecture I gave to the Enugu State House of Assembly on 23 June, 1999: "Overview of the 1999 Constitution with Special Reference to the State House of Assembly." Consider esp., ss. 214, 215 and 216; and items 38, 45 and 48 of the Exclusive Legislative List; in the 1999 Constitution.

do not even have a well-developed office of Sergeant-at-Arms.

Another immediate concern this Book attempts to address is the matter of judicial power. Our extension of Kelsen's "rules of law in a descriptive sense" may well provide material to save the Supreme Court from its newfound dalliance with anti-citizen judgments. In *Attorney General of the Federation v. Guardian Newspaper Ltd. and 5 ors*[5], the mutually repellent reasoning and conclusions signify the Supreme Court's desire to do some good but its inability to surmount and grasp the conceptual materials necessary for attainment of this honourable goal. If, as the judgment implies, the sole function of the judge is faithful application of the legislative will — even a senseless, tyrannical legislator's, then the courts lose their legitimating aspect[6]! If the Supreme Court judge thinks himself trained only to decipher and apply the decrees of a demented General, then the time and money invested in his long, expensive, education and professional training has been time and money not usefully spent. For

---

[5] [1999] 5 S.C.N.J. 324 to 430. Uwaifo, J.S.C.,'s leading judgment is reported from the start of 334 and the rest of the full court of seven Justices took the remaining pages including the whole of 430 (97 pages in all)!
[6] The condonation of contempt in this case is even more worrisome. The Federal Government had studiously ignored the Court of Appeal judgment to unseal the Guardian premises before it came to taunt the same judiciary with this appeal. By *Mobil Oil v. Assan* [1996] 9 S.C.N.J. 97, the Supreme Court forbids such nonsense except in four circumstances none of which is presently applicable. Courts should not grant audience to contemnors: *Shugaba v. U.B.N.* [1999] 7 S.C.N.J. 125 esp. (per Wali, J.S.C.) at 137.

this, a Sergeant Major could do a cheaper and better job.

So long as there is judicial power, there is latitude for interpretation – even subversive interpretation. If, as they professed in the *Guardian case*, the justices believed injustice would be done by faithful application of the usurper's unpopular laws, they had (and have) jurisdiction, even within the subsisting constitution, to exercise their hermeneutic powers. This, even in a manner as might subvert the apparent meaning of that law in preference for doing justice.[7] The tyrannous General must be deemed to have meant something different from what ostensibly appears from the Gazette or such-like official representation of his normative dictates. If Decrees 8 and 12 of 1994 purport an ouster of jurisdiction, this would merely be the Government Printer's description of what he thinks Legislator Abacha's norms for Nigeria are. The Supreme Court as the final constitution-interpreter is entitled to determine otherwise. This is what the Supreme Court failed to realize in the *Guardian case* and this failure is sad. The nature of sovereign power is different from its location at any given time and space. Decree 107, the 1993 constitution of Nigeria, could quite legally assign ultimate judicial power to General Abacha. However, it chose not to do so. Its conferment upon the Supreme Court makes that institution, part wielder of preponderant force. The court ought to have represented the populace in this uneven power equation. It is

---

[7] Strangely enough, in *P.D.P. and Bonnie Haruna v. I.N.E.C. and ors.* [1999] 7 S.C.N.J. 297, from 311 to 410, the Supreme Court by a four to three majority seemed to appreciate this power but in circumstances hopelessly inappropriate.

therefore depressing that the Supreme Court goes on as if it is a confused child. What the tyrant has not dared to take, our own Supreme Court unwittingly gives to him! Oputa has repeatedly warned against misapplication of legal principles[7a]. Like a disembodied spirit, the principle of faithful application of the legislative will is taken from the West without a care for first reviving its democratic body. Faint glimpses of our point seem evident in the part of the decision, which, in the *Guardian case*, favoured the 2nd to 6th respondents. If the mechanistic basis for denying judicial access to the first respondent is as impenetrable as the court would imply, there seems no warrant to lift the veil of the ouster clause just because totally unconcerned bystanders were equally affected or injured.

Various permutations of the results of this research can fruitfully lead to other such practical consequences. However, the part that gives us special satisfaction is the impact of this research on streamlining the system for the study of Constitutional Law in Nigerian Universities.

Our conclusion is that a constitution consists of two facets: the macro-plane of preponderant force and the micro-plane of the day-to-day framework for governance. From this conclusion, we see a logical possibility for the study of Constitutional Law (which we consider as solely concerned with the analysis of constitutions). Since University work is divided in Nigeria into two semesters for each course of study, we derive the inference that study of each of the two facets of the

---

[7a] See, for eg., *Adegoke Motors v. Adesanya* [1989] 5 S.C.N.J. 80.

constitution may usefully be taken up in each of the semesters. Since the first facet embraces and gives imprimatur even to the second, it seems logical that it be taken first as the general, introductory part of the course. Because it is general jurisprudence and mainly theoretical, the student is afforded the opportunity of understanding what a constitution means irrespective of the peculiar format adopted by any particular locale.

The second semester picks the domestic framework currently in place and dissects its particular provisions. Because this distinction has not earlier been fully understood, matters properly fitted to particular frameworks are indiscriminately joined for study with, and as if necessary to, general principles of Constitutional Theory. When in practice the student finds such particulars inapplicable to other regions applying different frameworks, there is embarrassment to the confused lecturer and much loss of faith in the integrity of the subject matter in both tutor and tutee.

RECOMMENDATIONS.

It is suggested that future research should concentrate on discovering a system to make the doctrine of preponderant force less vague in its practical application. It is easy to say that the wielder of this force determines the law of the relevant locale. But how do you apply this, for example, to the Democratic Republic of Congo (DRC) or even to present day Kosovo [in 1999]? Even though Laurent Kabila's forces defeated Mobutu and transformed Zaire to the DRC, it is difficult in 1999 to insist that Kabila's constitution has application in rebel-controlled Kisangani. Kisangani is still, at least formally, part of

Congo. So, what constitution applies there? Arafat's Palestine is not yet an independent state and is putatively part of Israel. But the Oslo, Wye River, etc., agreements all suggest what is true – that it is under a different constitutional regime from that governing the state of Israel.

A constitution is therefore judged in point of time and space. What is one this minute may not be so the next. Preponderant force is violently mobile. The combination of forces constituting the preponderant force may include one visible character in all its changes for a length of time, but this does not mean it is the same at those different times. In eight years of General Babangida, preponderant force, and thus the constitution, mutated rapidly and violently at various times. Sometimes, in him alone; other times in his junta with General Abacha; with the Langtang Generals; with his favourite Majors; the AFRC; etc. Sometimes, his dalliance with the press shifted the location of sovereign power and at other times, such as during the May, 1989, riots and June 12 imbroglio, preponderant force lay with the masses but with IBB's great dexterity at statecraft, he allowed himself to flow with the tide and remain the symbol of its force. It is at such times that the Courts are most potent. A courageous and knowledgeable judiciary can and should symbolize the preponderant force re-asserted by the populace. When it does so, it is able to make pronouncements against the interest of the ostensible sovereign and, thus, resolve the so-called auto-obligation question in Constitutional Law.

A constitution is also judged in point of space. It is such only to the extent of territory in which it is effective. The Nigerian constitution has no application in China. Even in Nigeria, it had no application for 30 months in that part which seceded as the Republic of Biafra. The intriguing thing is that even the constitution of this rebel enclave had no application to its supposed capital immediately federal troops recaptured Enugu.

All these demonstrate the need for circumspection before any generalizations. It is not enough to look at the formal document or its official title. Much more is needed. Mere text may be deceptive to the lazy analyst. Real and other evidence of preponderant force is required for a proper investigation. This book is only a seminal impetus for the much wider inquiry that is required. The search cannot be restricted to the lawyer. For the best result, we must engage the sociologist, the political scientist and, especially, the philosopher, amongst other such specialists.

We recommend, too, a shift in our current academic paradigm for the study of Constitutional Law. Unless we conceptually detach the study from its object, we remain doomed to confusion. Let us tear the constitution apart from Constitutional Law. Constitutional Law becomes a clearer subject when it realizes its distinct existence from the object of its enquiry. With this background, there is call for re-evaluation of the NUC syllabus on Constitutional Law.

Section 4, sub section (1) paragraph (m) of the National Universities Commission (NUC) Act, 1974[8], empowers the NUC:

---

[8] Now, in cap. 283, L.F.N., 1990.

> To lay down minimum standards for all
> universities in the federation …

The longest serving law lecturer in Nigeria
observes that indeed,

> Minimum academic standards was approved by
> the Federal military Government in 1989 on
> the recommendation of the NUC, for all
> disciplines taught in Nigerian
> Universities[9]

In paragraph 2.8 entitled "Synopses of
courses," the NUC[10] expresses "a desire to
ensure uniformity of courses taught in various
law faculties." And to effect this purpose, it
announces that the:

> Following is approved as the contents of
> syllabuses of the core and optional law
> courses …
> 1. LEGAL METHODS
> …
> …
>
> 2. Constitutional Law
> *FIRST SEMESTER – PART I*
> 1. Definition and sources … classification
> of the constitutions …
> 2. The concepts of separation … rule of
> law, federalism, supremacy of
> constitution/parliament. The legal
> consequences of the change of

---

[9] Prof. C.O. Okonkwo, S.A.N., "A Historical Overview of
Legal Education in Nigeria," paper presented at the
N.I.A.L.S. conference on legal education, Federal
Secretariat, Abuja, 20 April, 1999, at p. 11 of the
typed paper.
[10] See the "National Universities Commission Approved
Minimum Academic Standards in Law for Nigerian
Universities," excerpted from p. 8 of the cyclostyled
Abia State University copy given to me when I was part
of the Law Faculty there at Uturu in the 1994/1995
session.

government by extra-constitutional means (e.g. coup d' etat).
3. Constitutional history of Nigeria from the advent of British rule up-to date[11].

SECOND SEMESTER – PART II

1. The Military and constitution making in Nigeria (a) … (d) The military and the search for constitutional and political order.
2. The study of the current constitution.
   (a) Supremacy of the constitution, citizenship …
   (b) Legislative power …
   (c) Judicial power…
   (d) Executive power …
3. Law of Contract …" etc.

No doubt, the syllabus is adequate for an introductory course of Constitutional Law at the level of undergraduate study. Much of the content reflects our concerns and can be fleshed out for higher study. Our only worry now is as to procedure and as to system. Nothing in the scheme we have quoted above reflects the underlying philosophy for this study. There seems an implication, for example, under the first lectures for the 2nd semester, that the constitution is something mutually exclusive or, at any rate, mutually antagonistic with military rule. But this is absurd. Military regimes have constitutions although, usually, these are peculiarly

---

[11] No. 2.3 (on History) is mistakenly omitted from the Abia State University copy but supplied in the version published by the Faculty of Law, Nnamdi Azikiwe University, Awka (where I presently teach).

unattractive from the standpoint of the hapless citizen.

The second lectures in the first semester are made to deal with constitutional concepts. This is not bad. What is however odious is the implication that there are certain liberty-sensitive provisions without which a phenomenon cannot qualify to the status of a constitution. We recommend a clearer provision. The NUC would do better to specify that these constitutional concepts have been known to facilitate liberty-sensitive, progressive, constitutions but that constitutions exist which do not satisfy some or all of those requirements. In addition, as we have tried to show in Chapter 5, the specification for lectures on "The legal consequences of the change of government by extra-constitutional means" is unduly austere. It is better to require lectures on constitutional change in all its ramifications and not merely the revolutionary aspect.

Constitutional history of Nigeria should be extracted from the general principles of the 1st semester to the very first topic in the second. The military and constitution making should be taken as part of the lecture on classification of constitutions. It is a matter of general theory and has no place in the 2nd semester. It should be replaced by constitutional history, which the lecturer should be encouraged to divest of its very boring details. Any historical epoch included must be justified by its conformity with a relevant constitutional theme. Unless the teacher can pin it to, say, the constitutional attainment of a "representative legislature," there is clearly no warrant to bore the student with the piece of pedantry that at such and such a time under colonial domination, there was this or that number of official and unofficial members of the government's deliberative assembly.

Constitutional history should start the 2nd semester for another good reason. Having dealt with general jurisprudence of constitutions in the 1st semester, it is appropriate in the second to introduce the special local framework currently in place with a historical foundation. Now in Nigeria, for example, having considered all types of constitutions in the 1st semester, it is meet that before studying the current 1999 framework, something is said of its ancestors at the very start of the 2nd semester.

From what has been said so far, it may be prudent to discard the rather rigid formulation for the second series of lectures billed by the NUC for the 2nd semester. It assumes that future constitutional frameworks will retain the 1989 model upon which the guidelines are obviously patterned. This may not be very far-sighted. In any case, even in the model copied, executive power is treated before the judicial. The NUC guidelines reverse this order with no evident justification. A longer-lasting structure of lectures would be one where:

(a) Neutral provisions such as supremacy clauses, citizenship and fundamental objectives and directive principles of state policy are considered;

(b) Legislative powers (without undue specification) are treated according to the nature of whatever constitutional framework the lecturer has currently to contend with; similar treatment should extend to:

(c) Executive powers; and

(d) Judicial powers.

445

The judicial powers will deal with the hierarchy, structure and jurisdiction of the courts directly and indirectly set up under the current constitution and it is possible under this heading to deal with the matter of fundamental rights as a sub-heading. This proposal will remove the topic from the first part of the lectures in the second series mapped out for the 2nd semester. We propose its transplantation to the penultimate part. Similarly to be removed from the earlier lectures is the matter of "Creation of states and constitutional amendment." The issue of change will arise only after we have properly understood the thing to be changed.

One controlling theme evident in this report of our research is that we must discard much of our preconceived notions. A constitution has no set form inherently its own. Indeed, even for voting, no special pattern is dictated by nature. The ballot box is modern. Military revolutionaries (accepted whether tacitly or openly) could sometimes satisfy the requirements of popular sovereignty better than civilian brigands whose manipulations of electoral results have imposed charlatans on an unwilling populace.

Principles of any epistemological verity are, in this field, unusually fluid and highly elusive. In this tiresome travel, our approach will, we should hope, provide for the weary academic a higher ground and, therefore, a clearer view of the daunting terrain.

Our object of research has been to discover the relationship between force and law. As a result of this investigation, our thesis is that the constitution is the embodiment and junction of force and law. The body of knowledge devoted to the study of constitutions is known as Constitutional Law and we claim that the doctrine of preponderant force is the device of Constitutional Law with which the peculiar conjunction of force and law is best studied and appreciated.

BIBLIOGRAPHY

"The Colonel Dismounted or the Rector Vindicated" (Williamsburg, 1764) 118

"A sermon preached to his Excellency Francis Bernard..." 118

"Declaration of Delhi" (1959) 2 Jo. Int. Com. of Jurists, 7 to 43. Done at Delhi the 10th day of January, 1959. .... 264, 265, 266

"Hard Sell", Tempo, 20 June, 1996, 11 and 12 13

Abrams, Robert H. "Sing Muse: Legal Scholarship for New Law Teachers" (1987) 37 J. of Legal Educ. at 8 17

Abrams, Robert H., "Sing Muse: Legal Scholarship for New Law Teachers" (1987) 37 J. of Legal Educ. at 8 17

Achara, R.A.C.E. "Bare Text and the Constitutional Case for Abiola" (2003) vol. 1, no. 1, Nigerian Bar Journal, 71. 86

Achara, R.A.C.E. "Constitutional Law and the Autonomy Debate: Synthesis from Autopoiesis" (1998-1999) 7 Nig. J. Rev. 206. 419

Achara, R.A.C.E. "The Jurisprudence of Hermeneutics (Judicial and Executive Functions of Interpretation as a Limit on the Legislative Powers for Ousting Jurisdiction)" (2001) UNIZIK Law Journal, vol. 1, no. 3, 79. 72

Achara, R.A.C.E. "What is Constitutional Law" (2004) vol. 4, no. 1, UNIZIK Law Journal 38-51. 154

Achara, R.A.C.E., "Textual Fetishism and the Ambiguities of Constitutional Definition", in I.A. Umezulike and C.C. Nweze, eds., Perspectives in Law and Justice (Enugu: F.D.P., 1996), chapter 12, 274 to 295.140, 160, 355

Achara, R.A.C.E., ed. The DOILJ Discourses (Awka: Dept. of International Law and Jurisprudence, NAU, 2004) 4th Monthly Colloquium [3 Nov. 2004]. 20

Achara, R.A.C.E., Meta-Constitutional Conceptions: Subjective Legitimacy in the Jurisprudence of June 12 (Enugu: Mike Lawrence Publishers, 1998) 393

Achike, O., Groundwork of Military Law and Military Rule in Nigeria (Enugu, Nigeria: Fourth Dimension Publishers, 1978 and 1980) 51, 371

African Conference on the Rule of Law, Lagos, Nigeria, January 3-7, 1961... .... 243, 265, 266

Agbakoba, O. and Sam Amadi in Human Rights Newsletter, vol. 1, No. 2 [1998] Jan - March, 18 to 20 401

Bagehot, Walter, The English Constitution (1867; Oxford: Oxford University Press, 1928). 358

Bailyn, Bernard, The Ideological Origins of the American Revolution (Cambridge, Mass: The Belknap Press of Harvard University Press, 1967) 118, 120, 121, 122, 125, 126, 132, 133, 135, 136, 137, 139, 140, 198, 199, 201, 312, 334, 335, 338

Barker, Sir E., ed. and transl., The Politics of Aristotle (New York: Oxford University Press/Galaxy Books, 1962) 250

Becker, Dr. Peter, Rule of Fear: The Life and Times of Dingane King of the Zulu (England: Penguin Books Ltd., (1964) 1979) 197, 268

Belov, G., What is the State? (Moscow: Progress Publishers, 1986) 292

Bentham, J., Pannomial Fragments in John Bowring, supt., The Works of Jeremy Bentham (Edinburgh, 1938-43) vol. VIII 377

Blaustein, A.P., and G.H. Flanz, Constitutions of the Countries of the World: A Series of Updated Texts (New York: Dobbs Ferry, 1972). 223

Bogdanor, V., Power and the People: A Guide to Constitutional Reform (London: Victor Gollancz, 1997) 118

Bowring, J., supt., The Works of Jeremy Bentham (Edinburgh, 1938-43) vol. VIII. 377

Bracton, Henry, De Legibus et Consuetidinibus Angliae, fol. 5b, Woodbine (ed), vol. 2., 33 . . . . . . 248, 249, 252

Bradley, A.W., et al, E.C.S. Wade and A.W. Bradley: Constitutional and Administrative Law, 10th edition (U.S.A.: Longman Inc., New York, 1986) . . . 141, 142, 385

Brigham, John. The Constitution of Interests: Beyond the Politics of Rights (New York and London: New York University Press, 1996) at 135. 39

Brownlie, Ian, Treaties and Indigenous Peoples (The Robb Lectures) F.M. Brookfield, ed. (New York, USA: Oxford Univ. Press. 1982) 378

Burrow, J.W., Gibbon, in Keith Thomas, Gen. ed., Past Masters (Oxford: Oxford 255

C.F.R.N. 1979 218

Cable News Network (CNN) political talk-show; "Evans & Novak, Hunt & Shields" at 210

Cain, Maureen; and Carol Smart, series eds., Sociology of Law and Crime (New York: Routledge, 1991) . . 27, 260, 396

Chambers 20th Century Dictionary of 1983 63

451

453

Joye, E. Michael and Kingsley Igweike, Introduction to the 1979 Constitution (London and Basingstoke: The Macmillan Press, 1982) 27, 28, 184, 194, 195, 214, 217, 300

Joye, E. Michael and Kingsley Igweike, Introduction to the 1979 Nigerian Constitution ..27, 28, 184, 194, 195, 214, 217, 235, 299, 300

June 12 and the Future of Nigerian Democracy (Nigeria: Fed. Min. of Information and Culture, 1996) 11, 13, 15, 25, 90, 99, 108, 368, 386, 399

Kachikwu and Ozekhome in [1978-1988] 3 Nig. J.R. at 78. .... 125, 129, 130, 141

Kant, Immanuel, Critique of Pure Reason, Phillip Wheelwright and Peter Fuss, eds., Five Philosophers (New York: The Odyssey Press Inc., 1963) 43

Kelsen, H., 2nd edition, Reine Rechtslehre (1960)... 145, 150

Kelsen, H., General Theory of Law and State, transl. Anders Wedberg (Cambridge, Mass: Harvard University Press, 1949) (20th Century Legal Philosophy Series, vol. 1). 32, 388

Kelsen, H., The Pure Theory of Law, Max Knight, transl. (Berkeley: University of California Press, 1967)29, 31, 35, 64, 147, 149, 150, 153, 388

Kelsen, Hans, "Professor Stone and the Pure Theory of Law" (1965) 17 Stan. L.R. 1,130 144

Kerruish, V., Jurisprudence As Ideology, Maurice Cain and Carol Smart, Series eds., Sociology of Law and Crime (New York: Routledge, 1991)43, 55, 259, 260, 262, 263, 396, 397

Landau, S.I., et al, eds., Chambers English Dictionary (Edinburgh; W. & R. Chambers 123, 187

Lane, Prof. Jan-Erik, Constitutions and Political Theory (Manchester and New York: Manchester University Press, 1996) 216, 217, 222, 223, 224, 237, 239, 242, 282, 295, 296, 301, 303, 304, 333, 398

Langguth, A.J., Patriots: The Men who Started the American Revolution (New York: Simon and Schuster, 1988) 69, 118, 135, 334

Lee, Arthur, "Monitor III" Virgina Gazette (r), March 10, 1768. 139

Lloyd, Lord of Hampstead, Introduction to Jurisprudence, M.D.A. Freeman, co-ed., ... 144, 418

Locke, John, Two Treatises of Civil Government (London: Everyman's library, 1962).295, 296, 297, 298, 299, 300, 302, 309

Palmer, R. E., Hermeneutics (Evanston: North-Western University Press, 1969) 76

Parliament Acts of 1911 and 1949 110

Parry, G. and Michael Moran, "Introduction" in Parry and Moran, eds., Democracy and Democratization (New York: Routledge, 1994) 1 and 2 .... 170, 171

Plucknett, T.F.T., "Bonham's Case and Judicial Review" (1926) 40 Harv. Law Rev., 30 334

Podgorecki, A. and Vittorio Olgiati, eds. Totalitarian and Post-Totalitarian Law (England: Dartmouth Publishing Coy. Ltd. for the Onati International Institute for the Sociology of Law, 1996 295

Podgorecki, Adam, "Totalitarian Law: Basic Concepts and Issues", Chapt. 1 in Adam Podgorecki and Vittorio Olgiati, eds. Totalitarian and Post-Totalitarian Law (England: Dartmouth Publishing Coy. Ltd. for the Onati International Institute for the Sociology of Law, 1996) 295

Posner, Richard A., "The Decline of Law as an Autonomous Discipline: 1962 - 1987" in (1987) 100 Harv. L. Rev., no. 4, 769 40

Poulantzas, N., Political Power and Social Classes (London: New Left Books and Sheed & Ward, 1973) 27

Rasmussen, D., Symbol and Interpretation (The Hague: Martinus Nijhoff, 1974) 75

Raz, Joseph, The Concept of a Legal System: An Introduction to the Theory of Legal System (Oxford: Clarendon Press, 1970) 392

Reference Services, Central Office of Information (R.S., C.O. I.) History and Functions of Government Departments (London: Her Majesty's Stationery Office (HMSO), 1993) Aspects of Britain Series 203

Reisman, "A Hard Look at Soft Law", (1988) 82 Amer. Soc. of Intl. Law Procds., 371 240

Reismnn, W.H., "The Concept and Functions of Soft Law in International Politics" in E. G. Bello and B.A. Ajibola, eds., Essays in Honour of Judge Taslim Olawale Elias (Dordrecht: Martinus Nijhoff, 1992) at 135 ... 241

Ricoeur, Conflict of Interpretation: Essay in Hermeneutics, Don Hide, ed. (Evanston: Northwestern University Press, 1974) 75

Ricoeur, Hermeneutics and the Human Sciences: Essays on Language, Action and Interpretation, J.B. Thompson, transl. (Cambridge: Cambridge University Press, 1981) 75

461

The Concise Columbia Encyclopedia (Columbia: C.U.P., 1991) in Microsoft Office Professional & Bookshelf (1987-1994) 65

The Growth of the English Constitution 1st ed. (1872) . 125

The Guardian Newspaper of 15 May, 1999, 1. 422

Thorne, S.E., Dr. Bonham's Case" (1938) 54 L.Q.R. 543. 334

Tobi, Justice Niki, "Keynote Address" delivered on 24/8/92 at the Annual General Conference of the Nigeria Bar Association held in Port-Harcourt 71

Tobi, Prof. Niki Legal Impact of the Constitution (Suspension and Modification) Decree 1984 on the Constitution of the Federal Republic of Nigeria 1979 Calabar: Centaur Press Limited, 1985. .... 6, 22, 71

Tobi, Prof. Niki, J.C.A., Justice A.B.N. Obayi memorial lecture, "The Judiciary in a Democracy", 29 May, 1996, Hotel Presidential Enugu. 337

Triska, J.F., ed., Constitutions of the Communist Party States (1968) 127

Tur, Richard, "The Kelsenian Enterprise" in Richard Tur and William Twining, eds. Essays on Kelsen (Oxford: Clarendon Press, 1986) 29

Tushnet, Mark, Red, White and Blue: A Critical Analysis of Constitutional Law (Cambridge, Massachusetts and London, England: Harvard University Press, 1988) 40, 41, 50, 85, 140

Udoma, Sir Udo, History and the law of the Constitution of Nigeria (Lagos, Ibadan...Oxford: Malthouse Press Ltd., 1994) 267 to 307 400

Ukhuegbe, S.O., 'The Word "Constitution": From Antiquity to Our Time', Chapter 2 in Epiphany Azinge, ed., New Frontiers in Law (Benin City: Oliz Publishers, 1993). 116, 121

Umezulike, I.A., ed. Democracy Beyond the Third Republic vol. 14 (Nigeria: Fourth Dimension Publishers for the Federal Ministry of Justice, 1993) 316

Umezulike, I.A., ed. Towards the Stability of the Third Republic (Enugu: F.D.P. for the Fed. Min. of Justice, Lagos, Nigeria, 1993). 310

Umezulike, Justices I.A. and C.C. Nweze, eds. Perspectives in Law and Justice (Enugu: Fourth Dimension Publishers, 1996) 55, 115, 132, 160

Uzoukwu, Livy, Grundnorm of Nigeria (Lagos and Orlu: Greg Groupe and Friends..., 1991). 402

Voegelin, Eric, The Nature of the Law (unpublished paper available at the Institut fur Politische Wissenschaft, University of Munich) 387

Wacks, R., Swot Jurisprudence, C.J. Carr, Series ed., Fourth Edition (Great Britain: Blackstone Press Ltd., 1995) 27, 30, 59, 64, 243

Wade, H.W.R. in (1955) Cambridge Law Journal. 258

Watchman, Paul, "Palm Tree Justice and the Lord Chancellor's Foot" in Peter Robson and Paul Watchman, eds., Justice, Lord Denning and the Constitution (England: Gower Publication Co. Ltd., 1981) . 16, 78, 79

Wheare, K.C., Modern Constitutions 1st ed. (with revisions) 125, 141, 142

Williams, Chief F.R.A., S.A.N., "The Nigerian Judiciary and Military Governments" (1995) J.N.L., vol. 2, 1 181, 285, 370, 417, 418

Yardley, D.C.M., Introduction to British Constitutional law Sixth ed. (London: Butterworths, 1984) ... 127, 167, 170, 278, 291, 293, 295, 303, 305

Young, Eric, "Developing a System of Administrative Law?", in Peter Robson and Paul Watchman, eds., Justice, Lord Denning and the Constitution (England: Gower Publishing Co. Ltd., 1984) at 157 16

About the Author

RACE Achara has been Head of the Department of International Law and Jurisprudence at the Nnamdi Azikiwe University, Awka, Nigeria, where he has taught Constitutional Law for a decade. Winner of the University of Nigeria Postgraduate Prize for Law, he has recently been appointed professor of Constitutional Law at the Enugu State University of Science and Technology.

With some 18 years of practical experience as a trial lawyer, Professor Achara who was the millenial Chairman of the Nigerian Bar Association, Enugu Branch, provides in this, as in his numerous other academic works, practical insights tempered by taxonomic gridlines of intellectual rigour.

Winner of the competitive Five College African Scholars fellowship at the University of Massachusetts, Amherst, Dr. RACE Achara is author of some 32 academic books and articles some of which include: *Meta-Constitutional Conceptions: Subjective Legitimacy in the Jurisprudence of June 12*, "Textual Fetishism and the Ambiguities of Constitutional Definition," "Judicial Assault on Constitutional Access: Revisiting the Constitutional Obit of the Salati Obiter," "Constitutional Law and the Autonomy Debate: Synthesis from Autopoiesis" and "Relevancy and the Nigerian Hearsay Rule: *Subramaniam* and the Limits of Purpose."

Printed in the United States
41578LVS00004B/26

9 781420 849462